Microsoft®
Office 97
Visual Basic®
Programmer's Guide

PUBLISHED BY
Microsoft Press
A Division of Microsoft Corporation
One Microsoft Way
Redmond, Washington 98052-6399

Library of Congress Cataloging-in-Publication Data
Microsoft Office 97/Visual Basic Programmer's Guide / Microsoft
  Corporation.
      p.   cm.
    Includes bibliographical references (p.   -).
    ISBN 1-57231-340-4
    1. Integrated software.   2. Microsoft Office. 3. Microsoft Visual
BASIC. I. Microsoft Corporation.
QA76.76.I57M458   1997
005.369--dc21

96-29988
     CIP

Printed and bound in the United States of America.

4 5 6 7 8 9 QMQM 2 0 1 9 8

Distributed to the book trade in Canada by Macmillan of Canada, a division of Canada Publishing Corporation.

A CIP catalogue record for this book is available from the British Library.

Microsoft Press books are available through booksellers and distributors worldwide. For further information about international editions, contact your local Microsoft Corporation office. Or contact Microsoft Press International directly at fax (206) 936-7329.

Acquisitions Editor: Casey D. Doyle
Project Editor: Maureen Williams Zimmerman

Contents

Chapter 4   Microsoft Excel Objects   77

Contents

Chapter 8   Menus and Toolbars   177

Chapter 11   Data Access Objects   247

Introduction

Welcome to Microsoft® Visual Basic® for Applications version 5.0, the shared development environment that provides you the means to accomplish a wide range of programmatic results—everything from automating individual tasks to creating full-fledged custom applications in Microsoft Office 97. Whatever your programming background—Visual Basic (Standard, Professional, or Enterprise Edition), a previous version of Visual Basic for Applications, WordBasic, Access Basic, XLM, or another programming language—you'll find a number of powerful new capabilities in this version of Visual Basic for Applications, including those described in the following paragraphs.

Programmatic access to the functionality of each Office application Each Office application exposes its functionality as a set of programmable objects. Using Visual Basic for Applications gives you access to these objects, making it possible for you to do anything in the application programmatically that you can do manually with the user interface.

Consistent syntax across applications You no longer need to learn a different programming language for each Office application. This makes it much easier for you to apply the skills you acquire while learning to program one application to other Office applications. This uniformity of language also makes it easier to create solutions that involve more than one Office application and to reuse code across applications.

A powerful, full-featured development environment The integrated development environment of Visual Basic for Applications is available with Microsoft Excel, Microsoft Word, and Microsoft PowerPoint®; it looks exactly the same no matter which of these applications you start it from. This integrated programming environment runs in its own window, and it includes advanced debugging features, property- and code-editing features (including compile-time syntax checking and tools for constructing statements), an enhanced Object Browser, and code organization and tracking features.

Support for ActiveX controls You now have the ability to add ActiveX™ controls— prebuilt, reusable software components that have interactive capabilities—to dialog boxes and to embed them in documents.

A new way to create dialog boxes You can use Microsoft Forms to create custom dialog boxes in any application that supports the integrated development environment.

Support for integration with databases, messaging systems, and the Internet You have programmatic access to databases (using Data Access Objects, or DAO), to messaging (using the Microsoft Outlook™ object model), and to the Internet-ready features of the Office applications (using each application's object model).

Getting Started with Visual Basic

Use the following suggestions to get the most from the time you spend learning Visual Basic for Applications (referred to as "Visual Basic" for the remainder of this book).

Learn Microsoft Office first The more you know about Office, the better prepared you'll be to venture into Visual Basic. Most Visual Basic procedures perform a sequence of actions in Office, and most instructions in a procedure are equivalent to Office commands or actions. Consequently, working with Visual Basic is a little like working with Office without a user interface; instead of choosing commands and selecting options in dialog boxes, you write Visual Basic instructions. The statements and functions you use to write instructions are much easier to understand if you're already familiar with the features they represent in Office.

Also, if you know Office well, you can better answer the question you're most likely to ask yourself when writing a macro: "What's the best way to do this?" People have been known to write long macros for tasks that could have been handled by a single Office command.

Learn what you need, when you need it Learn what you need for the task at hand. Visual Basic can seem overwhelming at first, particularly if you don't have any experience with programming languages. A great way to begin learning Visual Basic is to investigate how to accomplish a particular task programmatically. As you gain experience writing procedures that automate different types of tasks, you'll cover a lot of ground.

Use the macro recorder The macro recorder—a feature that's available with Microsoft Excel, Word, and PowerPoint—can record the corresponding Visual Basic instruction for virtually every action you take in Office. You can use the macro recorder to see how actions performed in Office translate into Visual Basic instructions, and vice versa. Also, you'll find that recording part of a macro is often faster and easier than writing out the instructions.

Use Visual Basic Help Help is a powerful tool for learning Visual Basic. In a Visual Basic module, you can type a keyword and, with the insertion point positioned somewhere in the keyword, press F1 to immediately display the Visual Basic Help topic for that keyword. Most Visual Basic Help topics for keywords include examples you can copy and paste into your macros. For more information, see the following section, "Using Online Help."

Using Online Help

Microsoft Office provides an extensive Help system for the Visual Basic language, the objects that Office supports, and the properties and methods of those objects.

If you clicked **Typical** when you installed Office, you'll need to run Setup again to install Help for Visual Basic for the applications you want to program in.

You can access Visual Basic Help in any module in the Visual Basic Editor or in a Microsoft Access module in any of the following three ways:

- Position the insertion point anywhere in an object name, property name, method name, event name, function name, or other keyword you've typed, and then press F1 to get context-sensitive Help for that keyword.

- Click **Microsoft Visual Basic Help** (in the Visual Basic Editor) or **Microsoft Access Help** (in Microsoft Access) on the **Help** menu. You can then ask the Office Assistant a question, click **Search**, and click the topic you want to read in the **What would you like to do?** balloon.

- Click **Object Browser** on the **View** menu, and then either press F1 or click the **Help** button (the question-mark button above the **Members of** box) for information about the selected object, method, property, event, or function.

After you've displayed a Help topic, you can click the **Help Topics** button in the Help window to display the **Help Topics** dialog box, which contains three tabs: **Contents**, **Index**, and **Find**. You can then either look up a specific topic or Visual Basic term on the **Contents** or **Index** tab or perform a full-text search from the **Find** tab.

Note In the Visual Basic Editor, clicking **Contents and Index** on the **Help** menu displays the contents and index of Help for the Visual Basic Editor itself. From the **Contents** tab in Visual Basic Editor Help, you can display the contents and index of Visual Basic Help for Microsoft Excel, Word, or PowerPoint by double-clicking the book title that includes the name of the application you're working in (for example, "Microsoft Word Visual Basic Reference"), and then double-clicking the shortcut in that book (for example, "Shortcut to Microsoft Word Visual Basic Reference"). The **Help Topics** dialog box should reappear, displaying the contents and index for Visual Basic Help for your application.

Other Resources

Following are descriptions of the various resources you can use to get additional information about programming with Visual Basic in Office.

Technical Support Services

Microsoft offers a variety of support options to help you get the most from your Microsoft product. For more information about available support services, see *Getting Results with Microsoft Office 97*.

For basic technical support outside the United States, contact the Microsoft subsidiary office that serves your area. Microsoft subsidiary offices and the countries they serve are listed in *Getting Results with Microsoft Office 97*.

Microsoft Office Developer Forum

You can get the latest information about developing custom applications for Office at the Microsoft Office Developer Forum Web site at http://www.microsoft.com/officedev

Microsoft Press Books

In addition to the *Microsoft Office 97/Visual Basic Programmer's Guide*, Microsoft Press® offers a number of books to help you get started programming in Visual Basic. These books help you learn how to automate Office tasks and create custom applications as easily and as quickly as possible. The easy-to-follow lessons include clear objectives and real-world business examples so that you can learn exactly what you need to know, at your own speed.

- *Microsoft Word 97/Visual Basic Step by Step*, ISBN 1-57231-388-9, by Michael Halvorson and Chris Kinata
- *Microsoft Excel 97/Visual Basic Step by Step*, ISBN 1-57231-318-8, by Reed Jacobson
- *Microsoft Access 97/Visual Basic Step by Step*, ISBN 1-57231-319-6, by Evan Callahan
- *Microsoft Office 97/Visual Basic Step by Step*, ISBN: 1-57231-389-7, by David Boctor

For a technical exploration of the wide range of line-of-business development opportunities available to Office 97 developers, see the *Microsoft Office 97 Developer's Handbook*, ISBN 1-57231-440-0, by Christine Solomon.

Building Microsoft Outlook 97 Applications, ISBN 1-57231-5736-9, by Peter Krebs is a results-oriented book that offers both the nonprogrammer and the experienced IS professional the information, strategies, and sample applications they need to get started building useful groupware and mail-enabled applications.

For information about other Microsoft Press titles, see the Microsoft Press Web site at http://www.microsoft.com/mspress

Mastering Office 97 Development

Mastering Office 97 Development is a CD-ROM product available from Microsoft. Use this self-paced training tool to develop real-world skills that you can put to work right away. Become proficient with Visual Basic for Applications, Office 97 object modules, and more. More than 40 hours of labs, demos, sample code, and articles— plus valuable tips and techniques—get you up to speed fast. Use the powerful Boolean search engine and comprehensive index to find just information you need when you need it. Narrated demonstrations and interactive lab exercises walk you through complex concepts and help you design your own Office 97-based applications.

How This Book Is Organized

The chapters in this book cover basic concepts pertaining to object models and Visual Basic programming, the object models for the Office applications, and major feature areas of Visual Basic.

Chapter 1, "Programming Basics," provides a brief overview of the mechanics of writing Visual Basic code.

Chapter 2, "Understanding Object Models," is an introduction to the concept of programmable object models.

Chapter 3, "Microsoft Access Objects," discusses the Microsoft Access object model in detail.

Chapter 4, "Microsoft Excel Objects," discusses the Microsoft Excel object model in detail.

Chapter 5, "Microsoft Outlook Objects," discusses the Microsoft Outlook object model in detail.

Chapter 6, "Microsoft PowerPoint Objects," discusses the Microsoft PowerPoint object model in detail.

Chapter 7, "Microsoft Word Objects," discusses the Microsoft Word object model in detail.

Chapter 8, "Menus and Toolbars," and Chapter 12, "ActiveX Controls and Dialog Boxes," show you how to add interactive, custom user-interface elements to your Visual Basic applications.

Chapter 9, "Microsoft Office Assistant" discusses the Office Assistant object model in detail.

Chapter 10, "Shapes and the Drawing Layer," discusses the Office Art object model in detail.

Chapter 11, "Data Access Objects," explains how to use Data Access Objects (DAO) to import and export information stored in a database.

Chapter 13, "Optimizing for Size and Speed," provides several easy techniques that can make your Visual Basic code faster and more concise.

Chapter 14, "Debugging and Error Handling," shows you how to find and eliminate bugs in your code before you run it and how to handle errors that occur while your code is running.

Chapter 15, "Developing Applications for the Internet and World Wide Web," provides information about how to control the new Internet-ready features in Office applications programmatically.

The appendixes provide helpful information for experienced users of XLM or WordBasic who are switching to Visual Basic.

Document Conventions

This book uses the typographic conventions listed in the following table. You might not recognize all the terms or Visual Basic keywords yet, but you'll learn more about them later.

Example of convention	Description
setup	Words or characters you're instructed to type are formatted as bold.
Sub, If, ChDir, MsgBox, True, Add, Height, Application, Range, Row	Bold words with the initial-letter capitalization indicate either a language-specific term (a property, method, event, or object name), another Visual Basic keyword, or an interface element (such as a menu command or a toolbar button).
object	In text, italic type indicates important new terms, usually the first time they occur in the book.
PropertyName	In code syntax, italic type indicates placeholders for information you're to supply.
ENTER	Small capital letters are used for the names of keys and key combinations, such as ENTER and CTRL+R.

Example of convention	Description
CTRL+V	A plus sign (+) between key names indicates a key combination, or shortcut keys. For example, CTRL+V means to hold down the CTRL key while pressing the V key.
DOWN ARROW	Individual arrow keys are referred to by the direction of the arrow on the key (LEFT, RIGHT, UP, or DOWN). The phrase "arrow keys" is used to describe these keys collectively.
BACKSPACE, HOME	Other navigational keys are referred to by their specific names.
myVar	This font is used for example code.

Sub StockSale ( )
   .
   .
   .
End Sub
	A column of three periods indicates that part of an example has been intentionally omitted.

Programming Basics

This chapter introduces you to the fundamentals of the Visual Basic for Applications programming language: how to get to the Visual Basic programming environment and how to write, edit, store, and run code in that environment. This chapter also briefly discusses the control structures, data types, and built-in constants available to Visual Basic programmers.

Note The information in this chapter applies to the integrated development environment of Visual Basic for Applications in Microsoft Excel 97, Word 97, and PowerPoint 97. For information about writing Visual Basic code in Microsoft Access 97, see *Building Applications with Microsoft Access 97*, available in Microsoft Access 97 and Microsoft Office 97, Developer Edition. An online version of *Building Applications with Microsoft Access 97* is available in the ValuPack on CD-ROM in Microsoft Access 97 and Microsoft Office 97, Professional Edition. For information about writing VBScript code in Microsoft Outlook 97, see Chapter 5, "Microsoft Outlook Objects," and *Building Microsoft Outlook 97 Applications* by Peter Krebs, available from Microsoft Press (ISBN 1-57231-5736-9).

Contents
- Writing, Editing, and Running Code in the Visual Basic Editor
- Variables, Constants, and Data Types
- Control Structures

Writing, Editing, and Running Code in the Visual Basic Editor

Microsoft Excel 97, Word 97, and PowerPoint 97 come equipped with a full-featured development environment called the Visual Basic Editor. Using the Visual Basic Editor, you can create, edit, debug, and run code associated with Microsoft Office documents. To open the Visual Basic Editor, click the **Visual Basic Editor** button on the **Visual Basic** toolbar.

A First Look at the Visual Basic Editor

If you're used to writing, editing, and debugging code in a macro-editing window within the Word application window, on an XLM macro sheet, or on a module in a Microsoft Excel workbook, the Visual Basic Editor may seem complex to you the first time you open it, with many windows and buttons you aren't familiar with. This section explains some of these features of the Visual Basic Editor.

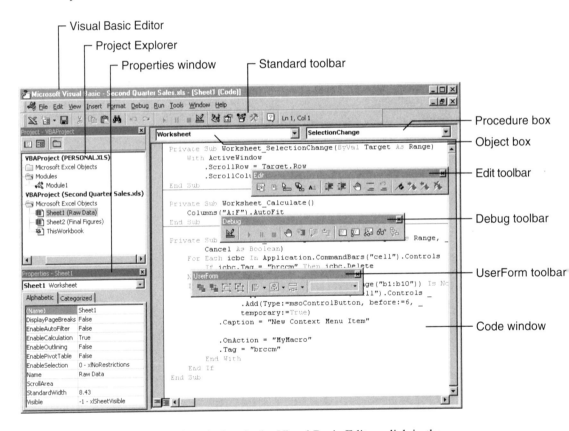

For information about a particular window in the Visual Basic Editor, click in the window and then press F1 to open the appropriate Help topic. To see the Help topic for any other element of the Visual Basic Editor, such as a particular toolbar button, search Help for the name of the element.

The Properties Window

A property is a characteristic of an object, such as the object's color or caption. You set a property to specify a characteristic or behavior of an object. For example, you can set the **ShowSpellingErrors** property of a Word document to **True** to show spelling errors in the document.

You can use the **Properties** window to set the properties of an object at design time. The **Properties** window is very useful when you're working with custom dialog boxes and ActiveX controls. For more information about using the **Properties** window to set properties of dialog boxes and controls, see Chapter 12, "ActiveX Controls and Dialog Boxes." For most objects, however, it's easier to set these properties at design time by using familiar commands in the user interface. For example, you can set the **ShowSpellingErrors** property of a Word document to **True** by selecting the **Hide spelling errors in this document** check box on the **Spelling & Grammar** tab in the **Options** dialog box (**Tools** menu).

If you don't think you'll be using the **Properties** window right now, you can close it to simplify your work space a little. You can open it again at any time by clicking **Properties Window** on the **View** menu.

The Project Explorer

All the code associated with a workbook, document, template, or presentation is stored in a *project* that's automatically stored and saved with the workbook, document, template, or presentation. In the **Project Explorer** of the Visual Basic Editor, you can view, modify, and navigate the projects for every open or referenced workbook, document, template, or presentation. You can resize the **Project Explorer** and either dock it to or undock it from any of the sides of the Visual Basic Editor window to make it easier to use.

Note In Word, because the Normal template is available from every Word document, there's always a project for Normal in the **Project Explorer**.

Within a project, there can be application objects that have events associated with them, custom dialog boxes (called *forms* in the **Project Explorer**), standard modules, class modules, and references.

View Code button

View Object button

Toggle Folders button

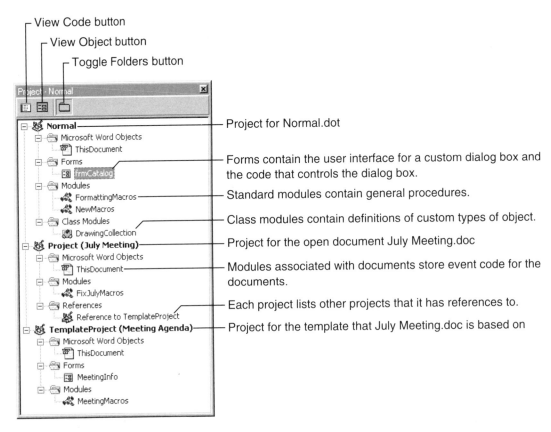

Project for Normal.dot

Forms contain the user interface for a custom dialog box and the code that controls the dialog box.

Standard modules contain general procedures.

Class modules contain definitions of custom types of object.

Project for the open document July Meeting.doc

Modules associated with documents store event code for the documents.

Each project lists other projects that it has references to.

Project for the template that July Meeting.doc is based on

Tip   Folders in the **Project Explorer** divide project elements into categories. If you don't see any folders, click the **Toggle Folders** button at the top of the **Project Explorer**.

In the **Project Explorer**, there's one project for each open or referenced workbook, document, template, or presentation. In each project, you may find objects (such as **Document** objects, **Workbook** objects, and **Worksheet** objects) that recognize events; forms (also called *UserForms*), which are custom dialog box interfaces and the code that controls how the user interacts with a particular dialog box; standard modules, which contain code that isn't associated with a particular object or form; class modules, which contain information about a custom object type; and references to other projects. To see the code in a module or the code associated with an object or form, click the element in the **Project Explorer**, and then click the **View Code** button at the top of the **Project Explorer**. To see the user interface for a particular object or form, click the object or form in the **Project Explorer**, and then click the **View Object** button at the top of the **Project Explorer**.

The Code Window

To view the code in a project, go to the **Project Explorer**, click the element that contains the code, and then click the **View Code** button at the top of the **Project Explorer**.

Tip If you want to be able to see more than one procedure in the code window at a time, select the **Default to Full Module View** check box on the **Editor** tab in the **Options** dialog box (**Tools** menu). To view just one procedure at a time, clear this check box.

You can navigate the **Code** window by using the items listed in the **Object** and **Procedure** boxes at the top of the window. In the **Object** box, click **(General)**, and then click a procedure name in the **Procedure** box to see a procedure that isn't associated with a specific event. In the **Object** box, click an object, and then click an event in the **Procedure** box to see the code that runs when a specific event occurs.

Making Room in the Visual Basic Editor

If all you want to do is write a simple procedure or edit a macro you've recorded, you may want to forego some of the advanced features of the Visual Basic Editor in the interest of a simpler workspace. Here are a few ways you can simplify your coding environment:

- Close the **Properties** window. If you aren't working with custom dialog boxes or ActiveX controls, the **Properties** window probably won't be of much use to you. To reopen **Properties** window, just click **Properties Window** on the **View** menu.

- Hide any toolbars you aren't currently using. To redisplay the **Debug**, **Edit**, **Standard**, or **UserForm** toolbar, right-click the Visual Basic Editor menu bar, and then click the name of the toolbar you want to display.

- If you're only working with code in a standard module and you don't need to navigate to other code in the project or to code in other projects, consider closing the **Project Explorer**. To reopen the **Project Explorer**, just click **Project Explorer** on the **View** menu.

Recording a Macro

You can use the macro recorder to translate user-interface actions into Visual Basic code. Recording a simple macro can give you a jump start on creating a more complex macro, and can help you become familiar with the objects, properties, and methods of an application.

▶ **To record a macro**

1 To display the **Visual Basic** toolbar, point to **Toolbars** on the **View** menu in your application window (not in the Visual Basic Editor), and then click **Visual Basic** if it isn't already selected.

2 On the **Visual Basic** toolbar, click the **Record Macro** button.

3 In the **Record Macro** dialog box, replace the default macro name in the **Macro name** box if you want, and click **OK**.

You can use the **Store macro in** box to choose where your macro will be stored. For now, click **This Workbook** in Microsoft Excel, **All Documents (Normal.dot)** in Word, or the name of the active presentation in PowerPoint.

4 Perform the actions for which you want to generate Visual Basic code.

5 On the **Stop Recording** toolbar, click the **Stop Recording** button.

Your macro has been recorded. To look at the macro code, point to **Macro** on the **Tools** menu, and then click **Macros**. In the **Macros** dialog box, select the appropriate macro name, and then click **Edit**.

Getting Around in Your Projects

You use the **Project Explorer** to navigate to any procedure in any open project. Start by finding the object that contains your macro. Most general procedures, including recorded macros, are stored in a standard module. If you have folders displayed in the **Project Explorer**, standard modules are located in the Modules folder.

Tip If you don't see folders in the **Project Explorer**, click the **Toggle Folders** button to display them.

After you locate the object that contains your code, double-click the object to view the procedures it contains. You can use this method to get to either procedures you've written from scratch or macros you've recorded.

Where a recorded macro is stored depends on what location you specified in the **Store macro in** box in the **Record Macro** dialog box when you recorded your macro. In Microsoft Excel, if you clicked **This Workbook** in the **Store macro in** box when you recorded your macro, your macro will be stored in Module1 in the Modules folder of the project for the workbook you recorded the macro in. In Word, if you clicked **All documents (Normal.dot)** in the **Store macro in box** when you recorded your macro, your macro will be stored in the NewMacros module in the Modules folder of the Normal project. In PowerPoint, if you clicked the name of the active presentation in the **Store macro in** box when you recorded your macro, your macro will be stored in Module1 in the Modules folder of the project for the presentation you recorded the macro in.

Tip If you want to be able to see more than one procedure in the code window at a time, make sure that the **Default to Full Module View** check box is selected on the **Editor** tab in the **Options** dialog box (**Tools** menu). Otherwise, you have to use the **Procedure** box in the code window to move from one procedure to another.

Writing a New Procedure

If you want to write code that isn't associated with a specific object or event, you can create a *procedure* in a standard module in the Visual Basic Editor. A procedure is a unit of code enclosed either between the **Sub** and **End Sub** statements or between the **Function** and **End Function** statements.

To create a blank standard module, go to the **Project Explorer**, click anywhere in the project you want to add the module to, and then click **Module** on the **Insert** menu.

To open an existing standard module, select the module in the **Project Explorer**, and then click the **View Code** button in the **Project Explorer**.

To add a procedure to a module, select the module in the **Project Explorer**, click **Procedure** on the **Insert** menu, select whatever options you want in the **Add Procedure** dialog box, and then click **OK**. For more information about the options in the dialog box, press F1 while the dialog box is displayed. For example, in the dialog box, type **Test1** in the **Name** box, click **Sub** under **Type**, click **Public** under **Scope**, and then click **OK**. The procedure that appears in your module should look like the following example.

```
Public Sub Test1()

End Sub
```

After you've added a procedure to a module, you can add code to the procedure. The following example adds to the preceding code a line that displays a message box.

```
Public Sub Test1()
    MsgBox "This is the Test1 procedure running"
End Sub
```

If you want to write code that runs automatically when a certain event occurs—for instance, when a document is opened, a worksheet is calculated, or a button in a custom dialog box is clicked—you should write a procedure associated with the event for the object or form. For general information about writing event procedures, see "Writing Code to Respond to Events" later in this chapter. For specific information about writing event procedures for custom dialog boxes and ActiveX controls, see Chapter 12, "ActiveX Controls and Dialog Boxes."

What's the Difference Between a Macro and a Procedure?

Although the terms *macro* and *procedure* are sometimes used interchangeably, they actually have distinct meanings. Procedure is the broader term; it applies to any unit of code enclosed either between the **Sub** and **End Sub** statements or between the **Function** and **End Function** statements. Macro is a specific term that applies only to public **Sub** procedures that take no arguments. All macros are procedures, but not all procedures are macros. All procedures you generate with the macro recorder and all procedures you can run from the **Macros** dialog box in the Office application are macros.

Sub Procedures vs. Function Procedures

With Visual Basic, you can create two types of procedures: **Sub** procedures and **Function** procedures.

A **Sub** procedure is a unit of code enclosed between the **Sub** and **End Sub** statements that performs a task but doesn't return a value. The following example is a **Sub** procedure.

```
Sub DisplayWelcome()
    MsgBox "Welcome"
End Sub
```

A **Function** procedure is a unit of code enclosed between the **Function** and **End Function** statements. Like a **Sub** procedure, a **Function** procedure performs a specific task. Unlike a **Sub** procedure, however, a **Function** procedure also returns a value. The following example is a **Function** procedure.

```
Function AddThree(OriginalValue As Long)
    AddThree = OriginalValue + 3
End Function
```

Public Procedures vs. Private Procedures

You can call a public procedure, declared with the **Public** keyword, from any procedure in any module in your application. You can call a private procedure, declared with the **Private** keyword, only from other procedures in the same module. Both **Sub** procedures and **Function** procedures can be either public or private. The following are examples of private procedures.

```
Private Sub Test1()
    MsgBox "This is the Test1 procedure running"
End Sub

Private Function AddThree(OriginalValue As Long)
    AddThree = OriginalValue + 3
End Function
```

The following are examples of public procedures.

```
Public Sub Test1()
    MsgBox "This is the Test1 procedure running"
End Sub

Public Function AddThree(OriginalValue As Long)
    AddThree = OriginalValue + 3
End Function
```

If you don't use either the **Public** or **Private** keyword to declare a procedure, the procedure will be public by default. Therefore, the following are also examples of public procedures.

```
Sub Test1()
    MsgBox "This is the Test1 procedure running"
End Sub

Function AddThree(OriginalValue As Long)
    AddThree = OriginalValue + 3
End Function
```

Although it's not necessary to use the **Public** keyword when creating a public procedure, including it in procedure declarations makes it easier to see at a glance which procedures are public and which are private. For more information, see "Public" or "Private" in Help.

Using the Value Returned from a Function

For a function to return a value, it must include a function assignment statement that assigns a value to the name of the function. In the following example, the value assigned to ConeSurface will be the value returned by the function.

```
Function ConeSurface(radius, height)
    Const Pi = 3.14159
    coneBase = Pi * radius ^ 2
    coneCirc = 2 * Pi * radius
    coneSide = Sqr(radius ^ 2 + height ^ 2) * coneCirc / 2
    ConeSurface = coneBase + coneSide
End Function
```

The information that must be supplied to a **Sub** procedure or **Function** procedure for it to perform its task (radius and height in the preceding example) is passed in the form of arguments. For more information about arguments, see "Passing Arguments to a Procedure" later in this chapter.

When the **Function** procedure returns a value, this value can then become part of a larger expression. For example, the following statement in another procedure incorporates the return value of the ConeSurface and ScoopSurface functions in its calculations.

```
totalSurface = ConeSurface(3, 11) + 2 * ScoopSurface(3)
```

Running a Sub Procedure

You can have a **Sub** procedure run in response to a specific event, you can run it from the Visual Basic Editor or your application window, or you can call it from another procedure.

- If you want a **Sub** procedure to run automatically every time a specific event occurs, you should add the code to the event procedure for the event. For more information, see "Writing Code to Respond to Events" later in this chapter.

- To run a **Sub** procedure from the Visual Basic Editor, position the insertion point anywhere in the procedure, and then either press F1 or click the **Run Sub/UserForm** button on the **Standard** or **Debug** toolbar.

- To run a **Sub** procedure that's a macro (see "What's the Difference Between a Macro and a Procedure?" earlier in this chapter), select the macro name in the **Macros** dialog box in the application, and then click **Run**.

- To call a **Sub** procedure from another procedure, name it in your code, just as you do with built-in keywords. The procedure in the following example calls the DisplayWelcome procedure.

```
Sub TestCall()
    DisplayWelcome
End Sub
```

You cannot call a procedure you've declared as private from any procedure outside the module in which the private procedure resides. However, you can call a public procedure from outside the module in which it resides. For an explanation of the terms "public" and "private" in this context, see "Sub Procedures vs. Function Procedures" earlier in this chapter.

When you call a public procedure that isn't located in the current module, Visual Basic searches other modules and runs the first public procedure it finds that has the name you called. If the name of a public procedure isn't unique, you can specify the module it's located in when you call the procedure. The following example runs a **Sub** procedure named "DisplayWelcome" that's stored in a module named "TestTools."

```
TestTools.DisplayWelcome
```

If necessary, you can also specify the project that the procedure resides in. The following example runs a **Sub** procedure named "DisplayWelcome" that's stored in a module named "TestTools" in a project named "TestDocument."

```
TestDocument.TestTools.DisplayWelcome
```

Note that the name of the project you specify is the project's code name, not the name of the document the project is associated with. You can check and modify the project's code name in the space to the right of (**Name**) in the **Properties** window for the project. To see the **Properties** window, select the project in the **Project Explorer**, and then click **Properties Window** on the **View** menu. You can also change the code name of a project by typing a new name in the **Project Name** box on the **General** tab in the **Project Properties** dialog box. You display this dialog box by right-clicking the project in the **Project Explorer**, and then clicking **Properties** on the shortcut menu (the command appears on the shortcut menu preceded by the current name of the project). For more information about the options in the **Project Properties** dialog box, click a tab and press F1.

Tip If you want to be able to call a procedure from other modules in the same project but not from other projects, declare the procedure as public, but make the module private to the project by adding the **Option Private Module** statement to the **(Declarations)** section of the module.

If you want to be able to call procedures in one project from another project, there must be a reference from the project containing the calling code to the project containing the called code. To create a reference to a project, use the **References** dialog box (**Tools** menu).

Note If you get an error when you try to create a reference from one project to another one, make sure that the project you're trying to reference doesn't have the same code name as the other project. (Multiple projects in an application may be given the same default code name, such as "Project" in Word or "VBAProject" in Microsoft Excel.) To check a project's code name, click the project name in the **Project Explorer**, and then click and then click **Properties Window** on the **View** menu. The text to the right of **(Name)** in the **Properties** window is the project's code name. To change the code name for a project, select the current code name and then type a new one. Keep in mind that you cannot have circular references—that is, if you have a reference to project A from project B, you cannot have a reference from project B to project A.

Passing Arguments to a Procedure

If your procedure needs information to perform its task that it cannot get from the context in which it's being run, you can pass that information to the procedure in the form of arguments. To indicate that a given procedure takes arguments, include an argument list between the parentheses that follow the procedure name in the procedure declaration. The argument list can contain multiple argument declarations, separated by commas.

When you declare an argument, you can specify the data type of the argument by using the **As** keyword (whether or not the procedure can change the argument's value by using the **ByVal** and **ByRef** keywords), and you can specify whether the argument is required or optional by using the **Optional** keyword. For more information about a specific keyword, see the appropriate topic in Help. For more information about the available data types in Visual Basic, see "Visual Basic Data Types" later in this chapter.

The following example shows the declaration line of a **Sub** procedure that takes three arguments.

```
Sub UpdateRecord(ByVal custId As Long, ByRef custName As String, _
    Optional custRepeat As Boolean)
```

The first argument, `custID`, is a required argument that will be passed as a value of type **Long** and will be passed *by value*. If you pass an argument by value when calling a procedure, the called procedure receives only a copy of the variable passed from the calling procedure. If the called procedure changes the value, the change affects only the copy and not the variable in the calling procedure.

The second argument, `custName`, is a required argument that will be passed as a value of type **String** and will be passed *by reference*. If you pass an argument by reference when calling a procedure, the procedure has access to the actual variable in memory. As a result, the variable's value can be changed by the procedure.

The third argument, `custRepeat`, is an optional argument that will be passed as a value of type **Boolean** and will be passed *by reference* (passing by reference is the default).

The following example calls UpdateRecord.

```
Dim newId As Long
Dim newName As String
Dim newRepeat As Boolean

newId = 3452
newName = "Mary Boyd"
newRepeat = True
UpdateRecord newId, newName, newRepeat
```

Note that the name of the variable you pass from the calling procedure doesn't have to match the name of the argument declared in the called procedure.

Using Named Arguments

If either a procedure you create or a built-in function, statement, or method takes more than one optional argument, you may want to pass arguments to it by name rather than by position.

For example, the **Open** method of the Microsoft Excel **Workbooks** object, which opens a workbook, takes 13 arguments. If you want to write code that opens the workbook Book2.xls and adds it to the list of recently used files, you could write the code shown in the following example.

```
Workbooks.Open "book2.xls", , , , , , , , , , , , True
```

However, this code is difficult to write correctly without introducing bugs, because you have to count the number of commas to insert between the arguments. The code is also very difficult to read, and it gives no clues about what the arguments represent. The following example shows a better way to write this code.

```
Workbooks.Open FileName:="book2.xls", AddToMru:=True
```

Because every argument has a name, you can use the name and the **:=** operator to assign a value to an argument. When you use named arguments, you don't have to remember the order of the arguments. For instance, the preceding code could have been written with the order of the arguments reversed, as in the following example.

```
Workbooks.Open AddToMru:=True, FileName:="book2.xls"
```

You can also use named arguments with the procedures you create. Visual Basic automatically associates argument names with their corresponding procedures. For instance, assume that you've created a FormatList procedure that takes two required arguments and two optional arguments, as shown in the following declaration.

```
Sub FormatList(startRow As Integer, startCol As Integer, _
    Optional redText, Optional sortList)
```

The DoList procedure in the following example uses named arguments to call the FormatList procedure.

```
Sub DoList()
    FormatList redText:=True, startCol:=2, startRow:=2
End Sub
```

The arguments are now out of order, and one of the optional arguments was omitted.

Note Using named arguments doesn't negate the need to enter required arguments.

Writing Code to Respond to Events

Certain objects in the Office 97 applications recognize a predefined set of events, which can be triggered either by the system or by the user. Examples of events recognized by objects in Office include the Open and Close events for Word documents; the Open, BeforePrint, BeforeSave, and BeforeClose events for Microsoft Excel workbooks; the Calculate and SelectionChange events for Microsoft Excel worksheets; the Click, Initialize, and Terminate events for custom dialog boxes; and the Click, GotFocus, and LostFocus events for ActiveX controls. For detailed information about the events available in Microsoft Excel and Word, see Chapter 7, "Microsoft Word Objects," and Chapter 4, "Microsoft Excel Objects." For detailed information about using custom dialog boxes and ActiveX controls, see Chapter 12, "ActiveX Controls and Dialog Boxes."

You can control how your application responds to a recognized event by writing code in the **Code** window for the object. Every time an event occurs, the code, or *event procedure*, associated with that event runs. For instance, if you write a procedure that's associated with the Open event for a Word document, every time that document is opened, the procedure automatically runs.

Where Event Code Is Stored

An event procedure is stored in the document, workbook, worksheet, slide, or UserForm where the event can be triggered. For example, the procedure that runs when you calculate the worksheet named "Last Quarter" in the workbook named "Sales" would be stored in the Last Quarter worksheet in the project associated with the Sales workbook. To view the code in a document, workbook, worksheet, slide, or UserForm, click the object in the **Project Explorer**, and then click the **View Code** button to open the **Code** window.

Note   PowerPoint presentations and slides don't recognize events. Therefore, unless you can place ActiveX controls (which recognize events) on a PowerPoint slide, there can be no event procedures associated with the slide, and you won't see the slide in the **Project Explorer**. For more information about adding ActiveX controls to documents, see Chapter 12, "ActiveX Controls and Dialog Boxes."

How Event Procedures Are Named

The name of an event procedure is the name of the object that recognizes the event— such as "Document," "Worksheet," "UserForm," or "CommandButton1"—followed by an underscore (_), followed by the name of the event that the procedure runs in response to — such as "Open," "Calculate," or "Click." For example, the procedure that runs when you open a Word document is Document_Open.

Note   Whereas the name of an event procedure for most objects is linked to the class name (such as **Document**, **Worksheet**, or **UserForm**), the name of an event procedure for an ActiveX control is linked to the control's code name—either the default name or a name you assign. If you change the code name of a control after writing event procedures, you must rename your procedures to match; otherwise, they will never run in response to the events for that control.

To view an event procedure, open the **Code** window for the document, workbook, worksheet, slide, or UserForm where the event can be triggered; select the name of the object that recognizes the event (this can be either the object where the event can be triggered itself or an ActiveX control contained in the object) in the **Object** box; and then select the name of the specific event you want to respond to in the **Procedure** box.

Note   If you want a procedure to be associated with a specific document, workbook, worksheet, slide, or custom dialog box, but not with a specific event—for instance, if you want to be able to call the procedure from several different event procedures—store it in the **(General)** section of the document, workbook, worksheet, or slide module.

Timesaving Tools for Writing Code

Many keywords used in Visual Basic are extremely long and difficult to type without making mistakes. To reduce the time you spend typing and the number of typing errors in your code, Visual Basic includes tools that complete words and build expressions for you.

When you've typed enough letters for Visual Basic to recognize a word, press CTRL+SPACE or click the **Complete Word** button on the **Edit** toolbar to have Visual Basic automatically complete the word for you.

In the **Options** dialog box (**Tools** menu), you can turn on tools that automatically do the following after you enter a line of code: verify correct syntax, display information, and give you appropriate options to choose from at each stage of building your expression.

You can also use the **List Properties/Methods**, **List Constants**, **Quick Info**, **Parameter Info**, and **Complete Word** buttons on the **Edit** toolbar to get help completing a word or an expression at any time. For more information about using a specific tool to help you complete words and statements, see the Help topic for that button or option. For information about using these tools to build statements using Office properties and methods, see Chapter 2, "Understanding Object Models."

Writing Code That's Easy to Read and Navigate

There are many ways to make your Visual Basic code more readable, as described in the following paragraphs.

Add comments to your code by using an apostrophe ('). At run time, Visual Basic ignores everything between the apostrophe and the end of the line. Each line in the following example includes a comment.

```
'This procedure calculates the burdened cost
'of the specified employee
Dim baseSalary As Currency          'salary not including benefits or bonuses
baseSalary = employeeLevel * 2500   'employeeLevel passed as argument
```

To add the comment character to the beginning of each line in a selected block of code, click the **Comment Block** button on the **Edit** toolbar. To remove the comment character from the beginning of each line in a selected block of code, click the **Uncomment Block** button.

Break a long statement into multiple lines in the Code window by using the *line-continuation character*, which is a space followed by an underscore (_). The following example shows the same statement expressed two different ways: on a single line, and continued over two lines:

```
Set myField = ActiveDocument.Fields.Add(Range:=Selection.Range, Type:=wdFieldDate)

Set myField = ActiveDocument.Fields.Add(Range:=Selection.Range, _
    Type:=wdFieldDate)
```

Note that you cannot use the line-continuation character in the middle of a literal string. If you have to break the line within a literal string, break the string with the concatenation character (&), as shown in the following example.

```
MsgBox "This is a string that I have to break up " & _
    "so that I can continue it on another line"
```

You cannot follow a line-continuation character with a comment on the same line.

Use indentation levels to show logical levels in your code. Press TAB or click the **Indent** button on the **Edit** toolbar to shift each line in a selected block of code one indentation level to the right. Lines within the selection retain their indentation levels relative to one another. Press SHIFT+TAB or click the **Outdent** button on the **Edit** toolbar to shift each line in a selected block of code one indentation level to the right.

Use bookmarks to mark key areas in your code that you want to be able to move between quickly without having to navigate manually. Add a bookmark to a line by clicking the **Toggle Bookmark** button on the **Edit** toolbar. A blue, rounded rectangle appears in the margin to indicate a bookmark. To navigate between bookmarks, click the **Next Bookmark** or **Previous Bookmark** button on the **Edit** toolbar.

For more information about a specific feature, see the appropriate topic in Help.

Document Projects vs. Template Projects

If you're writing procedures that are specifically designed to be run on a single document, workbook, or presentation, you can store the code in the project associated with that document, workbook, or presentation.

If, however, you want to be able to get to a procedure from more than one document, workbook, or presentation, you can store the code in the project associated with a particular template.

When you apply a template to a Word document, the template is attached to the Word document. All procedures in the attached template are available to the document. If you change the code in a template, the changed code is available for use in all documents based on that template. If you want a procedure to be available to all Word documents, regardless of which templates they're based on, store the procedure in Normal.dot, which is automatically referenced by all documents.

When you apply a template to a workbook or a presentation, any code in the template project is copied to the project for the workbook or presentation. Unlike Word, Microsoft Excel and PowerPoint don't attach the template to the workbook, so changes you make to the code in the template project won't be reflected in the workbook or presentation projects after the template has been applied. If you want a procedure to be available to all Microsoft Excel workbooks, regardless of which templates they're based on, store the procedure in Personal.xls.

Class Modules

You use class modules to create your own custom objects when you want to create encapsulated, reusable units of code. The **Sub** and **Function** procedures you define in a class module become methods of the custom object. The properties you define with the **Property Get**, **Property Let**, and **Property Set** statements become properties of the custom object. For more information about creating and using custom classes, see Mastering Office 97 Development, a CD-ROM product available from Microsoft.

If you've added class modules to your project, either by clicking **Class Module** on the **Insert** menu or by copying modules from another project, you'll see a Class Modules folder under the project name in the **Project Explorer**. You get to the code for a particular class by clicking the class name and then clicking the **View Code** button at the top of the **Project Explorer**.

Variables, Constants, and Data Types

In Visual Basic, as in all high-level programming languages, you use variables and constants to store values. Variables can contain data represented by any supported data type.

Visual Basic Data Types

The following table lists the fundamental data types that Visual Basic supports.

Data type	Description	Range
Byte	1-byte binary data	0 to 255.
Integer	2-byte integer	−32,768 to 32,767.
Long	4-byte integer	−2,147,483,648 to 2,147,483,647.
Single	4-byte floating-point number	−3.402823E38 to −1.401298E−45 (negative values).
		1.401298E−45 to 3.402823E38 (positive values).
Double	8-byte floating-point number	−1.79769313486231E308 to −4.94065645841247E − 324 (negative values).
		4.94065645841247E− 324 to 1.79769313486231E308 (positive values).
Currency	8-byte number with a fixed decimal point	−922,337,203,685,477.5808 to 922,337,203,685,477.5807.
String	String of characters	Zero to approximately two billion characters.
Variant	Date/time, floating-point number, integer, string, or object. 16 bytes, plus 1 byte for each character if the value is a string value.	Date values: January 1, 100 to December 31, 9999. Numeric values: same range as **Double**. String values: same range as **String**. Can also contain **Error** or **Null** values.
Boolean	2 bytes	**True** or **False**.
Date	8-byte date/time value	January 1, 100 to December 31, 9999.
Object	4 bytes	Any object reference.

Declaring a Constant, Variable, or Array

You declare a constant for use in place of a literal value by using the **Const** statement. You can specify private or public scope, specify a data type, and assign a value to the constant, as shown in the following declarations.

```
Const MyVar = 459
Public Const MyString = "HELP"
Private Const MyInt As Integer = 5
Const MyStr = "Hello", MyDouble As Double = 3.4567
```

If you don't specify scope, the constant has private scope by default. If you don't explicitly specify a data type when you declare a constant, Visual Basic gives the constant the data type that best matches the expression assigned to the constant. For more information, see "Const Statement," "Public Statement," "Private Statement," and "As" in Help.

You declare a variable by using the **Dim**, **Private**, **Public**, or **Static** keyword. Use the **As** keyword to explicitly specify a data type for the variable, as shown in the following declarations.

```
Private I
Dim Amt
Static YourName As String
Public BillsPaid As Currency
Private YourName As String, BillsPaid As Currency
Private Test, Amount, J As Integer
```

If you don't declare a variable as static, when a procedure that contains it ends, the variable's value isn't preserved and the memory that the variable used is reclaimed. If you don't explicitly declare a data type, Visual Basic gives the variable the **Variant** data type by default.

Note Not all variables in the same declaration statement have the same specified type. For example, the variables Test and Amount in the last line in the preceding example are of the **Variant** data type.

The steps you take to declare an array are very similar to the steps you take to declare a variable. You use the **Private**, **Public**, **Dim**, and **Static** keywords to declare the array, you use integer values to specify the upper and lower bounds for each dimension, and you use the **As** keyword to specify the data type for the array elements. You must explicitly declare an array before you can use it; you cannot implicitly declare an array.

When you declare an array, you specify the upper and lower bounds for each dimension within the parentheses following the array name. If you specify only one value for a dimension, Visual Basic interprets the value as the upper bound and supplies a default lower bound. The default lower bound is 0 (zero) unless you set it to 1 by using the **Option Base** statement. The following declarations declare one-dimensional arrays containing 15 and 21 elements, respectively.

```
Dim counters(14) As Integer
Dim sums(20) As Double
```

You can also specify the lower bound of a dimension explicitly. To do this, separate the lower and upper bounds with the **To** keyword, as in the following declarations.

```
Dim counters(1 To 15) As Integer
Dim sums(100 To 120) As String
```

In the preceding declarations, the index numbers of counters range from 1 to 15, and the index numbers of sums range from 100 to 120.

Tip   You can use the **LBound** and **UBound** functions to determine the existing lower and upper bounds of an array.

You can declare arrays of up to 60 dimensions. The following declaration creates an array with three dimensions, whose sizes are 4, 10, and 15. The total number of elements is the product of these three dimensions, or 600.

```
Dim multiD(4, 1 To 10, 1 To 15)
```

Tip   When you start adding dimensions to an array, the total amount of storage needed by the array increases dramatically, so use multidimensional arrays with care. Be especially careful with **Variant** arrays, because they're larger than arrays of other data types.

You declare a dynamic array just as you would declare a fixed-size array, but without specifying dimension sizes within the parentheses following the array name, as in the following declaration.

```
Dim dynArray() As Integer
```

Somewhere in a procedure, allocate the actual number of elements with a **ReDim** statement, as in the following example.

```
ReDim DynArray(X + 1)
```

Use the **Preserve** keyword to change the size of an array without losing the data in it. You can enlarge an array by one element without losing the values of the existing elements, as in the following example.

```
ReDim Preserve myArray(UBound(myArray) + 1)
```

For more information, see "ReDim Statement" in Help.

Setting an Object Variable

You declare an object variable by specifying for the data type either the generic **Object** type or a specific class name from a referenced object library. The following declaration declares an object variable of the generic type **Object**.

```
Dim mySheet As Object
```

When an object variable is declared as the generic type **Object**, Visual Basic doesn't know what type of object the variable will later be used with. Therefore, Visual Basic

cannot verify at compile time that the object exists, cannot verify that any properties or methods used with the object are specified correctly, and cannot bind this information to the object variable—in other words, Visual Basic cannot *early bind* the object variable. Not until the code runs and actually assigns an object to the object variable can Visual Basic verify this information and *late bind* the object variable. Generic object variables are useful when you don't know the specific type of object that the variable will contain, or when the variable must at different times contain objects from several different classes. If possible, however, you should provide a specific class name when declaring an object variable, as shown in the following declarations.

```
Dim mySheet As Worksheet
Dim myPres As Presentation
Dim myRange As Range
Dim myApp As Application
```

In addition to providing a specific class name, you may want to qualify the object variable type with the name of the application that's supplying the object, as in the following declarations. This is useful if you write code using the objects from more than one library, especially if the different libraries contain objects with the same name.

```
Dim wndXL As Excel.Window
Dim wndWD As Word.Window
Dim appWD As Word.Application
```

To assign an object to an object variable, use the **Set** statement, as shown in the following example.

```
Dim myRange As Excel.Range
Set myRange = Worksheets("Sheet1").Range("A1")
```

If you don't explicitly declare an object variable and you forget the **Set** statement in your assignment, Visual Basic attempts to use the default property of the object to assign a value to the variable. The following example assigns to the variable myRange the value of the default property of the **Range** object (which is the **Value** property) rather than the **Range** object itself.

```
myRange = Worksheets("Sheet1").Range("A1")   ' forgot the Set statement!
```

Using Built-in Constants

The object library in each Office 97 application provides a set of built-in constants, which you can use to set properties or pass arguments to properties or methods. An enumerated type is a set of built-in constants that represent the possible values that a specific property can be set to or that a specific property or method can accept as an argument. In the Object Browser, many properties or methods will display the name of an enumerated type for a return type or an argument type instead of displaying a basic data type. To open the Object Browser in the Visual Basic Editor, press F2. You can use the Object Browser to see which constants are included in an enumerated type and what literal value each constant represents. For example, click **Application** in the **Classes** box in the Object Browser, and click **DisplayAlerts** in the **Members of** box. In the pane at the bottom of the Object Browser, you see the following phrase:

Property **DisplayAlerts** As <u>WdAlertLevel</u>

WdAlertLevel is an enumerated type that contains a set of constants that represent all the valid values for the **DisplayAlerts** property. You can recognize an enumerated type name because it begins with a prefix that indicates the object library that supplied it—such as **Mso**, **Wd**, **Xl**, **Ac**, **Pp**, **VB**, or **Fm**—just as built-in constant names do. To see the constants included in this enumerated type, click **WdAlertLevel**. Built-in constant names begin with the same prefixes as enumerated types. The **Classes** box in the Object Browser will scroll to the **WdAlertLevel** enumerated type, and you'll see the constants of this type listed in the **Members of** box. If you click one of the constants, you'll see the literal value that it represents in the pane at the bottom of the Object Browser. For more information about using the Object Browser, see Chapter 2, "Understanding Object Models."

You use built-in constants to replace literal values in your code. The two lines of code in the following example, each of which sets Word to display all alerts and message boxes when it's running a procedure, are equivalent to one another.

```
Application.DisplayAlerts = -1
Application.DisplayAlerts = wdAlertsAll
```

Code that uses these constants instead of literal values is easier to read. In addition, code that uses built-in constants is less likely to need to be updated if values are remapped in future versions. That is, whereas the literal value -1 might not always represent the option of displaying all alerts and message boxes, the constant **wdAlertsAll** always will.

Control Structures

Using control structures, you can control the flow of your program's execution. If left unchecked by control-flow statements, a program's logic will flow through statements from left to right, and from top to bottom. Although you can write very simple programs with only this unidirectional flow, and although you can control a certain amount of flow by using operators to regulate precedence of operations, most of the power and utility of any programming language comes from its ability to change statement order with structures and loops.

Decision Structures

Visual Basic procedures can test conditions and then, depending on the results of that test, perform different operations. The Visual Basic decision structures are listed in the following table.

To test	Use
A single condition and run a single statement or a block of statements	**If...Then**
A single condition and choose between two statement blocks	**If...Then...Else**
More than one condition and run one of several statement blocks	**If...Then...ElseIf**
A single condition and run one of several statement blocks	**Select Case**

If...Then

Use the **If...Then** statement to run one or more statements when the specified condition is **True**. You can use either a single-line syntax or a multiple-line "block" syntax. The following pair of examples illustrate the two types of syntax.

```
If thisVal < 0 Then thisVal = 0

If thisVal > 5 Then
    thatVal = thisVal + 25
    thisVal = 0
End If
```

Notice that the single-line form of the **If...Then** statement doesn't use an **End If** statement. If you want to run more than one line of code when the condition is **True**, you must use the multiple-line **If...Then...End If** syntax.

Note   When the condition you're evaluating contains two expressions joined by an **Or** operator—for example, If (thisVal > 5 Or thatVal < 9)—both expressions are tested, even if the first one is **True**. In rare circumstances, this behavior can affect the outcome of the statement; for example, it can cause a run-time error if a variable in the second expression contains an error value.

If...Then...Else

Use the **If...Then...Else** statement to define two blocks of statements, as in the following example. One of the statements runs when the specified condition is **True**, and the other one runs when the condition is **False**.

```
If age < 16 Then
    MsgBox "You are not old enough for a license."
Else
    MsgBox "You can be tested for a license."
End If
```

If...Then...ElseIf

You can add **ElseIf** statements to test additional conditions without using nested **If...Then** statements, thus making your code shorter and easier to read. For example, suppose that you need to calculate employee bonuses using bonus rates that vary according to job classification. The **Function** procedure in the following example uses a series of **ElseIf** statements to test the job classification before calculating the bonus.

```
Function Bonus(jobClass, salary, rating)
    If jobClass = 1 Then
        Bonus = salary * 0.1 * rating / 10
    ElseIf jobClass = 2 Then
        Bonus = salary * 0.09 * rating / 10
    ElseIf jobClass = 3 Then
        Bonus = salary * 0.07 * rating / 10
    Else
        Bonus = 0
    End If
End Function
```

The **If...Then...ElseIf** statement block is very flexible. You can start with a simple **If...Then** statement and add **Else** and **ElseIf** clauses as necessary. However, this approach is unnecessarily tedious if each **ElseIf** statement compares the same expression with a different value. For this situation, you can use the **Select Case** statement.

Select Case

You can use the **Select Case** statement instead of multiple **ElseIf** statements in an **If...Then...ElseIf** structure when you want to compare the same expression with several different values. A **Select Case** statement provides a decision-making capability similar to the **If...Then...ElseIf** statement; however, **Select Case** makes the code more efficient and readable.

For instance, to add several more job classifications to the example in the preceding section, you can add more **ElseIf** statements, or you can write the function using a **Select Case** statement, as in the following example.

```
Function Bonus(jobClass, salary, rating)
    Select Case jobClass
        Case 1
            Bonus = salary * 0.1 * rating / 10
        Case 2
            Bonus = salary * 0.09 * rating / 10
        Case 3
            Bonus = salary * 0.07 * rating / 10
        Case 4, 5'The expression list can contain several values...
            Bonus = salary * 0.05 * rating / 5
        Case 6 To 8 '...or be a range of values
            Bonus = 150
        Case Is > 8 '...or be compared to other values
            Bonus = 100
        Case Else
            Bonus = 0
    End Select
End Function
```

Notice that the **Select Case** structure evaluates a single expression at the top of the structure. In contrast, the **If...Then...ElseIf** structure can evaluate a different expression for each **ElseIf** statement. You can replace an **If...Then...ElseIf** structure with a **Select Case** structure only if each **ElseIf** statement evaluates the same expression.

Looping Structures

You can use loop structures to repeatedly run a section of your procedure. The Visual Basic loop structures are listed in the following table.

To	Use
Test a condition at the start of the loop, run the loop only if the condition is **True**, and continue until the condition becomes **False**	**Do While...Loop**
Test a condition at the start of the loop, run the loop only if the condition is **False**, and continue until the condition becomes **True**	**Do Until...Loop**
Always run the loop once, test a condition at the end of the loop, continue while the condition is **True**, and stop when the condition becomes **False**	**Do...Loop While**
Always run the loop once, test a condition at the end of the loop, continue while the condition is **False**, and stop when the condition becomes **True**	**Do...Loop Until**
Run a loop a set number of times, using a loop counter that starts and ends at specified values and that changes value by a specified amount each time through the loop	**For...Next**
Run a loop once for each object in a collection	**For Each...Next**

Note   Visual Basic also includes the **While...Wend** statement, but it's a good idea to use the more flexible variations of the **Do...Loop** statement (such as **Do While...Loop** or **Do...Loop While**) instead.

Do...Loop

Use a **Do...Loop** statement to run a block of statements an indefinite number of times—that is, when you don't know how many times you need to run the statements in the loop. There are several variations of the **Do...Loop** statement, but each one evaluates a condition to determine whether or not to continue running. As with an **If...Then** statement, the condition must be a value or an expression that evaluates to either **True** or **False**. The different **Do...Loop** variations are described in this section. For more information about the **Do...Loop** statement, see "Do...Loop Statement" in Help.

Note   If you want to run a block of statements a specific number of times, use a **For...Next** loop.

Do While...Loop

Use the **Do While...Loop** statement when you want to test a condition before you run the loop and then continue to run the loop while the condition is **True**.

Note   The statements in a **Do While...Loop** structure must eventually cause the condition to become **False**, or the loop will run forever (this is called an *infinite loop*). To stop an infinite loop, press CTRL+BREAK.

The **Function** procedure in the following example counts the occurrences of a target string within another string by looping as long as the target string is found. Because the test is at the beginning of the loop, the loop runs only if the string contains the target string.

```
Function CountStrings(longstring, target)
    position = 1
    Do While InStr(position, longstring, target) 'Returns True/False
        position = InStr(position, longstring, target) + 1
        Count = Count + 1
    Loop
    CountStrings = Count
End Function
```

Do Until...Loop

Use the **Do Until...Loop** statement if you want to test the condition at the beginning of the loop and then run the loop until the test condition becomes **True**. If the condition is initially **True**, the statements inside the loop never run. With the test at the beginning of the loop in the following example, the loop won't run if **Response** is equal to **vbNo**.

```
Response = MsgBox("Do you want to process more data?", vbYesNo)
Do Until Response = vbNo
    ProcessUserData    'Call procedure to process data
    Response = MsgBox("Do you want to process more data?", vbYesNo)
Loop
```

Do...Loop While

When you want to make sure that the statements in a loop will run at least once, use **Do...Loop While** to put the test at the end of the loop . The statements will run as long as the condition is **True**. In the following Microsoft Excel example, the loop runs only if the **Find** method finds a cell that contains "test." If the text is found, the loop sets the color of the cell, and then searches for the next instance of "test." If no other instance is found, the loop ends.

```
Sub MakeBlue()
    Set rSearch = Worksheets("sheet1").Range("a1:a10")
    Set c = rSearch.Find("test")
    If Not c Is Nothing Then
        first = c.Address
        Do
            c.Font.ColorIndex = 5
            Set c = rSearch.FindNext(c)
        Loop While (Not c Is Nothing) And (c.Address <> first)
    Else
        MsgBox "not found"
    End If
End Sub
```

Do...Loop Until

With the **Do...Loop Until** statement, which puts the test at the end of the loop, the loop runs at least once and stops running when the condition becomes **True**, as shown in the following example.

```
Do
    ProcessUserData    'Call procedure to process data
    response = MsgBox("Do you want to process more data?", vbYesNo)
Loop Until response = vbNo
```

For...Next

When you know that you must run the statements a specific number of times, use a **For...Next** loop. Unlike the many variations of **Do...Loop**, a **For...Next** loop uses a counter variable that increases or decreases in value during each repetition of the loop. Whereas the variations of **Do...Loop** end when a test condition becomes **True** or **False**, a **For...Next** loop ends when the counter variable reaches a specified value.

The **Sub** procedure in the following example sounds a tone however many times you specify.

```
Sub BeepSeveral()
    numBeeps = InputBox("How many beeps?")
    For counter = 1 To numBeeps
        Beep
    Next counter
End Sub
```

Because you didn't specify otherwise, the counter variable in the preceding example increases by 1 each time the loop repeats. You can use the **Step** keyword to specify a different increment for the counter variable (if you specify a negative number, the counter variable decreases by the specified value each time through the loop). In the following **Sub** procedure, which replaces every other value in an array with 0 (zero), the counter variable increases by 2 each time the loop repeats.

```
Sub ClearArray(ByRef ArrayToClear())
   For i = LBound(ArrayToClear) To UBound(ArrayToClear) Step 2
      ArrayToClear(i) = 0
   Next i
End Sub
```

Note The variable name after the **Next** statement is optional, but it can make your code easier to read, especially if you have several nested **For** loops.

For Each...Next

A **For Each...Next** loop is similar to a **For...Next** loop, except that it repeats a group of statements for each element in a collection of objects or in an array, instead of repeating the statements a specified number of times. This is especially useful if you don't know how many elements are in a collection, or if the contents of the collection might change as your procedure runs. The **For Each…Next** statement uses the following syntax.

For Each *element* **In** *group*
   statements
Next *element*

When Visual Basic runs a **For Each...Next** loop, it follows these steps:

1. It defines *element* as naming the first element in *group* (provided that there's at least one element).

2. It runs *statements.*

3. It tests to see whether *element* is the last element in *group.* If so, Visual Basic exits the loop.

4. It defines *element* as naming the next element in *group.*

5. It repeats steps 2 through 4.

The following Microsoft Excel example examines each cell in the current region for cell A1 on the worksheet named "Sheet3" and formats its contents as red if its value is less than −1.

```
For Each c In Worksheets("sheet3").Range("a1").CurrentRegion.Cells
   If c.Value < -1 Then c.Font.ColorIndex = 3
Next c
```

The following Word example loops through all the revisions in the current selection and accepts each one.

```
For Each myRev In Selection.Range.Revisions
   myRev.Accept
Next myRev
```

The variable name after the **Next** statement—c in the Microsoft Excel example and myRev in the Word example—is optional, but it can make your code easier to read, especially if you have several nested **For Each** loops.

Important   If you want to delete all the objects in a collection, use a **For...Next** loop instead of a **For Each...Next** loop. The following example deletes all the slides in the active PowerPoint presentation.

```
Set allSlides = ActivePresentation.Slides
For s = allSlides.Count To 1 Step -1
    allSlides.Item(s).Delete
Next
```

The code in the following example, on the other hand, won't work (it will delete every other slide in the presentation).

```
For Each s In ActivePresentation.Slides
    s.Delete
Next
```

Keep the following restrictions in mind when using the **For Each...Next** statement:

- For collections, *element* can only be a **Variant** variable, a generic **Object** variable, or a specific object type in a referenced object library. For arrays, *element* can only be a **Variant** variable.

- You cannot use the **For Each...Next** statement with an array of user-defined types, because a **Variant** variable cannot contain a user-defined type.

Nesting Control Structures

You can place control structures inside other control structures; for instance, you can place an **If...Then** block within a **For Each...Next** loop within another **If...Then** block, and so on. A control structure placed inside another control structure is said to be *nested*.

The following example searches the range of cells you specify with an argument and counts the number of cells that match the value you specify.

```
Function CountValues(rangeToSearch, searchValue)
    If TypeName(rangeToSearch) <> "Range" Then
        MsgBox "You can search only a range of cells."
    Else
        For Each c in rangeToSearch.cells
            If c.Value = searchValue Then
                counter = counter + 1
            End If
        Next c
    End If
    CountValues = counter
End Function
```

Notice that the first **End If** statement closes the inner **If...Then** block and that the last **End If** statement closes the outer **If...Then** block. Likewise, in nested **For...Next** and **For Each...Next** loops, the **Next** statements automatically apply to the nearest prior **For** or **For Each** statement. Nested **Do...Loop** structures work in a similar fashion, with the innermost **Loop** statement matching the innermost **Do** statement.

Exiting Loops and Procedures

Usually, your macros will run through loops and procedures from beginning to end. There may be situations, however, in which leaving, or exiting, a loop or procedure earlier than normal can save you time by avoiding unnecessary repetition.

For example, if you're searching for a value in an array using a **For...Next** loop and you find the value the first time through the loop, there's no reason to search the rest of the array—you can stop repeating the loop and continue with the rest of the procedure immediately. If an error occurs in a procedure that makes the remainder of the procedure unnecessary, you can exit the procedure immediately. You can cut a control structure off early by using one of the **Exit** statements.

Although the **Exit** statements can be convenient, you should use them only when it's absolutely necessary and only as a response to an extraordinary condition (not in the normal flow of a loop or procedure). Overusing **Exit** statements can make your code difficult to read and debug.

Also , there may be a better way to skip portions of your macro. For instance, instead of using an **Exit** statement inside a **For...Next** loop while searching for a value in an array, you could use a **Do...Loop** to search the array only while an incremented index value is smaller than the array's upper bound and a **Boolean** variable value is **False**, as shown in the following example. When you find the array value, setting the **Boolean** value to **True** causes the loop to stop.

```
i = LBound(searchArray)
ub = UBound(searchArray)
foundIt = False
Do
    If searchArray(i) = findThis Then foundIt = True
    i = i + 1
Loop While i <= ub And Not foundIt
```

You use the **Exit Do** statement to exit directly from a **Do...Loop**, and you use the **Exit For** statement to exit directly from a **For** loop, as shown in the following example.

```
For Each c in rangeToSearch
    If c.Value = searchValue Then
        found = True
        Exit For
    End If
Next
```

You use the **Exit Sub** and **Exit Function** statements to exit a procedure. The following example demonstrates the use of **Exit Function**.

```
For Each c in rangeToSearch
   If c.Value = searchValue Then
      counter = counter + 1
   ElseIf c.Value = "Bad Data" Then
      countValues = Null
      Exit Function   'Stop testing and exit immediately.
   End If
Next c
```

CHAPTER 2

Understanding Object Models

Objects are the fundamental building blocks of the Microsoft Office 97 applications; nearly everything you do in Visual Basic involves manipulating objects. Every unit of content and functionality in Office—each workbook, worksheet, document, range of text, slide, and so on—is an object that you can control programmatically in Visual Basic. When you understand how to work with objects, you're ready to automate tasks in Office.

This chapter gives you a conceptual overview of objects and object models and the tools and techniques you use to explore and use them. For more information about using the object model for a particular application, see the chapter in this book that's devoted to working with that object model.

Contents
- Overview of Object Models
- Automating a Task by Using Objects
- Programming Another Application's Objects

Overview of Object Models

Before you can programmatically gain access to an application's content and functionality, it's important to understand how the content and functionality of the application is partitioned into discrete objects and how these objects are arranged in a hierarchical model.

What Are Objects and Object Models?

An application consists of two things: content and functionality. Content refers to the documents the application contains and the words, numbers, or graphics included in the documents; it also refers to information about attributes of individual elements in the application, such as the size of a window, the color of a graphic, or the font size of a word. Functionality refers to all the ways you can work with the content in the application—for example, opening, closing, adding, deleting, copying, pasting, editing, or formatting elements in the application.

The content and functionality in an application are broken down into discrete units of related content and functionality called *objects*. You're already familiar with some of these objects, as elements of the user interface: Microsoft Excel workbooks, worksheets, and cell ranges; Word documents and sections; and PowerPoint presentations and slides.

The top-level object in an application is usually the **Application** object, which is the application itself. For instance, Microsoft Excel itself is the **Application** object in the Microsoft Excel object model. The **Application** object contains other objects that you have access to only when the **Application** object exists (that is, when the application is running). For example, the Microsoft Excel **Application** object contains **Workbook** objects, and the Word **Application** object contains **Document** objects. Because the **Document** object depends on the existence of the Word **Application** object for its own existence, the **Document** object is said to be the *child* of the **Application** object; conversely, the **Application** object is said to be the *parent* of the **Document** object.

Many objects that are children have children of their own. For example, the Microsoft Excel **Workbook** object contains, or is parent to, the collection of **Worksheet** objects that represent all the worksheets in the workbook. A parent object can have multiple children; for instance, the Word **Window** object has as children the **Panes**, **Selection**, and **View** objects. Likewise, a child object can have multiple parents; for instance, the Word **Windows** collection object is the child of both the **Application** object and the **Document** object.

The way the objects that make up an application are arranged relative to each other, together with the way the content and functionality are divided among the objects, is called the *object hierarchy* or the *object model*. To see a graphical representation of the object model for a particular application, see "Microsoft Access Objects," "Microsoft Excel Objects," "Microsoft Word Objects," or "Microsoft PowerPoint Objects" in Visual Basic Help for that application. For information about using Help and the Object Browser to explore an object model, see "Getting Help Writing Code" later in this chapter.

Note If you clicked **Typical** when you installed Microsoft Office, you'll need to run Setup again to install Visual Basic Help for the application you want to program in.

In addition to containing lower-level objects, each object in the hierarchy contains content and functionality that apply both to the object itself and to all objects below it in the hierarchy. The higher an object is in the hierarchy, the wider the scope of its content and functionality. For example, in Microsoft Excel, the **Application** object contains the size of the application window and the ability to quit the application; the **Workbook** object contains the file name and format of the workbook and the ability to save the workbook; and the **Worksheet** object contains the worksheet name and the ability to delete the worksheet.

You often don't get to what you think of as the contents of a file (such as the values on a Microsoft Excel worksheet or the text in a Word document) until you've navigated through quite a few levels in the object hierarchy, because this specific information belongs to a very specific part of the application. In other words, the value in a cell on a worksheet applies only to that cell, not to all cells on the worksheet, so you cannot store it directly in the **Worksheet** object. The content and functionality stored in an object are thus intrinsically appropriate to the scope of the object.

In summary, the content and functionality in an application are divided among the objects in the application's object model. Together, the objects in the hierarchy contain all the content and functionality in the application. Separately, the objects provide access to very specific areas of content and functionality.

What Are Properties and Methods?

To get to the content and functionality contained in an object, you use properties and methods of that object. The following Microsoft Excel example uses the **Value** property of the **Range** object to set the contents of cell B3 on the worksheet named "Sales" in the workbook named "Current.xls."

```
Workbooks("Current.xls").Worksheets("Sales").Range("B3").Value = 3
```

The following example uses the **Bold** property of the **Font** object to apply bold formatting to cell B3 on the Sales worksheet.

```
Workbooks("Current.xls").Worksheets("Sales").Range("B3").Font.Bold = True
```

The following Word example uses the **Close** method of the **Document** object to close the file named "Draft 3.doc."

```
Documents("Draft 3.doc").Close
```

In general, you use properties to get to content, which can include the text contained in an object or the attribute settings for the object; and you use methods to get to functionality, which entails everything you can do to the content. Be aware, however, that this distinction doesn't always hold true; there are a number of properties and methods in every object model that constitute exceptions to this rule.

How Is the Object Model Related to the User Interface?

There are two ways to interact with an application's objects: manually (using the user interface) or programmatically (using a programming language). In the user interface, you use the keyboard or the mouse, or both, to navigate to the part of the application that controls the data you want to change or the commands you want to use. For example, in Microsoft Excel, to enter a value into cell B3 on the worksheet named "Sales" in the workbook named "Current.xls," you open the Current.xls workbook, you click the tab for the Sales worksheet, you click in cell B3, and then you type a value.

In Visual Basic statements, you navigate through the object model from the top-level object to the object that contains the content and functionality you want to work with, and you use properties and methods of that object to get to the content and functionality. For example, the following Microsoft Excel example navigates to cell B3 on the Sales worksheet in the Current.xls workbook and sets the contents of the cell.

```
Workbooks("Current.xls").Worksheets("Sales").Range("B3").Value = 3
```

Because the user interface and Visual Basic are two ways of gaining access to the exact same content and functionality, many objects, properties, and methods share names with elements in the user interface, and the overall structure of the object model resembles the structure of the user interface. This also means that for every action you can take in the user interface, there's a Visual Basic code equivalent. For information about using the macro recorder to translate user interface actions into their Visual Basic code equivalents, see "Using the Macro Recorder" later in this chapter.

Why Does It Matter Where an Object Is in the Object Model?

It's important to understand an object's place in the object model, because before you can work with an object, you have to navigate through the object model to get to it. This usually means that you have to step down through all the objects above it in the object hierarchy to get to it. For example, in Microsoft Excel, you cannot get to a particular cell on a worksheet without first going through the application , which contains the workbook that contains the worksheet that contains the cell. The following example inserts the value 3 in cell B3 on the worksheet named "Second Quarter" in the workbook named "Annual Sales.xls."

```
Application.Workbooks("Annual Sales.xls").WorkSheets("Second
Quarter").Range("B3").Value = 3
```

Similarly, the following Word example applies bold formatting to the second word in the third paragraph in the first open document.

```
Application.Documents(1).Paragraphs(3).Range.Words(2).Bold = True
```

What Are Collection Objects?

When using Visual Basic Help graphics to explore the object model for the application in which you want to program, you may notice that there are many boxes in the graphics that contain two words—usually the singular and plural forms of the same object name, such as "Documents (Document)" or "Workbooks (Workbook)." In these cases, the first name (usually the plural form) is the name of a *collection object*. A collection object is an object that contains a set of related objects. You can work with the objects in a collection as a single group rather than as separate entities. The second name (usually the singular form), enclosed in parentheses, is the name of an individual object in the collection. For example, in Word, you can use the **Documents** collection to work with all the **Document** objects as a group.

Although the **Documents** collection object and the **Document** object are both objects in their own right, each with its own properties and methods, they're grouped as one unit in most object model graphics to reduce complexity. You can use a collection object to get to an individual object in that collection, usually with the **Item** method or property. The following PowerPoint example uses the **Item** property of the **Presentations** collection object to activate the presentation named "Trade Show" and then close it. All other open presentations are left open.

```
Presentations.Item("Trade Show").Close
```

Note   The **Item** property or method is the default method for most collections. Therefore, `Presentations("Trade Show").Close` is equivalent to the preceding example.

You can also create new objects and add them to a collection, usually by using the **Add** method of that collection. The following Word example creates a new document based on the Normal template.

```
Documents.Add
```

You can find out how many objects there are in the collection by using the **Count** property. The following Microsoft Excel example displays the number of open workbooks in a message box if more than three workbooks are open.

```
If Workbooks.Count > 3 Then MsgBox "More than 3 workbooks are open"
```

Collections are useful in other ways as well. For instance, you can perform an operation on all the objects in a given collection, or you can set or test a value for all the objects in the collection. To do this, you use a **For Each...Next** or **For...Next** structure to loop through all the objects in the collection. For more information about looping through a collection, see Chapter 1, "Programming Basics."

Automating a Task by Using Objects

To automate a task in Microsoft Office, you first return a reference to the object that contains the content and functionality you want to get to, and then you apply properties and methods to that object. If you don't know which properties and methods you need to apply to what object to accomplish the task, or how to navigate through the object model to get to that object, see "Getting Help Writing Code" later in this chapter.

Returning a Reference to an Object

Before you can do anything with an object, you must return a reference to the object. To do this, you must build an expression that gains access to one object in the object model and then uses properties or methods to move up or down through the object hierarchy until you get to the object you want to work with. The properties and methods you use to return the object you start from and to move from one object to another are called *object accessors*, or just *accessors*. As you build an expression with accessors to return a reference to an object, keep the following guidelines in mind.

- A common place to gain access to the object model is the top-level object, which is usually the **Application** object. Use the **Application** property to return a reference to the **Application** object. The following expression returns a reference to the **Application** object (for any object library that contains an **Application** object).

```
Application
```

- To drill down to an object from the top-level object in a hierarchy, you must step down through all the objects above it in the hierarchy, using accessors to return one object from another. For example, the **Documents** property of the Word **Application** object returns the **Documents** collection object, which represents all open documents. The following expression returns a reference to the Word **Documents** collection object.

```
Application.Documents
```

- There are shortcut accessors you can use to gain direct access to objects in the model without having to drill down from the **Application** object. These shortcuts include accessors—such as the **Documents**, **Workbooks**, and **Presentations** properties—that you can use by themselves to return a reference to the document collection for a particular application. For example, in Word, you can use either of the following statements to open MyDoc.doc.

```
Application.Documents.Open FileName:="C:\DOCS\MYDOC.DOC"
Documents.Open FileName:="C:\DOCS\MYDOC.DOC"
```

There are other shortcut accessors—such as the **ActiveWindow**, **ActiveDocument**, **ActiveWorksheet**, or **ActiveCell** properties—that return a direct reference to an active part of an application. The following statement closes the active Word document. Notice that the **Application** object and the **Documents** collection object are never mentioned.

```
ActiveDocument.Close
```

Tip You can use any accessor that appears in the **Members of** pane of the Object Browser when **<globals>** is selected in the **Classes** pane as a shortcut; that is, you don't have to return the object that the property or method applies to before you use the property or method, because Visual Basic can determine from the context in which your code runs which object a global property or method applies to. For more information about the Object Browser, see "Getting Help Writing Code" later in this chapter.

- Many objects—such as workbooks, worksheets, documents, presentations, and slides—are members of collections. Because collections are always one level higher that individual objects in the hierarchy, you usually have to access a collection before you can get to an object in that collection. The accessor that returns a collection object often has the same name as the collection object itself.

For example, in Microsoft Excel, the following expression returns a reference to the **Workbooks** collection, which represents all open workbooks.

```
Workbooks
```

- To return a single member of a collection, you usually use the **Item** property or method with the name or index number of the member. For example, in Microsoft Excel, the following expression returns a reference to an open workbook named "Sales."

```
Workbooks.Item("Sales")
```

The **Item** property or method is the default method for most collections. Therefore, the following two expressions are equivalent.

```
Workbooks.Item("Sales")
Workbooks.("Sales")
```

- To navigate from an object higher up in the object hierarchy, you can often use the **Parent** property of the object. Note that the **Parent** property doesn't always return the immediate parent of an object—it may return the object's "grandparent," especially if the object is a member of a collection. That is, the **Parent** property of an object in a collection may return the collection's parent instead of the collection itself. For example, the **Parent** property of a Word **Document** object returns the **Application** object, not the **Documents** collection. Use the **TypeName** function to find out what kind of object the **Parent** property of an object returns a reference to. For example, in Microsoft Excel, the following statement displays the type of object that the **Parent** property of the **Worksheet** object refers to.

```
MsgBox TypeName(Workbooks(1).Worksheets(1).Parent)
```

Tip   You can use the **TypeName** function to determine the type of object returned by any expression, not just expressions containing the **Parent** property.

- To navigate from an object to the **Application** object at the top of the hierarchy, you can often use the **Application** property of the object. This is especially useful for getting at the objects in the application in which an embedded object was created. For example, in PowerPoint, the following expression returns a reference to the **Application** object for the application in which the OLE object in shape three on slide one in the active presentation was created.

```
ActivePresentation.Slides(1).Shapes(3).Object.Application
```

Applying Properties and Methods to an Object

After you've returned a reference to the object you want to work with it, you can apply properties and methods to the object to set an attribute for it or perform an action on it. You use the "dot" operator (.) to separate the expression that returns a reference to an object from the property or method you apply to the object. The following example, which can be run from Microsoft Excel, Word, or PowerPoint, sets the left position of the active window by using the **Left** property of the **Window** object that the **ActiveWindow** property returns a reference to.

```
ActiveWindow.Left = 200
```

The following Word example closes the active document by using the **Close** method of the **Document** object that the **ActiveDocument** property returns a reference to.

```
ActiveDocument.Close
```

Properties and methods can take arguments that qualify how they perform. In the following Word example, the **PrintOut** method of the **Document** object that the **ActiveDocument** property returns a reference to takes arguments that specify the range of pages it should print.

```
ActiveDocument.PrintOut From:="3", To:="7"
```

You may have to navigate through several layers in an object model to get to what you consider the real data in the application, such as the values in cells on a Microsoft Excel worksheet or the text in a Word document. The following Word example uses the following properties and methods to navigate from the top of the object model to the text of a document:

- The **Application** property returns a reference to the **Application** object.
- The **Documents** property of the **Application** object returns a reference to the **Documents** collection.
- The **Item** method of the **Documents** collection returns a reference to a single **Document** object.
- The **Words** property of the **Document** object returns a reference to the **Words** collection.
- The **Item** method of the **Words** collection returns a reference to a single **Range** object.
- The **Text** property of the **Range** object sets the text for the first word of the document.

```
Application.Documents.Item(1).Words.Item(1).Text = "The "
```

Because the **Documents** property is a global property, it can be used without the **Application** qualifier, and because **Item** is the default property or method for collection objects, you don't need to explicitly mention it in your code. You can therefore shorten the preceding statement to the statement shown in the following example. This example implicitly drills down through the same levels as the previous example does explicitly.

```
Documents(1).Words(1).Text = "The "
```

Similarly, the following Microsoft Excel example drills all the way down to the **Range** object that represents cell B3 on the worksheet named "New" in the workbook named "Sales.xls."

```
Workbooks("Sales.xls").Worksheets("New").Range("B3").Value = 7
```

Getting Help Writing Code

Sometimes you can guess what object you need to return a reference to, how to build the expression to return it, and what property or method you need to apply to it to accomplish a task. For instance, if you want to close the active Word document, you might guess that the functionality of closing a document would be controlled by a **Close** method that applied to the **Document** object that was returned by the **ActiveDocument** property—and you'd be right. Most of the time, however, figuring out which object, property, and method you want to use isn't that simple. Fortunately, the Office applications include a host of tools that help you write the code to perform your tasks.

Using the Macro Recorder

If you don't know which properties and methods you need to use to accomplish a task but you know how to perform the task (or something very similar to it) with the user interface, you can use the macro recorder to translate that series of user-interface actions into a series of Visual Basic instructions. For example, if you don't know which property or method to use to indent a paragraph in Word, record the actions you take to indent a paragraph.

▶ **To record user-interface actions in Microsoft Excel, Word, or PowerPoint**

1 On the **Tools** menu, point to **Macro**, and then click **Record New Macro**.

2 Change the default macro name and location if you want, and then click **OK** to start the macro recorder.

3 In the user interface, perform the tasks you want to accomplish.

4 When you finish your tasks, click the **Stop Recording** button on the **Stop Recording** toolbar.

5 On the **Tools** menu, point to **Macro**, and then click **Macros**.

6 Select the macro name from step 2, and then click **Edit**.

Examine the Visual Basic code, and try to correlate specific properties and methods to specific actions you took in the user interface.

Although this code can give you a good idea of what properties and methods to get more information about, you probably won't want to use the code without editing it, because the code the macro recorder generates is usually not very efficient or robust. For example, recorded code generally starts with an object that's selected or activated when you begin recording and navigates through the rest of the object model from that object, as shown in the following Word example.

```
Selection.ParagraphFormat.LeftIndent = InchesToPoints(0.5)
```

The following is another example of selection-based code in PowerPoint:

```
ActiveWindow.Selection.ShapeRange.Delete
```

The problem with code like that in the preceding examples, besides being inefficient, is that it relies on a particular element being selected or activated when you run the code for it to work properly. Your code will be much more robust and flexible if it contains expressions to navigate through the object model that don't begin with the selected or activated object. For example, in Word, if instead of applying the **ParagraphFormat** property to the **Selection** object that's returned by the **Selection** property, you apply the **Format** property to the **Paragraph** object that represents a specific paragraph (as shown in the following example), your code will run correctly no matter what's selected when you run it.

```
Documents("Test Document.doc").Paragraphs(1).Format.LeftIndent = InchesToPoints(0.5)
```

For ideas on how to improve your recorded code, position the insertion point within a property or method in your code, and then press F1 to see a Help topic with example code for that property or method. For more information about using Visual Basic Help to write code, see the following section. For more information about editing recorded code to make it more efficient, see Chapter 13, "Optimizing for Size and Speed."

Help Files and Graphics

Visual Basic Help for any given Office application contains a topic on each object, property, method, and event in the object model. To see a graphical depiction of an application's entire object model, see "Microsoft Access Objects," "Microsoft Excel Objects," "Microsoft Word Objects," or "Microsoft PowerPoint Objects" in Visual Basic Help for that application.

How Do I Display Visual Basic Help for Microsoft Excel, Word, and PowerPoint?

To use Visual Basic Help for Microsoft Excel, Word, or PowerPoint, you must click **Custom** during Setup and select the **Online Help for Visual Basic** check box for that application. Otherwise, Visual Basic Help won't be installed. If you've already installed your application, you can run Setup again to install Visual Basic Help.

To see the contents and index of Visual Basic Help for Microsoft Excel, Word, or PowerPoint, click **Contents and Index** on the **Help** menu in the Visual Basic Editor. On the **Contents** tab in the **Help Topics** dialog box, double-click the book title that includes the name of the application you're working in (for example, "Microsoft Word Visual Basic Reference"), and then double-click the shortcut in that book (for example, "Shortcut to Microsoft Word Visual Basic Reference"). The **Help Topics** dialog box should reappear, displaying the contents and index for Visual Basic Help for your application.

If you cannot tell by looking at an object's name what content and functionality the object encompasses, you can click that object in the graphic to open its Help topic and learn more about it. The Help topic for an individual object contains the following information:

- A graphic at the top of the topic that shows significant objects immediately above and below the object in the hierarchy (object model). You can click any object in the graphic to read more about it.

- An explanation of the content and functionality that the object encompasses.

- Instructions and examples that explain how to navigate through the object model to get to the object and how to then apply properties and methods to it. Note that you can copy code from Help topics to use in your own code.

- Jumps at the top of the topic that display lists of the properties and methods that apply to the object. You can click the name of a property or method to open its Help topic.

The Help topic for an individual property or method contains both a description of the content or functionality that the property or method gives you access to and a jump to an example that uses the property or method. You can copy code from Help topics to the Clipboard and then paste this code into your own module.

Object Browser

Each Office application provides a file called an *object library*, or *type library*, that contains information about the objects, properties, methods, events, and built-in constants that the application exposes. You can use a tool called the Object Browser to look at the information in this file and to browse the object model it describes.

To open the Object Browser from the Visual Basic Editor (Microsoft Excel, Word, and PowerPoint) or from a module (Microsoft Access), click **Object Browser** on the **View** menu. In the **Project/Library** box, click the name of the object library whose objects you want to see, or click **<All Libraries>** to view a master list of all the objects in all the referenced object libraries. If the object library whose objects you want to view doesn't appear in the **Project/Library** box, you must create a reference to that object library by using the **References** dialog box (**Tools** menu).

The **Classes** box in the Object Browser displays the names of all the objects and enumerated types in all the referenced object libraries.

Note A *class* is a type, or description, of object. An object is an actual instance of a class. For example, the **Workbook** class contains all the information you need to create a workbook. A **Workbook** object only comes into existence when you use the information in the **Workbook** class to create an actual workbook (an instance of the **Workbook** class). Despite this technical distinction, these terms are often used interchangeably. The term "object" is used generically for both "class" and "object" in this chapter.

When you click the name of an object in the **Classes** box in the Object Browser, you see all the properties, methods, and events associated with that object in the **Members of** box.

Tip   An *event* is an action recognized by an object, such as clicking the mouse or pressing a key. You can write code to respond to such actions. For general information about events, see Chapter 1, "Programming Basics." For information about events for a specific application, see the chapter on that application's object model, or see the topic for a specific event in Help.

Click a property or method in the **Members of** box. You can press F1 to see the Help topic for the selected keyword, or you can look in the **Details** pane at the bottom of the Object Browser window to see the following: syntax information, a property's read-only or read/write status, the object library that the object belongs to, and the type of data or object that the property or method returns. If a word in the **Details** pane is a jump, you can click it to get more information. This is useful if you want to figure out how to drill down to an object. For example, in Word, if you click the **Application** object in the **Classes** box and then click the **ActiveDocument** property in the **Members of** box, you see the following phrase in the **Details** pane:

Property **ActiveDocument** As **Document**

This tells you that the **ActiveDocument** property returns a reference to a **Document** object. If you click the return type (the object type or data type after the keyword **As**), which in this case is **Document**, the Object Browser will display the properties and methods of the **Document** object.

The **Details** pane can also be helpful if you cannot remember the exact syntax—the names and order of arguments that a given property or method takes, and which arguments are required or optional. For instance, in Word, if you click the **ComputeStatistics** method of the **Document** object that you've just navigated to, you'll see the following phrase in the **Details** pane:

Function **ComputeStatistics**(*Statistic* As **WdStatistic**, [*IncludeFootnotesAndEndnotes*]) As Long

This tells you that you can apply the **ComputeStatistics** method to the **Document** object and get back a value of type **Long**, but that you have to supply some additional information in the form of arguments for the method to work. Because the argument *Statistic* isn't in brackets, it's a required argument—that is, you must supply a value for it for the method to work. *IncludeFootnotesAndEndnotes*, which is in brackets, is an optional argument. If you don't supply a value for it, Visual Basic will use the default value.

If you're already familiar with the **ComputeStatistics** method, the information in the **Details** pane alone may jog your memory enough that you can use this method in code such as the following example.

```
MsgBox ActiveDocument.ComputeStatistics(Statistic:=wdStatisticWords, _
    IncludeFootnotesAndEndnotes:=True) & " words"
```

You can copy text from the **Details** pane and then either paste it into a module or just drag it and drop it into a module to save yourself some typing. If you cannot remember what the possible values for the *Statistic* argument are, click **WdStatistic** to see a list of valid constants. If you still don't have enough information to use the **ComputeStatistics** method in code, click F1 to get Help.

Note that if you have references to object libraries that contain objects of the same name and you have **<All Libraries>** selected in the **Project/Library** box in the Object Browser, you'll see duplicate names in the Object Browser. For example, if you have a reference to the Microsoft Excel and Word object libraries, you'll see duplicates of the **AddIn** object, the **AddIns** object, the **Adjustments** object, the **Application** object, and so on. You can tell these duplicate objects apart by clicking one of them and looking in the **Details** pane. The **Details** pane shows you which object library the selected keyword is a member of.

For more information about the Object Browser, see "Object Browser" in Help.

Statement-Building Tools

There are a number of tools built in to the development environment that help you build expressions and statements in Visual Basic. To turn these tools on or off in the Visual Basic Editor (Microsoft Excel, Word, or PowerPoint), select one or more of the following check boxes under **Code Settings** on the **Editor** tab in the **Options** dialog box (**Tools** menu). In Microsoft Access, select one or more of the following check boxes under **Coding Options** on the **Module** tab in the **Options** dialog box (**Tools** menu).

Option	Effect
Auto Syntax Check	Determines whether Visual Basic should automatically verify correct syntax after you enter a line of code.
Require Variable Declaration	Determines whether explicit variable declarations are required in modules. Selecting this check box adds the **Option Explicit** statement to general declarations in any new module.
Auto List Member	Displays a list that contains information that would logically complete the statement at the current location of the insertion point.
Auto Quick Info	Displays information about functions and their parameters as you type.
Auto Data Tips	Displays the value of the variable that the pointer is positioned over. Available only in break mode.
Auto Indent	Repeats the indent of the preceding line when you press ENTER. That is, all subsequent lines will start at that indent. You can press BACKSPACE to remove automatic indents.
Tab Width	Sets the tab width, which can range from 1 to 32 spaces (the default is 4 spaces).

These tools automatically display information and give you appropriate options to choose from at each stage of building your expression or statement. For example, with the **Auto List Member** option selected, type the keyword **Application** followed by the dot operator. You should see a box that lists the properties and methods that apply to the **Application** object in the first object library you have referenced. (If you have several object libraries referenced, you may want to qualify your statements with the library name to make sure you are returning a reference to the right object. For instance, you may want to use `Excel.Application` or `Word.Application` instead of just `Application`). You can select an item from the list and continue typing.

You can get also get help building expressions at any time by clicking **List Properties/Methods**, **List Constants**, **Quick Info**, **Parameter Info**, or **Complete Word** on the shortcut menu in a module. For more information about these commands in Microsoft Excel, Word, and PowerPoint, search for the command names in Visual Basic Help.

Early Binding and the Statement-Building Tools

When you create an object variable in one application that refers to an object supplied by another application, Visual Basic must verify that the object exists and that any properties or methods used with the object are specified correctly. This verification process is known as *binding*. Binding can occur at run time (late binding) or at compile time (early binding). Late-bound code is slower than early-bound code. In addition, many of the coding aids that are built into the development environment work only on early-bound code.

▶ To make your code early bound

1   Set a reference to the type library that contains the objects you want to refer; do this in the **References** dialog box (**Tools** menu).

2   Declare your object variables as specific types. For example, if an object variable is going to contain a reference to a **Document** object, declare the variable as follows.

```
Dim wdObject As Document
```

Don't declare the variable as the generic **Object** type, as shown in the following declaration.

```
Dim wdObject As Object
```

3   If you'll be writing code that uses objects from more than one library, specify the name of the application when declaring object variables, especially if the different libraries contain objects with the same name, as shown in the following two declarations.

```
Dim wndXL As Excel.Window
Dim wndWD As Word.Window
```

If a property or method that you use in your code to return a reference to an object has the generic return type **Object** instead of a specific object type, you must take additional steps to ensure that your code is early bound and that the statement-building tools will work.

For example, in Microsoft Excel, the **Item** method of the **Worksheets** object returns the type **Object**, instead of **Worksheet**, so you won't get any more help from the statement-building tools after you reach the following point in your statement.

```
Workbooks(1).Worksheets(1).
```

Because the returned object type is **Object**, which is the generic type for all objects, the statement-building tools don't know what the available properties and methods are. To get around this, you must explicitly declare an object variable that has the specific type **Worksheet**, and you must set that object variable to the expression that returns a reference to the **Worksheet** object, as shown in the following example.

```
Dim testWS As Worksheet
Set testWs = Workbooks(1).Worksheets(1)
```

From this point on, when you type the name of the object variable followed by a period, the **List Properties/Methods** command will suggest properties and methods for the **Workbook** object that the variable refers to.

Programming Another Application's Objects

You can run code in one Microsoft Office application that works with the objects in another application.

▶ To program another application's objects

1   Set a reference to the other application's type library in the **References** dialog box (**Tools** menu). After you've done this, the objects, properties, and methods will show up in the Object Browser and the syntax will be checked at compile time. You can also get context-sensitive Help on them.

2   Declare object variables that will refer to the objects in the other application as specific types. Make sure that you qualify each type with by the name of the application exposes the object. The following example declares a variable that will point to a Word document and another variable that refers to a Microsoft Excel workbook.

```
Dim appWD As Word.Application, wbXL As Excel.Workbook
```

3   Use the **CreateObject** function with the OLE programmatic identifier of the object you want to work with in the other application, as shown in the following example. If you want to see the session of the other application, set the **Visible** property to **True**.

```
Dim appWD As Word.Application

Set appWD = CreateObject("Word.Application.8")
appWd.Visible = True
```

For specific information about the programmatic identifiers exposed by each Office application, see "OLE Programmatic Identifiers" in Help.

4 Apply properties and methods to the object contained in the variable. The following example creates a new Word document.

```
Dim appWD As Word.Application

Set appWD = CreateObject("Word.Application.8")
appWD.Documents.Add
```

5 When you finish working with the other application, use the **Quit** method to close it, as shown in the following example.

```
appWd.Quit
```

CHAPTER 3

Microsoft Access Objects

A Microsoft Access database is made up of different types of objects. Some types are used to display the data in your database, while others are used to store and manage the data itself, or to assist you in programming in Visual Basic. You can use Visual Basic to create, control, and manage all of the different types of objects in a Microsoft Access database.

Some of the objects that are available to you from Visual Basic in Microsoft Access are supplied by Microsoft Access; others are provided by different components. The objects provided by Microsoft Access represent the forms, reports, controls, and modules in your application. This chapter explains how to program with Microsoft Access objects in Visual Basic.

Contents

Objects Available in Microsoft Access

When you program in Visual Basic, you work with *objects* that correspond to different parts of your Microsoft Access database. *Collections* are sets of objects of the same type. Programming with objects and collections gives you added flexibility in that you can design your Microsoft Access application to respond to user actions and input in a customized way.

Microsoft Access includes several components, each of which supplies its own set of objects. The component's *object library* contains information about the component's objects and their properties and methods. A component's objects are available to Microsoft Access only if a *reference* exists to the component's object library. A reference notifies Microsoft Access that the objects in a particular object library are available from Visual Basic. To view existing references, open a module and click **References** on the **Tools** menu. To set a reference, select the check box next to the object library you want to reference.

Microsoft Access automatically sets references to the following object libraries:

- The Microsoft Access 8.0 object library. This object library provides objects that you use to display your data, contain your code, and work with the Microsoft Access application. For example, the **Form**, **Module**, and **Application** objects are provided by the Microsoft Access 8.0 object library. These objects are discussed in this chapter.

- The Microsoft DAO 3.5 object library. This object library provides Data Access Objects (DAO), such as the **TableDef** and **QueryDef** objects, which determine the structure of your database and which you can use to manipulate data in Visual Basic. These objects are discussed in Chapter 11, "Data Access Objects."

- The Visual Basic for Applications object library. Visual Basic provides three objects that give you more flexibility in programming: the **Debug**, **Err**, and **Collection** objects. For more information on these objects, search Microsoft Access Help for the name of the object.

Microsoft Access also includes the Microsoft Office 8.0 object library. However, Microsoft Access doesn't automatically set a reference to the Microsoft Office 8.0 object library. If you want to work with objects provided by Microsoft Office, such as the **CommandBar**, **FileSearch**, and **Assistant** objects, from within Microsoft Access, you must first set a reference to the Microsoft Office 8.0 object library. In other Office applications, this reference is set automatically. The objects provided by the Microsoft Office 8.0 object library are discussed in Chapter 8, "Menus and Toolbars," and Chapter 9, "Microsoft Office Assistant."

You can also set references to object libraries supplied by other applications or components when you want to use objects in those libraries for Automation. For example, if you want to perform Automation operations with Microsoft Excel objects from Microsoft Access, you can set a reference to the Microsoft Excel object library.

If you want to work with Microsoft Access objects from another application that supports Automation, set a reference to the Microsoft Access 8.0 object library from that application. You can then work with the objects in the Microsoft Access object hierarchy from within that application. For more information, see "Using the Application Object for Automation Operations" later in this chapter.

The Microsoft Access Objects

The following table describes the objects and collections provided by the Microsoft Access 8.0 object library. Each of these objects and collections is discussed in more detail later in this chapter.

Object or collection	Description
Application object	Represents the Microsoft Access application.
Form object	Represents an open form.
Forms collection	Contains all currently open forms.
Report object	Represents an open report.
Reports collection	Contains all currently open reports.
Control object	Represents a control on a form, report, or section, or within another control.
Controls collection	Contains all controls on a form or report.
Module object	Represents a standard module or a class module.
Modules collection	Contains all currently open modules.
Reference object	Represents a reference to an object library.
References collection	Contains all references that are currently set.
DoCmd object	Runs a macro action in Visual Basic.
Screen object	Represents the current arrangement of objects on the screen.

Microsoft Access objects are organized in a hierarchical relationship. Objects contain collections, and collections contain other objects. The following illustration shows the hierarchy of Microsoft Access objects.

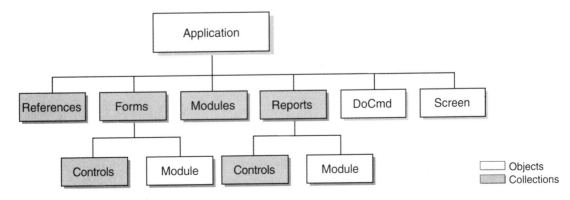

Each Microsoft Access object has properties, methods, and events associated with it. You can view these properties, methods, and events in the Object Browser. To open the Object Browser, open a module, and then click **Object Browser** on the **View** menu. You can also open the Object Browser by pressing F2 when a module is open.

The Application Object

The **Application** object represents the Microsoft Access application and is the top-level object in the Microsoft Access object hierarchy. It contains all the other Microsoft Access objects and collections. It's also the object you must first reference in order to use Microsoft Access objects through Automation.

The **Application** object is the default object in the object hierarchy. When you're working within Microsoft Access, you don't need to explicitly refer to the **Application** object when you use one of its methods or properties, or when you refer to an object or collection that the **Application** object contains. The only time you need to explicitly refer to the **Application** object is when you're working with Microsoft Access objects from another application through Automation. However, you can refer to the **Application** object explicitly from within Microsoft Access if you want to.

Using the Application Object for Automation Operations

If you want to work with Microsoft Access objects from another application that supports Automation, such as Microsoft Excel or Microsoft Visual Basic, you should begin by setting a reference to the Microsoft Access 8.0 object library from that application. Once you've set a reference to the Microsoft Access object library, you can work with the Microsoft Access objects, beginning with the **Application** object. The **Application** object is the top-level object in the Microsoft Access object hierarchy, so you must first refer to it in code before you can work with the other objects in the object hierarchy.

To work with Microsoft Access objects from another application, you must perform the following steps from within that application:

1. Set a reference to the Microsoft Access object library from the application in which you are working.

2. Declare an object variable to represent the Microsoft Access **Application** object.

3. Return a reference to the **Application** object and assign that reference to the object variable.

To set a reference to the Microsoft Access object library, open a module, click **References** on the **Tools** menu, and then select the **Microsoft Access 8.0 Object Library** check box in the **Available References** box.

After you've set a reference to the Microsoft Access object library, you can declare a variable of type **Application** to represent the Microsoft Access **Application** object. Because other applications have their own **Application** objects, you must qualify an object variable of type **Application** when you declare it so that Visual Basic creates the Microsoft Access **Application** object.

You qualify an object variable with the Visual Basic name of the object library that supplies it. Once you've set a reference to an object library, its name is available in the **Project/Library** box in the Object Browser. The Visual Basic name of the Microsoft Access object library is **Access**. The following example declares a variable to represent the **Application** object.

```
Dim appAccess As Access.Application
```

You can also declare an object variable to represent the **Application** object as type **Object**. However, your code will run faster if you declare the object variable as type **Application**.

Note Whenever you're working with multiple components through Automation, it's a good idea to qualify objects with the name of the object library that supplied them. If you qualify all objects, you can always be sure that you're referring to the correct object.

After you've declared an object variable to represent the **Application** object, you must return a reference to the **Application** object and assign that reference to the object variable. You can return a reference to the **Application** object by using either the **CreateObject** or the **GetObject** function, and you can assign that reference to the object variable with the **Set** statement. Use the **CreateObject** function to open Microsoft Access and return a reference to the **Application** object if Microsoft Access is not already running. Use the **GetObject** function to return a reference to the **Application** object when Microsoft Access is already running. The following example uses the **CreateObject** function to open Microsoft Access 97 and return a reference to the **Application** object, and then assigns it to an object variable of type **Application**.

```
Dim appAccess As Access.Application
Set appAccess = CreateObject("Access.Application.8")
```

Note If your code may run on a computer that has more than one version of Microsoft Access, you can include the version number you want to use in the argument for the **CreateObject** or **GetObject** function. The preceding example opens Microsoft Access 97, which is version 8.0. Microsoft Access 95 is version 7.0.

If the application in which you are working supports the **New** keyword, you can use the **New** keyword to declare an object variable, return a reference to the **Application** object, and assign it to the object variable all in one step, as shown in the following example.

```
Dim appAccess As New Access.Application
```

When a procedure that contains this code runs, Visual Basic returns a reference to the **Application** object and assigns it to the object variable. However, Visual Basic doesn't actually open Microsoft Access until you begin working with the object variable in code. In the following example, the declaration that contains the **New** keyword assigns a reference to the **Application** object to the object variable, but Microsoft Access doesn't open until the **NewCurrentDatabase** method runs.

```
Dim appAccess As New Access.Application
appAccess.NewCurrentDatabase "NewDb.mdb"
```

After you've created an object variable that represents the **Application** object, you can use it to work with any object in the Microsoft Access object hierarchy. For example, you can open the Northwind sample database, use the **DoCmd** object to open the Employees form, and then work with the **Form** object that represents the Employees form. To do this, add the following procedure to a Visual Basic module in Microsoft Excel and then run it.

```
Sub OpenNorthwindEmployees()
    Dim appAccess As New Access.Application

    Const conPath As String = "C:\Program Files\Microsoft Office\Office" _
        & "\Samples\Northwind.mdb"

    With appAccess
        ' Open the Northwind sample database.
        .OpenCurrentDatabase conPath
        ' Open the Employees form.
        .DoCmd.OpenForm "Employees"
        ' Set the form's caption.
        .Forms!Employees.Caption = "Northwind Employees"
    End With
End Sub
```

To work with **CommandBar** objects, you must first set a reference to the Microsoft Office 8.0 object library. You can set the reference from within Microsoft Access in the **References** dialog box (**Tools** menu). If you're working with Microsoft Access through Automation, you can set a reference to the Office object library from the other application. You can then use the **CommandBars** property of the Microsoft Access **Application** object to return a reference to the Office **CommandBars** collection.

You can also work with Data Access Objects (DAO) by first setting a reference to the Microsoft DAO 3.5 object library, then by using the **DBEngine** property of the Microsoft Access **Application** object to return a reference to the DAO **DBEngine** object. You can access all objects in the DAO object hierarchy through the **DBEngine** object, which is the top-level object in the hierarchy.

For more information about using Office **CommandBar** objects and DAO objects, see Chapter 8, "Menus and Toolbars," and Chapter 11, "Data Access Objects."

The Form Object and the Forms Collection

The **Form** object represents a Microsoft Access form that is open in Design view, Form view, or Datasheet view. **Form** objects are grouped in the **Forms** collection, which is a member of the Microsoft Access **Application** object. The **Forms** collection contains only the forms that are currently open in the database.

The following table shows the relationship between the **Form** object and the **Forms** collection and other objects and collections in the Microsoft Access object hierarchy.

Object or collection	Is contained by	Contains
Form object	**Forms** collection	**Controls** collection
		Properties collection
		Module object
Forms collection	**Application** object	**Form** objects

Referring to Form Objects

To work with a **Form** object in Visual Basic, you need to refer to the **Form** object in the **Forms** collection. To refer to a form, you must make sure that the form is open. To open a form with Visual Basic, use the **OpenForm** method of the **DoCmd** object.

If you refer to an individual **Form** object repeatedly within a procedure, you should declare an object variable to represent the **Form** object. If you know the name of the form, you can use the **!** operator syntax to refer to the **Form** object in the **Forms** collection by name. For example, the following code returns a reference to the Employees form and assigns it to a variable of type **Form**.

```
Dim frm As Form
Set frm = Forms!Employees
```

If you need to return a reference to a **Form** object and you won't know its name until run time, you can use the parentheses syntax to refer to the **Form** object within the **Forms** collection. This is useful if you want to pass the name of the form to a procedure as a variable, as shown in the following example.

```
Function SetFormCaption(strFormName As String)
   Dim frm As Form

   ' Open the form.
   DoCmd.OpenForm strFormName
   ' Return a reference to the Form object.
   Set frm = Forms(strFormName)
   ' Change the form's caption.
   frm.Caption = Date
End Function
```

You can also refer to an individual **Form** object by its index number, which indicates its position within the **Forms** collection. The **Forms** collection is indexed beginning with zero. That is, the index number for the first **Form** object in the **Forms** collection is 0, the second is 1, and so on.

Finally, if you need to set a **Form** object's property or call a method, but you don't need to use the **Form** object repeatedly throughout the procedure, you can refer to the form's class module directly in order to set the property or call the method. For example, the following code makes the form visible on the screen.

```
Form_Employees.Visible = True
```

For more information about class modules, see "Standard Modules vs. Class Modules" later in this chapter.

Properties of the Form Object

The properties of the **Form** object are too numerous to include in this chapter, so this section discusses only a few that deserve special consideration. To see all of the available properties of the **Form** object, search Microsoft Access Help for "Form object," or view the members of the **Form** object in the Object Browser.

The Me Property

The **Me** property returns a reference to the form in which code is currently running. You can use the **Me** property in procedures within a form module as shorthand for the full form reference. You can also use it to pass a **Form** object to a procedure without knowing the name of the form. If you use the **Me** property in code behind a form, you can rename the form without having to update your code.

The following example shows how you can use the **Me** property within an event procedure in a form module. This procedure sets the **BackColor** property of the form's detail section to a random color.

```
' Add this procedure to form module.
Private Sub Form_Load()
    ' Initializes random number generator.
    Randomize
    ' Sets BackColor property of form section.
    Me.Section(acDetail).BackColor = RGB(Rnd * 256, Rnd * 256, Rnd * 256)
End Sub
```

The following example also sets the detail section's **BackColor** property, but the Load event procedure passes a reference to the **Form** object to a procedure in a standard module. This strategy is preferable, because you can call the procedure in the standard module from any form, not just the one that contains the Load event.

```
' Add this procedure to form module.
Private Sub Form_Load()
    ' Passes reference to current form to ChangeBackColor procedure.
    ChangeBackColor Me
End Sub
```

```
' Add this procedure to standard module.
Public Sub ChangeBackColor(frm As Form)
    Randomize
    frm.Section(acDetail).BackColor = RGB(Rnd * 256, Rnd * 256, Rnd * 256)
End Sub
```

Note that when you're working with a Microsoft Access form from another application through Automation, you can't use the **Me** property to refer to the form from that application. You can only use the **Me** property to refer to a form in code within that form's module. The same is true for reports.

The Section Property

A form is divided into five sections: detail, header, footer, page header, and page footer. The **Section** property returns a reference to a particular section of a form. Once you've returned a reference to a form section, you can set properties for that section.

A number of properties apply to a form section rather than a **Form** object. For example, the **BackColor** property applies to a form section, not to a form, as shown in the preceding example. A section also has a **Controls** property, which returns a reference to the **Controls** collection for that section. The following example prints the names of all controls in the detail section of a form to the Debug window.

```
Sub ControlsBySection(frm As Form)
    Dim ctl As Control

    ' Enumerate the controls in the detail section.
    For Each ctl In frm.Section(acDetail).Controls
        Debug.Print ctl.Name
    Next ctl
End Sub
```

The Properties Property

The **Properties** property returns a reference to the **Properties** collection of a **Form** object. The **Properties** collection contains all of the properties of the form. You can enumerate the **Properties** collection with the **For Each...Next** statement. Note that you can't add a new property to the **Properties** collection. The following example prints all the properties of a **Form** object to the Debug window.

```
Sub EnumerateFormProperties(frm As Form)
    Dim prp As Property

    ' Enumerate the properties of a form.
    For Each prp In frm.Properties
        Debug.Print prp.Name, prp.Value
    Next prp
End Sub
```

The Module Property

The **Module** property returns a reference to the **Module** object associated with a form. You can assign this reference to a variable of type **Module**.

The module associated with a form doesn't automatically exist when the form is created. When you refer to the **Module** property, the module is created if it doesn't already exist. For more information, see the following section, "Form Modules."

The RecordSource Property

The **RecordSource** property binds a table or query to a form. After you've set the **RecordSource** property to the name of a table or query or to an SQL statement, you can display data from that table, query, or SQL statement on the form.

Form Modules

A **Form** object can have an associated module, which is represented by a **Module** object. However, the module does not exist when you first create the form. There are three ways to specify that Microsoft Access should create a module for a form:

- Click **Code** on the **View** menu when the form is open in Design view. The module opens and is subsequently saved with the form, even if you don't add any code to it.

- Set the form's **HasModule** property to **True**. You can set this property in the Microsoft Access property sheet or in Visual Basic. Note that setting this property to **False** removes the module and all code within it.

- Refer to the form's **Module** property in Visual Basic. The **Module** property returns a reference to the **Module** object associated with the form, creating it first if it does not already exist.

If you don't need to add code to a particular form, then you don't need to create a module for it. Forms without modules open more quickly. Also, eliminating unnecessary modules reduces the size of your database.

A form module contains any event procedures that you define for the form. You can also add other procedures to the form module. However, you should include only procedures that are specific for that form. If you want a procedure to be available to other procedures throughout the database, place that procedure in a standard module.

Creating Forms at Run Time

If you want to create a new form at run time, you can use the **CreateForm** function. This can be useful if you are creating an add-in for Microsoft Access. For example, you may want to create an add-in that adds a custom address book form to a database based on information provided by the user at run time. You can use the **CreateForm** function to generate the form in Visual Basic. You can also use the **CreateControl** function and the **DeleteControl** statement to add controls to or delete controls from the new form.

You can also add code to the form module at run time by using the methods and properties of the **Module** object. For example, the **CreateEventProc** method of the **Module** object creates an event procedure for a specified object—a form, report, section, or control. The **InsertLines** method inserts lines of code at a specified position in the module. The following example creates a new form and adds an event procedure to its module.

```
Function CreateFormWithCode () As Boolean
   Dim frm As Form, mdl As Module
   Dim lngLine As Long, strLine As String

   ' Enable error handling.
   On Error GoTo Error_CreateFormWithCode
   ' Create new form and return reference to Form object.
   Set frm = CreateForm
   ' Return reference to form module.
   Set mdl = frm.Module
   ' Create Load event procedure in form module.
   lngLine = mdl.CreateEventProc("Load", "Form")
   strLine = vbTab & "Me.Caption = " & Date
   ' Set form's caption in Load event.
   mdl.InsertLines lngLine + 1, strLine
   ' Return True if function is successful.
   CreateFormWithCode = True

Exit_CreateFormWithCode:
   Exit Function

Error_CreateFormWithCode:
   MsgBox Err & ": " & Err.Description
   CreateFormWithCode = False
   Resume Exit_CreateFormWithCode
End Function
```

For more information about writing and manipulating code with methods and properties of the **Module** object, see "The Module Object and the Modules Collection" later in this chapter, or search Microsoft Access Help for "Module object."

The Report Object and the Reports Collection

The **Report** object represents a Microsoft Access report that is open in Design view, Print Preview, or Layout Preview. **Report** objects are grouped in the **Reports** collection, which is a member of the Microsoft Access **Application** object. The **Reports** collection contains only the reports that are currently open in the database.

The following table shows the relationship between the **Report** object and the **Reports** collection and other objects and collections in the Microsoft Access object hierarchy.

Object or collection	Is contained by	Contains
Report object	**Reports** collection	**Controls** collection
		Properties collection
		Module object
Reports collection	**Application** object	**Report** objects

Report objects and **Form** objects have similar characteristics. This section only summarizes the characteristics of the **Report** object, because the same characteristics have been described in detail in the previous section, "The Form Object and the Forms Collection." For a list of the properties, methods, and events of the **Report** object, search Microsoft Access Help for "Report object," or view the members of the **Report** object in the Object Browser.

Referring to Report Objects

To work with a **Report** object in Visual Basic, you need to refer to the **Report** object in the **Reports** collection. To refer to a report, you must make sure that the report is open. To open a report with Visual Basic, use the **OpenReport** method of the **DoCmd** object.

You can refer to a **Report** object and assign it to an object variable in one of the following ways:

```
Dim rpt As Report
Set rpt = Reports!Invoice      ' Returns a reference to the Invoice report.
Set rpt = Reports("Invoice")   ' Returns a reference to the Invoice report.
Set rpt = Reports(0)           ' Returns a reference to the first report in
                               ' the collection.
```

Report Modules

Like a **Form** object, a **Report** object can have an associated module that is a class module. This module doesn't exist until you create it. You can create a report module by clicking **Code** on the **View** menu while the report is open in Design view, by setting the report's **HasModule** property to **True**, or by referring to the report's **Module** property in Visual Basic.

Creating Reports at Run Time

To create a new report at run time, use the **CreateReport** function. To add controls to or delete controls from a report at run time, use the **CreateReportControl** function or the **DeleteReportControl** statement.

The following example uses Automation from Microsoft Excel to create a linked table in a Microsoft Access database, and then creates a Microsoft Access report based on the data in the linked table. To use this example, you need to create a Microsoft Excel workbook named Revenue.xls, add some data to a worksheet in that workbook, and create a named range called DataRange that includes this data. Then, enter the following code in a module in the Microsoft Excel workbook. Before you run this example, you must set a reference to the Microsoft Access 8.0 object library and the DAO 3.5 object library from Microsoft Excel.

Important Before you run this code, make sure that the Microsoft Excel ISAM driver (Msexcl35.dll) is installed on your system. If it's not, you need to run Setup again to install it. The Microsoft Excel ISAM driver enables Microsoft Excel 97 files to work with the Microsoft Jet database engine. For more information on working with the Microsoft Excel ISAM driver, search Microsoft Access Help for "Microsoft Excel driver."

```
' Enter in Declarations section of a module.
Dim appAccess As New Access.Application

Sub PrintReport()

    Dim rpt As Access.Report, ctl As Access.TextBox
    Dim dbs As DAO.Database, tdf As DAO.TableDef, fld As DAO.Field
    Dim strDB As String, intLeft As Integer

    ' Set this constant to the path to your Northwind sample database.
    Const conPath As String = "C:\Program Files\Microsoft Office\Office\Samples\"

    ' Open database in Microsoft Access, specifying full path name.
    appAccess.OpenCurrentDatabase conPath & "Northwind.mdb"
    ' Return reference to current database.
    Set dbs = appAccess.CurrentDb
    ' Create new TableDef object.
    Set tdf = dbs.CreateTableDef("XLData")
    ' Specify connection string for Microsoft Excel ISAM driver.
    tdf.Connect = "EXCEL 8.0; Database=C:\My Documents\Revenue.xls"
    ' Specify source table as a named range in a worksheet.
    tdf.SourceTableName = "DataRange"
    ' Append new linked table to database.
    dbs.TableDefs.Append tdf
    ' Create new report in Microsoft Access.
    Set rpt = appAccess.CreateReport
    ' Specify linked table as report's record source.
    rpt.RecordSource = tdf.Name

    ' Create control on report for each field in linked table.
    For Each fld In tdf.fields
        Set ctl = appAccess.CreateReportControl(rpt.Name, acTextBox, , , _
            fld.Name, intLeft)
        intLeft = intLeft + ctl.Width
    Next fld
```

```
' Open report in Print Preview.
appAccess.DoCmd.OpenReport rpt.Name, acViewPreview
' Restore report.
appAccess.DoCmd.Restore
' Display Microsoft Access as active application.
AppActivate "Microsoft Access"
End Sub
```

The Control Object and the Controls Collection

The **Control** object represents a control on a Microsoft Access form or report. **Control** objects are grouped in **Controls** collections. The following table shows the relationship between the **Control** object and the **Controls** collection and other objects and collections in the Microsoft Access object hierarchy.

Object or collection	Is contained by	Contains
Control object	**Controls** collection	**Controls** collection, if the control is either an option group or a tab control
		Properties collection
		Hyperlink object
Controls collection	**Form** objects	**Control** objects
	Report objects	
	Control objects, if the control is an option group, tab control, text box, option button, toggle button, check box, combo box, list box, command button, bound object frame, or unbound object frame	

Two types of controls are available to you in Microsoft Access. The Microsoft Access 8.0 object library provides built-in controls, which are available in the toolbox. In addition to the built-in controls that appear in the toolbox, Microsoft Access supports *ActiveX controls*, formerly called *OLE controls* or *custom controls*.

The Microsoft Access Controls

The following table describes the built-in controls available in Microsoft Access. The controls are listed by their class names, as they appear in the Object Browser.

Control	Description
BoundObjectFrame	Displays a picture, chart, or OLE object stored in a Microsoft Access table.
CheckBox	Indicates whether an option is selected.

Control	Description
ComboBox	Combines a list box and a text box.
CommandButton	Starts an operation when the user clicks it.
Image	Displays a picture.
Label	Displays descriptive text.
Line	Displays a horizontal, vertical, or diagonal line.
ListBox	Displays a list of values.
ObjectFrame	Displays a picture, chart, or OLE object that is not stored in a table.
OptionButton	Indicates whether an option is selected.
OptionGroup	Displays a set of options together.
Page	Displays controls on a page of a tab control.
PageBreak	Marks the start of a new screen or printed page.
Rectangle	Displays a rectangle.
SubForm/SubReport	Displays a form within another form or a report within another report.
TabControl	Displays multiple pages, each of which can contain controls.
TextBox	Displays text data.
ToggleButton	Indicates whether an option is on or off.

For a list of the properties, methods, and events supported by each control, search
Microsoft Access Help for the name of that control, or view the control's members in
the Object Browser.

ActiveX Controls

An ActiveX control, like a built-in control, is an object that you place on a form to
display data or perform an action. However, unlike a built-in control, the code that
supports the ActiveX control is stored in a separate file or files which you must install
in order to use the control.

The following ActiveX controls are available for you to use with Microsoft Access:

- The Calendar control, which makes it easy to display and update a monthly
  calendar on a form. You can choose to install this control when you install
  Microsoft Access.

- The WebBrowser control, which you can use to display Web pages and other
  documents in a Microsoft Access form. The WebBrowser control is supplied by
  Microsoft Internet Explorer version 3.0, which is available in the ValuPack folder on
  the Microsoft Office 97 or Microsoft Access 97 CD-ROM. Alternatively, if you have
  access to the World Wide Web, you can download Microsoft Internet Explorer
  version 3.0 from the Microsoft home page, at http://www.microsoft.com/. When you
  install Microsoft Internet Explorer, the WebBrowser control is automatically
  available for you to use in Microsoft Access.

For examples of the Calendar control and the WebBrowser control, see the Developer Solutions sample application that's included with Microsoft Access.

If you have Microsoft Office 97, Developer Edition, you have additional ActiveX controls, as described in the following table.

Control	Description
Animation	Displays animations stored in .avi files.
TabStrip	Displays multiple pages, each of which can contain multiple controls.
ListView	Displays data items in one of four list views.
TreeView	Displays data in an expandable tree format.
ImageList	Contains a set of images for use with other ActiveX controls.
ToolBar	Displays a custom toolbar with buttons.
StatusBar	Displays status information associated with a form.
ProgressBar	Shows the progress of a lengthy operation by filling a rectangle with blocks from left to right.
Slider	Reflects a value or a range of values with a movable slider.
RichTextBox	Displays text with rich text formatting features.
CommonDialog	Displays one of a standard set of dialog boxes for operations such as opening, saving, and printing files or selecting colors and fonts.
UpDown	Increments or decrements numbers, or scrolls through a range of values or a list of items.
Winsock	Provides easy access to Transfer Control Protocol (TCP) and User Datagram Protocol (UDP) network services.

For more information about using ActiveX controls, see Chapter 12, "ActiveX Controls and Dialog Boxes," or search Microsoft Access Help for the name of the control. For information on the properties, methods, and events supported by an ActiveX control, see the documentation for that control, or set a reference to the control's object library and view its members in the Object Browser.

Referring to Control Objects

If you refer to a particular **Control** object repeatedly throughout a procedure, you may want to declare a variable to represent the **Control** object. If the control is a Microsoft Access control and you know what type of control it is, you can declare a variable of a specific control type. The following example declares a variable of type **TextBox**.

```
Dim txt As TextBox
```

If you don't know what type of control your code may refer to when it runs, or if it will refer to an ActiveX control, you must declare a variable of the more generic type **Control** to represent the control. For example, if you define a procedure to which you can pass different types of controls, then you should declare an argument of type

Control, as shown in the following code. You can pass any control to this function, but the function will return **True** only for controls that contain a valid hyperlink.

```
Function FollowControlHyperlink(ctl As Control) As Boolean
   Const conNoHyperlink As Integer = 7976

   ' Enable error handling.
   On Error GoTo Error_FollowControlHyperlink
   ' Follow control's hyperlink.
   ctl.Hyperlink.Follow
   ' Return True if successful.
   FollowControlHyperlink = True

Exit_FollowControlHyperlink:
   Exit Function

Error_FollowControlHyperlink:
   If Err = conNoHyperlink Then
      FollowControlHyperlink = False
   End If
End Function
```

To refer to an individual **Control** object in a **Controls** collection when you know the control's name, use the **!** operator syntax, as shown in the following example. Note that you use the **Set** statement when you're returning a reference to an object and assigning it to an object variable.

```
Set txt = Forms!Employees!LastName    ' Returns reference to LastName
                                      ' control on Employees form.
```

If you're referring to a control on the form in which code is currently running, you can use the **Me** keyword to represent the form, as shown in the following example.

```
Set txt = Me!LastName       ' Returns reference to LastName control on
                            ' form in which code is running.
```

If you need to return a reference to a **Control** object and you don't know its name when you're writing the procedure, you can use the parentheses syntax to refer to the **Control** object within the **Controls** collection. This is useful if you want to pass the name of the control to a procedure as a variable. You can also refer to an individual **Control** object by its index number, which indicates its position within the **Controls** collection. The **Controls** collection is indexed beginning with 0 (zero). That is, the index number for the first **Control** object in the **Controls** collection is 0, the second is 1, and so on.

Properties of the Control Object

The properties that apply to controls are too numerous to include in this chapter, so this section discusses only two that deserve special consideration. To see all of the available properties of the **Control** object, search Microsoft Access Help for "Control object," or view the members of the **Control** object in the Object Browser.

The Hyperlink Property

The **Hyperlink** property returns a reference to a **Hyperlink** object. A **Hyperlink** object represents a text or graphic that contains a jump to a file, a location in a file, an HTML page on the World Wide Web, or an HTML page on an intranet.

The controls that support the **Hyperlink** property include the combo box, command button, image, label, and text box controls. Each of these controls can display a hyperlink that the user can click to follow. When you have a reference to a **Hyperlink** object in a control, you can use the **Follow** method of the **Hyperlink** object to follow the hyperlink, as shown in the example in the previous section.

For more information about hyperlinks, see Chapter 15, "Developing Applications for the Internet and World Wide Web."

The ControlType Property

The **ControlType** property indicates what type of control a particular **Control** object is. For example, the following procedure checks the **ControlType** property for each control on a form and sets the **Locked** property of text boxes and combo boxes to **True**.

```
Function LockTextControls(frm As Form) As Boolean
    Dim ctl As Control

    ' Enable error handling.
    On Error GoTo Error_LockTextControls

    ' Enumerate controls on form.
    For Each ctl In frm.Controls
        ' If control is text box or combo box, set Locked property to True.
        If ctl.ControlType = acTextBox Or ctl.ControlType = acComboBox Then
            ctl.Locked = True
        End If
    Next ctl
    ' Return True if successful.
    LockTextControls = True

Exit_LockTextControls:
    Exit Function

Error_LockTextControls:
    MsgBox Err & ": " & Err.Description
    LockTextControls = False
    Resume Exit_LockTextControls
End Function
```

Data-Bound Controls

Some controls in Microsoft Access can be *data-bound*, which means they display data that is stored in a table, query, or SQL statement. The Microsoft Access data-bound controls include the bound object frame, check box, combo box, list box, option button, option group, text box, subform, and subreport controls. Some ActiveX controls, such as the Calendar control, can also be data-bound. Data-bound controls have a **ControlSource** property, which you can set to the name of a field in a table, query, or SQL statement to specify that the control should display data from that field. Note that before you can set the **ControlSource** property of a control, you must set the **RecordSource** property of the form or report to specify which table, query, or SQL statement supplies the data to the form or report.

The following example sets the **RecordSource** property of a form and the **ControlSource** property of a text box control in the form's Load event.

```
Private Sub Form_Load()
   ' Sets form's record source to Employees table.
   Me.Recordsource = "Employees"
   ' Sets ControlSource property of text box to LastName field.
   Me!Text0.ControlSource = "LastName"
End Sub
```

Controls That Have a Controls Collection

Several controls have a **Controls** collection that can contain other controls. The option group control and the tab control can both contain multiple controls. The option group control has a **Controls** collection, which can contain option button, toggle button, check box, and label controls. The tab control has a **Pages** collection, and each **Page** object in the **Pages** collection has a **Controls** collection. The **Controls** collection for a **Page** object contains the **Control** objects on that page.

The following example displays the name of the first control on the first page of a tab control on an Employees form.

```
Dim tbc As TabControl, pge As Page
Dim txt As TextBox

' Return reference to tab control.
Set tbc = Forms!Employees!TabCtl0
' Return reference to first page.
Set pge = tbc.Pages(0)
' Return reference to text box on page.
Set txt = pge.Controls(0)
MsgBox txt.Name
```

Other controls have a **Controls** collection that can contain a single control: an attached label. These controls include the text box, option group, option button, toggle button, check box, combo box, list box, command button, bound object frame, and unbound object frame controls.

The Module Object and the Modules Collection

The **Module** object represents a module in Microsoft Access. **Module** objects are contained in the **Modules** collection, which is a member of the Microsoft Access **Application** object. A **Form** or **Report** object can also contain a single **Module** object.

The set of all modules in a Microsoft Access database make up the Visual Basic *project* for that database. The **Modules** collection contains all the currently open modules in the project. **Modules** that are not open for editing are not included in the **Modules** collection. To open a module in Visual Basic, use the **OpenModule** method of the **DoCmd** object.

The following table shows the relationship between the **Module** object and the **Modules** collection and other objects in the Microsoft Access object hierarchy.

Object or collection	Is contained by	Contains
Module object	**Modules** collection	None
	Form objects	
	Report objects	
Modules collection	**Application** object	**Module** objects

Referring to Module Objects

To work with a **Module** object in Visual Basic, you need to refer to the **Module** object in the **Modules** collection. To refer to a module, you must make sure that the module is open. You can refer to a standard or class **Module** object and assign it to an object variable in any of the following ways:

```
Dim mdl As Module
Set mdl = Modules![Utility Functions]      ' Returns a reference to the
                                           ' Utility Functions module.
Set mdl = Modules("Utility Functions")     ' Returns a reference to the
                                           ' Utility Functions module.
Set mdl = Modules(0)                       ' Returns a reference to the first
                                           ' module in the collection.
```

A form or report class module that's open is included in the **Modules** collection. To refer to a form or report class module that's not open, use the **Module** property of the form or report to return a reference to the associated **Module** object, as discussed earlier in this chapter.

Standard Modules vs. Class Modules

Microsoft Access contains two types of modules: *standard modules* and *class modules*. Both types of modules are available in the **Modules** tab of the Database window. A form or report can also have an associated class module.

When you write code that you want to be available to any procedure in the project, you should put that code in a standard module. Standard modules are public by default, which means that any procedure in the project can call a procedure or use a module-level variable defined in a standard module. Also, if you set a reference to a project in a Microsoft Access database from another Microsoft Access project, you can call code in a standard module in the project to which you've set the reference.

Class modules, on the other hand, are always private. You can use class modules to create custom objects to use within the current project. However, you can't share those objects with other projects. The **Sub** and **Function** procedures that you define within a class module become methods of the custom object defined by the class module, and any **Property Let**, **Property Get**, and **Property Set** procedures become its properties.

You use the class module associated with a form or report to define event procedures for the form or report and its controls. You can also add any procedures that you want to be available only to that particular form or report.

For more information about standard modules and class modules, search Microsoft Access Help for "standard modules" or "class modules."

Properties of the Module Object

The following table describes the properties of the **Module** object.

Property	Description
Application	Returns a reference to the **Application** object.
CountOfDeclarationLines	Returns the number of lines of code in the Declarations section of a module.
CountOfLines	Returns the number of lines of code in a module.
Lines	Returns the text of a specified line or lines of code.
Name	Returns the name of a module.
Parent	Returns a reference to the object or collection that contains the module.
ProcBodyLine	Returns the number of the line on which the procedure definition begins.
ProcCountLines	Returns the number of lines in a procedure.
ProcOfLine	Returns the name of the procedure that contains a particular line.

Property	Description
ProcStartLine	Returns the number of the line on which a procedure begins.
Type	Indicates whether a module is a class module or a standard module.

Determining the Number of Lines in a Module

The lines in a module are numbered beginning with 1. The number of the last line in a module is equal to the value of the **CountOfLines** property. The number of the last line in the Declarations section of a module is equal to the value of the **CountOfDeclarationLines** property.

Note Line numbers don't actually appear in a module; they're used only for reference.

Working with Procedures

You can use the **Lines**, **ProcBodyLine**, **ProcCountLines**, **ProcOfLine**, and **ProcStartLine** properties to get information about a procedure in a module. Procedures can be one of four types: a **Sub** or **Function** procedure, a **Property Get** procedure, a **Property Let** procedure, or a **Property Set** procedure. **Sub** and **Function** procedures are considered the same type. Most of your procedures will be of this type. You don't need to be concerned with the last three unless you're creating properties within class modules.

The **ProcBodyLine** property returns the number of the line on which the procedure definition begins; that is, the line that includes a **Sub**, **Function**, **Property Get**, **Property Let**, or **Property Set** statement. The **ProcStartLine** property returns the number of the line immediately following the procedure separator, if you have the **Full Module View** and **Procedure Separator** options set on the **Module** tab of the **Options** dialog box (**Tools** menu). This line number may or may not be the same as the one returned by the **ProcBodyLine** property. Any comments, module-level declarations, or empty lines that precede the procedure definition are considered part of the procedure. The **ProcStartLine** property returns the number of the first line of the full procedure.

The following example uses the **ProcCountLines**, **ProcStartLine**, **ProcBodyLine**, and **Lines** properties to print a procedure in a module to the Debug window.

```
Function ProcLineInfo(strModuleName As String, strProcName As String) As Boolean
    Dim mdl As Module
    Dim lngStartLine As Long, lngBodyLine As Long
    Dim lngCount As Long, lngEndProc As Long

    On Error GoTo Error_ProcLineInfo
    ' Open specified Module object.
    DoCmd.OpenModule strModuleName
    ' Return reference to Module object.
    Set mdl = Modules(strModuleName)
```

```
' Count lines in procedure.
lngCount = mdl.ProcCountLines(strProcName, vbext_pk_Proc)
' Determine start line.
lngStartLine = mdl.ProcStartLine(strProcName, vbext_pk_Proc)

' Determine body line.
lngBodyLine = mdl.ProcBodyLine(strProcName, vbext_pk_Proc)
Debug.Print

' Print all lines in procedure preceding body line.
Debug.Print "Lines preceding procedure " & strProcName & ": "
Debug.Print mdl.Lines(lngStartLine, lngBodyLine - lngStartLine)

' Determine line number of last line in procedure.
lngEndProc = (lngBodyLine + lngCount - 1) - Abs(lngBodyLine - lngStartLine)

' Print all lines in body of procedure.
Debug.Print "Body lines: "
Debug.Print mdl.Lines(lngBodyLine, (lngEndProc - lngBodyLine) + 1)
ProcLineInfo = True

Exit_ProcLineInfo:
    Exit Function

Error_ProcLineInfo:
    MsgBox Err & " :" & Err.Description
    ProcLineInfo = False
    Resume Exit_ProcLineInfo
End Function
```

You can call this function from the Northwind sample database with a procedure such as the following.

```
Sub GetProcInfo()
    ProcLineInfo "Utility Functions", "IsLoaded"
End Sub
```

Methods of the Module Object

The following table describes the methods of the **Module** object.

Method	Description
AddFromFile	Adds the contents of a text file to a module.
AddFromString	Adds the contents of a string to a module.
CreateEventProc	Creates an event procedure within a class module.
DeleteLines	Deletes specified lines from a module.
Find	Finds specified text in a module.
InsertLines	Inserts a line or group of lines of code at a specified point in a module.
ReplaceLine	Replaces a line in a module with specified text.

Adding Text to a Module

If you want to add a string of text to a module, use the **InsertLines** method. With this method, you can specify at which line in the procedure you want the text to be added.

The following example creates a new form, adds a command button, creates a Click event procedure for the command button, and inserts a line of code with the **InsertLines** method.

```
Function ClickEventProc() As Boolean
    Dim frm As Form, ctl As Control, mdl As Module
    Dim lngReturn As Long

    On Error GoTo Error_ClickEventProc
    ' Create new form.
    Set frm = CreateForm
    ' Create command button on form.
    Set ctl = CreateControl(frm.Name, acCommandButton, , , , 1000, 1000)
    ctl.Caption = "Click here"
    ' Return reference to form module.
    Set mdl = frm.Module
    ' Add event procedure.
    lngReturn = mdl.CreateEventProc("Click", ctl.Name)
    ' Insert text into body of procedure.
    mdl.InsertLines lngReturn + 1, vbTab & "MsgBox ""Way cool!"""
    ClickEventProc = True

Exit_ClickEventProc:
    Exit Function

Error_ClickEventProc:
    MsgBox Err & " :" & Err.Description
    ClickEventProc = False
    Resume Exit_ClickEventProc
End Function
```

Creating a New Module

You can create a new module with the **RunCommand** method of the **Application** object. The following example creates a new module and opens it in Design view. Note that this code may not run in every view.

```
RunCommand acCmdNewObjectModule
```

You may want to add a new module with Visual Basic in order to add text from a file. The following example uses the **AddFromFile** method to add the contents of a text file to a new module. The procedure saves the new module with the same name as the text file.

```
Function AddFromTextFile(strFileName) As Boolean
    Dim strModuleName As String, intPosition As Integer
    Dim intLength As Integer
    Dim mdl As Module
```

```
    ' Store file name in variable.
    strModuleName = strFileName

    ' Remove directory path from string.
    Do
        ' Find \ character in string.
        intPosition = InStr(strModuleName, "\")
        If intPosition = 0 Then
            Exit Do
        Else
            intLength = Len(strModuleName)
            ' Remove path from string.
            strModuleName = Right(strModuleName, Abs(intLength - intPosition))
        End If
    Loop

    ' Remove file extension from string.
    intPosition = InStr(strModuleName, ".")
    If intPosition > 0 Then
        intLength = Len(strModuleName)
        strModuleName = Left(strModuleName, intPosition - 1)
    End If

    ' Create new module.
    RunCommand acCmdNewObjectModule
    ' Save module with name of text file, excluding path and extension.
    DoCmd.Save , strModuleName
    ' Return reference to Module object.
    Set mdl = Modules(strModuleName)
    ' Add contents of text file.
    mdl.AddFromFile strFileName
    ' Save module with new text.
    DoCmd.Save
End Function
```

When you run this procedure, avoid stepping through the line that first saves the module. If you enter break mode by stepping through this line, the module in which the code is running gets the focus, rather than the module that the code has just created. Visual Basic then tries to save the module in which the code is running rather than the new module.

Note that to create a new module with the **RunCommand** method, the **Module** command on the **Insert** menu must be available.

Class Module Events

Class modules that aren't associated with a form or report have two events: the Initialize event and the Terminate event. The Initialize event occurs when you create a custom object in memory from its class definition. The Terminate event occurs when you remove a custom object from memory.

To create event procedures for the Initialize and Terminate events, open the class module and click **Class** in the **Object** box. Then click **Initialize** or **Terminate** in the **Procedure** box.

You can use these events to run code when you create a custom object in memory or remove it from memory. For example, you may want to initialize a module-level variable defined in the class module when you create a custom object. The following example declares a module-level variable. When the Initialize event procedure runs, Visual Basic assigns the variable a value.

```
' Declare module-level variable.
Public intX As Integer

Private Sub Class_Initalize()
    intX = 10
End Sub
```

The Reference Object and the References Collection

The **Reference** object represents a reference from Microsoft Access to another project or object library. **Reference** objects are contained in the **References** collection. Each **Reference** object in the **References** collection corresponds to a reference that is set in the **References** dialog box (**Tools** menu).

You can use the **Reference** object and **References** collection to add references with Visual Basic, to check existing references, or to remove references that are no longer needed.

The following table shows the relationship between the **Reference** object and the **References** collection and other objects in the Microsoft Access object hierarchy.

Object or collection	Is contained by	Contains
Reference object	**References** collection	None
References collection	**Application** object	**Reference** object

Referring to Reference Objects

To work with a **Reference** object in Visual Basic, you need to refer to the **Reference** object in the **References** collection. You can refer to a **Reference** object and assign it to an object variable in any of the following ways:

```
Dim ref As Reference
Set ref = References!VBA          ' Assigns Reference object to a variable.
Set ref = References("VBA")       ' Assigns Reference object to a variable.
Set ref = References(1)           ' Returns a reference to the first Reference
                                  ' in the collection.
```

Properties of the Reference Object

The following table describes the properties of the **Reference** object.

Property	Description
BuiltIn	Indicates whether a **Reference** object points to a default reference that's necessary for Microsoft Access to function properly.
Collection	Returns a reference to the **References** collection.
FullPath	Returns the path and file name of the referenced project or object library.
GUID	Returns the globally unique identifier (GUID) for a referenced project or object library. A GUID is stored in the Windows registry.
IsBroken	Indicates whether a **Reference** object points to a valid reference.
Kind	Indicates whether a **Reference** object points to a Visual Basic project or to an object library.
Major	Returns the value to the left of the decimal point in the version number of a file to which a reference has been set.
Minor	Returns the value to the right of the decimal point in the version number of a file to which a reference has been set.
Name	Returns the name of the project or object library to which a reference has been set.

For more information about each of these properties, search Microsoft Access Help for the name of the property.

Methods of the References Collection

The following table describes the methods of the **References** collection.

Method	Description
AddFromFile	Creates a reference to a file that contains a project or object library.
AddFromGUID	Creates a reference to a project or object library based on its GUID, which is stored in the Windows registry.
Item	Returns a particular member of the **References** collection.
Remove	Removes a **Reference** object from the **References** collection.

For more information about each of these methods, search Microsoft Access Help for "References collection."

Setting a Reference in Visual Basic

You can use the **AddFromFile** or **AddFromGUID** method to set a reference in Visual Basic. The following example creates a reference at run time.

```
Function AddReference(strFilePath As String) As Boolean
   Dim ref As Reference

   Const conReferenceExists As Long = 32813

   On Error GoTo Error_AddReference
   ' Add reference to project or object library.
   Set ref = References.AddFromFile(strFilePath)
   AddReference = True

Exit_AddReference:
   Exit Function

Error_AddReference:
   If Err <> conReferenceExists Then
      MsgBox Err & ": " & Err.Description
   End If
   AddReference = False
   Resume Exit_AddReference
End Function
```

You can call this function to set a reference to the Developer Solutions sample application, as shown in the following example.

```
Sub SetSolutionsReference()
   Const strRefPath As String = "C:\Program Files\Microsoft Office" _
      & "\Office\Samples\Solutions.mdb"

   If AddReference(strRefPath) = True Then
      MsgBox "Reference set successfully."
   Else
      MsgBox "Reference not set successfully."
   End If
End Sub
```

The DoCmd Object

You can use the **DoCmd** object to carry out macro actions in Visual Basic. Macro actions perform common operations that aren't supported by other objects. For example, you can use methods of the **DoCmd** object to open, save, or close tables, forms, queries, reports, macros, and modules in Visual Basic. You can also use methods of the **DoCmd** object to maximize, minimize, or restore a window. Several of the examples in this chapter demonstrate the uses of the **DoCmd** object—for example, the ProcLineInfo procedure in "Properties of the Module Object" earlier in this chapter.

To see a list of the methods of the **DoCmd** object, search for "DoCmd" in the Object Browser. You can also see a list of the methods of the **DoCmd** object, as well as get more information on each method, by searching Microsoft Access Help for "DoCmd object."

The Screen Object

The **Screen** object refers to the form, report, datasheet, or control that has the focus. You use the **Screen** object to work with a particular object on the current screen. For example, you can use the **ActiveForm** property of the **Screen** object to return a reference to the form in the active window without knowing the form's name. This is useful when you need to work with the active form but don't necessarily know which form that will be.

Properties of the Screen Object

The following table describes the properties of the **Screen** object.

Property	Description
ActiveControl	Returns a reference to the control that has the focus.
ActiveDatasheet	Returns a reference to the datasheet that has the focus.
ActiveForm	Returns a reference to the form that has the focus.
ActiveReport	Returns a reference to the report that has the focus.
Application	Returns a reference to the **Application** object.
MousePointer	Sets or returns a value that specifies the type of mouse pointer currently displayed.
Parent	Returns a reference to the object that contains the **Screen** object.
PreviousControl	Returns a reference to the control that last had the focus.

When you use the **Screen** object, you may want to implement error handling because an object other than the one you expect may have the focus when your code runs. It may be preferable to first use the **SetFocus** method of a form, report, or control to set the focus to the object you want, so that you can always be certain that the correct object has the focus. Also, avoid using the **Screen** object with the **OutputTo** method of the **DoCmd** object.

Note that the **ActiveForm** property and the **Me** property do not necessarily return a reference to the same form. The **Me** property represents the form in which code is currently running. The **ActiveForm** property returns a reference to the form that is active on the screen, which may not be the form in which code is currently running. For example, a Timer event may occur on a form that is not the active form. You can use the **Me** property to refer to the form on which the Timer event is occurring, and the **ActiveForm** property to refer to the form that is active on the screen while the Timer event is occurring.

The following example uses a Timer event to requery the active form at regular intervals. The form on which the Timer event occurs may or may not be the active form.

```
Private Sub Form_Load()
    Me.TimerInterval = 30000
End Sub

Private Sub Form_Timer()
    Const conFormNotActive As Integer = 2475
    Const conFormInDesignView As Integer = 2478

    On Error GoTo Error_Timer
    ' Requery record source for active form.
    Screen.ActiveForm.Requery

Exit_Timer:
    Exit Sub

Error_Timer:
    If Err = conFormNotActive Or Err = conFormInDesignView Then
        Resume Exit_Timer
    Else
        MsgBox Err & ": " & Err.Description
    End If
End Sub
```

CHAPTER 4

Microsoft Excel Objects

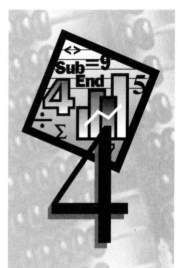

Visual Basic supports a set of objects that correspond directly to elements in Microsoft Excel, most of which you're familiar with from the user interface. For example, the **Workbook** object represents a workbook, the **Worksheet** object represents a worksheet, and the **Range** object represents a range of cells on a worksheet. Every element in Microsoft Excel—each workbook, worksheet, chart, cell, and so on—can be represented by an object in Visual Basic. By creating procedures that control these objects, you automate tasks in Microsoft Excel. The object model in Microsoft Excel 97 contains extensive changes and modifications. To view a graphical representation of the Microsoft Excel 97 object model, see "Microsoft Excel Objects" in Help. For a list of changes and additions, see "Changes to the Microsoft Excel 97 Object Model" in Help.

Microsoft Excel 97 adds support for event-driven programming to Visual Basic. An *event* is any action recognized by a Microsoft Excel object. Several objects in Microsoft Excel recognize a predefined set of events; when you want an object to respond to an event in a particular way, you can write a Visual Basic *event procedure* for that event.

Contents
- Working with the Application Object
- Working with the Workbook Object
- Working with the Range Object
- Working with Events

How Do I Display Visual Basic Help for Microsoft Excel?

To use Visual Basic Help for Microsoft Excel, you must click **Custom** during Setup and select the **Online Help for Visual Basic** check box for Microsoft Excel. Otherwise, Visual Basic Help won't be installed. If you've already installed Microsoft Excel, you can run Setup again to install Visual Basic Help.

To see the contents and index of Visual Basic Help for Microsoft Excel, click **Contents and Index** on the **Help** menu in the Visual Basic Editor. On the **Contents** tab in the **Help Topics** dialog box, double-click "Microsoft Excel Visual Basic Reference," and then double-click "Shortcut to Microsoft Excel Visual Basic Reference." The **Help Topics** dialog box should reappear, displaying the contents and index for Visual Basic Help for Microsoft Excel.

Working with the Application Object

Most properties of the Microsoft Excel **Application** object control the appearance of the application window or the global behavior of the application. For example, the value of the **DisplayFormulaBar** property is **True** if the formula bar is visible, and the value of the **ScreenUpdating** property is **False** if screen updating is turned off.

In addition, properties of the **Application** object provide access to objects lower in the object hierarchy, such as the **Windows** collection (representing all currently open windows) and the **Workbooks** collection (representing all currently open workbooks). You use these properties, sometimes called *accessors*, to move down the object hierarchy from the top-level **Application** object to objects lower in the hierarchy (such as the **Workbook**, **Worksheet**, and **Range** objects). For more information about navigating through an object model, see Chapter 2, "Understanding Object Models."

Some methods and properties that apply to the **Application** object also apply to objects lower in the object hierarchy. Using these properties or methods at the **Application** level usually changes all open workbooks or sheets. For example, the **Calculate** method applies to the **Application**, **Workbook**, and **Worksheet** objects. Using `Application.Calculate` recalculates all worksheets in all open workbooks, whereas using this method on the **Workbook** or **Worksheet** object provides greater control.

Working with the Workbook Object

When you open or save a file in Microsoft Excel, you're actually opening and saving a workbook. In Visual Basic, the methods for manipulating files are methods of the **Workbook** object or the **Workbooks** collection.

Opening Workbooks

When you open a workbook, you use the **Open** method. The **Open** method always applies to the **Workbooks** collection, which you return using the **Workbooks** property. The following code opens the file Book1.xls (in the current folder) and then displays the value that's in cell A1 on the first worksheet in the workbook.

```
Sub OpenBook1()
    Set myBook = Workbooks.Open(Filename:="BOOK1.XLS")
    MsgBox myBook.Worksheets(1).Range("A1").Value
End Sub
```

Notice that the return value of the **Open** method is a **Workbook** object that refers to the workbook that was just opened.

The file name in this example doesn't contain a path; therefore, the file is assumed to be in the current folder. This is guaranteed to cause a run-time error, because as soon as the user changes the current folder, Visual Basic can no longer find the file.

There are two relatively safe places to store a workbook you want to open programmatically. One place is the folder that contains the executable file for Microsoft Excel. The other place is the Library folder, which is created automatically during setup; this folder is one level down from the folder that contains the executable file.

If you want to open a workbook that's saved in the folder that contains the executable file, you can use the **Path** property to return a string that specifies the folder. The **PathSeparator** property returns the correct separator character for the current file system (for example, a backslash (\) for MS-DOS®/Windows® FAT, or a colon (:) for the Macintosh®). The following example shows file-system-independent code you can use to open Book1.xls, assuming that Book1.xls is saved in the folder that contains the executable file.

```
Sub OpenBook1()
    EXEPath = Application.Path & Application.PathSeparator
    fName = EXEPath & "BOOK1.XLS"
    Set myBook = Workbooks.Open(Filename:=fName)
    MsgBox myBook.Worksheets(1).Range("A1").Value
End Sub
```

The other relatively safe place to store a workbook is in the Library folder. You can use the **LibraryPath** property instead of the **Path** property to return a string that specifies the Library folder. The following code shows how you would alter the preceding example to use the **LibraryPath** property.

```
Sub OpenBook1()
    LibPath = Application.LibraryPath & Application.PathSeparator
    fName = LibPath & "BOOK1.XLS"
    Set myBook = Workbooks.Open(Filename:=fName)
    MsgBox myBook.Worksheets(1).Range("A1").Value
End Sub
```

Instead of hard-coding a file name with the **Open** method, you may want to give the user the option of selecting a file to open. The **GetOpenFilename** method displays the standard **Open** dialog box, but the method returns a string instead of opening a file. The string contains the fully qualified path and file name. The following example demonstrates the **GetOpenFilename** method by displaying the return value in a message box and then opening the file.

```
Sub DemoGetOpenFilename()
    Do
        fName = Application.GetOpenFilename
    Loop Until fName <> False
    MsgBox "Opening " & fName
    Set myBook = Workbooks.Open(Filename:=fName)
End Sub
```

Creating and Saving Workbooks

You create a new workbook by applying the **Add** method to the **Workbooks** collection. Remember to set the return value of the **Add** method to an object variable so that you can refer to the new workbook in your code.

When you save a new workbook for the first time, use the **SaveAs** method. For subsequent saves, use the **Save** method. The **GetSaveAsFilename** method is very similar to the **GetOpenFilename** method, which is described in the preceding section. The following example shows how to create a new workbook and then save it using the **GetSaveAsFilename** method.

```
Sub CreateAndSave()
    Set newBook = Workbooks.Add
    Do
        fName = Application.GetSaveAsFilename
    Loop Until fName <> False
    newBook.SaveAs Filename:=fName
End Sub
```

Closing Workbooks

To close a workbook, use the **Close** method of the **Workbook** object. You can close a workbook without saving changes, as shown in the following example.

```
Sub OpenChangeClose()
    Do
        fName = Application.GetOpenFilename
    Loop Until fName <> False
    Set myBook = Workbooks.Open(Filename:=fName)
    ' Make some changes to myBook
    myBook.Close savechanges:=False
End Sub
```

This code uses the **GetOpenFilename** method to select the workbook to open, makes some changes to the workbook (indicated by the comments), and then closes the workbook without saving the changes.

Working with the Range Object

The **Range** object can represent a single cell, a range of cells, an entire row or column, a selection containing multiple areas, or a 3-D range. The **Range** object is somewhat unusual in that it can represent both a single cell and multiple cells. There's no separate collection object for the **Range** object; you can think of it as being either a single object or a collection, depending on the situation. There are many different properties and methods that return a **Range** object, as shown in the following list.

ActiveCell	**DirectDependents**	**RowFields**
BottomRightCell	**DirectPrecedents**	**RowRange**
Cells	**EntireColumn**	**Rows**
ChangingCells	**EntireRow**	**Selection**
CircularReference	**Next**	**TableRange1**
Columns	**Offset**	**TableRange2**
CurrentArray	**PageRange**	**TopLeftCell**
CurrentRegion	**Precedents**	**UsedRange**
Dependents	**Range**	**VisibleRange**

For more information about these properties and methods, see the individual property and method topics in Help.

Using an A1-Style String Reference or Range Name

One of the most common ways to return a **Range** object is to use an A1-style reference or the name of a range, as shown in the following table.

To do this	Use the following code
Set the value of cell A1 on Sheet1	`Worksheets("Sheet1").Range("A1").Value = 3`
Set the formula for cell B1 on the active sheet	`Range("B1").Formula = "=5-10*RAND()"`
Set the value of each cell in the range C1:E3 on the active sheet	`Range("C1:E3").Value = 6`
Clear the contents of the range A1:E3 on the active sheet	`Range("A1", "E3").ClearContents`
Set the font style for the range named "myRange" (a workbook-level name) to bold	`Range("myRange").Font.Bold = True`
Set the value of each cell in the range named "yourRange" (a sheet-level name)	`Range("Sheet1!yourRange").Value = 3`
Set an object variable to refer to a range	`Set objRange = Range("myRange")`

Remember that expressions such as `Range("C1:E3").Value` = 6 assume that the **Range** property operates on the active sheet. If you try to run this code with a chart sheet active, a run-time error occurs (error 1004, "Range method of Application class failed").

Another cause of errors is the use of the **Range** property in an argument to another method, without fully qualifying the **Worksheet** object to which the **Range** property applies. The following example, which is supposed to sort a range of cells on Sheet1, also causes run-time error 1004.

```
Sub SortRange()
Worksheets("Sheet1").Range("A1:B10").Sort _
    key1:=Range("A1"), order1:=xlDescending
End Sub
```

This error is more difficult to find, because the line that contains the **Sort** method is correct. The error is caused by the second line, which contains the *Key1* argument. This code will run correctly if Sheet1 is the active sheet, but it will fail when it's run from another worksheet or from a module. To avoid the error, use the **Worksheets** property in the argument.

```
Sub SortRange()
    Worksheets("Sheet1").Range("A1:B10").Sort _
        key1:=Worksheets("Sheet1").Range("A1"), order1:=xlDescending
End Sub
```

Using Numeric Row and Column Indexes

You can also return a specific cell by specifying its row and column numbers, or indexes. You specify the row index first, followed by the column index, as shown in the following table.

To do this	Use the following code
Set the value of cell A1 on Sheet1	`Worksheets("Sheet1").Cells(1, 1).Value = 3`
Set the formula for cell B1 on the active sheet	`Cells(1, 2).Formula = "=5-10*RAND()"`
Set an object variable	`Set objRange = Worksheets("Sheet1").Cells(1, 1)`

Numeric row and column indexes are useful when you want to refer to cells by using loop counters. For example, the following code loops through cells A1:D10 on Sheet1. If any of the cells has a value less than 0.01, the example replaces the value with 0 (zero).

```
Sub RoundToZero()
    For rwIndex = 1 to 4
        For colIndex = 1 to 10
            If Worksheets("Sheet1").Cells(rwIndex, colIndex) < .01 Then
                Worksheets("Sheet1").Cells(rwIndex, colIndex).Value = 0
            End If
```

```
      Next colIndex
   Next rwIndex
End Sub
```

The following example shows a quick and easy way to display items in a
multiple-column list. The code creates a new worksheet and sets the object variable
newSheet to refer to the worksheet. The code then creates a list of all the names in
the active workbook and displays their formulas in A1-style notation.

```
Sub ListNames()
   Set newSheet = Worksheets.Add
   i = 1
   For Each nm In ActiveWorkbook.Names
      newSheet.Cells(i, 1).Value = nm.Name
      newSheet.Cells(i, 2).Value = "'" & nm.RefersTo
      i = i + 1
   Next nm
   newSheet.Columns("A:B").AutoFit
End Sub
```

Using the Offset Property

You often need to return a range of cells that's a certain number of rows or columns
away from another range of cells. The **Offset** property applies to a **Range** object,
takes a *RowOffset* argument and a *ColumnOffset* argument, and returns a new range.
The following example determines the type of data in each cell in the range A1:A10.
The code writes the data types in the column to the right of the input cells.

```
Sub ScanColumn()
   For Each c In Worksheets("Sheet1").Range("A1:A10").Cells
      If Application.IsText(c.Value) Then
         c.Offset(0, 1).Formula = "Text"
      ElseIf Application.IsNumber(c.Value) Then
         c.Offset(0, 1).Formula = "Number"
      ElseIf Application.IsLogical(c.Value) Then
         c.Offset(0, 1).Formula = "Boolean"
      ElseIf Application.IsError(c.Value) Then
         c.Offset(0, 1).Formula = "Error"
      ElseIf c.Value = "" Then
         c.Offset(0, 1).Formula = "(blank cell)"
      End If
   Next c
End Sub
```

Using the CurrentRegion and UsedRange Properties

These two properties are very useful when your code operates on ranges whose size
you have no control over. The current region is a range of cells bounded by empty
rows and empty columns, or by a combination of empty rows, empty columns, and the
edges of the worksheet.

The **CurrentRegion** property applies to a **Range** object. There can be many different current regions on a worksheet, depending on the **Range** object to which you apply the **CurrentRegion** property.

Suppose that Sheet1 contains a list to which you want to apply a number format. The only thing you know about the list is that it begins at cell A1; you don't know how many rows or columns it contains. The following example shows how to format the list by using the **CurrentRegion** property.

```
Sub FormatRange()
    Set myRange = Worksheets("Sheet1").Range("A1").CurrentRegion
    myRange.NumberFormat = "0.0"
End Sub
```

The used range is bounded by the farthest upper-left and farthest lower-right nonempty cells on a worksheet. It's a range that contains every nonempty cell on the worksheet, as well as all the empty cells that are interspersed among them. There can be only one used range on a worksheet; the **UsedRange** property applies to a **Worksheet** object, not to a **Range** object.

Suppose that the active worksheet contains data from a timed experiment. The used range contains the dates in the first column, the times in the second column, and the measurements in the third and fourth columns. You want to write code that combines each separate date and time into a single value, converts that value from Greenwich Mean Time (GMT) to Pacific Standard Time (PST), and then applies a date format to the value. The data table can contain empty rows and columns. You can use the **UsedRange** property to return the entire used range, including any embedded blank rows. The following example shows one way to convert and format the dates and times.

```
Sub ConvertDates()
    Set myRange = ActiveSheet.UsedRange
    myRange.Columns("C").Insert
    Set dateCol = myRange.Columns("C")
    For Each c In dateCol.Cells
        If c.Offset(0, -1).Value <> "" Then
            c.FormulaR1C1 = "=RC[-2]+RC[-1]-(8/24)"
        End If
    Next c
    dateCol.NumberFormat = "mmm-dd-yyyy hh:mm"
    dateCol.Copy
    dateCol.PasteSpecial Paste:=xlValues
    myRange.Columns("A:B").Delete
    dateCol.AutoFit
End Sub
```

Notice that the code uses the expression `ActiveSheet.UsedRange.Columns("C")` to return the third column from the used range (although this is the third column in the used range, it can appear in any column on the worksheet—that is, the used range can be preceded by empty columns). You can use other **Range** object properties and methods in a similar way to build complex expressions that return subranges or super-ranges of a **Range** object. Some properties and methods commonly used in this way are **Areas**, **Cells**, **Columns**, **EntireColumn**, **EntireRow**, **Range**, and **Rows**.

Looping on a Range of Cells

There are several different ways to loop on the cells in a range. The examples in this section show the **For Each...Next** statement and the **Do...Loop** statement applied to looping on a range of cells.

Using For Each...Next

The recommended way to loop on the cells in a range is to use the **For Each...Next** loop, which is also the recommended way to loop on the elements in a collection.

The following example shows how to loop through the range A1:D10 on Sheet1, setting any number whose absolute value is less than 0.01 to 0 (zero).

```
Sub RoundToZero()
    For Each r In Worksheets("Sheet1").Range("A1:D10").Cells
        If Abs(r.Value) < 0.01 Then
            r.Value = 0
        End If
    Next r
End Sub
```

Suppose that you want to modify this code to loop over a range of cells that a user selects. One way of doing this is to use the **InputBox** method to prompt the user to select a range of cells. The **InputBox** method returns a **Range** object that represents the selection. By using the *Type* argument and error handling, you can ensure that the user selects a valid range of cells before the input box is dismissed.

```
Sub RoundToZero()
    Worksheets("Sheet1").Activate
    On Error GoTo PressedCancel
    Set r = Application.InputBox( _
        prompt:="Select a range of cells", _
        Type:=8)
    On Error GoTo 0
    For Each c In r.Cells
        If Abs(c.Value) < 0.01 Then
            c.Value = 0
        End If
    Next c
    Exit Sub

PressedCancel:
    Resume
End Sub
```

If you don't want the user to select the range, you may be able to use the **CurrentRegion** property or the **UsedRange** property to return a **Range** object. For example, if you know that the data on Sheet1 begins at cell A1 and includes no empty rows or columns, you can use the **CurrentRegion** property to return the entire range automatically.

```
Sub RoundToZero()
    Set r = Worksheets("Sheet1").Range("A1").CurrentRegion
    For Each c In r.Cells
        If Abs(c.Value) < 0.01 Then
            c.Value = 0
        End If
    Next c
End Sub
```

The following two examples show two different ways to hide every other column in the used range on Sheet1. The first example shows a **For Each...Next** loop in which the **Column** property of the object variable is tested.

```
Sub HideColumns()
    Set r = Worksheets("Sheet1").UsedRange
    For Each col In r.Columns
        If col.Column Mod 2 = 0 Then
            col.Hidden = True
        End If
    Next col
End Sub
```

The second example shows a **For...Next** loop that tests the loop counter.

```
Sub HideColumns()
    Set r = Worksheets("Sheet1").UsedRange
    For i = 1 To r.Columns.Count
        If i Mod 2 = 0 Then
            r.Columns(i).Hidden = True
        End If
    Next i
End Sub
```

Using Do...Loop

Occasionally, the **For Each...Next** loop isn't the best way to loop on a range. Suppose that you have a column of data and you want to write a macro that sorts the data and then deletes rows that contain duplicate data. You could try to use a **For Each...Next** loop, as shown in the following example.

```
Sub BuggyRemoveDuplicates()    ' DON'T USE THIS CODE!
    Worksheets("Sheet1").Range("A1").Sort _
        key1:=Worksheets("Sheet1").Range("A1")
    Set r = Worksheets("Sheet1").Range("A1").CurrentRegion.Columns("A")
    For Each c In r.Cells
        If c.Offset(1, 0).Value = c.Value Then
            c.Offset(1, 0).EntireRow.Delete
        End If
    Next c
End Sub
```

Unfortunately, this code doesn't work correctly because the **Delete** method is modifying the range on which **For Each...Next** is looping. This causes duplicates not to be deleted in some cases.

A better solution is to use a **Do...Loop** structure, as shown in the following example.

```
Sub GoodRemoveDuplicates()
    Worksheets("Sheet1").Range("A1").Sort _
        key1:=Worksheets("Sheet1").Range("A1")
    Set currentCell = Worksheets("Sheet1").Range("A1")
    Do While Not IsEmpty(currentCell)
        Set nextCell = currentCell.Offset(1, 0)
        If nextCell.Value = currentCell.Value Then
            currentCell.EntireRow.Delete
        End If
        Set currentCell = nextCell
    Loop
End Sub
```

The loop tests the object variable `currentCell`, exiting when it encounters an empty cell at the bottom of the column of data. You could build an equivalent loop by testing the value in `currentCell` against an empty string, as shown in the following example.

```
Do While currentCell.Value <> ""
    ' Code to run on cells with values
Loop
```

In either case, don't forget to increment the cell at the bottom of the **Do...Loop** structure (`Set currentCell = nextCell`, for example).

Using the Address Property to Debug Range Object Code

You can apply the **Address** property to any **Range** object. The **Address** property returns the cell address of a range, as a string. The following example shows how to use the **Address** property to debug the HideColumns procedure.

```
Sub HideColumns()
    Set r = Worksheets("Sheet1").UsedRange
    MsgBox r.Address    ' debugging only!
    For i = 1 To r.Columns.Count
        If i Mod 2 = 0 Then
            r.Columns(i).Hidden = True
            MsgBox r.Columns(i).Address   ' debugging only!
        End If
    Next i
End Sub
```

You can also set *watch expressions* instead of using message boxes. For the preceding example, you could set two watch expressions—`r.Address` and `r.Columns(i).Address`—and then examine the values of the watch expressions in the **Immediate** window. For more information about debugging, see Chapter 14, "Debugging and Error Handling."

Working with Events

If you've used Visual Basic (Standard, Professional, or Enterprise Edition), you're familiar with event-driven programming; most of your Visual Basic code was probably written to respond to events, such as when the user clicks a button or when a form is loaded. In Microsoft Excel, you may have used properties such as **OnSheetActivate** or **OnEntry** to cause a macro to run when a sheet is activated or changed. This is also event-driven programming. Microsoft Excel 97 expands the available list of events and adds event procedures that receive arguments.

With Microsoft Excel 97, you can write event procedures at the worksheet, chart, workbook, or application level. For example, the Activate event occurs at the sheet level, and the SheetActivate event is available at both the workbook and application levels. The SheetActivate event for a workbook occurs when any sheet in that workbook is activated. At the application level, the SheetActivate event occurs when any sheet in any open workbook is activated.

Worksheet and workbook event procedures are created by default for any open worksheet, chart sheet, or workbook. To write event procedures for an embedded chart or for the application, you must create a new object using the **WithEvents** keyword in a class module. You can also use a class module to create event procedures that can be used for more than one worksheet or workbook. For more information , see "Using Class Modules with Events" later in this chapter.

Enabling or Disabling Events

Use the **EnableEvents** property to enable or disable events. For example, using the **Save** method to save a workbook causes the BeforeSave event to occur. You can prevent this by setting the **EnableEvents** property to **False** before you call the **Save** method, as in the following example.

```
Application.EnableEvents = False
ActiveWorkbook.Save
Application.EnableEvents = True
```

Using Events on Sheets

Events on sheets are enabled by default. To view the event procedures for a particular sheet, use either of the following techniques:

- Right-click the sheet tab, and then click **View Code** on the shortcut menu. In the **Procedure** box, click the event name.

- On the **Tools** menu, point to **Macro** and then click **Visual Basic Editor**. Select the sheet in the Project Explorer, and then either click the **View Code** button or click **Code** on the **View** menu. In the **Object** box, click either **Worksheet** or **Chart**, and then click the event name in the **Procedure** box.

Worksheet Events

Worksheet-level events occur when the user activates a worksheet or changes a worksheet cell, as shown in the following table.

Event	Description
Activate	Occurs when the user activates the sheet. Use this event instead of the **OnSheetActivate** property.
BeforeDoubleClick	Occurs when the user double-clicks a worksheet cell. Use this event instead of the **OnDoubleClick** property.
BeforeRightClick	Occurs when the user right-clicks a worksheet cell.
Calculate	Occurs when the user recalculates the worksheet. Use this event instead of the **OnCalculate** property.
Change	Occurs when the user changes a cell formula. Use this event instead of the **OnEntry** property.
Deactivate	Occurs when the sheet is active and the user activates a different sheet. Doesn't occur when the user shifts the focus from one window to another window showing the same sheet. Use this event instead of the **OnSheetDeactivate** property.
SelectionChange	Occurs when the user selects a worksheet cell.

For more information about an event, see the corresponding Help topic.

Examples

The following example adjusts the size of columns A through F whenever the worksheet is recalculated.

```
Private Sub Worksheet_Calculate()
    Columns("A:F").AutoFit
End Sub
```

Some events can be used to substitute an action for the default application behavior, or to make a small change to the default behavior. The following example traps the right-click event and adds a new menu item to the shortcut menu for cells B1:B10.

```
Private Sub Worksheet_BeforeRightClick(ByVal Target As Range, _
     Cancel As Boolean)
   For Each icbc In Application.CommandBars("cell").Controls
       If icbc.Tag = "brccm" Then icbc.Delete
   Next icbc
   If Not Application.Intersect(Target, Range("b1:b10")) Is Nothing Then
          With Application.CommandBars("cell").Controls _
              .Add(Type:=msoControlButton, before:=6, _
              temporary:=True)
          .Caption = "New Context Menu Item"
          .OnAction = "MyMacro"
          .Tag = "brccm"
       End With
   End If
End Sub
```

Chart Events

Like worksheet-level events, chart-level events occur when the user activates or changes a chart, as shown in the following table.

Event	Description
Activate	Occurs when the user activates the chart sheet (doesn't work with embedded charts). Use this event instead of the **OnSheetActivate** property.
BeforeDoubleClick	Occurs when the user double-clicks the chart. Use this event instead of the **OnDoubleClick** property.
BeforeRightClick	Occurs when the user right-clicks the chart.
Calculate	Occurs when the user plots new or changed data on the chart.
Deactivate	Occurs when the sheet is active and the user activates a different sheet. Doesn't occur when the user shifts the focus from one window to another window showing the same sheet. Use this event instead of the **OnSheetDeactivate** property.
DragOver	Occurs when the user drags data over the chart.
DragPlot	Occurs when the user drags a range of cells over the chart.
MouseDown	Occurs when the user clicks a mouse button while the pointer is positioned over the chart.
MouseMove	Occurs when the user moves the pointer over the chart.
MouseUp	Occurs when the user releases a mouse button while the pointer is positioned over the chart.
Resize	Occurs when the user changes the size of the chart.
Select	Occurs when the user selects a chart element.
SeriesChange	Occurs when the user changes the value of a chart data point.

For more information about an event, see the corresponding Help topic.

Events for chart sheets are available by default in the Visual Basic Editor. To write event procedures for an embedded chart, you must create a new object using the **WithEvents** keyword in a class module. For more information, see "Using Class Modules with Events" later in this chapter.

Example

The following example changes a point's border color when the user changes the point's value.

```
Private Sub Chart_SeriesChange(ByVal SeriesIndex As Long, _
    ByVal PointIndex As Long)
    Set p = ActiveChart.SeriesCollection(SeriesIndex).Points(PointIndex)
    p.Border.ColorIndex = 3
End Sub
```

Workbook Events

Workbook events occur when the user changes a workbook or any sheet in the workbook.

Event	Description
Activate	Occurs when the user activates the workbook.
AddInInstall	Occurs when the user installs the workbook as an add-in. Use this event instead of the Auto_Add macro.
AddInUninstall	Occurs when the user uninstalls the workbook as an add-in. Use this event instead of the Auto_Remove macro.
BeforeClose	Occurs before the workbook closes. Use this event instead of the Auto_Close macro.
BeforePrint	Occurs before the workbook is printed.
BeforeSave	Occurs before the workbook is saved. Use this event instead of the **OnSave** property.
Deactivate	Occurs when the workbook is active and the user activates a different workbook.
NewSheet	Occurs after the user creates a new sheet.
Open	Occurs when the user opens the workbook. Use this event instead of the Auto_Open macro.
SheetActivate	Occurs when the user activates a sheet in the workbook. Use this event instead of the **OnSheetActivate** property.
SheetBeforeDoubleClick	Occurs when the user double-clicks a worksheet cell (not used with chart sheets). Use this event instead of the **OnDoubleClick** property.
SheetBeforeRightClick	Occurs when the user right-clicks a cell on a worksheet (not used with chart sheets).

Event	Description
SheetCalculate	Occurs after the user recalculates a worksheet (not used with chart sheets). Use this event instead of the **OnCalculate** property.
SheetChange	Occurs when the user changes a cell formula (not used with chart sheets). Use this event instead of the **OnEntry** property.
SheetDeactivate	Occurs when the user activates a different sheet in the workbook. Use this event instead of the **OnSheetDeactivate** property.
SheetSelectionChange	Occurs when the user changes the selection on a worksheet (not used with chart sheets).
WindowActivate	Occurs when the user shifts the focus to any window showing the workbook. Use this event instead of the **OnWindow** property.
WindowDeactivate	Occurs when the user shifts the focus away from any window showing the workbook. Use this event instead of the **OnWindow** property.
WindowResize	Occurs when the user opens, resizes, maximizes, or minimizes any window showing the workbook.

For more information about an event, see the corresponding Help topic.

Example

The following example maximizes the Microsoft Excel application window when the workbook is opened.

```
Sub Workbook_Open()
    Application.WindowState = xlMaximized
End Sub
```

Application Events

Application events occur when the user creates or opens a workbook or when the user changes any sheet in any open workbook.

Event	Description
NewWorkbook	Occurs when the user creates a new workbook.
SheetActivate	Occurs when the user activates a sheet in an open workbook. Use this event instead of the **OnSheetActivate** property.
SheetBeforeDoubleClick	Occurs when the user double-clicks a worksheet cell in an open workbook (not used with chart sheets). Use this event instead of the **OnDoubleClick** property.

Event	Description
SheetBeforeRightClick	Occurs when the user right-clicks a worksheet cell in an open workbook (not used with chart sheets).
SheetCalculate	Occurs after the user recalculates a worksheet in an open workbook (not used with chart sheets). Use this event instead of the **OnCalculate** property.
SheetChange	Occurs when the user changes a cell formula in an open workbook (not used with chart sheets). Use this event instead of the **OnEntry** property.
SheetDeactivate	Occurs when the user deactivates a sheet in an open workbook. Use this event instead of the **OnSheetDeactivate** property.
SheetSelectionChange	Occurs when the user changes the selection on a sheet in an open workbook.
WindowActivate	Occurs when the user shifts the focus to an open window. Use this event instead of the **OnWindow** property.
WindowDeactivate	Occurs when the user shifts the focus away from an open window. Use this event instead of the **OnWindow** property.
WindowResize	Occurs when the user resizes an open window.
WorkbookActivate	Occurs when the user shifts the focus to an open workbook.
WorkbookAddInInstall	Occurs when the user installs a workbook as an add-in.
WorkbookAddInUninstall	Occurs when the user uninstalls a workbook as an add-in.
WorkbookBeforeClose	Occurs before an open workbook is closed.
WorkbookBeforePrint	Occurs before an open workbook is printed.
WorkbookBeforeSave	Occurs before an open workbook is saved.
WorkbookDeactivate	Occurs when the user shifts the focus away from an open workbook.
WorkbookNewSheet	Occurs when the user adds a new sheet to an open workbook.
WorkbookOpen	Occurs when the user opens a workbook.

For more information about an event, see the corresponding Help topic.

Using Class Modules with Events

Unlike sheet events, embedded charts and the **Application** object don't have events enabled by default. Before you can use events with an embedded chart or with the **Application** object, you must create a new class module and declare an object of type **Chart** or **Application** with events. You use the **Class Module** command (**Insert** menu) in the Visual Basic Editor to create a new class module.

To enable the events of the **Application** object, you'd add the following declaration to the class module.

```
Public WithEvents App As Application
```

After the new object has been declared with events, it appears in the **Object** box in the class module, and you can write event procedures for the new object. (When you select the new object in the **Object** box, the valid events for that object are listed in the **Procedure** box.)

Before the procedures will run, however, you must connect the declared object in the class module to the **Application** object. You can do this from any module by using the following declaration (where "EventClass" is the name of the class module you created to enable events).

```
Public X As New EventClass
```

After you've created the X object variable (an instance of the EventClass class), you can set the App object of the EventClass class equal to the Microsoft Excel **Application** object.

```
Sub InitializeApp()
    Set X.App = Application
End Sub
```

After you run the InitializeApp procedure, the App object in the EventClass class module points to the Microsoft Excel **Application** object, and the event procedures in the class module will run whenever the events occur.

Although this may seem like a lot of work, one advantage is that you can use the same event procedure for many objects. For example, suppose that you declare an object of type **Chart** with events in a class module, as follows.

```
Public WithEvents cht As Chart
```

You can then use the following code to cause the event procedures to run whenever an event occurs for either chart one or chart two.

```
Dim C1 As New EventClass
Dim C2 As New EventClass

Sub InitializeCharts
    Set C1.cht = Worksheets(1).ChartObjects(1).Chart
    Set C2.cht = Worksheets(1).ChartObjects(2).Chart
End Sub
```

You can declare **Worksheet** or **Workbook** objects with events in a class module and use the events in the new class with several sheets, in addition to the default event procedures. You might use this technique to write an Activate event handler that runs only when either sheet one or sheet five is activated. Or you can use a **Chart** object declared in a class module to write an event handler for both embedded charts and chart sheets.

CHAPTER 5

Microsoft Outlook Objects

Microsoft Outlook 97, the desktop information management program included in Microsoft Office 97, is fully programmable and can be automated to build useful group software and mail-enabled applications. Although Outlook doesn't contain Visual Basic for Applications version 5.0, it does include a complete type library and Visual Basic Scripting Edition (VBScript). Using the Outlook type library and VBScript, you can write procedures that respond to specific events—such as opening or replying to a mail message or clicking a control on a form—and store those procedures in a custom form. Using the type library and Visual Basic in Microsoft Access, Microsoft Excel, Microsoft Word, or Microsoft PowerPoint, you can control an entire Outlook session by using Automation (formerly OLE Automation).

This chapter provides a general overview of the objects exposed by the Outlook type library, and then it focuses on techniques for handling Outlook folders and items programmatically. Finally, the chapter compares Automation and VBScript and discusses the restrictions and guidelines for using each one.

Note This chapter doesn't discuss designing and distributing custom Outlook solutions. For information about developing Outlook solutions, see *Building Microsoft Outlook 97 Applications* by Peter Krebs, available from Microsoft Press (ISBN 1-57231-5736-9).

Contents

- The Outlook Object Model
- Working with Outlook Folders
- Working with Outlook Items and Events
- Using Automation and VBScript

How Do I Display Visual Basic Help for Outlook?

Visual Basic Help for Outlook isn't installed during setup; instead, you must copy the files Vbaoutl.hlp and Vbaoutl.cnt from the ValuPack folder to the folder in which you've installed Outlook. For more information about installing and using Visual Basic Help for Outlook, see "Getting Help for Visual Basic in Microsoft Outlook" in Outlook Help.

To see the table of contents and index for Visual Basic Help for Outlook, you must display the Script Editor window while an Outlook item is open in design mode. To design an Outlook item, open any item except a note, and then click **Design Outlook Form** on the **Tools** menu. In design mode, click **View Code** on the **Form** menu to display the Script Editor. In the Script Editor, click **Microsoft Outlook Object Library Help** on the **Help** menu. The **Help Topics** dialog box should appear, displaying the table contents and index for Visual Basic Help for Outlook.

The Outlook Object Model

In the Outlook object model, the **Application** object contains the **NameSpace** object, which contains **MAPIFolder** objects that represent all the available folders in a given data source (for example, a MAPI message store). The **MAPIFolder** objects contain objects that represent all the Outlook items in the data source, and each item contains some useful programmable objects for controlling that item. In addition, there's an **Explorer** object associated with each folder and an **Inspector** object associated with each item.

For a visual representation of the Outlook object model, see "Microsoft Outlook Objects" in Help.

Application Object

The **Application** object is the root object of the object model; it gives you easy access to all the other objects in the model. It gives you direct access to new items you create by using **CreateItem**, without having to traverse the object model, and it gives you access to the objects that represent the Outlook interface (the **Explorer** and **Inspector** objects). The **Application** object is the only Outlook object you can return by using the **CreateObject** or **GetObject** function in another application.

NameSpace Object

The **NameSpace** object can represent any recognized data source, such as a MAPI message store. The object itself provides methods for logging in and out, returning objects directly by ID, returning default folders directly, and gaining access to data sources owned by other users.

Note MAPI message stores, which are returned by the expression `GetNameSpace("MAPI")`, are the only data sources currently supported by Microsoft Outlook.

Folders Collection and MAPIFolder Object

The **Folders** collection contains all the **MAPIFolder** objects in the specified message store (or other recognized data source) or in a folder in that message store. For more information about using the objects that represent Outlook folders, see "Working with Outlook Folders" later in this chapter.

Items Collection

The **Items** collection contains all the Outlook items in the specified folder. Items and controls on items are the only objects in Outlook that support programmable events. For information about using the objects that represent Outlook items (such as **MailItem** and **AppointmentItem**) and the objects contained in Outlook items (such as **Attachments** and **Recipients**), as well as the events they support, see the following section, "Working with Outlook Items and Events."

Explorer and Inspector Objects

The **Explorer** object represents the window in which the contents of a folder are displayed. The **Inspector** object represents the window in which an Outlook item is displayed.

For information about using the **Explorer** and **Inspector** objects, see "Using Automation and VBScript" later in this chapter.

Working with Outlook Folders

Just as you can use Outlook to explore the contents of any folder in your message store, you can automate Outlook to add folders or items to folders or to move and copy items and folders among folders in your message store.

To return the **Folders** collection from a **NameSpace** object or another **MAPIFolder** object, use the **Folders** property. To return a single **MAPIFolder** object, use **Folders**(*index*), where *index* is the folder's name or index number.

Note Folder names are case-sensitive.

The following Automation example returns the folder named "Urgent" from the message store for Shannon Boyd. This example assumes that Shannon Boyd is **currently logged on in Outlook.**

```
Set olMAPI = GetObject("","Outlook.Application").GetNameSpace("MAPI")
Set urgentFolder = olMAPI.Folders("Mailbox - Shannon Boyd").Folders("Urgent")
```

Certain folders within an Outlook message store support the default functionality of Outlook and are created the first time Outlook is run. Each folder contains Outlook items of the same type. The following table describes these default folders.

Default folder	Description
Calendar	Default container for **AppointmentItem** objects.
Contacts	Default container for **ContactItem** objects.
Deleted Items	Storage area into which all item objects are moved when they're marked for deletion. The application has options to retain such items indefinitely, archive them after a user-defined period of time or purge them when the application is closed.
Inbox	Default container for **MailItem** objects.
Journal	Default container for **JournalItem** objects.
Notes	Default container for **NoteItem** objects.
Outbox	Storage area for items that are completed but not sent.
Sent Mail	Storage area into which copies of user-generated **MailItem** objects are moved when they're sent.
Tasks	Default container for **TaskItem** objects.

You can quickly return a default folder by using the **GetDefaultFolders** method with the appropriate **OlDefaultFolders** constant. The following VBScript example returns the Inbox folder for the user who's currently logged on to Outlook.

```
Set olMAPI = Application.GetNameSpace("MAPI")
Set curInbox= olMAPI.GetDefaultFolder(6)
```

One of the most useful features of Outlook is delegation, where one user delegates access to another user for one or more of their default folders. Most often, this will be a shared Calendar folder through which members of a group will coordinate their individual schedules with a joint schedule or even a master schedule for the group as a whole. To return a **MAPIFolder** object that represents a shared default folder for a specific user, use the **GetSharedDefaultFolder** method. The following Automation example returns Kim Buhler's shared Calendar folder.

```
Set olMAPI = GetObject("","Outlook.Application").GetNameSpace("MAPI")
Set myRecipient = olMAPI.CreateRecipient("Kim Buhler")
myRecipient.Resolve
If myRecipient.Resolved Then
    Set schedKim = olMAPI.GetSharedDefaultFolder(myRecipient, _
        olFolderCalendar)
End If
```

You can set folders in the Outlook message store to contain only certain types of objects. For example, you can have the Calendar folder contain only **AppointmentItem** objects and have the Contacts folder contain only **ContactItem** objects.

Note When items of a specific type are saved, they're saved directly into their corresponding default folder. For example, when the **GetAssociatedAppointment** method is applied to a **MeetingRequestItem** object in the Inbox folder, the **AppointmentItem** object that's returned will be saved to the default Calendar folder.

To add a folder to the **Folders** collection, use the **Add** method. The **Add** method has an optional argument you can use to specify the type of items that can be stored in that folder. By default, a folder created inside another folder inherits the parent folder's type. The following VBScript example adds a new folder named "Caterers" to the current (default) Contacts folder.

```
Set olMAPI = Application.GetNameSpace("MAPI")
Set myContacts = olMAPI.GetDefaultFolder(10)
Set caterers = myContacts.Folders.Add("Caterers")
```

If you've used the **ActiveExplorer** property to return the **Explorer** object that represents the currently displayed folder in an Outlook session, you can use the **CurrentFolder** property to return the corresponding **MAPIFolder** object, as shown in the following Automation example.

```
Set olApp = GetObject("","Outlook.Application")
Set currFldr = olApp.ActiveExplorer.CurrentFolder
```

To return an **Explorer** object associated with a given **MAPIFolder** object, use the **GetExplorer** method.

Working with Outlook Items and Events

Outlook items are represented by the fundamental objects in the Outlook object model. These objects represent mail messages, appointments or meetings, meeting requests, tasks, task requests, contacts, journal entries, posts, mail delivery reports, remote mail items, and notes. The following table describes the objects that represent Outlook items.

Object	Description
AppointmentItem	Represents an appointment in the Calendar folder. An **AppointmentItem** object can represent either a one-time or recurring meeting or appointment. An appointment becomes a meeting when the **MeetingStatus** property is set to **olMeeting** and one or more resources (either personnel, in the form of required or optional attendees, or physical resources, such as a conference room) are designated. These actions result in the creation of a **MeetingRequestItem** object.

Object	Description
ContactItem	Represents a contact in a Contacts folder. A contact can represent any person with whom you have any personal or professional contact.
JournalItem	Represents a journal entry in a Journal folder. A journal entry represents a record of all Outlook-moderated transactions for any given period of time.
MailItem	Represents a mail message in the Inbox folder or another mail folder. The **MailItem** object is the default item object and, to some extent, the basic element of Outlook. In addition to the **MailItem** object, Outlook also has a parallel **PostItem** object that has all of the characteristics of the mail message, differing only in that it's posted (written directly to a folder) rather than sent (mailed to a recipient), and it has two subordinate objects—**RemoteItem** and **ReportItem** objects—that are subsets of the mail message used to handle remote mail items and mail transport system reports, respectively.
MeetingRequestItem	Represents a change to the recipient's Calendar folder, initiated either by another party or as a result of a group action. Unlike with other Outlook objects, you cannot create a **MeetingRequestItem** object or find an existing one in the **Items** collection. This object is created automatically when you set the **MeetingStatus** property of an **AppointmentItem** object to **olMeeting** and send it to one or more users.

To return the **AppointmentItem** object associated with a **MeetingRequestItem** object and work directly with the AppointmentItem object to respond to the request, use the **GetAssociatedAppointment** method. |
NoteItem	Represents a note (an annotation attached to a document) in a Notes folder.
PostItem	Represents a post in a public folder that other users can browse. This object is similar to the **MailItem** object, differing only in that it's posted (saved) directly to the target public folder, not sent (mailed) to a recipient. You use the **Post** method, which is analogous to the **Send** method for the **MailItem** object, to save the post to the target public folder instead of mailing it.
RemoteItem	Represents a remote item in the Inbox folder or another mail folder. This object is similar to the **MailItem** object, but it contains only the **Subject**, **Received**, **Date**, **Time**, **Sender**, and **Size** properties and the first 256 characters of the body of the message. You use it to give someone who's connecting in remote mode enough information to decide whether or not to download the corresponding mail message.

Object	Description
ReportItem	Represents a mail-delivery report in the Inbox folder or another mail folder. This object is similar to the **MailItem** object, and it contains a report (usually the nondelivery report) or error message from the mail transport system.
TaskItem	Represents a task (an assigned, delegated, or self-imposed task to be performed within a specified time frame) in a Tasks folder. Like appointments or meetings, tasks can be delegated. Tasks are delegated when you assign them to one or more delegates, using the **Assign** method.
TaskRequestItem	Represents a change to the recipient's task list, initiated either by another party or as a result of a group assignment. Unlike with other Outlook objects, you cannot create a **TaskRequestItem** object or find an existing one in the **Items** collection. It's created automatically when you apply the **Assign** method to a **TaskItem** object to assign (delegate) the associated task to another user.
	To return the **TaskRequestItem** object and work directly with the **TaskItem** object to respond to the request, use the **GetAssociatedTask** method.

The **Items** collection of a **MAPIFolder** object contains the objects that represent all the Outlook items in the specified folder. If a given folder doesn't contain any Outlook items, the **Count** property for the **Items** collection is 0 (zero).

To return the **Items** collection of a **MAPIFolder** object, use the **Items** property. To return a single **AppointmentItem**, **ContactItem**, **JournalItem**, **MailItem**, **NoteItem**, **PostItem**, or **TaskItem** object from its respective **Items** collection, use **Items**(*index*), where *index* is the item's name or index number.

The following example returns the first item with the subject "Need your advice" in myFolder.

```
Set myItem = myFolder.Items("Need your advice")
```

The following example returns the first item in myFolder.

```
Set myItem = myFolder.Items(1)
```

To add items to the **Items** collection, use the **Add** method.

Note   If you don't specify item type, it defaults to the type of the parent folder, or to **MailItem** if this folder doesn't have a type assigned to it. You can also assign to an item any valid message class as a type. You'll want to do this when you're creating customs forms.

The following Automation example gets the current Contacts folder and adds a new **ContactItem** object to it.

```
Set olMAPI = GetObject("","Outlook.Application").GetNameSpace("MAPI")
Set myItem = olMAPI.GetDefaultFolder(olFolderContacts).Items.Add
```

The following VBScript example adds a custom form to the default Tasks folder.

```
Set olMAPI = Application.GetNameSpace("MAPI")
Set myForm = olMAPI.GetDefaultFolder(13).Items _
    .Add("IPM.Task.myTask")
```

The easiest way to return a new **AppointmentItem**, **ContactItem**, **JournalItem**, **MailItem**, **NoteItem**, **PostItem**, or **TaskItem** object directly from the **Application** object is to use the **CreateItem** method with the appropriate **OlItems** constant. The following VBScript example uses the **Application** object to create a new contact.

```
Set myContact = Application.CreateItem(2)
```

If you've used the **ActiveInspector** property to return an **Inspector** object, you can use the **CurrentItem** property to return the object that represents the Outlook item displayed in the inspector. The following Automation example returns the active **Inspector** object and displays the name of the item that the inspector is displaying.

```
Set olApp = GetObject("","Outlook.Application")
Set currInspect = olApp.ActiveInspector
MsgBox "The active item is " & currInspect.CurrentItem.Subject
```

To return an **Inspector** object associated with an Outlook item, use the **GetInspector** method.

Objects Supported by Outlook Items

Every Outlook item can be analyzed or modified by reading or setting its properties or applying its methods. In addition, every Outlook item can contain other objects that represent more complex qualities or behaviors of the item; for example, there are objects that represent the recipients of the item, the files attached to the item, and the customized pages and controls of the item. The following table describes the objects contained in Outlook items.

Object	Description
Actions (Action)	Represent specialized actions (for example, the voting options response) that you can perform on an item.
Attachments (Attachment)	Represent linked or embedded objects contained in an item.
FormDescription	Represents the general properties of the form for an item.
Pages	Represents the customized pages of an item. Every **Inspector** object has a **Pages** collection, whose count is 0 (zero) if the item has never been customized before.
Recipients (Recipient)	Represent users or resources in Outlook; generally, recipients are mail message addressees.
RecurrencePattern	Represents the pattern of incidence of recurring appointments and tasks for the associated **AppointmentItem** or **TaskItem** object.
UserProperties (UserProperty)	Represent the custom fields added to an item at design time.

For more information about these objects, as well as examples of using them in code, see the corresponding topics in Help.

Events Supported by Outlook Items

The events supported by Outlook items are the key to programming Outlook in VBScript. While designing a form, you can write event procedures in the Script Editor and save that script with the form. You can write procedures that respond to changes in the item or that respond to the user's clicking a control on the form. Within an event procedure, you can use any of the objects exposed by the Outlook type library. For information about the features and restrictions of VBScript, see "Using Automation and VBScript" later in this chapter.

The names of event procedures for items are composed of the word "Item" followed by an underscore character (_) and the name of the event (for example, "Item_Open"). Within an event procedure, you can use the word "Item" to refer to the object that represents the Outlook item where the event occurred. The following example adds the date and time that the Outlook item was opened to the end of the item's subject line.

```
Function Item_Open()
Item.Subject = Item.Subject & " [opened " & Now & "]"
End Function
```

For information about adding event procedures to a script in Outlook, see "Using Automation and VBScript" later in this chapter.

Your procedures can respond to some events in Outlook by preventing the default behavior of Outlook from occurring—that is, the procedures can interrupt the events. For example, if the user clicks **Save** on the **File** menu of an item, you can prompt the user for confirmation and prevent the item from being saved if the user reconsiders. Procedures that interrupt events can be declared as **Function** procedures; to indicate whether a given event should be allowed to finish, you assign **True** or **False** to the function value before the procedure ends. Events that can be interrupted include the following: Close, CustomAction, Forward, Open, Reply, ReplyAll, Send, and Write.

Note   If you don't intend to interrupt an event that can be interrupted, you can declare your procedure as a **Sub** procedure rather than a **Function** procedure. Procedures that respond to events that cannot be interrupted must be declared as **Sub** procedures.

Close Event

The Close event occurs when the inspector associated with the item is being closed. When the event occurs, the inspector is still open on the desktop. You can prevent the inspector from closing by setting the function value to **False**. The following example automatically saves an item without prompting the user when the item closes.

```
Function Item_Close()
If not Item.Saved Then
    Item.Save
End If
Item_Close = True
End Function
```

CustomAction Event

The CustomAction event occurs when one of the item's custom actions is executed. Both the name of the custom action and the object that represents the newly created item resulting from the custom action are passed to the event. You can prevent the custom action's behavior and prevent the item from being displayed by setting the function value to **False**. The following example sets a property of the response item created by Action1.

```
Function Item_CustomAction(ByVal myAction, ByVal myResponse)
Select Case myAction.Name
    Case "Action1"
        myResponse.Subject = "Changed by VBScript"
    Case Else
End Select
Item_CustomAction = True
End Function
```

CustomPropertyChange Event

The CustomPropertyChange event occurs when one of the item's custom properties is changed. These properties are the nonstandard properties added to the item at design time. The property name is passed to the procedure, making it possible for the procedure to determine which property was changed. The following example enables a control when a **Boolean** field is set to **True**.

```
Sub Item_CustomPropertyChange(ByVal myPropertyName)
Select Case myPropertyName
    Case "RespondBy"
        Set cstPages = Item.GetInspector.ModifiedFormPages
        Set ctlRespond = cstPages("Page 2").Controls("DateToRespond")
        If Item.UserProperties("RespondBy").Value Then
            ctlRespond.Enabled = True
            ctlRespond.Backcolor = 1
        Else
            ctlRespond.Enabled = False
            ctlRespond.Backcolor = 0
        End If
    Case Else
End Select
End Sub
```

Forward Event

The Forward event occurs when the user selects the **Forward** action for an item. The newly created item is passed to the procedure. **You can** prevent the new item from being displayed on the desktop by setting the function value to **False**. The following example disables forwarding an item and displays a message that the item cannot be forwarded.

```
Function Item_Forward(ByVal myForwardItem)
MsgBox "You cannot forward this message."
Item_Forward = False
End Function
```

Open Event

The Open event occurs when the inspector for an item is being opened. When this event occurs, the **Inspector** object is initialized but not yet displayed. You can prevent the **Inspector** object from being opened on the desktop by setting the function value to **False**. The following example opens an item in its inspector and displays the All Fields page.

```
Function Item_Open()
Item.GetInspector.SetCurrentFormPage "All Fields"
Item_Open = True
End Function
```

PropertyChange Event

The PropertyChange event occurs when one of the item's standard properties (such as **Subject** or **To**) is changed. The property name is passed to the procedure, making it possible for the procedure to determine which property was changed. The following example disables setting a reminder for an item.

```
Sub Item_PropertyChange(ByVal myPropertyName)
Select Case myPropertyName
    Case "ReminderSet"
        MsgBox "You cannot set a reminder on this item."
        Item.ReminderSet = False
    Case Else
End Select
End Sub
```

Read Event

The Read event occurs each time the user opens an existing item for editing. This event differs from the Open event in that Read is called whenever the user modifies the item in an explorer view that supports editing or whenever the user opens the item in an inspector. The following example increments a counter to track how often an item is read.

```
Sub Item_Read()
    Set myProperty = Item.UserProperties("ReadCount").Value
    myProperty.Value = myProperty.Value + 1
    myItem.Save
End Sub
```

Reply Event

The Reply event occurs when the user replies to an item's sender. The newly created item is passed to the procedure. You can prevent the new item from being displayed on the desktop by setting the function value to **False**. The following example sets the Sent Items folder for the new item to the folder in which the original item resides.

```
Function Item_Reply(ByVal myResponse)
Set myResponse.SaveSentMessageFolder = Item.Parent
Item_Reply = True
End Function
```

ReplyAll Event

The ReplyAll event occurs when the user replies to an item's sender and recipients. The newly created item is passed to the procedure. You can prevent the new item from being displayed on the desktop by setting the function value to **False**. The following example reminds the user that he or she is replying to all the original recipients of an item and, depending on the user's response, either makes it possible for the action to continue or prevents it from continuing.

```
Function Item_ReplyAll(ByVal myResponse)
myResult = MsgBox ("Do you really want to reply to all original recipients?", _
    289, "Flame Protector")
If myResult = 1 Then
    Item_ReplyAll = True
Else
    Item_ReplyAll = False
End If
End Function
```

Send Event

The Send event occurs when the user sends an item. You can prevent the item from being sent by setting the function value to **False**. If you interrupt this event, the item's inspector remains displayed on the desktop. The following example sends an item that has an automatic expiration date of one week.

```
Function Item_Send()
Item.ExpiryTime = Date + 7
Item_Send = True
End Function
```

Write Event

The Write event occurs each time an item is saved—either explicitly, as with the **Save** or **SaveAs** method, or implicitly, as in response to a prompt when the item's inspector is being closed. You can prevent the item from being saved by setting the function value to **False**. The following example warns the user that item is about to be saved and will overwrite any existing item and, depending on the user's response, either makes it possible for the action to continue or prevents it from continuing.

```
Function Item_Write()
myResult = MsgBox ("The item is about to be saved. Do you wish to overwrite the _
    existing item?", 289, "Save")
If myResult = 1 Then
    Item_Write = True
Else
    Item_Write = False
End If
End Function
```

Click Event

The Click event occurs when the user clicks a form control (such as an ActiveX control or a custom field). You can create as many Click event procedures as you have controls on a form. The name of each event procedure is the name of the control (such as "CommandButton1"), followed by an underscore character (_) and the word "Click." The following example displays a greeting containing the logon name of the current user whenever the button named "CommandButton1" is clicked.

```
Sub CommandButton1_Click()
MsgBox "Hello " & Application.GetNameSpace("MAPI").CurrentUser
End Sub
```

Unlike with the word "Item" in other event procedures, you cannot use the name of a control to gain access to the object in a Click event procedure. The properties and methods of the control itself aren't accessible from VBScript.

Note   The Message and Note form controls don't support the Click event.

Using Automation and VBScript

There are two ways to program Outlook objects: remotely from another Office application by using Visual Basic and Automation, or locally in Outlook by using VBScript. You use Automation when you want to control an entire Outlook session; for example, you can copy data from a Microsoft Excel worksheet into a new mail message and send it to a list of recipients, all without leaving Microsoft Excel. You use VBScript when you want to design an Outlook-based solution; for example, you can create a custom mail message form that contains custom controls, fields, and backup processes for a particular workgroup.

Using Automation

Automating Outlook from another Office application is the same as automating any other Office application remotely. You must first reference the Outlook type library; then, use the **CreateObject** function to start a new session of Outlook, or use the **GetObject** function to automate a session that's already running. After returning the Outlook **Application** object by using one of these two functions, you can write code in your controlling module that directly uses the objects, properties, methods, and constants defined in the Outlook type library.

Note If you use Automation to control Outlook, you cannot write event procedures to respond to the events supported by Outlook items.

For more information about using Automation to control one Office application from another one, see Chapter 2, "Understanding Object Models."

For up-to-date information about VBScript, see the Visual Basic Scripting Edition Web site at http://www.microsoft.com/vbscript

Using VBScript

If you're creating an Outlook-based solution, you can program Outlook from within your custom forms by writing scripts using VBScript at design time (while you're adding controls and fields to forms after clicking **Design Outlook Form** on the **Tools** menu). To view and edit scripts on a form, click **View Code** on the **Form** menu in design mode. The Script Editor has templates for all the item events. To add an event template to your script in the Script Editor, click **Event** on the **Script** menu, click an event name in the list, and then click **Add**. The appropriate **Sub...End Sub** or **Function...End Function** statement is inserted, with its arguments (if any) specified. (You cannot add Click event procedures by using the **Event** command on the **Script** menu; you must type the **Sub...End Sub** statement for those procedures from scratch.)

Note You can write **Sub** and **Function** procedures that don't respond to events, but they won't run unless they're called from valid event procedures.

In Outlook, users cannot run your scripts using Outlook commands. Instead, scripts run automatically in response to events that the user triggers. For example, when the user opens an item based on your form template, the Open event occurs; if an Open event procedure exists, it runs automatically. Only Outlook items and controls on those items support events; folders don't support events.

VBScript is a subset of the Visual Basic language. It's designed to be a small, lightweight interpreted language, so it doesn't use strict types (only **Variant**). VBScript is also intended to be a safe subset of Visual Basic, so it doesn't include file input/output functions or Automation functions, and it doesn't allow declarations to external functions. The following sections describe the capabilities and restrictions of VBScript in detail.

VBScript Features

The following table shows the Visual Basic features and keywords that were included in VBScript.

Category	Feature or keyword
Array handling	**Dim**, **ReDim**
	IsArray
	Erase
	LBound, **UBound**
Assignment	**=**
	Set
Comment	**Rem**
Constants and literals	**Empty**
	Nothing
	Null
	True, **False**
Control flow	**Do ... Loop**
	For ... Next
	If ... Then ... Else
	Select Case
	While ... Wend
Conversion	**Abs**
	Asc, **AscB**, **AscW**
	Chr, **ChrB**, **ChrW**
	CBbool, **CByte**
	CDate, **CDbl**, **CInt**
	CLng, **CSng**, **CStr**
	DateSerial, **DateValue**
	Hex, **Oct**
	Fix, **Int**
	Sgn
	TimeSerial, **TimeValue**
Date and time	**Date**, **Time**
	DateSerial, **DateValue**
	Day, **Month**, **Weekday**, **Year**
	Hour, **Minute**, **Second**
	Now
	TimeSerial, **TimeValue**

Category	Feature or keyword
Declaration	**Dim**, **ReDim**
	Function, **Sub**
Error handling	**Err**
	On Error
Input and output	**InputBox**
	MsgBox
Math	**Atn**, **Cos**, **Sin**, **Tan**
	Exp, **Log**, **Sqr**
	Randomize, **Rnd**
Objects	**IsObject**
Operators	Addition (+), subtraction (−)
	Exponentiation (^)
	Modulus arithmetic (**Mod**)
	Multiplication (*), division (/), integer division (\)
	Negation (−)
	String concatenation (&)
	Equality (=), inequality (<>)
	Less than (<), less than or equal to (<=)
	Greater than (>), greater than or equal to (>=)
	Is
	And, **Or**, **Xor**
	Eqv, **Imp**
Options	**Option Explicit**
Procedures	**Call**
	Function, **Sub**
Strings	**Asc**, **AscB**, **AscW**
	Chr, **ChrB**, **ChrW**
	InStr, **InStrB**
	Len, **LenB**
	LCase, **UCase**
	Left, **LeftB**
	Mid, **MidB**
	Right, **RightB**
	Space
	StrComp
	String
	LTrim, **RTrim**, **Trim**

Category	Feature or keyword
Variants	**IsArray**
	IsDate
	IsEmpty
	IsNull
	IsNumeric
	IsObject
	VarType

Visual Basic Features Omitted from VBScript

The following table shows the Visual Basic features and keywords that were omitted from VBScript.

Category	Omitted feature or keyword
Array handling	**Array** function
	Option Base
	Private, **Public**
	Declaring arrays with lower bound <> 0
Collection	**Add, Count, Item, Remove**
	Access to collections using the ! character (for example, `myCollection!Foo`)
Conditional compilation	**#Const**
	#If ... Then ... Else
Constants and literals	**Const**
	All intrinsic constants
	Type declaration characters (for example, 256&)
Control flow	**DoEvents**
	For Each ... Next
	GoSub ... Return, GoTo
	On Error GoTo
	On ... GoSub, On ... GoTo
	Line numbers, line labels
	With ... End With
Conversion	**CCur, CVar, CVDate**
	Format
	Str, Val
Data types	All intrinsic data types except **Variant**
	Type ... End Type

Category	Omitted feature or keyword
Date and time	**Date** statement, **Time** statement
	Timer
DDE	**LinkExecute**, **LinkPoke**, **LinkRequest**, **LinkSend**
Debugging	**Debug.Print**
	End, **Stop**
Declaration	**Declare** (for declaring DLLs)
	Property Get, **Property Let**, **Property Set**
	Public, **Private**, **Static**
	ParamArray, **Optional**
	New
Error handling	**Erl**
	Error
	On Error ... Resume
	Resume, **Resume Next**
File input and output	All
Financial	All financial functions
Object manipulation	**CreateObject** function
	GetObject function
	TypeOf
Objects	**Clipboard**
	Collection
Operators	**Like**
Options	**Def** *type*
	Option Base
	Option Compare
	Option Private Module
Strings	Fixed-length strings
	LSet, **RSet**
	Mid statement
	StrConv
Using objects	**TypeName**
	Collection access using ! character (for example, `myCollection!Foo`)

Variables in VBScript

Variable names follow the standard rules for naming anything in VBScript. A variable name:

- Must begin with an alphabetic character.
- Cannot contain an embedded period.
- Must not exceed 255 characters.
- Must be unique in the scope in which it's declared.

Generally, when you declare a variable within a procedure, only code within that procedure can get to or change the value of that variable; it has *local* scope and is known as a *procedure-level* variable. When you declare a variable outside a procedure, you make it recognizable to all the procedures in your script; it has *script-level* scope and is known as a script-level variable.

When you're using variables in VBScript, the following limitations apply:

- There can be no more than 127 procedure-level variables (arrays count as a single variable).
- Each script is limited to no more than 127 script-level variables.

The length of time a variable exists is called its *lifetime*. A script-level variable's lifetime extends from the time it's declared until the time the script is finished running. A local variable's lifetime begins when its declaration statement is encountered as the procedure begins, and it ends when the procedure concludes. Local variables are thus ideal as temporary storage space while a procedure is running. You can have local variables with the same name in different procedures, because each variable is recognized only by the procedure in which it's declared.

A variable's scope is determined by where you declare it. At script level, the lifetime of a variable is always the same; it exists while the script is running. At procedure level, a variable exists only while the procedure is running; when the procedure exits, the variable is destroyed.

Constants in VBScript

When you automate Outlook by using an Automation object in an application that supports Visual Basic, you can use built-in constants to specify property and argument values. However, when you automate Outlook by using VBScript, you must use the numeric values that the built-in constants represent. For lists of the numeric values of built-in Outlook constants, see "Microsoft Outlook Constants" in Help.

Variants in VBScript

VBScript has only one data type, called **Variant**. **Variant** is a special kind of data type that can contain different kinds of information, depending on how the value is used. Because **Variant** is the only data type in VBScript, it's also the data type returned by all functions in VBScript.

At its simplest, **Variant** can contain either numeric or string information. **Variant** behaves as a number when it's used in a numeric context and as a string when it's used in a string context. If you're working with data that resembles numeric data, VBScript treats it as such and processes it accordingly. If you're working with data that's clearly string data, VBScript treats it as such. As in other Microsoft languages, numbers enclosed in quotation marks are treated as strings.

Beyond the simple numeric or string classifications, a **Variant** can make further distinctions about the specific nature of numeric information, such as information that represents a date or time. When used with other date or time data, the result is always expressed as a date or a time. Variant can contain numeric information ranging in size from **Boolean** values to huge floating-point numbers. These various categories of information that can be contained in a **Variant** are called *subtypes*. Usually you'll be able to put the kind of data you want in a **Variant**, and it will most likely behave in a way that's suited to the data it contains.

The subtypes supported by VBScript correspond to the data types supported by Visual Basic. For information about the data types supported by Visual Basic, see Chapter 1, "Programming Basics."

The **VarType** function returns a value that indicates the subtype of a variable, giving you information about how your data is stored in a **Variant**. The following table shows values that can be returned by the **VarType** function and their respective **Variant** subtypes.

Subtype	Return value
Empty	0
Null	1
Integer	2
Long	3
Single	4
Double	5
Currency	6
Date (Time)	7
String	8
Automation Object	9
Error	10
Boolean	11

Subtype	Return value
Variant	12 (used only with an array of **Variant** types)
Non-Automation Object	13
Byte	17
Array	8192

Note   The **VarType** function never returns the value for **Array** by itself; it's always added to some other value to indicate an array of a particular type. The value for **Variant** is returned only after it's been added to the value for **Array** to indicate that the argument to the **VarType** function is an array. For example, the value returned for an array of integers is calculated as 2+8192, or 8194. If an object has a default property, **VarType**(*object*) returns the type of that property.

Microsoft PowerPoint Objects

This chapter discusses how to work with each of the primary objects in the Microsoft PowerPoint 97 object model: how to return it, what tasks you can use it to automate, and what lower-level objects you can access from it.

For general information about understanding and navigating Office object models, see Chapter 2, "Understanding Object Models." To view a graphical representation of the entire PowerPoint 97 object model, see "Microsoft PowerPoint Objects" in Help. For a detailed description of a specific object, click the name of that object on the diagram.

Contents
- Working with the Application Object
- Working with the Presentation Object
- Working with the Slide, SlideRange, and Slides Objects
- Working with the Selection Object
- Working with the View and SlideShowView Objects
- Controlling How Objects Behave During a Slide Show

How Do I Display Visual Basic Help for PowerPoint?

To use Visual Basic Help for PowerPoint, you must click **Custom** during Setup and select the **Online Help for Visual Basic** check box for PowerPoint. Otherwise, Visual Basic Help won't be installed. If you've already installed PowerPoint, you can run Setup again to install Visual Basic Help.

To see the contents and index of Visual Basic Help for PowerPoint, click **Contents and Index** on the **Help** menu in the Visual Basic Editor. On the **Contents** tab in the **Help Topics** dialog box, double-click "Microsoft PowerPoint Visual Basic Reference," and then double-click "Shortcut to Microsoft PowerPoint Visual Basic Reference." The **Help Topics** dialog box should reappear, displaying the contents and index for Visual Basic Help for PowerPoint.

Working with the Application Object

When you start a PowerPoint session, you create an **Application** object. You use properties and methods of the **Application** object to control application-wide attributes and behaviors, to control the appearance of the application window, and to get to the rest of the PowerPoint object model.

Note The following properties of the **Application** object can be used without the `Application` object qualifier: **ActivePresentation**, **ActiveWindow**, **AddIns**, **Assistant**, **CommandBars**, **Presentations**, **SlideShowWindows**, and **Windows**. All other properties and methods must have the object qualifier. For example, both of the following lines of code are valid.

```
Application.ActivePresentation.PrintOut
ActivePresentation.PrintOut
```

However, you cannot omit the object qualifier from the following line.

```
Application.Quit
```

Returning the Application Object

From code running in PowerPoint, you can use the **Application** keyword alone to return the PowerPoint **Application** object. The following example sets the left position for the application window.

```
Application.Left = 30
```

If you set an object variable to the **Application** object, declare it as
`PowerPoint.Application`. The following example sets an object variable to the
PowerPoint **Application** object.

```
Dim appPPT As PowerPoint.Application
Set appPPT = Application
```

You can also use the **Application** property of any PowerPoint object to return the
PowerPoint **Application** object. This is useful for returning the PowerPoint
Application object from a PowerPoint presentation embedded in a document created
in another application. The following example, when run from Microsoft Excel, sets
an object variable to the PowerPoint **Application** object. Shape one on worksheet one
must be an embedded PowerPoint presentation.

```
Dim appPPT As PowerPoint.Application
Set embeddedPres = Worksheets(1).Shapes(1)
embeddedPres.OLEFormat.Activate
Set appPPT = embeddedPres.OLEFormat.Object.Object.Application
```

Controlling the Appearance of the Application Window

You can use properties and methods of the **Application** object to control the
appearance of the application window. The following table shows which properties
and methods control which aspects of the application window's appearance.

To do this	Use this property or method
Activate the PowerPoint application window	**Activate** method
Check to see whether the PowerPoint application window is active	**Active** property
Set or return text that appears in the title bar of the PowerPoint application window	**Caption** property
Set or return the size and position of the PowerPoint application window on the screen	**Height**, **Left**, **Top**, and **Width** properties
Set or return a value that controls whether the application window is visible. You must set this property to **True** when you create a PowerPoint **Application** object in another application if you want to be able to see PowerPoint on your screen.	**Visible** property
Set or return a value that controls whether the PowerPoint application window is maximized, minimized, or floating.	**WindowState** property

Note that most of these properties and methods can also be applied to the
DocumentWindow object to control the appearance of the document window.

Controlling Application-Wide Attributes and Behavior

You can use other properties and methods of the **Application** object to control application-wide settings or behaviors, as shown in the following table.

To do this	Use this property or method
Return the name of the active printer	**ActivePrinter** property
Return the PowerPoint build number	**Build** property
Display a Help topic	**Help** method
Return the name of the operating system	**OperatingSystem** property
Return the path to the PowerPoint application.	**Path** property
Quit PowerPoint	**Quit** method
Run a Visual Basic procedure	**Run** method
Return the PowerPoint version number	**Version** property

Getting to Presentations, Document Windows, and Slide Show Windows

The properties of the **Application** object that you'll probably use most provide access to objects that represent presentations, document windows, slide show windows, and add-ins. Use the **Presentations** property of the **Application** object to return any open presentation, or use the **ActivePresentation** property to return the active presentation. Use the **AddIns** property to return any available add-in (an add-in is a special type of presentation you use to assemble and distribute custom features). Use the **Windows** property of the **Application** object to return any open document window, or use the **ActiveWindow** property to return the active document window. Use the **SlideShowWindows** property to return an open slide show window.

Getting to Shared Office Object Models

Other properties of the **Application** object provide access to objects that represent shared Office features, such as menus and toolbars, file searching, the Visual Basic Editor, and the Office Assistant. For more information about these properties, see "Application Object" in Help.

You can use other properties of the **Application** object to control application-wide settings and behavior, as shown in the following table.

To return a reference to	Use this property
Office Assistant	**Assistant** property
PowerPoint menus and toolbars	**CommandBars** property
File search	**FileSearch** property (**FileFind** property on the MacIntosh)
Visual Basic Editor	**VBE** property

Working with the Presentation Object

When you open or create a file in PowerPoint, you create a **Presentation** object. (You may notice that many properties and methods of the **Presentation** object correspond to items on the **File** menu.) You use properties and methods of the **Presentation** object or its collection to open, create, save, and close files; to control presentation-wide attributes and behavior; and to get to slides and masters in the presentation.

Returning the Presentation Object

Use the **ActivePresentation** property to return the presentation that's displayed in the active window. The following example saves the active presentation.

```
ActivePresentation.Save
```

You can return any open presentation by using the syntax **Presentations**(*index*), where *index* is the presentation's name or index number. The following example adds a slide to the beginning of Sample Presentation.

```
Presentations("Sample Presentation").Slides.Add 1, 1
```

Use the **Presentation** property to return the presentation that's currently displayed in the specified document window or slide show window. The following example displays the name of the slide show that's running in slide show window one.

```
MsgBox SlideShowWindows(1).Presentation.Name
```

To return a **Presentation** object that represents an embedded presentation, use the **Object** property of the **OLEFormat** object for the shape that contains the embedded presentation. The following example sets an object variable to the embedded presentation in shape three on slide one in the active presentation.

```
Dim embeddedPres As Presentation
Set embeddedPres = ActivePresentation.Slides(1).Shapes(3).OLEFormat.Object
```

Opening an Existing Presentation

To open an existing presentation, use the **Open** method. This method always applies to the **Presentations** collection, which you return by using the **Presentations** property. The following example opens the file Pres1.ppt and then displays the presentation in slide sorter view.

```
Dim myPres As Presentation
Set myPres = Presentations.Open(FileName:="c:\My documents\pres1.ppt")
myPres.Windows(1).ViewType = ppViewSlideSorter
```

Notice that the return value of the **Open** method is a **Presentation** object that refers to the presentation that was just opened.

Tip The file name in this example contains a path. If you don't include a path, the file is assumed to be in the current folder. Not including the path in the file name may cause a run-time error, because as soon as the user makes a different folder the current folder, Visual Basic can no longer find the file.

Creating a New Presentation

To create a new presentation, apply the **Add** method to the **Presentations** collection. The following example creates a new presentation.

```
Presentations.Add
```

The **Add** method returns the presentation that's just been created. When you add a presentation, you can set an object variable to the returned presentation so that you can refer to the new presentation in your code. The following example creates a new presentation and adds a slide to it.

```
Dim myPres As Presentation
Set myPres = Presentations.Add
myPres.Slides.Add 1, ppLayoutTitle
```

Another way to make it easy to refer to the presentation later in your code is to assign a meaningful name to the presentation as you add it. Use the **SaveAs** method to assign a name to a presentation. (The **Name** property of the **Presentation** object is read-only, so you cannot use it to set the presentation's name.) The following example creates a new presentation and immediately saves it under the name "Sales Report.ppt." The new name is then used to index the presentation within the **Presentations** collection and add a slide to it.

```
Presentations.Add.SaveAs "Sales Report"
Presentations("Sales Report").Slides.Add 1, ppLayoutTitle
```

Importing a Presentation from a Word Outline

To create a presentation from a Word outline, use the **PresentIt** method of the Word **Document** object. The following example, run from Word, exports Presentation Outline.doc as a presentation.

```
Document.Open("C:\Presentation Outline.doc")PresentIt
```

Activating a Presentation

There's no **Activate** method for the **Presentation** object. To activate a PowerPoint presentation, activate one of the document windows in which the presentation appears. The following example activates the first document window in which the Sales Report presentation appears.

```
Presentations("Sales Report").Windows(1).Activate
```

Controlling Slide Numbering, Size, and Orientation in a Presentation

Use the **PageSetup** property of the **Presentation** object to return the **PageSetup** object. This object contains settings for slide and notes page orientation, slide size and orientation, and slide numbering. The following example sets all slides in the active presentation to be 11 inches wide and 8.5 inches high and sets the slide numbering for the presentation to start at 17.

```
With ActivePresentation.PageSetup
    .SlideWidth = 11 * 72
    .SlideHeight = 8.5 * 72
    .FirstSlideNumber = 17
End With
```

Note that the values you specify for some of the properties of the **PageSetup** object can automatically set values for other properties in a common-sense way that mimics behavior in the **Page Setup** dialog box (**File** menu) in the user interface. For example, setting the **SlideOrientation** property will switch the values of the **SlideHeight** and **SlideWidth** properties, if appropriate. By the same token, explicitly setting the **SlideWidth** and **SlideHeight** properties automatically sets **SlideSize** to **ppSlideSizeCustom** and sets the **SlideOrientation** property to the appropriate value (based on whichever is greater—slide width or height).

Getting a Consistent Look Throughout a Presentation

You can use templates and masters to ensure a consistent look throughout your presentation. Use the **ApplyTemplate** method of the **Presentation** object to apply a design template to the presentation.

```
ActivePresentation.ApplyTemplate "c:\templates\presentation designs\meadow.pot"
```

Note The available color schemes change when you apply a template. If you've added a standard color scheme to the presentation, it will be lost when the **ApplyTemplate** method is applied.

Use the **HandoutMaster**, **NotesMaster**, **SlideMaster**, or **TitleMaster** property of the **Presentation** object to return a **Master** object that represents a slide, notes, or handout master. You can apply a background fill or color scheme to a master, add background graphics or ActiveX controls to a master, or format the text styles and layout of a master when you want to apply changes to all slides based on that master rather than applying them to one slide at a time. The following example sets the background fill for the slide master for the active presentation.

```
ActivePresentation.SlideMaster.Background.Fill.PresetGradient _
    msoGradientHorizontal, 1, msoGradientBrass
```

If you want a specific shape, such as a picture or an ActiveX control, to show up on all slides in a presentation, add it to the master. An ActiveX control on the master will respond to events during a slide show whenever you click the control, on any slide where it appears.

To make uniform changes to the text formatting in a presentation, use the **TextStyles** property of the **Master** object to return the **TextStyles** collection., This collection contains three **TextStyle** objects that represent the following: the style for title text, the style for body text, and the style for default text (text in AutoShapes). Each **TextStyle** object contains a **TextFrame** object that describes how text is placed within the text-bounding box and a **Ruler** object that contains tab stops and outline-indent formatting information. Use the **Levels** property of the **TextStyle** object to return the **TextStyleLevels** collection. This collection contains outline text formatting information for the five available outline levels (for title text and default text, always use level one). The following example sets the font name, the font size, and the space after paragraphs for level-one body text on all the slides in the active presentation that are based on the master.

```
With ActivePresentation.SlideMaster.TextStyles(ppBodyStyle).Levels(1)
    With .Font
        .Name = "Arial"
        .Size = 36
    End With
    With .ParagraphFormat
        .LineRuleAfter = False
        .SpaceAfter = 6
    End With
End With
```

Note You can set the title and body text styles to different values for each master. The default text style doesn't apply to each individual master but rather to the entire presentation.

Printing a Presentation

Use the **PrintOut** method of the **Presentation** object to print a presentation, as shown in the following example.

```
ActivePresentation.PrintOut
```

To set print options before printing, use the properties and methods of the **PrintOptions** object. Use the **PrintOptions** property of the **Presentation** object to return the **PrintOptions** object. The following example prints three collated copies of the active presentation.

```
With ActivePresentation.PrintOptions
    .NumberOfCopies = 3
    .Collate = True
    .Parent.PrintOut
End With
```

Note that the **Parent** property of the **PrintOption** object used in the preceding example returns the **Presentation** object.

Saving a Presentation

When you save a new presentation for the first time, or when you want to save an existing presentation under a new name, use the **SaveAs** method. The following example creates a new presentation, adds a slide to it, and saves it under the name "Sample."

```
With Presentations.Add
    .Slides.Add 1, ppLayoutTitle
    .SaveAs "Sample"
End With
```

For subsequent saves, use the **Save** method. The following example saves the active presentation.

```
ActivePresentation.Save
```

Closing a Presentation

To close a presentation, use the **Close** method of the **Presentation** object. If there are changes in any presentation, PowerPoint displays a message asking whether you want to save changes. The following example closes Pres1.ppt.

```
Presentations("pres1.ppt").Close
```

If you want to close a presentation without saving changes, set the **Saved** property to **True** before closing the presentation, as shown in the following example.

```
With Application.Presentations("pres1.ppt")
    .Saved = True
    .Close
End With
```

Setting Up and Running a Slide Show

Use the **SlideShowSettings** property of the **Presentation** object to return the **SlideShowSettings** object, which lets you set up and run the slide show for the presentation. The following example sets the slide show in the active presentation to start on slide two and end on slide four, to advance slides by using the timings set in the first section, and to run in a continuous loop until you press ESC. Finally, the example runs the slide show.

```
With ActivePresentation.SlideShowSettings
    .StartingSlide = 2
    .EndingSlide = 4
    .RangeType = ppShowSlideRange
    .AdvanceMode = ppSlideShowUseSlideTimings
    .LoopUntilStopped = True
    .Run
End With
```

Getting to the Slides in a Presentation

Use the **Slides** property of the **Presentation** object to get to the individual slides in a presentation and, from there, to the graphics and text on the slides. The following section discusses in detail how to work with slides.

Working with the Slide, SlideRange, and Slides Objects

There are three different objects in the PowerPoint object model that represent slides: the **Slides** collection, which represents all the slides in a presentation; the **SlideRange** collection, which represents a subset of the slides in a presentation; and the **Slide** object, which represents an individual slide. In general, you use the **Slides** collection to create slides and when you want to iterate through all the slides in a presentation; you use the **Slide** object when you want to format or work with a single slide; and you use the **SlideRange** collection when you want to format or work with multiple slides the same way you work with multiple slides in the user interface.

Returning the Slides Collection

To return the entire collection of slides in a presentation, use the **Slides** property. The following example inserts slides from the Clipboard at the end of the active presentation.

```
ActivePresentation.Slides.Paste
```

Returning the Slide Object

Use the **Item** method of the **Slides** collection to return a single **Slide** object that you specify by name or index number (because the **Item** method is the default method, you can omit it from your code). The following example copies the third slide in the active presentation to the Clipboard.

```
ActivePresentation.Slides(3).Copy
```

Because the index number of a particular slide can change when you add, delete, or reorder slides, you may find it more reliable to use the **FindBySlideID** property to specify a slide by its slide ID number, a unique identifier that's assigned to a slide when it's added to a presentation and that doesn't change if you change the order of the slides (if you copy the slide into another presentation, it's assigned a new ID number). The following example copies the slide with the ID number 256 to the Clipboard.

```
ActivePresentation.Slides.FindBySlideID(256).Copy
```

Use the **SlideID** property of the **Slide** object to get the slide's ID number. The following example adds a slide to the active presentation and sets a variable to the slide ID number for the new slide.

```
Dim newSlideID As Long
newSlideID = ActivePresentation.Slides.Add(1, ppLayoutTitleOnly).SlideID
```

To return the slide that's currently displayed in the specified document window or slide show window view, use the **Slide** property of the **View** object for the window. The following example copies the slide that's currently displayed in window two to the Clipboard.

```
Windows(2).View.Slide.Copy
```

To return a slide within the selection, use **Selection.SlideRange**(*index*), where *index* is the slide's name or index number. The following example sets the layout for slide one in the selection in the active window, assuming that the selection contains at least one slide.

```
ActiveWindow.Selection.SlideRange(1).Layout = ppLayoutTitle
```

Returning the SlideRange Object

Use **Slides.Range**(*index*), where *index* is either the slide's name or index number or an array of slide index names or slide index numbers, to return a **SlideRange** object from the **Slides** collection. The following example sets the background fill for slides one and three in the active presentation.

```
With ActivePresentation.Slides.Range(Array(1, 3))
    .FollowMasterBackground = False
    .Background.Fill.PresetGradient msoGradientHorizontal, 1, msoGradientLateSunset
End With
```

Adding a Slide

Use the **Add** method of the **Slides** collection to create a new slide and add it to the presentation. The following example adds a title slide to the beginning of the active presentation.

```
ActivePresentation.Slides.Add 1, ppLayoutTitleOnly
```

Inserting Slides from a Word Outline

To insert slides based on a Word outline, use the **InsertFromFile** method. The following example inserts the outline in Presentation Outline.doc as slides after slide three in the active presentation.

```
ActivePresentation.Slides.InsertFromFile FileName:="C:\Presentation Outline.doc", Index:=3
```

Setting the Slide Background and Color Scheme

If you want to set the background fill or color scheme for all the slides in a presentation, use the **Background** or **ColorScheme** property of the **Master** object, as discussed in the section "Getting a Consistent Look Throughout a Presentation" earlier in this chapter. If, however, you want to set the background fill or color scheme for a particular slide or set of slides, use the **Background** or **ColorScheme** property of the **Slide** or **SlideRange** object.

To set the background fill for a slide or a set of slides, use the **Background** property of the **Slide** or **SlideRange** object to return the **SlideRange** object that represents the slide background, and use the **Fill** property to return the **FillFormat** object that represents the background fill. You can then use the properties and methods of the **FillFormat** object to set properties for the fill. The following example sets a gradient fill for the background for slide one in the active presentation.

```
With ActivePresentation.Slides(1)
    .FollowMasterBackground = False
    .Background.Fill.PresetGradient msoGradientHorizontal, 1, msoGradientDaybreak
End With
```

Note To set the background for a slide independently of the slide master background, set the **FollowMasterBackground** property for the slide to **False**.

To set the color scheme for a slide or a set of slides, use the **ColorScheme** property of the **Slide** or **SlideRange** object to return the **ColorScheme** object that represents the color scheme. You can then set the **ColorScheme** object for the slide to another **ColorScheme** object, or you can use the **Colors** method to edit individual colors in the scheme. The following example sets the color scheme for slide one in the active presentation to the third standard color scheme (as counted from left to right and from top to bottom on the **Standard** tab in the **Color Scheme** dialog box).

```
With ActivePresentation
    .Slides(1).ColorScheme = .ColorSchemes(3)
End With
```

The following example uses the **Colors** method to access the title color in the color scheme for the active presentation and then uses the **RGB** property to access the red-green-blue (RGB) value for that color and set it to the RGB value for green that the **RGB** function generates.

```
ActivePresentation.Slides(1).ColorScheme.Colors(ppTitle).RGB = RGB(0, 255, 0)
```

Note   The set of available color schemes changes when you apply a template. If you've added a standard color scheme to a presentation, this color scheme will be lost when the **ApplyTemplate** method is applied.

Choosing the Slide Layout

When you add a slide to a presentation, you specify what layout it should have by using the *Layout* argument of the **Add** method. The following example adds a slide that contains only a title placeholder to the beginning of the active presentation.

```
ActivePresentation.Slides.Add 1, ppLayoutTitleOnly
```

You can check or change the layout of an existing slide by using the **Layout** property. The following example changes the layout of slide one in the active presentation to include a title placeholder, a text placeholder, and a chart placeholder.

```
ActivePresentation.Slides(1).Layout = ppLayoutTextAndChart
```

Note   When you switch slide layouts, any placeholders that contain text or an object remain on the slide, although they may have been repositioned at the time of the switch.

Adding Objects to a Slide

You add objects (such as AutoShapes, OLE objects, and pictures) to a slide by using one of the methods of the **Shapes** collection. You return the **Shapes** collection, which represents the entire drawing layer for a slide, using the **Shapes** property of the **Slide** object. For information about how to create and format objects on slides, see Chapter 10, "Shapes and the Drawing Layer." For information about controlling how an object on a slide behaves during a slide show, see "Controlling How Objects Behave During a Slide Show" later in this chapter.

Changing Slide Order

To change a slide's position in the presentation, cut the slide and then paste it in its new position. The following example moves slide four in the active presentation and makes it slide six. For this example to work, there must be at least six slides in the presentation.

```
With ActivePresentation.Slides
    .Item(4).Cut
    .Paste 6
End With
```

Setting Slide Transition Effects

The properties that control the transition effects for a slide are stored in the **SlideShowTransition** object, which you return by using the **SlideShowTransition** property of the **Slide** or **SlideRange** object. The following example specifies a Fast Strips Down-Left transition accompanied by the Bass.wav sound for slide one in the active presentation. The example also specifies that the slide advance automatically five seconds after the previous animation or slide transition.

```
With ActivePresentation.Slides(1).SlideShowTransition
    .Speed = ppTransitionSpeedFast
    .EntryEffect = ppEffectStripsDownLeft
    .SoundEffect.ImportFromFile "c:\sndsys\bass.wav"
    .AdvanceOnTime = True
    .AdvanceTime = 5
End With
ActivePresentation.SlideShowSettings.AdvanceMode = _
    ppSlideShowUseSlideTimings
```

Note For the timings you set for your slide transition to take effect, the **AdvanceMode** property of the **SlideShowSettings** object must be set to **ppSlideShowUseSlideTimings**.

Getting to the Speaker's Notes on the Notes Page for a Slide

To gain access to the text in the notes area on the notes page for a slide, use the **NotesPage** property to return a **SlideRange** collection that represents the specified notes page. The following example inserts text into placeholder two (the notes area) on the notes page for slide one in the active presentation. (If you've removed the slide image from the notes page, use Placeholders(1) to return the notes area.)

```
ActivePresentation.Slides(1).NotesPage.Shapes.Placeholders(2) _
    .TextFrame.TextRange.InsertAfter "Added Text"
```

Working with the Selection Object

The **Selection** object in PowerPoint represents the selection in a document window. You use methods of the **Selection** object to cut, copy, delete, or unselect the selection. You use the **Type** property of the **Selection** object to figure out what type of content is selected (slides, shapes, text, or nothing at all), and you use the **ShapeRange**, **SlideRange**, and **TextRange** properties to return only a certain type of selected object.

Note Selection-based code is inefficient and is usually unnecessary. For example, you can change the font properties of a text range directly without having to select the text. If you rely on the macro recorder to supply code for you, you should rewrite the code it generates to be selection-independent wherever possible.

Making a Selection

You can create a selection either manually or by applying the **Select** method to the **Shape**, **ShapeRange**, **Slide**, **SlideRange**, or **TextRange** object. The following example selects shapes one and three on slide one in the active presentation.

```
ActivePresentation.Slides(1).Shapes.Range(Array(1, 3)).Select
```

Note You can make a given selection programmatically only if you can make that same selection manually in the active document window. For example, if slide two is showing in the active document window, you cannot select shapes on slide one. Similarly, you cannot make a selection that's inappropriate to the current view in the active document window. For example, if the active document window is in slide sorter view, you cannot select a shape or text range on an individual slide.

Returning the Selection Object

Use the **Selection** property of the **DocumentWindow** object to return the selection. The following example cuts the selection in the active window.

```
ActiveWindow.Selection.Cut
```

Returning Shapes, Text, or Slides in a Selection

Use the **ShapeRange** property of the **Selection** object to return the **ShapeRange** collection that includes all the shapes in the selection. Use the **Item** method of the returned **ShapeRange** object to return a single selected shape. The following example cuts the third shape in the selection in the active window.

```
ActiveWindow.Selection.ShapeRange(3).Cut
```

Returning Selected Text

If only text is selected, use the **TextRange** property of the **Selection** object to return a **TextRange** object that represents the selected text. The following example applies bold formatting to the first three characters in the selected text in the active window.

```
ActiveWindow.Selection.TextRange.Characters(1, 3).Font.Bold = True
```

To get to the text in a selected shape, do the following: return the shape, use the **TextFrame** property to return the text area in the shape, and then use the **TextRange** property of the text frame to return the text in the shape. The following example applies bold formatting to the first three characters in the third shape in the selection in the active window

```
ActiveWindow.Selection.ShapeRange(3).TextFrame.TextRange _
    .Characters(1, 3).Font.Bold = True
```

Returning Selected Slides

Use the **SlideRange** property of the **Selection** object to return a **SlideRange** collection that includes all the selected slides. The following example cuts the selected slides in the active window.

```
ActiveWindow.Selection.SlideRange.Cut
```

Working with the View and SlideShowView Objects

When you open a file in PowerPoint, you simultaneously create a **Presentation** object, which represents the contents of the file; a **DocumentWindow** object, which represents the interface between the user and the file in design mode; and the **View** object, which represents a container for the contents of the file in design mode.

When you start a slide show, you create a **SlideShowWindow** object, which represents the interface between the user and the file in run mode, and a **SlideShowView** object, which represents a container for the contents of the file in run mode.

Understanding Presentations, Windows, and Views

When you're running PowerPoint and you make changes to what you see on the screen, you may be making changes to the **Presentation** object, the **DocumentWindow** object, or the **View** object.

- Changes made to the actual contents of slides—such as by adding, deleting, or formatting objects—are changes to the presentation and are controlled by properties and methods of the **Presentation** object and the objects below the **Presentation** object in the object hierarchy.

- Changes made to the interface that displays the contents—such as by changing the size of the window or switching black-and-white display on or off—are changes to the document window or slide show window and are controlled by properties and methods of the **DocumentWindow** or **SlideShowWindow** object. These changes don't affect the contents of the file. Changes to the document window are retained when you switch document views.

- Changes made to what information is displayed to you—such as whether you see text and graphics or only graphics, and how big the elements look on the screen— are changes to the view and are controlled by properties and methods of the **View** or **SlideShowView** objects. These changes don't affect the contents of the file, and they aren't retained when you switch views.

Returning the View and SlideShowView Objects

The **View** object represents the way information is displayed in a document window. Use the **View** property of the **DocumentWindow** object to return a **View** object. The following example sets the document window to automatically adjust (zoom) to fit the dimensions of the application window.

```
Windows(1).View.ZoomToFit = True
```

The **SlideShowView** object represents the way information is displayed in the slide show window. Use the **View** property of the **SlideShowWindow** object to return a **SlideShowView** object. The following example runs a slide show of the active presentation with shortcut keys disabled (the **Run** method of the **SlideShowSettings** object returns a **SlideShowWindow** object).

```
ActivePresentation.SlideShowSettings.Run.View.AcceleratorsEnabled = False
```

The following example sets the pointer color and pointer shape for the second slide show that's currently running. (There can be only one running slide show window per presentation, but there can be multiple presentations running slide shows at the same time.)

```
With SlideShowWindows(2).View
    .PointerColor.RGB = RGB(255, 0, 0)
    .PointerType = ppSlideShowPointerPen
End With
```

Navigating in a Slide Show in a Document Window View or Slide Show Window View

Use the **GotoSlide** method of the **View** or **SlideShowView** object to make a specific slide the active slide. The following example makes slide three in the presentation in document window one the active slide in the window.

```
Windows(1).View.GotoSlide 3
```

Note that depending on what document view you're in, the term "active slide" has slightly different meanings. In slide view or note view, the active slide is the one that's currently displayed in the window. In outline view or slide sorter view, the active slide is the selected slide.

The following example advances the presentation in slide show window one to the third slide.

```
SlideShowWindows(1).View.GotoSlide 3
```

You can also go to the first slide in a slide show by using the **First** method or to the last slide by using the **Last** method, or you can go to a custom slide show by using the **GotoNamedShow** method. For more information about these methods, see the topics for them in Help.

Pasting Clipboard Contents into a Document Window View

Use the **Paste** method to paste the contents of the Clipboard into the active document window view. The following example copies the selection in window one to the Clipboard and then copies it into the view in window two. If the Clipboard contents cannot be pasted into the view in window two—for example, if you try to paste a shape into slide sorter view—this example fails.

```
Windows(1).Selection.Copy
Windows(2).View.Paste
```

The following table shows what you can paste into each view.

Into this view	You can paste the following from the Clipboard
Slide view or notes page view	Shapes, text, or entire slides.
	Pasted shapes will be added to the top of the z-order and won't replace selected shapes.
	If one shape is selected, pasted text will be appended to the shape's text; if text is selected, pasted text will replace the selection; if anything else is selected, pasted text will be placed in it's own text frame.
	If you paste a slide from the Clipboard, an image of the slide will be inserted onto the slide, master, or notes page as an embedded object.

Into this view	You can paste the following from the Clipboard
Outline view	Text or entire slides.
	A pasted slide will be inserted before the slide that contains the insertion point.
	You cannot paste shapes into outline view.
Slide sorter view	Entire slides.
	A pasted slide will be inserted at the insertion point or after the last slide in the selection.
	You cannot paste shapes or text into slide sorter view.

For information about setting the view for a window before pasting the Clipboard contents into it, see the following section.

Setting or Checking the View Type in a Document Window

Use the **Type** property of the **View** object to see what the active document view is, and use the **ViewType** property of the **DocumentWindow** object to set the active document view. The following example copies the selection in window one to the Clipboard, makes sure that window one is in slide view, and then copies the Clipboard contents into the view in window two.

```
Windows(1).Selection.Copy
With Windows(2)
    .ViewType = ppViewSlide
    .View.Paste
End With
```

Returning the Slide That's Currently Showing in a Document Window View or Slide Show Window View

Use the **Slide** property to return the **Slide** object that represents the slide that's currently displayed in the specified slide show window view or document window view. The following example places on the Clipboard a copy of the slide that's currently displayed in slide show window one.

```
SlideShowWindows(1).View.Slide.Copy
```

Tip If the currently displayed slide is from an embedded presentation, you can use the **Parent** property of the **Slide** object returned by the **Slide** property to return the embedded presentation that contains the slide. (The **Presentation** property of the **SlideShowWindow** object or **DocumentWindow** object returns the presentation in which the window was created, not the embedded presentation.)

Controlling How Objects Behave During a Slide Show

The entire drawing layer on a slide is represented by the **Shapes** collection, and each object on a slide—whether it's a placeholder, AutoShape, or OLE object—is represented by a **Shape** object. Using properties and methods of the **Shapes** collection, you can add objects to slides and gain access to the individual objects on a slide. Using properties and methods of the **Shape** object, you cancontrol the shape's appearance, the text or OLE object it can contain, and the way it behaves during a slide show. This section discusses the properties and methods that control how a shape behaves during a slide show. For information about the properties and methods that control other attributes and behavior of shapes, see Chapter 10, "Shapes and the Drawing Layer."

Controlling How a Shape Becomes Animated During a Slide Show

The **AnimationSettings** object contains properties and methods that control how and when a shape appears on a specific slide during a slide show. The following example sets shape two on slide one in the active presentation to become animated automatically after five seconds.

```
With ActivePresentation.Slides(1).Shapes(2).AnimationSettings
    .AdvanceMode = ppAdvanceOnTime
    .AdvanceTime = 5
    .TextLevelEffect = ppAnimateByAllLevels
    .Animate = True
End With
```

When you work with the properties of the **AnimationSettings** object, it's important to keep in mind how individual properties work with each other and with the **AdvanceMode** property of the **SlideShowSettings** object.

You won't see the effects of setting any properties of the **AnimationSettings** object unless the specified shape is animated—that is, if the shape doesn't appear on the slide when the slide is initially displayed during a slide show but appears later. For a shape to be animated, the **TextLevelEffect** property must be set to something other than **ppAnimateLevelNone** and the **Animate** property must be set to **True**.

To put into effect animation timings, which determine when the shape will appear on the slide during a slide show, you must not only assign a number of seconds to the **AdvanceTime** property, but you must also set the **AdvanceMode** property of the **SlideShowSettings** object to **ppAdvanceOnTime** and set the **AdvanceMode** property to **ppSlideShowUseSlideTimings**.

You can use the **AfterEffect** property to specify what happens to a shape after it becomes animated. Obviously, unless a shape gets animated and at least one other shape on the slide gets animated after it, you won't see any of the aftereffects you set for the shape. Additionally, unless the **AfterEffect** property is set to **ppAfterEffectDim**, you won't see the effect of the **DimColor** property setting.

Controlling How a Shape Responds to Mouse Actions During a Slide Show

The **ActionSettings** collection for a shape contains two **ActionSetting** objects—one that contains properties and methods that control how a shape responds when it's clicked during a slide show (corresponds to the settings on the **Mouse Click** tab in the **Action Settings** dialog box), and another that contains properties and methods that control how a shape responds when the mouse pointer passes over it during a slide show (corresponds to the settings on the **Mouse Over** tab in the **Action Settings** dialog box). The following example specifies that when shape three on slide one in the active presentation is clicked during a slide show, the shape's color is momentarily inverted, the Applause sound plays, and the slide show returns to the first slide.

```
With ActivePresentation.Slides(1).Shapes(3).ActionSettings(ppMouseClick)
    .Action = ppActionFirstSlide
    .SoundEffect.Name = "applause"
    .AnimateAction = True
End With
```

Note that different action settings are available for different types of shapes (for example, you can use the **ActionVerb** property only for OLE objects). Thus, for any given shape, you should use only properties that correspond to the settings available in the user interface when the shape is selected.

If you set a property of the **ActionSetting** object but don't see the changes you made reflected in the slide show, make sure that you've set the correct value for the **Action** property, as shown in the following table.

If you use this property	To do this	Set the Action property to this value to put the change into effect
Hyperlink	Set properties for the hyperlink that will be followed in response to a mouse action on the shape during a slide show	**ppActionHyperlink**
Run	Return or set the name of the program to run in response to a mouse action on the shape during a slide show	**ppActionRunProgram**

If you use this property	To do this	Set the Action property to this value to put the change into effect
Run	Return or set the name of the macro to be run in response to a mouse action on the shape during a slide show	**ppActionRunMacro**
ActionVerb	Set the OLE verb that will be invoked in response to a mouse action on the shape during a slide show	**ppActionOLEVerb**
SlideShowName	Set the name of the custom slide show that will be run in response to a mouse action on the shape during a slide show	**ppActionNamedSlideShow**

Controlling How a Media Clip Plays During a Slide Show

The **PlaySettings** object, which you return by using the **PlaySettings** property of the **AnimationSettings** object, contains properties and methods that control how and when a media clip plays during a slide show. The following example inserts a movie named "Clock.avi" into slide one in the active presentation, sets it to play automatically after the previous animation or slide transition, specifies that the slide show continue while the movie plays, and specifies that the movie object be hidden during a slide show except when it's playing.

```
Set clockMovie = ActivePresentation.Slides(1).Shapes.AddMediaObject _
    (FileName:="C:\WINNT\clock.avi", Left:=20, Top:=20)
With clockMovie.AnimationSettings.PlaySettings
    .PlayOnEntry = True
    .PauseAnimation = False
    .HideWhileNotPlaying = True
End With
```

Depending on whether you inserted the media clip as an OLE object (using the **Object** command on the **Insert** menu, or using the **AddOLEObject** method) or as a native media object (using the **Movies and Sounds** menu or the **AddMediaObject** method), different properties of the **PlaySettings** object will apply to the clip. This mimics the way different options are available for native media objects and OLE objects on the **Play Settings** tab in the **Custom Animation** dialog box (**Slide Show** menu).

The preferred way to insert media clips is as native media objects, because native movies and sounds don't require the use of the Windows Media Player and therefore respond faster when they're clicked or activated. Most of the properties of the **PlaySettings** object apply only to native media clips. The **ActionVerb** property, which corresponds to the options listed in the **Object** box on the **PlaySettings** tab in the **Custom Animation** dialog box, is the only property of the **PlaySettings** object that doesn't apply to native media objects.

To determine whether a particular media clip is a native media object, check to see whether the value of the **Type** property of the **Shape** object that contains the clip is **msoMedia**. Use the **MediaType** property of the **Shape** object to determine whether the clip is a sound or a movie. The following example sets all native sound objects on slide one in the active presentation to loop during a slide show until they're manually stopped.

```
Dim so As Shape
For Each so In ActivePresentation.Slides(1).Shapes
    If so.Type = msoMedia Then
        If so.MediaType = ppMediaTypeSound Then
            so.AnimationSettings.PlaySettings.LoopUntilStopped = True
        End If
    End If
Next
```

CHAPTER 7

Microsoft Word Objects

Visual Basic supports a set of objects that correspond directly to elements in Microsoft Word 97, most of which you're familiar with from the user interface. For example, the **Document** object represents an open document, the **Bookmark** object represents a bookmark in a document, and the **Selection** object represents the selection in a document window pane. Every type of element in Word—documents, tables, paragraphs, bookmarks, fields, and so on—can be represented by an object in Visual Basic. To automate tasks in Word, use methods and properties of these objects.

For general information about understanding and navigating the object models in Microsoft Office 97, see Chapter 2, "Understanding Object Models." The object model in Microsoft Word 97 is extensive, encompassing approximately 180 objects. To view a graphical representation of the Word object model, see "Microsoft Word Objects" in Help. For a detailed description of a specific object, click the name of the object on the diagram, or search for the specific object name in the Help index.

Contents

- Working with the Application Object
- Working with the Document Object
- Working with the Range Object
- Working with the Selection Object
- Working with the Find and Replacement Objects
- Working with Table, Column, Row, and Cell Objects
- Working with Other Common Objects
- Determining Whether an Object Is Valid
- Modifying Word Commands
- Working with Events

- Using Auto Macros
- Using Automation

How Do I Display Visual Basic Help for Word?

To use Visual Basic Help for Word, you must click **Custom** during Setup and select the **Online Help for Visual Basic** check box for Word. Otherwise, Visual Basic Help won't be installed. If you've already installed Word, you can run Setup again to install Visual Basic Help.

To see the contents and index of Visual Basic Help for Word, click **Contents and Index** on the **Help** menu in the Visual Basic Editor. On the **Contents** tab in the **Help Topics** dialog box, double-click "Microsoft Word Visual Basic Reference," and then double-click "Shortcut to Microsoft Word Visual Basic Reference." The **Help Topics** dialog box should reappear, displaying the contents and index for Visual Basic Help for Word.

Working with the Application Object

When you start a Word session, you automatically create an **Application** object. You use properties or methods of the **Application** object to control or return application-wide attributes, to control the appearance of the application window, and to get to the rest of the Word object model. Use the **Application** property to return the Word **Application** object. The following example switches the view to print preview.

```
Application.PrintPreview = True
```

Some properties of the **Application** object control the appearance of the application. For example, if the **DisplayStatusBar** property is **True**, the status bar is visible, and if **WindowState** property is **wdWindowStateMaximize**, the application window is maximized. The following example sets the size of the application window on the screen.

```
With Application
    .WindowState = wdWindowStateNormal
    .Height = 450
    .Width = 600
End With
```

Properties of the **Application** object also provide access to objects lower in the object hierarchy, such as the **Windows** collection (representing all currently open windows) and the **Documents** collection (representing all currently open documents). You use properties, which are sometimes called *accessors*, to move down through the object hierarchy from the top-level **Application** object to the lower levels (**Document**, **Window**, **Selection**, and so forth). You can use either of following examples to open MyDoc.doc.

```
Application.Documents.Open FileName:="C:\DOCS\MYDOC.DOC"
Documents.Open FileName:="C:\DOCS\MYDOC.DOC"
```

Because the **Documents** property is *global*, the **Application** property is optional. Global properties and methods don't need the **Application** object qualifier. To view the list of global properties and methods in the Object Browser, click **<globals>** in the **Classes** box. The global items are listed in the **Members of** box.

Note   The **Options** object includes a number of properties that control the global behavior of Word. Many of the properties for the **Options** object correspond to items in the **Options** dialog box (**Tools** menu). Use the **Options** property of the **Application** object to return the **Options** object. The following example sets three application-wide options (because the **Options** property is global, the **Application** property isn't needed in this example).

```
With Application.Options
    .AllowDragAndDrop = True
    .ConfirmConversions = False
    .MeasurementUnit = wdPoints
End With
```

Working with the Document Object

When you open or create a file in Word, you create a **Document** object. You use properties and methods of the **Document** object or the **Documents** collection to open, create, save, activate, and close files.

Returning the Document Object

You can return any open document as a **Document** object, using the syntax **Documents**(*index*), where *index* is the document's name or index number. In the following example, the variable myDoc contains a **Document** object that refers to the open document named "Report.doc."

```
Set myDoc = Documents("Report.doc")
```

The index number represents the position of the document in the **Documents** collection. In the following example, the variable myDoc contains a **Document** object that refers to the first document in the **Documents** collection.

```
Set myDoc = Documents(1)
```

Note   Because the index number of a particular document can change when you add or close documents, it's best to use the document name to index a **Document** object in the **Documents** collection.

In addition to referring to a document by either its name or index number, you can use the **ActiveDocument** property to return a **Document** object that refers to the active document (the document with the focus). The following example displays the name of the active document; if there are no documents open, the example displays a message.

```
If Documents.Count >= 1 Then
    MsgBox ActiveDocument.Name
Else
    MsgBox "No documents are open"
End If
```

Opening Documents

To open an existing document, use the **Open** method. The **Open** method applies to the **Documents** collection, which you return using the **Documents** property. The following example opens the file Test.doc (from the current folder) and turns on change tracking.

```
Set myDoc = Documents.Open(FileName:="TEST.DOC")
myDoc.TrackRevisions = True
```

Notice that the return value of the **Open** method in the preceding example is a **Document** object that represents the document that was just opened. The file name in the example doesn't contain a path; therefore, the file is assumed to be in the current folder. This is guaranteed to cause a run-time error, because as soon as the user makes a different folder the current folder, Visual Basic can no longer find the file. You can, however, ensure that the correct file is opened by specifying the complete path, as shown in the following table.

Operating system	FileName
Windows	FileName:="C:\Documents\Temporary File.doc"
Macintosh	FileName:="Hard Drive:Documents:Temporary File"

If your macro is intended for only one file system, you can hard-code the path separator ("\" or ":") in the *FileName* argument, as shown in the preceding table. The following example shows file-system-independent code you can use to open Sales.doc, assuming that Sales.doc has been saved in the Word program folder.

```
programPath = Options.DefaultFilePath(wdProgramPath)
Documents.Open FileName:=programPath & Application.PathSeparator & "SALES.DOC"
```

The **PathSeparator** property returns the correct separator character for the current file system (for example, "\" for MS-DOS/Windows FAT or ":" for the Macintosh). The **DefaultFilePath** property returns folder locations such as the paths for the document folder, the program folder, and the current folder.

An error occurs if the specified file name doesn't exists in either the current folder (if a path isn't specified) or the specified folder (if a path is specified). The following example uses properties and methods of the **FileSearch** object to determine whether a file named "Test.doc" exists in the user's default document folder. If the file is found (`FoundFiles.Count = 1`), it's opened; otherwise, a message is displayed.

```
defaultDir = Options.DefaultFilePath(wdDocumentsPath)
With Application.FileSearch
    .FileName = "Test.doc"
    .LookIn = defaultDir
    .Execute
    If .FoundFiles.Count = 1 Then
        Documents.Open FileName:=defaultDir & Application.PathSeparator & "TEST.DOC"
    Else
        MsgBox "Test.doc file was not found"
    End If
End With
```

Instead of hard-coding the *FileName* argument of the **Open** method, you may want to allow a user to select a file to open. Use the **Dialogs** property with the **wdDialogFileOpen** constant to return a **Dialog** object that refers to the **Open** dialog box (**File** menu), as in the following example. The **Show** method displays and executes actions performed in the **Open** dialog box.

```
Dialogs(wdDialogFileOpen).Show
```

The **Display** method displays the specified dialog box without doing anything further. The following example checks the value returned by the **Display** method. If the user clicks **OK** to close the dialog box, the value –1 value is returned and the selected file, whose name is stored in the variable fSelected, is opened.

```
Set dlg = Dialogs(wdDialogFileOpen)
aButton = dlg.Display
fSelected = dlg.Name
If aButton = -1 Then
    Documents.Open FileName:=fSelected
End If
```

For more information about displaying Word dialog boxes, see "Displaying built-in Word dialog boxes" in Help.

To determine whether a particular document is open, you can enumerate the **Documents** collection by using a **For Each...Next** statement. The following example activates the document named "Sample.doc" if it's already open; if it's not currently open, the example opens it.

```
docFound = True
For Each aDoc In Documents
    If InStr(1, aDoc.Name, "sample.doc", 1) Then
        aDoc.Activate
    Exit For
    Else
        docFound = False
    End If
Next aDoc
If docFound = False Then Documents.Open _
    FileName:="C:\Documents\Sample.doc"
```

Use the **Count** property to determine how many documents are currently open. The **Count** property applies to the **Documents** collection, which you return using the **Documents** property. The following example displays a message if there are no documents open.

```
If Documents.Count = 0 Then MsgBox "No documents are open"
```

Creating and Saving Documents

To create a new document, apply the **Add** method to the **Documents** collection. The following example creates a new document.

```
Documents.Add
```

The **Add** method returns the document that was just created as a **Document** object. When you add a document, you can set the return value of the **Add** method to an object variable so that you can refer to the new document in your code. The following example creates a new document and sets its top margin to 1.25 inches.

```
Dim myDoc As Document
Set myDoc = Documents.Add
myDoc.PageSetup.TopMargin = InchesToPoints(1.25)
```

To save a new document for the first time, use the **SaveAs** method with a **Document** object. The following example saves the active document as "Temp.doc" in the current folder.

```
ActiveDocument.SaveAs FileName:="Temp.doc"
```

After a document is saved, you can use its document name to get to the **Document** object. The following example creates a new document and immediately saves it as "1996 Sales.doc." The example then uses the new name to index the document in the **Documents** collection and adds a table to the document.

```
Documents.Add.SaveAs FileName:="1996 Sales.doc"
Documents("1996 Sales.doc").Tables.Add _
    Range:=Selection.Range, NumRows:=2, NumColumns:=4
```

To save changes to an existing document, use the **Save** method with a **Document** object. The following instruction saves the document named "Sales.doc."

```
Documents("Sales.doc").Save
```

If you use the **Save** method with an unsaved document or template, the **Save As** dialog box will prompt the user for a file name. To save all open documents, apply the **Save** method to the **Documents** collection. The following example saves all open documents without prompting the user for their file names.

```
Documents.Save NoPrompt:=True
```

Activating a Document

To make a different document the active document, apply the **Activate** method to a **Document** object. The following example activates the open document (MyDocument.doc).

```
Documents("MyDocument.doc").Activate
```

The following example opens two documents and then activates the first one (Sample.doc).

```
Set Doc1 = Documents.Open(FileName:="C:\Documents\Sample.doc")
Set Doc2 = Documents.Open(FileName:="C:\Documents\Other.doc")
Doc1.Activate
```

Printing a Document

To print a document, apply the **PrintOut** method to a **Document** object, as shown in the following example.

```
ActiveDocument.PrintOut
```

To programmatically set print options that you'd otherwise set in the **Print** dialog box (**File** menu), use the arguments of the **PrintOut** method. You can use properties of the **Options** object to set print options that you'd otherwise set on the **Print** tab in the **Options** dialog box (**Tools** menu). The following example sets the active document to print hidden text and then prints the first three pages.

```
Options.PrintHiddenText = True
ActiveDocument.PrintOut Range:=wdPrintFromTo, From:="1", To:="3"
```

Closing Documents

To close a document, apply the **Close** method to a **Document** object. The following example closes the document named "Sales.doc."

```
Documents("Sales.doc").Close
```

If there are changes in the document, Word displays a message asking whether the user wants to save changes. You can prevent this prompt from appearing by using the **wdDoNotSaveChanges** or **wdSaveChanges** constant with the *SaveChanges* argument. The following example saves and closes Sales.doc.

```
Documents("Sales.doc").Close SaveChanges:=wdSaveChanges
```

To close all open documents, apply the **Close** method to the **Documents** collection. The following example closes all documents without saving changes.

```
Documents.Close SaveChanges:=wdDoNotSaveChanges
```

Accessing Objects in a Document

From the **Document** object, you have access to a number of properties and methods that return objects. To view a graphical representation of the objects available from the **Document** object, see "Microsoft Word Objects (Documents)" in Help. For example, the **Tables** property, which returns a collection of **Table** objects, is available from the **Document** object. Use the **Count** property with a collection object to determine how many items there are in the collection. The following example displays a message that indicates how many tables there are in the active document.

```
MsgBox ActiveDocument.Tables.Count & " table(s) in this document"
```

Use **Tables**(*index*), where *index* is the index number, to return a single **Table** object. In the following example, myTable refers to the first table in the document named "Sales.doc."

```
Set myTable = Documents("Sales.doc").Tables(1)
```

Information about returning a particular object is available in the object topic itself (for example, "Table Object") and in the corresponding collection object topic (for example, "Tables Collection Object") in Help.

Adding Objects to a Document

You can add objects, such as a footnotes, comments, or tables, to a document using the **Add** method with a collection object accessed from the **Document** object. For example, the following instruction adds a 3x3 table at the location specified by the myRange variable (myRange is an object variable that contains a **Range** object).

```
ActiveDocument.Tables.Add Range:=myRange, NumRows:=3, NumColumns:=3
```

This following example adds a footnote at the location specified by the variable myRange.

```
ActiveDocument.Footnotes.Add Range:=myRange, Text:="The Willow Tree"
```

For a list of collection objects that support the **Add** method, see "Add Method" in Help.

Working with the Range Object

A common task when using Visual Basic is to specify an area in a document and then do something with it, such as insert text or apply formatting. For example, you may want to write a macro that locates a word or phrase within a portion of a document. You can use a **Range** object to represent the portion of the document you want to search for the specified word or phrase. After you identify the **Range** object, you can apply methods and properties of this object to modify the contents of the range.

A **Range** object represents a contiguous area in a document. Each **Range** object is defined by a starting character position and an ending character position. Similar to the way you use bookmarks in a document, you use **Range** objects in Visual Basic procedures to identify specific portions of a document. A **Range** object can be as small as the insertion point or as large as the entire document. However, unlike a bookmark, a **Range** object exists only while the procedure that defined it is running.

Range objects are independent of the selection; that is, you can define and modify a range without changing the selection. You can also define multiple ranges in a document, while there is only one selection per document pane.

The **Start**, **End**, and **StoryType** properties uniquely identify a **Range** object. The **Start** and **End** properties return or set the starting and ending character positions of the **Range** object. The character position at the beginning of each story is 0 (zero), the position after the first character is 1, and so on. There are 11 different story types represented by the **WdStoryType** constants of the **StoryType** property. For example, if a **Range** object is in the footnote area, the **StoryType** property returns **wdFootnotesStory**. For more information about stories, see "Working with Stories" later in this section.

Using the Range Object Instead of the Selection Object

The macro recorder will often create a macro that uses the **Selection** property to manipulate the **Selection** object. However, you can usually accomplish the same task with fewer instructions by using one or more **Range** objects. The following example was created using the macro recorder. This macro applies bold formatting to the first two words in the document.

```
Selection.HomeKey Unit:=wdStory
Selection.MoveRight Unit:=wdWord, Count:=2, Extend:=wdExtend
Selection.Font.Bold = wdToggle
```

The following example accomplishes the same task without using the **Selection** object.

```
ActiveDocument.Range(Start:=0, End:=ActiveDocument.Words(2).End).Bold = True
```

The following example applies bold formatting to the first two words in the document, and then it inserts a new paragraph.

```
Selection.HomeKey Unit:=wdStory
Selection.MoveRight Unit:=wdWord, Count:=2, Extend:=wdExtend
Selection.Font.Bold = wdToggle
Selection.MoveRight Unit:=wdCharacter, Count:=1
Selection.TypeParagraph
```

The following example accomplishes the same task as the preceding example without using the **Selection** object.

```
Set myRange = ActiveDocument.Range(Start:=0, End:=ActiveDocument.Words(2).End)
myRange.Bold = True
myRange.InsertParagraphAfter
```

Both of the preceding examples change the formatting in the active document without changing the selection. In most cases, **Range** objects are preferred over the **Selection** object for the following reasons:

- You can define and use multiple **Range** objects, whereas you can only have one **Selection** object per document window.

- Manipulating **Range** objects doesn't change the selected text.

- Manipulating **Range** objects is faster than working with the selection.

Using the Range Method to Return a Range Object

You use the **Range** method to create a **Range** object in the specified document. The **Range** method (which is available from the **Document** object) returns a **Range** object located in the main story, with a given starting point and ending point. The following example creates a **Range** object that's assigned to the variable myRange.

```
Set myRange = ActiveDocument.Range(Start:=0, End:=10)
```

In the preceding example, myRange represents the first 10 characters in the active document. You can see that the **Range** object has been created when you apply a property or method to the **Range** object stored in the myRange variable. The following example applies bold formatting to the first 10 characters in the active document.

```
Set myRange = ActiveDocument.Range(Start:=0, End:=10)
myRange.Bold = True
```

When you need to refer to a **Range** object multiple times, you can use the **Set** statement to set a variable equal to the **Range** object. However, if you need to perform only a single action on a **Range** object, there's no need to store the object in a variable. You can achieve the same results by using just one instruction that identifies the range and changes the **Bold** property, as in the following example.

```
ActiveDocument.Range(Start:=0, End:=10).Bold = True
```

Like a bookmark, a range can span a group of characters or mark a location in a document. In the following example, the starting and ending points of the **Range** object are the same, and the range doesn't include any text. The example inserts text at the beginning of the active document.

```
ActiveDocument.Range(Start:=0, End:=0).InsertBefore Text:="Hello "
```

You can define the beginning and ending points of a range by using the character position numbers as shown in the preceding example, or by using the **Start** and **End** properties with the **Selection**, **Bookmark**, or **Range** object. The following example creates a **Range** object that refers to the third and fourth sentences in the active document.

```
Set myDoc = ActiveDocument
Set myRange = myDoc.Range(Start:=myDoc.Sentences(3).Start, _
    End:=myDoc.Sentences(4).End)
```

Tip A **Range** object doesn't have a visual representation in a document. You can, however, use the **Select** method to select a **Range** object to ensure that the **Range** object refers to the correct range of text. The **Range** object in the following example refers to the first three paragraphs in the active document. After this macro has been run, the selection indicates the range of text that was contained in the variable aRange.

```
Set aRange = ActiveDocument.Range(Start:=0, _
    End:=ActiveDocument.Paragraphs(3).Range.End)
aRange.Select
```

Using the Range Property to Return a Range Object

The **Range** property is available from multiple objects—for instance, **Paragraph**, **Bookmark**, **Endnote**, and **Cell**—and is used to return a **Range** object. The following example returns a **Range** object that refers to the first paragraph in the active document.

```
Set myRange = ActiveDocument.Paragraphs(1).Range
```

After you've created a reference to a **Range** object, you can use any of its properties or methods to modify the range. The following example copies the first paragraph in the active document.

```
Set myRange = ActiveDocument.Paragraphs(1).Range
myRange.Copy
```

This following example copies the first row in table one in the active document.

```
ActiveDocument.Tables(1).Rows(1).Range.Copy
```

The following example displays the text marked by the first bookmark in the active document. The **Range** property is available from the **Bookmark** object.

```
MsgBox ActiveDocument.Bookmarks(1).Range.Text
```

If you need to apply numerous properties or methods to the same **Range** object, you can use the **With…End With** statement. The following example formats the text in the first paragraph in the active document.

```
Set myRange = ActiveDocument.Paragraphs(1).Range
With myRange
    .Bold = True
    .ParagraphFormat.Alignment = wdAlignParagraphCenter
    .Font.Name = "Arial"
End With
```

For additional examples of returning **Range** objects, see "Range Property" in Help.

Modifying a Portion of a Document

Visual Basic includes objects you can use to modify the following types of document elements: characters, words, sentences, paragraphs, and sections. The following table includes the properties that correspond to these document elements and the objects they return.

This expression	Returns this object
Words(*index*)	**Range**
Characters(*index*)	**Range**
Sentences(*index*)	**Range**
Paragraphs(*index*)	**Paragraph**
Sections(*index*)	**Section**

When you use these properties without an index, a collection with the same name is returned—for example, the **Paragraphs** property returns the **Paragraphs** collection. However, if you identify an item within a collection by index, the object in the second column of the preceding table is returned—for example, Words(1) returns a **Range** object. You can use any of the range properties or methods to modify a **Range** object, as in the following example, which copies the first word in the selection to the Clipboard.

```
Selection.Words(1).Copy
```

The items in the **Paragraphs** and **Sections** collections are **Paragraph** and **Section** objects, respectively, rather than **Range** objects. However, the **Range** property (which returns a **Range** object) is available from both the **Paragraph** and **Section** objects. The following example copies the first paragraph in the active document to the Clipboard.

```
ActiveDocument.Paragraphs(1).Range.Copy
```

All the document element properties in the preceding table are available from the **Document**, **Selection**, and **Range** objects, as shown in the following three examples.

This example sets the case of the first word in the active document.

```
ActiveDocument.Words(1).Case = wdUpperCase
```

This example sets the bottom margin of the first selected section to 0.5 inch.

```
Selection.Sections(1).PageSetup.BottomMargin = InchesToPoints(0.5)
```

This example double-spaces the text in the active document (the **Content** property returns a **Range** object that represents the main document story).

```
ActiveDocument.Content.ParagraphFormat.Space2
```

Modifying a Group of Document Elements

To modify a range of text that consists of a group of document elements (characters, words, sentences, paragraphs, or sections), you can create a **Range** object that includes the document elements. Using the **Start** and **End** properties with a **Range** object, you can create a new **Range** object that refers to a group of document elements. The following example creates a **Range** object (myRange) that refers to the first three words in the active document and then changes the font for these words to Arial.

```
Set Doc = ActiveDocument
Set myRange = Doc.Range(Start:=Doc.Words(1).Start, End:=Doc.Words(3).End)
myRange.Font.Name = "Arial"
```

The following example creates a **Range** object beginning at the start of the second paragraph and ending after the fourth paragraph.

```
Set myDoc = ActiveDocument
Set myRange = myDoc.Range(Start:=myDoc.Paragraphs(2).Range.Start,
End:=myDoc.Paragraphs(4).Range.End)
```

The following example creates a **Range** object (aRange) beginning at the start of the second paragraph and ending after the third paragraph. The **ParagraphFormat** property is used to access paragraph formatting properties such as **SpaceBefore** and **SpaceAfter**.

```
Set Doc = ActiveDocument
Set aRange = Doc.Range(Start:=Doc.Paragraphs(2).Range.Start,
End:=Doc.Paragraphs(3).Range.End)
With aRange.ParagraphFormat
    .Space1
    .SpaceAfter = 6
    .SpaceBefore = 6
End With
```

Returning or Setting the Text in a Range

Use the **Text** property to return or set the contents of a **Range** object. The following example returns the first word in the active document.

```
strText = ActiveDocument.Words(1).Text
```

The following example changes the first word in the active document to "Hello."

```
ActiveDocument.Words(1).Text = "Hello"
```

Use the **InsertAfter** or **InsertBefore** method to insert text before or after a range. The following example inserts text at the beginning of the second paragraph in the active document.

```
ActiveDocument.Paragraphs(2).Range.InsertBefore Text:="In the beginning "
```

After you use either the **InsertAfter** or **InsertBefore** method, the range expands to include the new text. You can, however, collapse the range to its beginning or ending point by using the **Collapse** method. The following example inserts the word "Hello" before the existing text and then collapses the range to its beginning (before the word "Hello").

```
With ActiveDocument.Paragraphs(2).Range
    .InsertBefore Text:="Hello "
    .Collapse Direction:=wdCollapseStart
End With
```

Formatting the Text in a Range

Use the **Font** property to get to character-formatting properties and methods, and use the **ParagraphFormat** property to get to paragraph-formatting properties and methods. The following example sets character and paragraph formatting for the text in the first paragraph in the active document.

```
With ActiveDocument.Paragraphs(1).Range.Font
    .Name = "Times New Roman"
    .Size = 14
    .AllCaps = True
End With
With ActiveDocument.Paragraphs(1).Range.ParagraphFormat
    .LeftIndent = InchesToPoints(0.5)
    .Space1
End With
```

Redefining a Range Object

Use the **SetRange** method to redefine an existing **Range** object. The following example defines myRange as the current selection. The **SetRange** method redefines myRange so that it refers to the current selection plus the next 10 characters.

```
Set myRange = Selection.Range
myRange.SetRange Start:=myRange.Start, End:=myRange.End + 10
```

For additional information about and examples of redefining a **Range** object, see "SetRange Method" in Help.

You can also redefine a **Range** object by changing the values of the **Start** and **End** properties, or by using the **MoveStart** or **MoveEnd** methods. The following example redefines myRange so that it refers to the current selection plus the next 10 characters.

```
Set myRange = Selection.Range
myRange.End = myRange.End + 10
```

The following example uses the **MoveEnd** method to extend myRange to include the next paragraph.

```
Set myRange = ActiveDocument.Paragraphs(2)
myRange.MoveEnd Unit:=wdParagraph, Count:=1
```

Looping Through a Range of Paragraphs

There are several different ways to loop through the paragraphs in a range. This section includes examples of using the **For Each...Next** statement and the **Next** property and method to loop through a range of paragraphs. You can use these same techniques to loop through characters, words, or sentences in a range.

Using the For Each...Next Statement

The recommended way to loop through the paragraphs in a range is to use the **For Each...Next** statement, which is also the recommended way to loop on the elements in a collection. The following example loops through the first five paragraphs in the active document, adding text before each paragraph.

```
Set myDoc = ActiveDocument
Set myRange = myDoc.Range(Start:=myDoc.Paragraphs(1).Range.Start, _
    End:=myDoc.Paragraphs(5).Range.End)
For Each para In myRange.Paragraphs
    para.Range.InsertBefore "Question:" & vbTab
Next para
```

Suppose that you want to modify this code to loop through a range of paragraphs that a user selected. You can use the **Selection** property to refer to the paragraphs in the selection. The following example loops through the paragraphs in the selection, removing bold formatting.

```
For Each para In Selection.Paragraphs
    para.Range.Bold = False
Next para
```

Using the Next Property or Method

You can also use the **Next** property and method to loop through a range of paragraphs. The following example shows how you can loop through a range of words and increase the size of each word by 1 point. The example also uses the **Next** method to redefine myRange to represent the next word.

```
Set myRange = ActiveDocument.Words(1)
For i = 1 To 5
    myRange.Font.Size = myRange.Font.Size + i
    Set myRange = myRange.Next(Unit:=wdWord, Count:=1)
Next i
```

The following example loops through a range of paragraphs and changes the range's alignment from centered to left aligned. The example also uses the **Next** property to redefine myRange to represent the next paragraph.

```
Set myRange = ActiveDocument.Paragraphs(1).Range
For i = 1 To 5
    If myRange.Paragraphs(1).Alignment = wdAlignParagraphCenter Then
        myRange.Paragraphs(1).Alignment = wdAlignParagraphLeft
    End If
    Set myRange = myRange.Paragraphs(1).Next.Range
Next i
```

Assigning Ranges

There are several ways to assign an existing **Range** object to a variable. In the following examples, the variables Range1 and Range2 refer to **Range** objects. The instructions in the examples assign the first and second words in the active document to the variables Range1 and Range2, respectively.

```
Set Range1 = ActiveDocument.Words(1)
Set Range2 = ActiveDocument.Words(2)
```

Setting a Range Object Variable Equal to Another Range Object Variable

The following example creates the variable Range2 and assigns it to the same range as Range1.

```
Set Range2 = Range1
```

You now have two variables that represent the same range. When you manipulate the starting point, the ending point, or the text of Range2, your changes affect Range1 as well, and vice versa.

The following example assigns the value of the default property of Range1 (the **Text** property) to the default property of Range2. The code in this example is equivalent to Range2.Text = Range1.Text, which doesn't change what the **Range** objects actually represent; the only thing that's changed is the contents (text) of Range2.

```
Range2 = Range1
```

The two ranges (Range2 and Range1) have the same contents as one another, but they may point to different locations in the document, or even to different documents.

Using the Duplicate Property

The following example creates a new, duplicated **Range** object, Range2, which has the same starting point, ending point, and text as Range1.

```
Set Range2 = Range1.Duplicate
```

If you change the starting or ending point of Range1, this change doesn't affect Range2, and vice versa. However, because these two ranges point to the same location in the document, changing the text in one range changes the text in the other range as well.

Working with Stories

A story is a document area that contains a range of text distinct from other areas of text in that document. For example, if a document includes body text, footnotes, and headers, it contains a main text story, a footnotes story, and a headers story. There are 11 different types of stories you can have in a document, corresponding to the following **WdStoryType** constants: **wdCommentsStory**, **wdEndnotesStory**, **wdEvenPagesFooterStory**, **wdEvenPagesHeaderStory**, **wdFirstPageFooterStory**, **wdFirstPageHeaderStory**, **wdFootnotesStory**, **wdMainTextStory**, **wdPrimaryFooterStory**, **wdPrimaryHeaderStory**, and **wdTextFrameStory**.

Use the **StoryType** property to return the story type for the specified range, selection, or bookmark. The following example closes the footnote pane in the active window if the selection is contained in the footnote story.

```
ActiveWindow.View.Type = wdNormalView
If Selection.StoryType = wdFootnotesStory Then ActiveWindow.ActivePane.Close
```

The **StoryRanges** collection contains the first story range for each story type available in a document. Use the **NextStoryRange** method to return subsequent stories. The following example searches each story in the active document for the text "Microsoft Word." The example also applies italic formatting to any instances of this text that it finds.

```
For Each myStoryRange In ActiveDocument.StoryRanges
    myStoryRange.Find.Execute FindText:="Microsoft Word", Forward:=True
    While myStoryRange.Find.Found
        myStoryRange.Italic = True
        myStoryRange.Find.Execute FindText:="Microsoft Word", _
            Forward:=True, Format:=True
    Wend
    While Not (myStoryRange.NextStoryRange Is Nothing)
        Set myStoryRange = myStoryRange.NextStoryRange
        myStoryRange.Find.Execute FindText:="Microsoft Word", Forward:=True
        While myStoryRange.Find.Found
            myStoryRange.Italic = True
            myStoryRange.Find.Execute FindText:="Microsoft Word", _
                Forward:=True, Format:=True
        Wend
    Wend
Next myStoryRange
```

Working with the Selection Object

When you work on a document in Word, you usually select text and then perform an action, such as formatting existing text or typing new text. In Visual Basic, it's usually not necessary to select text before modifying it; instead, you create and manipulate a **Range** object that refers to a specific portion of the document. However, when you want your code to respond to or change the selection, you can do so with the **Selection** object.

Use the **Selection** property to return the **Selection** object. There can only be one **Selection** object per pane in a document window, and only one **Selection** object can be active at any given time. The selection can either encompass an area in the document or be collapsed to an insertion point. The following example changes the paragraph formatting of the paragraphs in the selection.

```
Selection.Paragraphs.SpaceBefore = InchesToPoints(0.25)
```

The **Selection** property is available from the **Application**, **Window**, and **Pane** objects. If you use the **Selection** property with the **Application** object, the **Selection** object refers to the active selection. The following example inserts text after the selection (because **Selection** is a global property, the **Application** property isn't included).

```
Selection.InsertAfter Text:="Next Text"
```

You can also use the **Selection** property with a **Window** or **Pane** object to return a **Selection** object in a particular window or window pane. The following example uses the **Selection** property with a **Window** object to insert text into the document window named "Document2."

```
Windows("Document2").Selection.InsertAfter Text:="New Text"
```

The following example uses the **Selection** property with a **Pane** object to insert text into the primary header pane.

```
With ActiveWindow
    .View.Type = wdPageView
    .View.SeekView = wdSeekPrimaryHeader
    .ActivePane.Selection.InsertAfter Text:="Header"
End With
```

After you use the **InsertAfter** or **InsertBefore** method, the selection expands to include the new text. You can, however, collapse the selection to its beginning or ending point by using the **Collapse** method. The following example inserts the word "Hello" after the text in the selection and then collapses the selection to an insertion point after the word "Hello."

```
Selection.InsertAfter Text:="Hello"
Selection.Collapse Direction:=wdCollapseEnd
```

Moving and Extending the Selection

There are a number of methods you can use to move or extend the selection represented by the **Selection** object (for instance, **Move** and **MoveEnd**). The following example moves the selection to the beginning of the next paragraph.

```
Selection.MoveDown Unit:=wdParagraph, Count:=1, Extend:=wdMove
```

You can also move or extend the selection by changing the values of the **Start** and **End** properties of the **Selection** object or by using the **MoveStart** and **MoveEnd** methods. The following example extends the selection by moving the ending position to the end of the paragraph.

```
Selection.MoveEnd Unit:=wdParagraph, Count:=1
```

Because there can be only one selection in a document window or pane, you can also move the selection by selecting another object. Use the **Select** method to select an item in a document. After using the **Select** method, you can use the **Selection** property to return a **Selection** object. The following example selects the first word in the active document and then changes the word to "Hello."

```
ActiveDocument.Words(1).Select
Selection.Text = "Hello "
```

You can also move the selection by using the **GoToNext**, **GoToPrevious**, or **GoTo** method. The following example moves the selection to the fourth line in the document.

```
Selection.GoTo What:=wdGoToLine, Which:=wdGoToAbsolute, Count:=4
```

The following example moves the selection just before the next field in the active document.

```
Selection.GoToNext What:=wdGoToField
```

Objects Available from the Selection Object

Many of the objects available from the **Range** and **Document** objects are also available from the **Selection** object, making it possible for you to manipulate the objects within a selection. For a complete list of the objects available from the **Selection** object, see "Microsoft Word Objects (Selection)" or "Selection Object" in Help.

The following example updates the results of the fields in the selection.

```
If Selection.Fields.Count >= 1 Then Selection.Fields.Update
```

The following example indents the paragraphs in the selection by 0.5 inch.

```
Selection.Paragraphs.LeftIndent = InchesToPoints(0.5)
```

Instead of manipulating all the objects in the collection, you can use **For Each...Next** to loop through the individual objects in the selection. The following example loops through each paragraph in the selection and left aligns any paragraphs it finds that are centered.

```
For Each para In Selection.Paragraphs
    If para.Alignment = wdAlignParagraphCenter Then para.Alignment =
wdAlignParagraphLeft
Next para
```

The following example displays the name of each bookmark in the selection.

```
For Each aBook In Selection.Bookmarks
    MsgBox aBook.Name
Next aBook
```

Properties and Methods of the Selection Object

This section highlights some of the commonly used properties and methods of the **Selection** object.

Returning or Setting the Text in the Selection

Use the **Text** property to return or set the contents of a **Selection** object. The following example returns the selected text.

```
strText = Selection.Text
```

The following example changes the selected text to "Hello World."

```
Selection.Text = "Hello World"
```

Use the **InsertBefore** or **InsertAfter** method to insert text before or after the selection. The following example inserts text at the beginning of the selection.

```
Selection.InsertBefore Text:="And furthermore "
```

Formatting the Selected Text

Use the **Font** property to gain access to character-formatting properties and methods, and use the **ParagraphFormat** property to gain access to paragraph-formatting properties and methods. The following example sets character and paragraph formatting for the selection.

```
With Selection.Font
    .Name = "Times New Roman"
    .Size = 14
End With
Selection.ParagraphFormat.LeftIndent = InchesToPoints(0.5)
```

Returning a Range Object

If a method or property is available from the **Range** object but not from the **Selection** object (the **CheckSpelling** method, for example), use the **Range** property to return a **Range** object from the **Selection** object. The following example checks the spelling of the selected words.

```
Selection.Range.CheckSpelling
```

Returning Information About the Selection

Use the **Information** property to return information about the selection. For example, you can determine the current page number, the total number of pages in a document, or whether or not the selection is in a header or footer. The **Information** property accepts 35 different constants (**wdActiveEndPageNumber**, **wdNumberOfPagesInDocument**, and **wdInHeaderFooter**, to name just a few) that you can use to return different types of information about the selection. If the selection is in a table, for instance, the following example displays the number or rows and columns in the table.

```
If Selection.Information(wdWithInTable) = True Then
    MsgBox "Columns = " & Selection.Information(wdMaximumNumberOfColumns) _
        & vbCr & "Rows = " & Selection.Information(wdMaximumNumberOfRows)
End If
```

For a complete list and description of the constants you can use with the **Information** property, see "Information Property" in Help.

Determining Whether Text Is Selected

Use the **Type** property to set or return the way you want the selection to be indicated in your document. For instance, you can use the **wdSelectionBlock** constant to determine whether a block of text is selected. The following example selects the paragraph that contains the insertion point if the selection is an insertion point.

```
If Selection.Type = wdSelectionIP Then
    Selection.Paragraphs(1).Range.Select
End If
```

Working with the Find and Replacement Objects

Use the **Find** and **Replacement** objects to find and replace specified ranges of text in your documents. The **Find** object is available from either the **Selection** or **Range** object (the find action differs slightly depending on whether you return the **Find** object from the **Selection** object or the **Range** object).

Using Selection.Find

If you return the **Find** object from the **Selection** object, the selection is changed when the find criteria are found. The following example selects the next occurrence of the word "Hello." If the end of the document is reached before the word "Hello" is found, the search is stopped.

```
With Selection.Find
    .Forward = True
    .Wrap = wdFindStop
    .Text = "Hello"
    .Execute
End With
```

The **Find** object includes properties that relate to the options in the **Find and Replace** dialog box (**Edit** menu). You can set the individual properties of the **Find** object, or you can use arguments with the **Execute** method, as shown in the following example.

```
Selection.Find.Execute FindText:="Hello", Forward:=True, Wrap:=wdFindStop
```

Using Range.Find

If you return the **Find** object from a **Range** object, the selection isn't changed but the range is redefined when the find criteria are found. The following example locates the first occurrence of the word "blue" in the active document. If the find operation is successful, the range is redefined and bold formatting is applied to the word "blue."

```
With ActiveDocument.Content.Find
    .Text = "blue"
    .Forward = True
    .Execute
    If .Found = True Then .Parent.Bold = True
End With
```

The following example performs the same action as the preceding example, using arguments of the **Execute** method.

```
Set myRange = ActiveDocument.Content
myRange.Find.Execute FindText:="blue", Forward:=True
If myRange.Find.Found = True Then myRange.Bold = True
```

Using the Replacement Object

The **Replacement** object represents the replace criteria for a find and replace operation. The properties and methods of the **Replacement** object correspond to the options in the **Find and Replace** dialog box (**Edit** menu).

The **Replacement** object is available from the **Find** object. The following example replaces all occurrences of the word "hi" with "hello." The selection changes when the find criteria are found because the code returns the **Find** object from the **Selection** object.

```
With Selection.Find
    .ClearFormatting
    .Text = "hi"
    .Replacement.ClearFormatting
    .Replacement.Text = "hello"
    .Execute Replace:=wdReplaceAll, Forward:=True, Wrap:=wdFindContinue
End With
```

The following example removes all bold formatting in the active document. The **Bold** property is **True** for the **Find** object and **False** for the **Replacement** object. To find and replace formatting, set the find and replace text to empty strings (**""**), and set the *Format* argument of the **Execute** method to **True**. The selection remains unchanged because the code returns the **Find** object from a **Range** object (the **Content** property returns a **Range** object).

```
With ActiveDocument.Content.Find
    .ClearFormatting
    .Font.Bold = True
    With .Replacement
        .ClearFormatting
        .Font.Bold = False
    End With
    .Execute FindText:="", ReplaceWith:="", Format:=True, Replace:=wdReplaceAll
End With
```

Working with Table, Column, Row, and Cell Objects

The Word object model includes an object for tables as well as objects for the various elements of a table. Use the **Tables** property with the **Document**, **Range**, or **Selection** object to return the **Tables** collection. Use **Tables**(*index*), where *index* is the table's index number, to return a single **Table** object. The index number represents the position of the table in the selection, range, or document. The following example converts the first table in the selection to text.

```
If Selection.Tables.Count >= 1 Then
    Selection.Tables(1).ConvertToText Separator:=wdSeparateByTabs
End If
```

Use the **Cells** property with the **Column**, **Range**, **Row**, or **Selection** object to return the **Cells** collection. You can get an individual **Cell** object by using the **Cell** method of the **Table** object or by indexing the **Cells** collection. The following two statements both set myCell to a **Cell** object that represents the first cell in table one in the active document.

```
Set myCell = ActiveDocument.Tables(1).Cell(Row:=1, Column:=1)
Set myCell = ActiveDocument.Tables(1).Columns(1).Cells(1)
```

Note To insert text into a cell in a table, use the **Text** property, the **InsertAfter** method, or the **InsertBefore** method with a **Range** object. Use the **Range** property with a **Cell** object to return a **Range** object. The following example inserts a sequential cell number into each cell in table one.

```
i = 1
For Each c In ActiveDocument.Tables(1).Range.Cells
    c.Range.InsertBefore Text:="Cell " & i
    i = i + 1
Next c
```

Use the **Columns** property with the **Table**, **Range**, or **Selection** object to return the **Columns** collection. Use **Columns**(*index*), where *index* is the index number, to return a single **Column** object. The following example selects the first column in table one.

```
ActiveDocument.Tables(1).Columns(1).Select
```

Use the **Rows** property with the **Table**, **Range**, or **Selection** object to return the **Rows** collection. Use **Rows**(*index*), where *index* is the index number, to return a single **Row** object. The following example applies shading to the first row in table one.

```
ActiveDocument.Tables(1).Rows(1).Shading.Texture = wdTexture10Percent
```

Modifying Rows and Columns in Drawn Tables

When you try to work with an individual row or column in a drawn table (or any table where two or more adjacent cells have been merged, leaving the rows and columns not uniform), a run-time error may occur. The following example generates an error if the first table in the active document doesn't have the same number of rows in each column.

```
ActiveDocument.Tables(1).Rows(1).Borders.Enable = False
```

You can avoid this error by first using the **SelectColumn** or **SelectRow** method to select the cells in a particular column or row. After you've selected the column or row you want, use the **Cells** property with the **Selection** object. The following example selects the first row in table one in the active document. The example uses the **Cells** property to return the selected cells (all the cells in the first row) so that borders can be removed.

```
If ActiveDocument.Tables(1).Uniform = False
    ActiveDocument.Tables(1).Cell(1, 1).Select
    With Selection
        .SelectRow
        .Cells.Borders.Enable = False
    End With
End If
```

The following example selects the first column in table one. The example uses a **For Each...Next** loop to add text to each cell in the selection (all the cells in the first column).

```
If ActiveDocument.Tables(1).Uniform = False
    ActiveDocument.Tables(1).Cell(1, 1).Select
    Selection.SelectColumn
    i = 1
    For Each oCell In Selection.Cells
        oCell.Range.Text = "Cell " & i
        i = i + 1
    Next oCell
End If
```

Working with Other Common Objects

This section provides information and tips about working the some common Word objects.

Using the HeaderFooter Object

The **HeaderFooter** object can represent either a header or a footer . The **HeaderFooter** object is a member of the **HeadersFooters** collection, which is available from the **Section** object. Use the **Headers**(*index*) or **Footers**(*index*) property, where *index* is one of the **WdHeaderFooterIndex** constants, to return a single **HeaderFooter** object.

The following example creates a **Range** object (oRange) that references the primary footer for section one in the active document. After the example sets the **Range** object, it deletes the existing footer text. It also adds the AUTHOR field to the footer, along with two tabs and the FILENAME field.

```
Set oRange = ActiveDocument.Sections(1).Footers(wdHeaderFooterPrimary).Range
With oRange
    .Delete
    .Fields.Add Range:=oRange, Type:=wdFieldFileName, Text:="\p"
    .InsertAfter Text:=vbTab
    .InsertAfter Text:=vbTab
    .Collapse Direction:=wdCollapseStart
    .Fields.Add Range:=oRange, Type:=wdFieldAuthor
End With
```

Note The **PageNumbers** collection is available only from a **HeaderFooter** object. Apply the **Add** method to the **PageNumbers** collection to add page numbers to a header or footer.

Using the Styles Collection

The **Styles** collection is available from the **Document** object. The following example changes the formatting of the Heading 1 style in the active document.

```
ActiveDocument.Styles(wdStyleHeading1).Font.Name = "Arial"
```

The **Styles** collection isn't available from the **Template** object. If you want to modify styles in a template, use the **OpenAsDocument** method to open a template as a document so that you can modify styles. The following example changes the formatting of the Heading 1 style in the template attached to the active document.

```
Set aDoc = ActiveDocument.AttachedTemplate.OpenAsDocument
With aDoc
    .Styles(wdStyleHeading1).Font.Name = "Arial"
    .Close SaveChanges:=wdSaveChanges
End With
```

Specifying the CommandBars Context

Before using the **CommandBars** collection (which represents menus and toolbars), use the **CustomizationContext** property to set the **Template** or **Document** object in which changes to menus and toolbars are stored. The following example adds the **Double Underline** command to the **Formatting** toolbar. Because the customization change is stored in the Normal template, all documents are affected.

```
CustomizationContext = NormalTemplate
CommandBars("Formatting").Controls.Add Type:=msoControlButton, _
    ID:=60, Before:=7
```

For more information about the scope of changes to menus and toolbars, see Chapter 8, "Menus and Toolbars."

Using the Dialogs Collection

Use the **Dialogs** property to return the **Dialogs** collection, which represents the built-in Word dialog boxes (for example, the **Open** and **File Save** dialog boxes). You cannot create a new built-in dialog box or add one to the **Dialogs** collection. For information about creating custom dialog boxes with ActiveX controls, see Chapter 12, "ActiveX Controls and Dialog Boxes."

Returning the MailMerge and Envelope Objects

Use the **MailMerge** property of the **Document** object to return a **MailMerge** object. The **MailMerge** object is available regardless of whether or not the specified document is a mail-merge document. Use the **State** property to determine the state of the mail-merge operation before you execute the merge by using the **Execute** method. The following example executes a mail merge if the active document is a main document with an attached data source.

```
Set myMerge = ActiveDocument.MailMerge
If myMerge.State = wdMainAndDataSource Then myMerge.Execute
```

Use the **Envelope** property of the **Document** object to return an **Envelope** object. The **Envelope** object is available regardless of whether or not you've added an envelope to the specified document. However, an error occurs if you use one of the following properties and you haven't added an envelope to the document: **Address**, **AddressFromLeft**, **AddressFromTop**, **FeedSource**, **ReturnAddress**, **ReturnAddressFromLeft**, **ReturnAddressFromTop**, or **UpdateDocument**.

The following example uses the **On Error GoTo** statement to trap the error that occurs if you haven't added an envelope to the active document. If, however, you've added an envelope to the document, the recipient address is displayed.

```
On Error GoTo ErrorHandler
MsgBox ActiveDocument.Envelope.Address
ErrorHandler:
If Err = 5852 Then MsgBox "Envelope is not in the specified document"
```

Adding and Editing Fields in a Document

You can add fields to a document by applying the **Add** method to the **Fields** collection. The following example adds a DATE field in place of the selection.

```
ActiveDocument.Fields.Add Range:=Selection.Range, Type:=wdFieldDate
```

After you've added a field, you can return or set the field result and field code by using the **Result** or **Code** property, either of which returns a **Range** object. The following example changes the first field code in the selection, updates the field, and then displays the field result.

```
If Selection.Fields.Count >= 1 Then
    With Selection.Fields(1)
        .Code.Text = "CREATEDATE \*MERGEFORMAT"
        .Update
        MsgBox .Result.Text
    End With
End If
```

InlineShape Objects vs. Shape Objects

A **Shape** object represents an object in the drawing layer, such as an AutoShape, freeform, OLE object, ActiveX control, or picture. **Shape** objects are anchored to a range of text but are free-floating in that you can positioned them anywhere on the page. For information about working with **Shape** objects, see Chapter 10, "Shapes and the Drawing Layer," and see "Shape Object" in Help.

An **InlineShape** object represents an object in the text layer of a document. An inline shape can be a picture, an OLE object, or an ActiveX control. **InlineShape** objects are treated like characters and are positioned as characters within a line of text. For information about **InlineShape** objects, see "InlineShapes Collection Object" or "InlineShape Object" in Help.

Using FormField Objects in Word Forms

You can create an Word online form that includes check boxes, text boxes, and drop-down list boxes. These form elements can be inserted using the **Forms** toolbar. The corresponding Visual Basic objects are **CheckBox**, **TextInput**, and **DropDown**. All these objects can be returned from any **FormField** object in the **FormFields** collection; however, you should return the object that corresponds to the type of the form field. For example, the following instruction selects the check box form field named "Check1" in the active document.

```
ActiveDocument.FormFields("Check1").CheckBox.Value = True
```

In addition to the form elements available on the **Forms** toolbar, you can add ActiveX controls to an online form. ActiveX controls can be inserted using the **Control Toolbox**. You can insert a control into the text layer or into the drawing layer; the control will be represented by an **InlineShape** object or a **Shape** object, respectively. For more information about working with ActiveX controls, see Chapter 12, "ActiveX Controls and Dialog Boxes."

Determining Whether an Object Is Valid

You can avoid many run-time errors in your code by including statements that determine whether a particular object returned by an expression or an object referenced by a variable is valid. This section discusses some techniques for checking the validity of a value returned by an expression or stored in a variable.

You can use the **TypeName** function with a variable or expression to determine the object type. The following example displays a message in the status bar if `Selection.NextField` returns a **Field** object.

```
If TypeName(Selection.NextField) = "Field" Then StatusBar = "A field was found"
```

The following example is functionally equivalent to the preceding example; it's different only in that it uses an object variable (`myField`) to store the return value of the **NextField** method.

```
Set myField = Selection.NextField
If TypeName(myField) = "Field" Then StatusBar = "A field was found"
```

If the specified variable or expression doesn't refer to an object, it evaluates to **Nothing**. The following example applies the **Update** method to `myField` if the **NextField** method doesn't return **Nothing** (that is, if the **NextField** method returns a **Field** object, its only other possible return value).

```
Set myField = Selection.NextField
If Not (myField Is Nothing) Then myField.Update
```

Word includes the global **IsObjectValid** property. You can use this property to determine whether an object referenced by a particular variable is valid. This property returns **False** if the object referenced by the variable has been deleted. The following example adds a table to the active document and assigns it to the variable `aTable`. The example deletes the first table from the document. If the table that `aTable` refers to wasn't the first table in the document (that is, if `aTable` is still a valid object), the example removes borders from the table.

```
Set aTable = ActiveDocument.Tables.Add(Range:=Selection.Range, NumRows:=2, NumColumns:=3)
ActiveDocument.Tables(1).Delete
If IsObjectValid(aTable) = True Then aTable.Borders.Enable = False
```

Modifying Word Commands

You can modify most Word commands by turning them into macros. For example, you can modify the **Open** command on the **File** menu so that instead of displaying a list of Word document files (in Windows, files ending with the .doc file name extension), Word displays every file in the current folder.

To display the list of built-in Word commands in the **Macro** dialog box (**Tools** menu), click **Word commands** in the **Macros in** box. Every available menu, toolbar, and shortcut key command is listed in this box. Each menu command begins with the menu name associated with that command. For example, the **Save** command on the **File** menu is listed as **FileSave**.

You can replace a Word command with a macro by giving a macro the same name as the Word command. For example, if you create a macro named "FileSave," Word runs this macro when you do any of the following: click **Save** on the **File** menu, click the **Save** button on the **Standard** toolbar, or press the shortcut key assigned to **FileSave**.

▶ **To modify a Word command**

1 On the **Tools** menu, point to **Macro**, and then click **Macros**.

2 In the **Macros in** box, click **Word Commands**.

3 In the **Macro name** box, click the Word command you want to modify (for example, **FileSave**).

4 In the **Macros in** box, select a template or document location where you want to store the macro. For example, click **Normal.dot (global template)** to create a global macro (the **FileSave** command will be automatically modified for all documents).

5 Click **Create**.

The Visual Basic Editor opens with a module displayed that contains a new procedure whose name is the same as the command you clicked. If you clicked the **FileSave** command, the FileSave macro appears as shown in the following example.

```
Sub FileSave()
'
' FileSave Macro
' Saves the active document or template
'
    ActiveDocument.Save

End Sub
```

You can add additional instructions or remove the existing `ActiveDocument.Save` instruction. Every time the **FileSave** command runs, your FileSave macro runs instead of the Word command. To restore the original **FileSave** command, you need to rename or delete your FileSave macro.

Note You can also replace a Word command by creating a code module whose name is the same as the Word command (for example, FileSave) with a subroutine named "Main."

Working with Events

An event is an action that's recognized by an object (such as opening a document or quitting the application) and for which you can write code to respond. Events can occur as a result of either a user action or program code, or they can be triggered by the system. Word supports the events listed in the following tables, as well as the ActiveX control events discussed in Chapter 12, "ActiveX Controls and Dialog Boxes."

For more information about working with Word events, see the following Help topics: "Using Events with the Document Object," "Using Events with ActiveX Controls," and "Using Events with the Application Object."

Document Events

Document events occur when the user opens or closes an existing document or creates a new document, as shown in the following table.

Event	Description
Close	Occurs when a document is closed.
New	Occurs when a new document based on the template is created.
Open	Occurs when a document is opened.

The scope of a document event procedure depends on where it is stored. If you store a Open or Close event procedure in a document, the procedure will run only when the user closes or opens that document; if you store a Open or Close event procedure in a template, the procedure will run when a document based on the template or the template itself is opened or closed. A New event procedure must be stored in a template; a New event procedure stored in a document will never run, because new documents can only be based on templates.

The following example maximizes the Word application window when the document is opened.

```
Private Sub Document_Open()
    Application.WindowState = wdWindowStateMaximize
End Sub
```

ActiveX Control Events

Word implements the LostFocus and GotFocus events for ActiveX controls in a Word document.

Event	Description
LostFocus	Occurs when the focus is moved from an embedded ActiveX control.
GotFocus	Occurs when the focus is moved to an embedded ActiveX control.

The following example leaves CommandButton1 disabled until the user enters a value in TextBox1.

```
Private Sub TextBox1_LostFocus()
    If TextBox1.Value = "" Then
        CommandButton1.Enabled = False
    Else
        CommandButton1.Enabled = True
    End If
End Sub
```

Additional ActiveX control events are documented in Microsoft Forms Help. For information about using ActiveX controls in custom dialog boxes and documents, see Chapter 12, "ActiveX Controls and Dialog Boxes."

Application Events

Application events occur when the user quits the application or the focus is shifted to another document. However, unlike document and ActiveX control events, the **Application** object doesn't have events enabled by default. Before you can use events with the **Application** object, you must create a new class module and declare an object of type **Application** with events. You use the **Class Module** command (**Insert** menu) in the Visual Basic Editor to create a new class module.

To enable the events of the **Application** object, you'd add the following declaration to the class module.

```
Public WithEvents App As Application
```

After the new object has been declared with events, it appears in the **Object** box in the class module, and you can write event procedures for the new object. (When you select the new object in the **Object** box, the valid events for that object are listed in the **Procedure** box.)

Before the procedures will run, however, you must connect the declared object in the class module to the **Application** object. You can do this from any module by using the following declaration (where "EventClass" is the name of the class module you created to enable events).

```
Public X As New EventClass
```

After you've created the X object variable (an instance of the EventClass class), you can set the App object of the EventClass class equal to the Word **Application** object.

```
Sub InitializeApp()
    Set X.App = Application
End Sub
```

After you run the InitializeApp procedure, the App object in the EventClass class module points to the Word **Application** object, and the event procedures in the class module will run whenever the events occur.

After you've enabled events for the **Application** object, you can create event procedures for the events described in the following table.

Event	Description
DocumentChange	Occurs when a new document is created, when an existing document is opened, or when another document is made the active document.
Quit	Occurs when the user quits Word.

The following example ensures that the **Standard** and **Formatting** toolbars are visible before the user quits Word. As a result, when Word is started again, these toolbars won't be visible.

```
Private Sub App_Quit()
    CommandBars("Standard").Visible = True
    CommandBars("Formatting").Visible = True
End Sub
```

Using Auto Macros

By giving a macro a special name, you can run it automatically when you perform an operation such as starting Word or opening a document. Word recognizes the following names as automatic macros, or "auto" macros.

Macro name	When it runs
AutoExec	Each time you start Word or load a global template
AutoNew	Each time you create a new document
AutoOpen	Each time you open an existing document
AutoClose	Each time you close a document
AutoExit	Each time you quit Word or unload a global template

For more information about using auto macros, see "Auto Macros" in Help.

Using Automation

In addition to working with Word data, you may want your application to exchange data with other applications, such as Microsoft Excel, Microsoft PowerPoint, or Microsoft Access. You can communicate with other applications by using Automation (formerly OLE Automation).

Automating Word from Another Application

Automation allows you to return, edit, and export data by referencing another application's objects, properties, and methods. Application objects that you can reference in another application are called *Automation objects*. The first step toward making Word available to another application for Automation is to create a reference to the Word type library. To create a reference to the Word type library, click **References** on the **Tools** menu in the Visual Basic Editor, and then select the check box next to **Microsoft Word 8.0 Object Library**.

Next, declare an object variable that will refer to the Word **Application** object, as in the following example.

```
Dim appWD As Word.Application.8
```

Use the Visual Basic **CreateObject** or **GetObject** function with the Word OLE Programmatic Identifier (Word.Application.8 or Word.Document.8), as shown in the following example. If you want to see the Word session, set the **Visible** property to **True**.

```
Dim appWD As Word.Application.8

Set appWD = CreateObject("Word.Application.8")
appWd.Visible = True
```

The **CreateObject** function returns a Word **Application** object and assigns it to appWD. Using the objects, properties, and methods of the Word **Application** object, you can control Word through this variable. The following example creates a new Word document.

```
appWd.Documents.Add
```

The **CreateObject** function starts a Word session that Automation won't close when the object variable that references the **Application** object expires. Setting the object reference to the **Nothing** keyword won't close Word either. Instead, use the **Quit** method to close Word. The following Microsoft Excel example inserts data from cells A1:B10 on Sheet1 into a new Word document and then arranges the data in a table. The example uses the **Quit** method to close the new instance of Word if the **CreateObject** function was used. If the **GetObject** function returns error 429, the example uses the **CreateObject** function to start a new session of Word.

```
Dim appWD As Word.Application
Err.Number = 0
On Error GoTo notloaded
Set appWD = GetObject(, "Word.Application.8")
notloaded:
If Err.Number = 429 Then
    Set appWD = CreateObject("Word.Application.8")
    theError = Err.Number
End If
appWD.Visible = True

With appWD
    Set myDoc = .Documents.Add
    With .Selection
        For Each c In Worksheets("Sheet1").Range("A1:B10")
            .InsertAfter Text:=c.Value
            Count = Count + 1
            If Count Mod 2 = 0 Then
                .InsertAfter Text:=vbCr
            Else
                .InsertAfter Text:=vbTab
            End If
        Next c
        .Range.ConvertToTable Separator:=wdSeparateByTabs
        .Tables(1).AutoFormat Format:=wdTableFormatClassic1
    End With
    myDoc.SaveAs FileName:="C:\Temp.doc"
End With
If theError = 429 Then appWD.Quit
Set appWD = Nothing
```

Automating Another Application from Word

To exchange data with another application by using Automation from Word, you must first set a reference to the other application's type library in the **References** dialog box (**Tools** menu). After you've done this, the other application's objects, properties, and methods will show up in the Object Browser and the syntax will be automatically checked at compile time. You can also get context-sensitive Help on these objects, properties, and methods.

Next, declare object variables that will refer to the objects in the other application as specific types. The following example declares a variable that will point to the Microsoft Excel **Application** object.

```
Dim xlObj As Excel.Application.8
```

You obtain a reference to the Automation object by using the **CreateObject** or **GetObject** function. Then, using the objects, properties, and methods of the other application, you add, change, or delete information. When you finish making your changes, close the application. The following Word example determines whether Microsoft Excel is currently running. If the specified Microsoft Excel task exists, the example uses the **GetObject** function; otherwise, it uses the **CreateObject** function.

The example then sends the selected text to cell A1 on Sheet1 in the active Microsoft Excel workbook. Use the **Set** statement with the **Nothing** keyword to clear the Automation object variable after the task has been completed.

```
Dim xlObj As Excel.Application.8
If Tasks.Exists("Microsoft Excel") = True Then
    Set xlObj = GetObject(, "Excel.Application.8")
Else
    Set xlObj = CreateObject("Excel.Application.8")
End If
xlObj.Visible = True
If xlobj.Workbooks.Count = 0 Then xlobj.Workbooks.Add
xlObj.Worksheets("Sheet1").Range("A1").Value = Selection.Text
Set xlObj = Nothing
```

The following Word example determines whether PowerPoint is currently running. If the PowerPoint task exists, the example uses the **GetObject** function; otherwise, it uses the **CreateObject** function. The example then creates a new presentation, with the first text box including the name of the active Word document and the second text box including the text from the first paragraph in the active document. Use the **Set** statement with the **Nothing** keyword to clear the automation object variable after the task has been completed.

```
Dim pptObj As PowerPoint.Application.8
If Tasks.Exists("Microsoft PowerPoint") = True Then
    Set pptObj = GetObject(, "PowerPoint.Application.8")
Else
    Set pptObj = CreateObject("PowerPoint.Application.8")
End If
pptObj.Visible = True
Set pptPres = pptObj.presentations.Add
Set aSlide = pptPres.Slides.Add(Index:=1, Layout:=ppLayoutText)
aSlide.Shapes(1).TextFrame.TextRange.Text = ActiveDocument.Name
aSlide.Shapes(2).TextFrame.TextRange.Text = ActiveDocument.Paragraphs(1).Range.Text
Set pptObj = Nothing
```

For information about automating Microsoft Access, see Chapter 3, "Microsoft Access Objects." For information about using Data Access Objects (DAO) from Word, see Chapter 11, "Data Access Objects," and see "Using DAO from Microsoft Word" in Help.

Communicating with Embedded Word Objects

You can use the **Application** property of any Word object to return the Word **Application** object. This is useful for returning the Word **Application** object from a Word document embedded in another application. The following example, run from Microsoft Excel, sets an object variable to the Word **Application** object. (For this example to work, shape one on the active worksheet must be an embedded Word document.) The final instruction in the example adds text at the beginning of the embedded Word document.

```
Dim appWRD As Word.Application
Set embeddedDoc = ActiveSheet.Shapes(1)
Set appWRD = embeddedDoc.OLEFormat.Object.Object.Application
appWRD.ActiveDocument.Range(Start:=0, End:=0).InsertBefore Text:="New text "
```

The following example, run from PowerPoint, sets an object variable to the Word
Application object. (For this example to work, shape one on slide one in the
presentation must be an embedded Word document.) The final instruction in the
example displays the text in the embedded Word document.

```
Dim appWRD As Word.Application
Set embeddedDoc = Presentations(1).Slides(1).Shapes(1)
embeddedDoc.OLEFormat.Activate
Set appWRD = embeddedDoc.OLEFormat.Object.Application
MsgBox appWRD.ActiveDocument.Content.Text
```

CHAPTER 8

Menus and Toolbars

An essential part of creating a useful custom application is providing a simple and consistent way for the user to interact with your Visual Basic application. Menus and toolbars provide a quick, convenient, and widely accessible way to expose simple commands and options to the user. In Microsoft Office 97, menus and toolbars are easy to design and modify; Microsoft Access 97, Microsoft Excel 97, Microsoft Word 97, and Microsoft PowerPoint 97 all share the same basic customization interface—the **Customize** dialog box. Because all menus and toolbars are represented by the same type of object—the **CommandBar** object—they're easy to customize and control from Visual Basic, as well.

The information in this chapter covers the shared menu and toolbar customization features of Microsoft Access, Microsoft Excel, Microsoft Word, and Microsoft PowerPoint. For more information about customizing menus and toolbars in Microsoft Access, see Chapter 1 in *Building Applications with Microsoft Access 97*, which is available in Microsoft Access 97 and Microsoft Office 97, Developer Edition. An online version of that book is available in the ValuPack on CD-ROM in Microsoft Access 97 and Microsoft Office 97, Professional Edition.

Note Microsoft Outlook doesn't provide an interface for customizing menus and toolbars. Therefore, none of the information in this chapter about the **Customize** dialog box applies to Microsoft Outlook.

Contents

- Tools for Modifying the User Interface
- Scope of Changes to the User Interface
- Choosing the Best User-Interface Enhancement
- The Menu System
- Design-Time Modifications to the Menu System

- Run-Time Modifications to the Menu System
- Toolbars
- Design-Time Modifications to Toolbars
- Run-Time Modifications to Toolbars
- Menu Item and Toolbar Control IDs

Tools for Modifying the User Interface

There are two tools for customizing menu bars and toolbars: the shared **Customize** dialog box and Visual Basic. Although the **Customize** dialog box differs slightly from one Office application to the next, the programmable objects used to modify menu bars and toolbars are the same across all applications. This section describes the **Customize** dialog box and the shared programmable objects, as well as when and how to use these tools.

The Customize Dialog Box

The Office applications (excluding Outlook) provide a common interface—the **Customize** dialog box—for making design-time changes to your Visual Basic application. Design-time changes to menu bars and toolbars are any changes you make before the application runs. This includes adding, deleting, moving, and restoring menu components and toolbar controls, as well as setting menu-component and toolbar-control properties that won't change in response to changing conditions at run time.

The sections in this chapter discuss how to modify menu bars and toolbars by using either the **Customize** dialog box or Visual Basic code. In cases where you can use either technique to make the same modifications, using the **Customize** dialog box to make design-time changes is quicker and easier. Therefore, you should be familiar with the elements of and techniques for using this dialog box.

▶ **To display the Customize dialog box**

- On the **View** menu, point to **Toolbars**, and then click **Customize**.

The following illustration shows the **Toolbars** tab in the **Customize** dialog box displayed by PowerPoint.

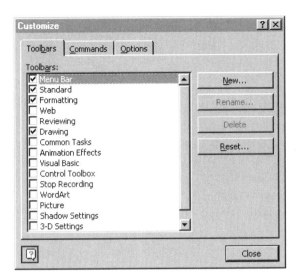

Microsoft Access, Microsoft Excel, and Microsoft Word all provide the same controls in the **Customize** dialog box (on the **Toolbars**, **Commands**, and **Options** tabs) as does PowerPoint, but these first three applications also include other elements on the **Toolbars** and **Commands** tabs that are specific to customizing those applications. Those elements are described in the following paragraphs.

Microsoft Access   The **Toolbars** tab contains a **Properties** button that displays the **Toolbar Properties** dialog box. Use this dialog box to set properties of built-in or custom menu bars and toolbars. For more information about using the **Toolbar Properties** dialog box, see Chapter 1 in *Building Applications with Microsoft Access 97.*

Microsoft Excel   The **Toolbars** tab contains an **Attach** button that displays the **Attach Toolbars** dialog box. You can use this dialog box to copy menu bars and toolbars from the application workspace to the active workbook. For more information, see "Scope of Changes to the User Interface" later in this chapter.

Microsoft Word   The **Commands** tab contains a **Save in** box you can use to specify the context of the design-time changes you make in the **Customize** dialog box. The **New Toolbar** dialog box that appears when you click the **New** button on the **Toolbars** tab contains the **Make toolbar available to** box. For more information, see "Scope of Changes to the User Interface" later in this chapter. The **Commands** tab also contains a **Keyboard** button that displays the **Customize Keyboard** dialog box; you can use this dialog box to assign shortcut keys to any macro or built-in Word command.

After you've opened the **Customize** dialog box in any Microsoft Office application, you follow the same general procedure for modifying any built-in or custom menu or toolbar, as described by the following steps.

1. In the **Toolbars** box on the **Toolbars** tab, select the check box next to the name of the menu bar or toolbar you want to display and modify. When you create a new menu bar or toolbar, it's automatically displayed.

2. Click any menu item (including menu and submenu captions) or toolbar control to select it. The command associated with the control doesn't run while the **Customize** dialog box is open.

3. Right-click the item or control you've selected to display the shortcut menu containing the available customization options. Options for menu commands and toolbar buttons include resetting the command; deleting the item or control; changing its name; specifying whether it should have a name, an image, or both displayed; modifying its image; and setting it to begin a group (that is, to appear with a line above or before it).

   Note One or more of these options may not be available for built-in commands or controls; unavailable options appear dimmed on the shortcut menu.

While the **Customize** dialog box is open, you can rearrange items and controls by dragging and dropping them, and you can add new items and controls from the **Commands** tab. For more information about adding new items and controls, see the corresponding procedures in "Design-Time Modifications to the Menu System" and "Design-Time Modifications to Toolbars" later in this chapter.

Visual Basic

In general, to create or modify the user interface of the Microsoft Office application in which you're delivering your Visual Basic application, you should use the **Customize** dialog box. Changes you make to the user interface by using the **Customize** dialog box are known as *design-time* changes.

You can also add to and modify menus and toolbars by using the command bar portion of the shared Microsoft Office object model in Visual Basic code: the top-level object is the **CommandBars** collection, which is returned by the **CommandBars** property in all the Microsoft Office applications. Every menu bar, shortcut menu, and toolbar is represented by a **CommandBar** object in this collection. Every **CommandBar** object contains a **CommandBarControls** collection; each control on a menu bar or toolbar is represented by a member of this collection.

For more information about the **CommandBars** collection, all the objects it contains, and the properties and methods of those objects, see "Overview of command bars" and the corresponding object, property, and method topics in Help.

You can write code that runs just once to create or change elements of menus or toolbars; in effect, the code simulates making design-time changes in the **Customize** dialog box. In some Microsoft Office applications, however, you may be required to use a combination of this kind of Visual Basic code and the **Customize** dialog box to design your Visual Basic application. The following are some common areas where you must use a combination of code and the container application's interface:

- If you cannot use the **Customize** dialog box to create a new menu bar, you'll need to create a menu bar by using Visual Basic. After you've created the menu bar in Visual Basic, you can design menus on that menu bar by using the **Customize** dialog box.

- If your container application doesn't provide a way to display built-in or custom shortcut menus while the **Customize** dialog box is open, you must use Visual Basic code to modify those shortcut menus.

- If your container application doesn't provide an interface for adding or modifying text boxes, drop-down list boxes, or combo boxes on toolbars, you must use Visual Basic code to add and design these controls.

You can also write code that exists in your Visual Basic application to make changes to the menu system while your application is running (for example, you can write code to disable a command on a menu under certain conditions, or to add a menu to a menu bar in response to a user's actions). Changes brought about by your code while your Visual Basic application is running are known as *run-time* changes.

Scope of Changes to the User Interface

Each Microsoft Office application uses slightly different rules regarding where and how changes to the user interface are stored. It's important to understand how you can control the scope of the changes, because the ability of your Visual Basic application to display your custom interface correctly depends on it.

Microsoft Access

The following information describes managing and storing menu bars and toolbars in Microsoft Access. For more information about working with menu bars and toolbars in Microsoft Access, see Chapter 1 in *Building Applications with Microsoft Access 97*.

You can use custom menu bars and shortcut menus in your custom application in three ways:

- Attached to a form or report. Microsoft Access displays your custom menu bar whenever you open the form or display the report in print preview. For more information, see "MenuBar Property" in Help.

- As a shortcut menu attached to a form, a control on a form, or a report. Microsoft Access displays your custom menu whenever you right-click the form, control, or report it's attached to. For more information, see "ShortCutMenuBar Property" in Help.

- As your application's global menu bar. Microsoft Access displays your custom menu bar in all windows, except in forms or reports that have their own custom menu bar. (A form or report's custom menu bar overrides a global custom menu bar.) You can specify a menu bar to use throughout your application by using the **Startup** dialog box.

You can use one or more custom toolbars in an application. Create the toolbars you want, and then use the appropriate method to display your custom toolbars:

- If your application has only one custom toolbar, just use the **Toolbars** command (**View** menu) to display it; it will appear each time your application starts.

- If your application has different custom toolbars for different forms or reports, you can specify a toolbar for each form or report in the form or report's **Toolbar** property.

  Note There is no need to create event procedures for the Activate and Deactivate events of the form to show and hide toolbars, as was required in previous versions of Microsoft Access. Setting the **Toolbar** property to a custom toolbar automatically hides the built-in **Form View** toolbar when your form is opened and hides your custom toolbar when a user closes the form or switches to another form.

- If you need to work with more than one custom toolbar for a form or report, or if you want to hide or show built-in Microsoft Access toolbars, you can use the **Visible** property of the **CommandBar** object in Visual Basic code or use the **ShowToolbar** action in macros to hide and show the toolbars.

- If you want your application to display only custom toolbars, you can hide all built-in toolbars by clicking the **Startup** command (**Tools** menu) and then clearing the **Allow Built-in Toolbars** check box.

Microsoft Excel

You can store custom menu bars and toolbars with the workspace or with the workbook. When you quit Microsoft Excel, the toolbars in the workspace are automatically saved in the file *Username*8.xlb (where *Username* is the current user's Windows 95 logon name). If the user isn't logged on, the file name is Excel8.xlb. The toolbars saved in a workbook are stored in the workbook file.

Workbook-level menu bars and toolbars make it easier for you to create a polished user interface for a custom application (an add-in, for instance) and to distribute custom toolbar buttons and their supporting procedures. If you're going to distribute a custom toolbar with a custom application, you should attach it to the workbook that contains that application so that the toolbar is stored in the same file as the application.

▶ To move a menu bar or toolbar from the workspace to a workbook

1 If the **Customize** dialog box isn't already open, point to **Toolbars** on the **View** menu, and then click **Customize**.

2 On the **Toolbars** tab, click **Attach**.

The **Attach Toolbars** dialog box is displayed.

3 In the **Custom toolbars** box, click the name of the menu bar or toolbar you want to copy to the active workbook.

4 Click **Copy**.

The name of the menu bar or toolbar you copied appears in the **Toolbars in workbook** box.

You can delete the original workspace-level menu bar or toolbar by clicking the **Toolbars** tab in the **Customize** dialog box, selecting the name of the menu bar or toolbar you want to delete, and then clicking **Delete**. If you don't delete the workspace version of the menu bar or toolbar, you can change it without affecting the version stored in the workbook. If you make changes to the workspace version of the menu bar or toolbar and would like to update the workbook version to match the current workspace version, you can copy the workspace version to the workbook again, thus replacing the previous workbook version.

After you've copied a menu bar or toolbar to a workbook, the menu bar or toolbar becomes available only after the user has opened that workbook. A workbook version of the menu bar or toolbar retains not only its name and contents, but also the code assignments for menu items or toolbar controls; the location, size, and shape of the menu bar or toolbar; its on-screen position; and whether it's visible or hidden.

You can also delete a workbook version of a menu bar or toolbar.

▶ To delete a workbook version of a menu bar or toolbar

1 If the **Customize** dialog box isn't already open, point to **Toolbars** on the **View** menu, and then click **Customize**.

2 On the **Toolbars** tab, click **Attach**.

The **Attach Toolbars** dialog box is displayed.

3 In the **Toolbars in workbook** box, click the name of the menu bar or toolbar you want to delete.

4 Click **Delete**.

Note You cannot use Visual Basic to attach menu bars or toolbars to a workbook or delete them from a workbook.

When you open a workbook that contains one or more menu bars or toolbars, Microsoft Excel first determines whether a workspace menu bar or toolbar with that name already exists. If not, Microsoft Excel creates a new workspace menu bar or toolbar and copies the workbook version into it. This way, the you get a fresh copy of the menu bar or toolbar, which you can alter by hiding it or by copying items or controls to or from the workspace-level copy. When you quit Microsoft Excel, changes made to this copy of the menu bar or toolbar are stored with the workspace file.

There's no way to rename a menu bar or toolbar, so when the workbook is reopened, the workspace already contains a menu bar or toolbar with the same name as the workbook version, and Microsoft Excel uses the workspace copy rather than reloading the workbook version. However, the procedures that support the menu items or toolbar buttons in the open workbook still run when the user clicks the corresponding item or control.

As a developer, you can design a menu bar or toolbar and then attach it to a workbook. When the user opens the workbook, the custom menu bar or toolbar is available. The user can then edit it and move items or controls from it to personal menu bars or toolbars, without affecting the copy stored in the workbook. The user's changed menu bars and toolbars are stored with the workspace file when he or she quits Microsoft Excel. When the user starts Microsoft Excel again, the edited menu bar or toolbar is available; clicking one of the developer's menu items or toolbar controls loads the workbook that contains the procedure attached to that item or control. To generate a fresh copy of the workbook menu bar or toolbar, the user can delete the edited copy.

Microsoft Word

Word stores custom menus and toolbars in templates, just as it does with macros. When you customize a menu or create a new toolbar, changes are stored by default in the Normal template and are available "globally"—that is, you can always display a custom toolbar stored in the Normal template, even if the active document is based on a different template. A toolbar stored in a template other than Normal is available under either of two circumstances: the template is attached to the active document, or the template is loaded as a global template (**Tools** menu, **Templates and Add-ins** command). When you store a toolbar in a document, you can display the toolbar only when the document itself is active.

If you're going to distribute a Visual Basic application with customized menus and toolbars, you should store your menu bars and toolbars in a custom template or in a document. Because every user has his or her own Normal template, your Visual Basic application shouldn't change the Normal template. It's also easier to remove custom menus and toolbars when the user quits your application if the customizations are in the template or document that contains your application. That is, when the user closes the document (if the document contains toolbars or the template it's attached to contains toolbars) or unloads your template, your custom toolbars are no longer available; only the built-in menus and toolbars or the user's custom toolbars remain.

If two custom toolbars with the same name are available at the same time (for example, if the Normal template and a loaded global template both have a toolbar named "Custom Tools"), both toolbars are listed in the **Customize** dialog box and can be displayed either separately or at the same time.

In Visual Basic, you can add, customize, or delete menu bars and toolbars in any document or template. However, because the **CommandBars** property applies only to the **Application** object, you must set the context for your change before you make the change. Similar to using the **Store in** box on the **Commands** tab in the **Customize** dialog box, you can use the **CustomizationContext** property in Visual Basic to specify a **Document** or **Template** object that represents the document or template in which you want to make changes. You must set the **CustomizationContext** property before using the **CommandBars** property; this ensures that a reference to the collection of menu bars and toolbars for that document or template is returned. For more information, see "Design-Time Modifications to Toolbars" later in this chapter.

Microsoft PowerPoint

Custom menu bars and toolbars are always stored with the workspace. When you quit PowerPoint, the toolbars in the workspace are saved in the file *Username*.pcb (where *Username* is the current user's Windows 95 logon name). If the user isn't logged on, the file name is Powerpnt.pcb.

Because menu bars and toolbars aren't visible while a presentation is running, customizing menus and toolbars in PowerPoint is limited to changing the available menu commands and toolbar controls in design mode. You can use either the **Customize** dialog box or Visual Basic to modify your own design environment. If your Visual Basic application delivers a custom interface for designing presentations, you must use Visual Basic to make changes to menus and toolbars. When the user finishes with your application, it's a good idea for you to remove changes you made in Visual Basic.

Choosing the Best User-Interface Enhancement

Menus are lists of user-interface commands from which the user can choose. Menus offer a convenient and consistent way to group commands and an easy way for users to get to them. Commands for performing related tasks can be listed on the same menu, and commands can also be grouped (separated by lines from other commands or groups of commands). Submenus offer additional levels of organization, and shortcut menus offer a way to group related commands that apply to the limited context of a specific task.

You can assign access keys to make commands accessible from the keyboard, and you can assign shortcut keys to provide the user even quicker access to the commands. In addition, menus take up less space than toolbars, as the items on a menu are displayed on demand and don't take up dedicated screen space. On the other hand, if you want quick, graphical access to a command, a toolbar may be a better choice.

Toolbars contain controls that perform frequently used commands. Toolbars are ideal for presenting individual property settings (such as bold or italic formatting, or font size), commands that are best represented visually, and commands you want to access with one click of the mouse. In addition, toolbars remain displayed while the user works, whereas menus are displayed only on demand; this makes scanning a toolbar for a particular button easier than scanning the menus on a menu bar for a particular command. However, if you need easy keyboard access to a command, if you want to display your commands hierarchically, or if you are short on screen space, a menu may be a better choice.

If you need to present a more complex set of options to the user, a dialog box may be a better choice than either a toolbar or a menu. If you want to place a tool closer to the data the user is working with, the best solution may be to place a control directly on a worksheet or document. For more information about these various types of user-interface enhancements, see Chapter 12, "ActiveX Controls and Dialog Boxes."

The Menu System

The *menu system* in each Microsoft Office application is composed of the entire set of menus and the items on each menu. Each menu is either a menu, a submenu, or a shortcut menu. Each menu item is usually either a command or a submenu caption. In this chapter, the term *component* refers generically to any menu or menu item.

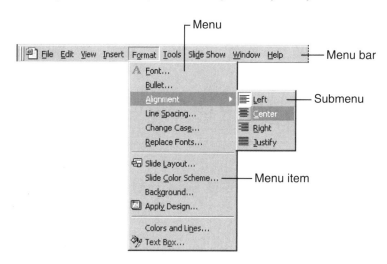

A menu bar is a bar at the top of the active window that displays the names of all the menus that are available in that application at any given time. That is, a Microsoft Office application can change the menu bar it displays in response to a change in the active window or in response to a Visual Basic instruction. For example, when you edit a chart in Microsoft Excel, the menu bar containing a set of menus that apply to the charting environment is automatically displayed.

A menu is a list of menu items that appears (drops down) when you click a menu name on the menu bar.

A submenu (or *child menu*) is a menu that's attached to the side of another menu (the *parent menu*), adjacent to a particular submenu caption on the parent menu. Each submenu caption is marked with an arrowhead pointing to the right. You can add submenus to menus or shortcut menus. A submenu is displayed when you point to the corresponding submenu caption on the parent menu.

A shortcut menu is a floating menu that contains a group of commands pertinent to a specific task. A shortcut menu appears when the user right-clicks an object.

Guidelines for Customizing the Menu System

You can modify the menu system in a Microsoft Office application in a wide range of ways: you can create new menu bars, add new menus to built-in or custom menu bars, add new menu items (commands or submenus) to built-in or custom menus or submenus, add and modify shortcut menus, and assign macros to menu items. In addition, you can restore the built-in menu system to its default state at any time.

Adding Custom Components or Modifying Built-in Components

Each Microsoft Office application comes with its own built-in menu system. You can modify components of this built-in system or create and modify custom menu components.

Modifying a built-in menu bar, menu, or menu item is appropriate if you're adding or changing a small number of components. For example, if you just want to provide menu access to a macro, you can add a menu item to a built-in menu and then link the macro to that item.

If you need to make more extensive changes, you may be better off creating a completely new component. For example, if you want to add several new menus—each of which will contain several new menu items—it may be more appropriate to create an entirely new menu bar to contain the new menus.

Using Submenus

If your menus become crowded and difficult to scan, you can use submenus to organize them more effectively and add clarity to your Visual Basic application by reducing the amount of information presented to the user at any one time. For example, suppose that you create a menu that presents a number of options, as shown in the following illustration.

Using submenus, you can present the same items in either of the ways shown in the following illustration.

With submenus, the user can browse through commands that might otherwise be available only through a series of custom dialog boxes. However, if you need to create a complicated array of submenus to present a set of commands, a dialog box may be a better solution.

Using Shortcut Menus

If you want to give the user access to a command that applies only to the limited context of a selected object, you can add the command to the built-in shortcut menu for that object. In Microsoft Access, you can also create custom shortcut menus and associate them with objects in your application. For information about creating and using custom shortcut menus in Access, see Chapter 1 in *Building Applications with Microsoft Access 97.*

Using Text Boxes, List Boxes, and Combo Boxes

Although it's possible to add built-in or custom text boxes, list boxes, and combo boxes to menus, shortcut menus, and submenus in your Visual Basic application, such controls are better suited to toolbars. Text boxes on menus can be useful in some instances to display or return a simple setting. List boxes and combo boxes also display the current setting when a menu is displayed. However, as soon as the user selects a new value in the box, the menu is closed (the user cannot see or revise the setting and must display the menu again to verify it).

If you want to add built-in text boxes, list boxes, and combo boxes to menus, use the same techniques given for adding built-in commands (see "Adding and Grouping Commands" later in this chapter). If you want to add custom text boxes, list boxes, and combo boxes, use the same techniques given for adding them to toolbars (see "Design-Time Modifications to Toolbars" later in this chapter).

Design-Time Modifications to the Menu System

Design-time changes to the menu system are any changes you make before the application runs. These include adding, deleting, moving, and restoring menu components, as well as setting menu component properties that won't change in response to changing conditions at run time.

Adding a Custom Menu Bar

If you want to design a set of menus that differs significantly from what's currently available on the Office application's built-in menu bar or menu bars, you may need to create a new menu bar. You can do this by using the **Customize** dialog box in Microsoft Access, or by using Visual Basic in Microsoft Excel, Word, or PowerPoint.

Using the Customize Dialog Box

In Microsoft Access, the **Customize** dialog box provides a convenient way to add a custom menu bar.

▶ **To add a menu bar in Microsoft Access**

1 If the **Customize** dialog box isn't already open, point to **Toolbars** on the **View** menu, and then click **Customize**.

2 On the **Toolbars** tab, click **New**.

3 In the **Toolbar name** box, type a name for the new menu bar, and then click **OK**.

An empty, floating menu bar with the name you typed is displayed.

4 Click **Properties** to display the **Toolbar Properties** dialog box.

5 In the **Type** box, click **Menu Bar**.

You can also set many other properties of your custom menu bar in the **Toolbar Properties** dialog box. For information about these properties and their uses, see Chapter 1 in *Building Applications with Microsoft Access 97*.

The new menu bar is added to the list of in the **Toolbars** box on the **Toolbars** tab.

Using Visual Basic

You use the **Add** method of the **CommandBars** collection to create a new menu bar; the *MenuBar* argument of the **Add** method determines whether the **CommandBar** object you're creating can be displayed as a menu bar. The following example creates a new menu bar named "Custom Menu Bar."

```
Set cstm = CommandBars.Add(Name:="Custom Menu Bar", Position:=msoBarTop, _
    MenuBar:=True, Temporary:=False)
```

In Microsoft Excel, Word, and PowerPoint, you must use Visual Basic to create a new menu bar. In Microsoft Access, you have the option of using either Visual Basic or the **Customize** dialog box.

Adding Menus

You can add a menu to any built-in or custom menu bar. Because a Microsoft Office application can display different built-in menu bars in different contexts, you may have to add a command to more than one menu bar to make sure that the user has access to the command regardless of the context. For example, in Microsoft Excel, you might want to add a special Accounting menu to each menu bar so that employees in a company can run the corresponding macros from any sheet.

When you add a menu to a menu bar, you can specify an access key for the menu; the access key appears underlined when the menu is displayed.

Note Although a Microsoft Office application may list toolbars that contain shortcut menus on the **Toolbars** tab in the **Customize** dialog box, you can neither add custom shortcut menus directly to these toolbars nor delete built-in shortcut menus from them. You can, however, add items to, delete items from, or customize items on shortcut menus. For information about customizing shortcut menus, see "Adding and Modifying Shortcut Menus" later in this section.

Using the Customize Dialog Box

The **Customize** dialog box provides a convenient way to add a menu to a built-in or custom menu bar.

▶ **To add a custom menu to a menu bar**

1   If the **Customize** dialog box isn't already open, point to **Toolbars** on the **View** menu, and then click **Customize**.

2   If the menu bar you want to modify isn't visible, select the check box next to the name of that menu bar in the **Toolbars** box on the **Toolbars** tab.

3   On the **Commands** tab, click **New Menu** in the **Categories** box.

4   Drag the **New Menu** item from the **Commands** box to the position on the menu bar where you want to add the menu.

    An I-beam on the menu bar indicates the position where the new menu will be added when you release the mouse button.

5 Right-click the new menu, and then type a name in the **Name** box. Type an ampersand (&) before the character you want to use as the access key for the menu.

When you click the menu name, an empty menu is displayed. For information about adding menu items to the new menu, see "Adding and Grouping Commands" later in this section.

The **Customize** dialog box also provides a quick way to add a copy of any built-in menu to a built-in or custom menu bar. You can customize the commands on the copy without affecting the original built-in menu.

▶ To add a copy of a built-in menu to a menu bar

1 If the **Customize** dialog box isn't already open, point to **Toolbars** on the **View** menu, and then click **Customize**.

2 If the menu bar you want to modify isn't visible, select the check box next to the name of that menu bar in the **Toolbars** box on the **Toolbars** tab.

3 On the **Commands** tab, click **Built-in Menus** in the **Categories** box.

4 Drag a built-in menu from the **Commands** box to the position on the menu bar where you want to add the copy.

An I-beam on the menu bar indicates the position where the menu will be added when you release the mouse button.

Tip You can also make a copy of any built-in menu by displaying the menu bar that contains that menu and holding down CTRL while you drag the menu to another menu bar.

Using Visual Basic

Use the **Add** method of the **CommandBarControls** collection to add a menu to a **CommandBar** object that represents a particular menu bar. Setting the *Type* argument of the **Add** method to **msoControlPopup** indicates that the control you're adding displays a menu. Controls that display menus are known as *pop-up controls*. The *Before* argument indicates the position of the new menu among the existing menus on the menu bar. Set the **Caption** property of the **CommandBarPopup** object returned by the **Add** method to specify the menu name and the access key. The following Microsoft Excel example adds a new menu named "Accounting" to the left of the **Window** menu on the menu bar for worksheets.

```
Set cstmAccounting = CommandBars("Worksheet Menu Bar").Controls _
    .Add(Type:=msoControlPopup, Before:=9)
cstmAccounting.Caption = "&Accounting"
```

Note You use an ampersand (&) in the menu name in front of the character that will be used as the access key for the menu. After you've added the menu, you can specify the menu name either with or without the ampersand when you reference the menu using **Controls**(*index*).

Adding Submenus

A submenu (child menu) is a menu attached to the side of another menu (the parent menu), adjacent to a particular menu item (the submenu caption). You can add submenus to menus, other submenus, and shortcut menus.

Just as you display the items on a menu by clicking the menu name on the menu bar, you display items on a submenu by pointing to the submenu caption on the parent menu. Similarly, just as you first add an empty menu (having a name but no menu items) to a menu bar and then add individual menu items, you first add an empty submenu to a parent menu and then add menu items.

Using the Customize Dialog Box

You use the **Customize** dialog box to add a submenu to another menu.

▶ **To add a submenu to a menu**

1 If the **Customize** dialog box isn't already open, point to **Toolbars** on the **View** menu, and then click **Customize**.

2 If the menu bar that contains the menu you want to modify isn't visible, select the check box next to the name of that menu bar in the **Toolbars** box on the **Toolbars** tab.

3 On the **Commands** tab, click **New Menu** in the **Categories** box.

4 Drag the **New Menu** item from the **Commands** box to the position on the menu where you want to add the submenu.

   To indicate the position for the new submenu, drag it over the menu name (and subsequent submenu captions, if necessary) to open the menu or submenu you want, drag the new submenu to the location where you want it on the menu or submenu, and then release the mouse button. A horizontal I-beam on the menu indicates the position where the submenu will be added when you release the mouse button.

5 Right-click the new submenu, and then type a name in the **Name** box. Type an ampersand (&) before the character you want to use as the access key for the submenu.

When you click the submenu caption, an empty submenu is displayed. For information about adding menu items to the new submenu, see "Adding and Grouping Commands" later in this section.

Using Visual Basic

Use the **Add** method of the **CommandBarControls** collection to add a submenu to a **CommandBar** object that represents another menu. Setting the *Type* argument of the **Add** method to **msoControlPopup** indicates that the control you're adding is a pop-up control—the same kind of control that indicates a menu on a menu bar. The

Before argument indicates the position of the new menu among the existing items on the menu. Set the **Caption** property of the **CommandBarPopup** object returned by the **Add** method to specify the submenu caption and the access key. The following Microsoft Excel example adds a new submenu named "Product" at the end of the Accounting menu on the menu bar for worksheets.

```
Set cstmAcctProduct = CommandBars("Worksheet Menu Bar").Controls("Accounting") _
    .Controls.Add(Type:=msoControlPopup)
cstmAccProduct.Caption = "&Product"
```

Note   You use an ampersand (&) in front of the character in the submenu caption that will be used as the access key for the submenu. After you've added the submenu, you can specify the submenu name either with or without the ampersand when you reference the submenu by using **Controls**(*index*).

Adding and Grouping Commands

You can add commands to any built-in or custom menu or submenu, modify their appearance, and visually separate them into logical groupings. This section deals with adding commands to menus and submenus. The following section addresses the specific issues of adding shortcut menus and then adding menu items to them.

Note   Although you can add text boxes, list boxes, and combo boxes to menus and submenus, they're not usually the best choice for presenting or returning information. If you want to add custom text boxes, list boxes, and combo boxes, use the same techniques given for adding them to toolbars (see "Design-Time Modifications to Toolbars" later in this chapter).

Using the Customize Dialog Box

The **Customize** dialog box provides an easy way to add items to menus and submenus.

▶ **To add a built-in command to a menu or submenu**

1   If the **Customize** dialog box isn't already open, point to **Toolbars** on the **View** menu, and then click **Customize**.

2   If the menu bar that contains the menu you want to modify isn't visible, select the check box next to the name of that menu bar in the **Toolbars** box on the **Toolbars** tab.

3   On the **Commands** tab, select a category of commands in the **Categories** box.

The commands in the category you select are listed in the **Commands** box.

4   Drag a command from the **Commands** box to the position on the menu or submenu where you want to add the command.

To indicate the position for the command, drag it over the menu name (and subsequent submenu captions, if necessary) to open the menu or submenu you want, drag the command to the location where you want it on the menu or submenu, and then release the mouse button. A horizontal I-beam on the menu indicates the position where the command will be added when you release the mouse button.

Tip You can also make a copy of any built-in command by displaying the menu bar that contains a menu with that command and holding down CTRL while you drag the command to another menu.

The **Customize** dialog box also provides a quick way to add a custom command to a built-in or custom menu bar. However, each Microsoft Office application involves a different technique for using the **Customize** dialog box to do this. The following paragraphs describe these differences.

Microsoft Access To add a menu item that runs a macro, follow the same steps as in the procedure for adding a built-in command to a menu. In the **Categories** box, click **All Macros**. Drag the macro you want from the **Commands** box to the position on the menu where you want it to appear. To add a menu item that runs a **Function** procedure, follow the same steps as in the procedure for adding a built-in command to a menu. In the **Categories** box, click any category, and then drag any item you want to the position on the menu where you want it to appear. Right-click the item, and then click **Control Properties** to display the **Control Properties** dialog box. In the **Caption** box, delete the current name, and then type a new name for your command. In the **On Action** box, type an expression to run your Visual Basic **Function** procedure. The expression must use the following syntax: *=functionname()*.

Microsoft Excel Follow the same steps as in the procedure for adding a built-in command to a menu; in the **Categories** box, click **Macros**, and then drag **Custom Menu Item** from the **Commands** box to the position on the menu where you want it to appear. Right-click the new item and then click **Assign Macro**. In the **Macro Name** box in the **Assign Macro** dialog box, enter the name of the macro you want to run.

Microsoft Word Follow the same steps as in the procedure for adding a built-in command to a menu; in the **Categories** box, click **Macros**, and then drag a macro from the **Commands** box to the position on the menu where you want it to appear.

Tip In Word, if you write a procedure whose name is the same as that of a built-in Word command (or if you write a procedure named "MAIN" in a module whose name is the same as that of a built-in Word command), that procedure will replace the built-in functionality of the command whenever the module that contains it is available. Every copy of the menu item on whatever menu it appears will run the replacement procedure. For more information about controlling the context of your customizations, see "Scope of Changes to the User Interface" earlier in this chapter. For more information about modifying Word commands, see Chapter 7, "Microsoft Word Objects."

Microsoft PowerPoint Follow the same steps as in the procedure for adding a built-in command to a menu; in the **Categories** box, click **Macros**, and then drag a macro from the **Commands** box to the position on the menu where you want it to appear.

Modifying the Appearance of a Command

Any command on a menu can have a button image displayed next to the command name. Whether a button image appears next to a command is determined by its "style." You set a command's style using commands on the shortcut menu while the **Customize** dialog box is open. The following table describes the effect of each style on menu commands.

Style	What appears on a menu
Default Style	Button image and name
Text Only (In Menus)	Name only
Text Only (Always)	Name only
Image And Text	Button image and name

Note By default, some built-in menu commands don't have a button image associated with them and won't display an image regardless of the style you set. However, you can add an image to any built-in menu command.

While the **Customize** dialog box is open, you can add or modify the button image next to a menu command. The following table describes the techniques you can use.

To	Do this
Use a predefined button image	Right-click the command, point to **Change Button Image**, and then click the image you want.
Copy and paste another command's button image	Right-click the command that has the image you want to use, and then click **Copy Button Image**. Right-click the command whose image you're customizing, and then click **Paste Button Image**.
Copy and paste an image from a graphics program	In a graphics program, open the image you want to copy. Select and copy the image (preferably a 16 x 16 pixel image or portion). Switch back to your application. Right-click the command, and then click **Paste Button Image**.
Edit the command's current button image	Right-click the command, and then click **Edit Button Image**. In the **Button Editor** dialog box, you can change the color and shape of the image, adjust the image's position on the control, and preview your changes to the image. When you finish editing the button image, click **OK**.
Reset a command to use its original button image (or no image)	Right-click the command, and then click **Reset Button Image**.

Tip In Microsoft Access, you can use the **Properties** dialog box to set many other properties of menu commands. For more information, see Chapter 1 in *Building Applications with Microsoft Access 97*.

Grouping Commands

You can group related commands on a menu by separating them with lines. The lines themselves aren't menu items; rather, you can set any item on a menu to appear with a line before it. You use the **Customize** dialog box to set a command to appear as the first item in a group of commands.

▶ To begin a group of commands on a menu

1   If the **Customize** dialog box isn't already open, point to **Toolbars** on the **View** menu, and then click **Customize**.

2   If the menu bar that contains the menu you want to modify isn't visible, select the check box next to the name of that menu bar in the **Toolbars** box on the **Toolbars** tab.

3   Right-click the menu item you want to appear with a line above it, and then click **Begin Group**.

The next time you right-click that item, a check mark will be displayed next to **Begin Group** on the shortcut menu. To remove the line before a menu item, right-click the item and then click **Begin Group** again (the check mark will no longer appear).

Using Visual Basic

Use the **Add** method of the **CommandBarControls** collection to add a new menu item to the **CommandBar** object that represents a particular menu or submenu. To add a built-in command, specify the ID number of the command by using the *Id* argument of the **Add** method. The following example adds the **Spelling** command to the menu named "Quick Tools" on the menu bar named "Custom Menu Bar."

```
Set mySpell = CommandBars("Custom Menu Bar").Controls("Quick Tools") _
    .Controls.Add(Id:=2)
```

For information about determining the built-in command ID numbers of a Microsoft Office application, see "Menu Item and Toolbar Control IDs" later in this chapter.

To add a custom command, you add a new menu item and then set the **OnAction** property to specify a Visual Basic procedure to run whenever that item is clicked. Setting the *Type* argument of the **Add** method to **msoControlButton** indicates that a menu item is a command. The following Microsoft Excel example adds an Open Database menu item to the **File** menu on the menu bar for worksheets. Microsoft Excel runs the OpenDatabaseProc Visual Basic procedure whenever the user clicks this menu item. Open Database appears directly above the **Close** command on the **File** menu.

```
Set databaseItem = CommandBars("Worksheet Menu Bar").Controls("File") _
    .Controls.Add(Type:=msoControlButton, Before:=3)
With databaseItem
    .Caption:="Open Database"
    .OnAction:="OpenDatabaseProc"
End With
```

There are many properties of the objects that represent menu commands that you can set in Visual Basic to modify the appearance of commands. For more information, see "Style Property" and "FaceID Property" in Help, as well as the Help topics for other properties and methods of the **CommandBarButton** object.

To set a menu item to begin a group of menu items (that is, to be preceded by a line), you just set the **BeginGroup** property of the **CommandBarButton**, **CommandBarPopup**, or **CommandBarComboBox** object that represents the menu item to **True**. To remove the line, set the **BeginGroup** property to **False**. Use **Controls**(*index*), where *index* is the caption or index number of a menu item, to return an object that represents the item. The following example adds a line before the Open Database command on the **File** menu (added by the preceding example).

```
Set databaseItem = CommandBars("Worksheet Menu Bar").Controls("File") _
    .Controls("Open Database")
databaseItem.BeginGroup = True
```

Adding and Modifying Shortcut Menus

You can add and modify custom shortcut menus by using the **Customize** dialog box in Microsoft Access, or by using Visual Basic in Microsoft Excel. In Microsoft Access, Word, and PowerPoint, you can modify built-in shortcut menus (and custom shortcut menus in Microsoft Access) by using the **Customize** dialog box.

With Microsoft Access, you can assign custom shortcut menus to reports, forms, and controls on forms; the assigned shortcut menu is displayed whenever the user right-clicks the corresponding object. For information about working with shortcut menus in Microsoft Access reports and forms, see Chapter 1 in *Building Applications with Microsoft Access 97*.

Microsoft Excel provides an event—BeforeRightClick—that you can respond to by modifying a built-in shortcut menu or displaying a custom shortcut menu.

Note   Word and PowerPoint don't provide a way to display a custom shortcut menu when the user right-clicks in the application window.

Using the Customize Dialog Box

In Microsoft Access, the **Customize** dialog box provides a convenient way to add a custom shortcut menu.

▶ **To add a shortcut menu in Microsoft Access**

1   If the **Customize** dialog box isn't already open, point to **Toolbars** on the **View** menu, and then click **Customize**.

2   On the **Toolbars** tab, click **New**.

3 In the **Toolbar name** box, type a name for the new shortcut menu, and then click **OK**.

An empty, floating toolbar with the name you typed is displayed.

4 Click **Properties** to display the **Toolbar Properties** dialog box.

5 In the **Type** box, click **Shortcut Menu**.

The empty, floating toolbar is no longer displayed. To display the shortcut menu from the **Customize** dialog box, click the **Toolbars** tab, and then select the check box next to **Shortcut Menus** in the **Toolbars** box. The toolbar that contains all the shortcut menus is displayed; the shortcut menu you just created appears on the last menu on the toolbar.

In Microsoft Access, Word, and PowerPoint, you can modify built-in shortcut menus by using the **Customize** dialog box. (In Microsoft Access, you can also modify custom shortcut menus in this way.) To add a submenu to a shortcut menu, follow the same steps as are given in "Adding Submenus" earlier in this section. To add a command, follow the same steps as are given in "Adding and Grouping Commands" earlier in this section. Remember to select the check box next to **Shortcut Menus** in the **Toolbars** box to display a toolbar that contains all the shortcut menus that are available while the **Customize** dialog box is open.

Using Visual Basic

You use the **Add** method of the **CommandBars** collection to create a new shortcut menu; setting the *Position* argument of the **Add** method to **msoBarPopup** indicates that the **CommandBar** object you're creating can be displayed as a shortcut menu. The following example creates a new shortcut menu named "Shortcuts1."

```
Set cstm = CommandBars.Add(Name:="Shortcuts1", Position:=msoBarPopup, _
    MenuBar:=False, Temporary:=False)
```

In Microsoft Excel, Word, and PowerPoint, you must use Visual Basic to create a new shortcut menu. In Microsoft Access, you have the option of using either Visual Basic or the **Customize** dialog box.

To modify a custom or built-in shortcut menu in any Microsoft Office application by using Visual Basic, you use the same techniques as are described earlier in this section for using Visual Basic to add submenus or commands to a menu. You use **CommandBars**(*name*), where *name* is the name of a shortcut menu, to return a **CommandBar** object that represents that shortcut menu. Then you can add or modify the elements of the **Controls** collection available from that **CommandBar** object.

Deleting Menu Components

You can delete built-in or custom items from menus, you can delete built-in or custom menus from menu bars, and you can delete custom menu bars. Note, however, that although you can delete all the items on shortcut menus and built-in menu bars, you cannot delete the shortcut menus or built-in menu bars themselves.

Deleting built-in menu components can help you tailor your Visual Basic application to the needs of the user. For example, you might want to delete a built-in command from a menu and replace it with a custom version of the command that performs specialized tasks for the user. Or you might want to remove certain menu items to simplify the interface or reduce the possibility that inexperienced users will choose commands you didn't intend for them to use.

Note You can restore built-in menu bars, menus, or menu items that you've deleted. However, you cannot restore custom menu bars, menus, or menu items that you've deleted; you must re-create them.

Using the Customize Dialog Box

With the **Customize** dialog box open, you can delete any menu component.

▶ **To delete a menu system component**

1 If the **Customize** dialog box isn't already open, point to **Toolbars** on the **View** menu, and then click **Customize**.

2 If the menu bar that contains the menu component you want to delete isn't visible, select the check box next to the name of that menu bar in the **Toolbars** box on the **Toolbars** tab.

3 Right-click the menu component you want to delete, and then click **Delete** on the shortcut menu.

To delete an entire custom menu bar, open the **Customize** dialog box, click the name of the menu bar in the **Toolbars** box on the **Toolbars** tab, and then click the **Delete** button. You cannot delete built-in menu bars.

Using Visual Basic

Use the **Delete** method to delete a custom menu bar, a custom or built-in drop-down menu or submenu, or a custom or built-in menu item. You cannot delete a built-in menu bar or a shortcut menu.

The following Microsoft Excel example deletes the **Edit** menu from the menu bar for charts.

```
CommandBars("Chart Menu Bar").Controls("Edit").Delete
```

The following example deletes the custom menu bar named "Custom Menu Bar."

```
CommandBars("Custom Menu Bar").Delete
```

For information about restoring built-in menu components that you've deleted, see the following section.

Restoring Built-in Menu Components

You can restore built-in menu bars, menus, or menu items that you've deleted. However, you cannot restore custom menu bars, menus, or menu items that you've deleted; you must re-create them.

Using the Customize Dialog Box

You can use the **Customize** dialog box to restore a built-in menu or submenu to once again contain its original, built-in set of menu items. Note that if you restore a menu, all the submenus on that menu are restored. Likewise, if you restore a built-in menu bar, all the menus and submenus on that menu bar are restored.

▶ To restore a built-in menu

1 If the **Customize** dialog box isn't already open, point to **Toolbars** on the **View** menu, and then click **Customize**.

2 If the menu bar that contains the menu you want to restore isn't visible, select the check box next to the name of that menu bar in the **Toolbars** box on the **Toolbars** tab.

3 Right-click the menu or submenu you want to delete, and then click **Restore** on the shortcut menu.

To restore a built-in menu bar, open the **Customize** dialog box, click the name of the menu bar in the **Toolbars** box on the **Toolbars** tab, and then click the **Restore** button.

Using Visual Basic

Use the **Reset** method to reset the components of a built-in menu bar, menu, or submenu.

The following Microsoft Excel example resets the **Edit** menu on the menu bar for charts.

```
CommandBars("Chart Menu Bar").Controls("Edit").Reset
```

The following Word example resets the built-in menu bar.

```
CommandBars("Menu Bar").Reset
```

Run-Time Modifications to the Menu System

You can program the menu system you created at design time to respond dynamically to changing conditions at run time. You can replace the default menu bar with a custom menu bar that you've designed. If a particular menu item is an inappropriate choice in certain contexts, you can remove it, hide it, or disable it to prevent the user from selecting it (disabling a menu item is also called *dimming* the menu item, or making it gray). If a menu item represents an option with two possible states, you can make the command's button image appear pushed down to show that the option is turned on or appear flat to show that it's turned off. Finally, you might want to rename a menu item in response to current conditions. For example, in Microsoft Excel, clicking the **Freeze Panes** command on the **Windows** menu causes the command to be renamed **Unfreeze Panes**.

Note that although you can make design-time changes to the menu system by using either the **Customize** dialog box or Visual Basic, you must use Visual Basic to make any run-time changes.

Displaying a Custom Menu Bar

To display a custom menu bar instead of the active menu bar, you set the **Visible** property of a **CommandBar** object that represents that custom menu bar to **True**. (For information about creating a menu bar that can replace the active menu bar, see "Adding a Custom Menu Bar" earlier in this chapter.) The newly visible menu bar replaces the active menu bar automatically. You set the **Visible** property to **False** to display the default menu bar again when your Visual Basic application finishes running.

Whenever a user starts a Microsoft Office application, the default menu bar is displayed. In Word, you can replace the default menu bar with a custom menu bar at startup—the last menu bar that was visible when the Normal template was saved before quitting is the default menu bar when Word is started again. You can also set the **Visible** property of a menu bar to **True** in an Open event procedure to replace the default menu bar. In Microsoft Excel and PowerPoint, you must use an event procedure or a macro to replace the default menu bar.

For information about specifying form, report, and global menu bars in Microsoft Access, see Chapter 1 in *Building Applications with Microsoft Access 97*.

Displaying Menu Components Dynamically

If a menu component applies only to a particular document, it's best if that menu component appears only when that document is active; this reduces needless clutter in the interface. You can limit the lifetime of a given menu component to the period during which the document it applies to is open or active.

If you want a menu or menu item to appear only for a specific document, you can set the **Visible** property to make the component visible every time the user activates the document, and hide it every time the user deactivates the document. If you want to associate a menu bar with a specific document, you can set the **Visible** property to make the menu bar appear whenever the user activates the document and then hide the menu bar whenever the user deactivates the document, rather than actually adding or deleting the menu bar each time.

To display menu components dynamically, you write the appropriate event procedure that enables the component or makes it visible, and you write the event procedure that disables the component or hides it. If the application whose menu bars you're modifying doesn't support events, you cannot customize the interface dynamically. An alternative in these applications is to assign similar procedures to the **OnAction** property of other menu items or toolbar buttons. If your application supports embedding ActiveX controls, you can also modify the interface of the container application in response to an event supported by that control.

Note   Because Word stores customizations in documents and templates, custom menu components are visible when the document or template is available in the current context, and they're hidden when the document or template isn't available. In contrast, because Microsoft Excel stores customizations at the workspace level, you need to use the **Visible** property in event code to dynamically change the interface.

Enabling or Disabling Menu Components

If you want to prevent the user from choosing a particular menu item under certain conditions, you can disable it. A disabled command still appears on the menu, but it appears dimmed and doesn't respond to user actions. Use the **Enabled** property to enable or disable a menu item. The **Enabled** property is **True** if the menu item is enabled, and it's **False** if the menu item is disabled (you cannot set the **Enabled** property for a built-in menu item). The following Microsoft Excel example adds the Open Database command to the **File** menu on the menu bar for worksheets and then disables the Open Database command.

```
CommandBars("Worksheet Menu Bar").Controls("File") _
    .Controls.Add("Open Database").Enabled = False
```

If you want to disable all the commands on a particular menu, you can disable the menu itself. This effectively disables all the commands on the menu, as the user no longer has access to them. The following Microsoft Excel example disables the entire **File** menu on the menu bar for worksheets.

```
CommandBars("Worksheet Menu Bar").Controls("File").Enabled = False
```

Note   You can disable all the menu items on a submenu, but you cannot disable the submenu itself.

Indicating the State of a Menu Item

If a menu item represents an option that has only two possible states, you can make the button image next to the item appear pushed down or appear flat to indicate the current state of the option. The appearance should be changed to the opposite of its current appearance—and the option turned on or off, accordingly—each time the user clicks the menu item. You change the appearance by setting the **State** property of the menu item.

To see how this works, suppose that the Microsoft Excel procedure in the following example is assigned to the custom menu item Database on the **View** menu on the menu bar for worksheets. This menu item offers the user the option of viewing a worksheet either in database view or in worksheet view. Every time the user clicks the Database menu item, the procedure switches the button image next to the menu item between appearing pushed down and appearing flat (that is, the procedure sets the **State** property and then switches views).

```
Sub DatabaseView()
   With CommandBars("Worksheet Menu Bar").Controls("View").Controls("Database")
   If .State = msoButtonUp Then
      .State = msoButtonDown
      'Switch to database view
   Else
      .State = mosButtonUp
      'Switch to worksheet view
   End If
   End With
End Sub
```

Every built-in and custom menu item has text and a button image; many built-in menu items have blank button images. When you add an item to a menu by using the **Customize** dialog box, you can specify and modify the item's button image. At run time, you set the menu item's **FaceId** property to specify the button image you want to display next to the menu item when its state changes. To specify the button image you want to display next to a menu item, you must find the built-in command with that button image, determine its ID, and then assign that value to the **FaceId** property. (Changing the **FaceId** property of a menu item doesn't change its functionality.) For information about determining the built-in command ID numbers of a Microsoft Office application, see "Menu Item and Toolbar Control IDs" later in this chapter.

The following Microsoft Excel example not only switches the state of the button image next to the menu item, but it changes the image as well. When the user switches to database view, the button image is switched to a grid (ID 987). Likewise, when the user switches out of database view, the image is set to a blank face (ID 1).

```
Sub DatabaseView()
   With CommandBars("Worksheet Menu Bar").Controls("View").Controls("Database")
   If .State = msoButtonUp Then
      .FaceId = 987
      .State = msoButtonDown
      'Switch to database view
   Else
      .FaceId = 1
      .State = mosButtonUp
      'Switch to worksheet view
   End If
   End With
End Sub
```

Renaming a Menu Item

You can use the **Caption** property of a menu item to change the item's name in response to changing conditions in your Visual Basic code. Suppose, for example, that you've created a menu command that opens a database. After the user has opened a database, you may want to replace the original command with a command that closes the database. The following example shows how you can accomplish this.

```
CommandBars("MyMenubar").Controls("File").Controls("Open Database") _
    .Caption = "Close &Database"
```

When you rename a menu item this way, make sure that the other procedures in your application reference the menu item by its new name (Close Database, in this example).

You can also use variables to refer to a menu item. An advantage of this technique is that variables continue to work even if the item's caption changes. The following example sets a variable to the Open Database menu item.

```
Set openData = CommandBars("My Menubar").Controls _
    ("File").Controls("Open Database")
```

You can change the caption later by using the code in the following example.

```
openData.Caption = "Close &Database"
```

Toolbars

Each Microsoft Office application provides a system of toolbars containing toolbar controls that the user can click to gain access to frequently used commands. Each toolbar can appear docked at the top, at the bottom, or on either the left or right side of the application window, or as a floating window positioned anywhere in the workspace. Each toolbar control is a simple, graphical control with which the user can exchange information with your Visual Basic application. To display any toolbar in an Office application, point to **Toolbars** on the **View** menu, and then click the name of the toolbar you want to display. To see additional available toolbars, open the **Customize** dialog box and browse through the toolbars listed in the **Categories** box.

There are several types of controls that are classified as toolbar controls; these are discussed in the following paragraphs.

The most common type of toolbar button is a simple button control that contains a graphic. The graphic, called the *button image*, is a visual representation of the command or option that the toolbar button activates. The user can click one of these toolbar buttons to execute a command (for example, clicking the **New** button on the **Standard** toolbar creates a new document) or to alternate between the two possible states of an option represented by a button (for example, clicking the **Bold** button on the **Formatting** toolbar alternately applies bold formatting to and removes it from the selected text).

Another type of toolbar control is a button control that contains a graphic and an attached drop-down palette. The user clicks the drop-down arrow to display a palette and then clicks an option on the palette. The user clicks the button control to apply the current option. For example, in Microsoft Excel, clicking the drop-down arrow for the **Font Color** button displays a palette of font colors from which the user can choose. Clicking this toolbar control's button applies the indicated color to the selected text.

A text box, list box, or combo box can also be a toolbar control. The user either types text in the box or clicks the drop-down arrow and then clicks an item in the list. For example, on the **Formatting** toolbar, you can set the font size for the selected text either by clicking an item in the drop-down list box contained in the **Font Size** button or by typing an entry in the text box.

The last type of toolbar control is the pop-up control, which displays a menu of other controls. A pop-up control on a toolbar is essentially the same as a menu name on a menu bar. The **Draw** button on the **Drawing** toolbar in Microsoft Excel, Word, or PowerPoint is an example of a pop-up control.

Note   Although they share similar appearances and behavior, toolbar controls and ActiveX controls aren't the same. You cannot add ActiveX controls to toolbars, and you cannot add toolbar controls to documents or forms.

Now that you understand what toolbars and the various types of toolbar controls are, you can study the specifics of modifying the toolbars and toolbar controls described in the preceding paragraphs. In the following sections, you'll learn how to make design-time and run-time changes to toolbars and toolbar controls.

Guidelines for Customizing Toolbars

The Microsoft Office applications offer you a wide range of ways to modify the built-in toolbars to better serve the needs of the user. You can create new toolbars; add new toolbar buttons to built-in or custom toolbars; modify the image on a toolbar button face; and assign macros, ToolTip text, and status bar text to toolbar buttons.

Whether you modify a built-in toolbar or create a new one depends on the extent of the changes you want to make. Modifying a built-in toolbar makes sense if you're adding or changing only a few toolbar buttons; creating a new toolbar may be more convenient if you want to provide an entirely different assortment of commands than are found on any of the built-in toolbars, or if you want to present a number of custom toolbar buttons as a distinct group. Regardless of how many changes you make, you can restore the built-in menu system to its default state whenever you want.

In addition to the above changes, which are usually made at design time, you can use Visual Basic procedures to change the properties of toolbars and toolbar buttons in response to user input while your application is running (that is, at run time). For example, you can hide a toolbar when the user no longer needs it, move or resize a toolbar to keep it out of the user's way, disable a toolbar button to prevent the user from clicking it at an inappropriate time, or switch the appearance of a toolbar button between pushed down and flat every time the user clicks it.

Using Menus

You can add pop-up controls—the same controls that display menus on menu bars and submenus on menus—to any built-in or custom toolbar. Often, adding a menu to a toolbar is a useful compromise between customizing a built-in menu bar (which may not be as convenient as adding toolbar controls) and adding a cumbersome number of toolbar controls (some of which may be dropped from a wide toolbar that's docked). The **Draw** button on the **Drawing** toolbar in Microsoft Excel, Word, or PowerPoint is an example of a menu on a toolbar.

To add menus, submenus, and menu items to toolbars, use the same steps as were presented for adding such components to menu bars in "Design-Time Modifications to the Menu System" earlier in this chapter.

Using Text Boxes, List Boxes, and Combo Boxes

In the Microsoft Office applications, you can add text boxes, list boxes, and combo boxes to built-in and custom toolbars. These controls can be useful for getting information from a user frequently, or for running a complex procedure that can use the value of the control to determine a range of possible results.

The **Customize** dialog box supports adding built-in text boxes, list boxes, and combo boxes to any toolbar, but it doesn't support adding custom ones; instead, you must use Visual Basic to add and design these controls. With the **Customize** dialog box open, you can change the width of any built-in or custom text box, list box, or combo box.

Design-Time Modifications to Toolbars

Design-time changes include creating a new toolbar;, adding new or built-in toolbar controls to a toolbar; deleting toolbar controls from a toolbar; grouping or ungrouping toolbar controls; and changing the width of text box, list box, and combo box toolbar controls. You can also select a new image or use the Button Editor to customize the image associated with a particular toolbar control.

Adding a Custom Toolbar

In many cases, you can present a new set of commands by adding custom toolbar controls to a built-in toolbar. But if you want to present a complete set of commands in an easily accessible form, distinct from all built-in commands, you can create a new toolbar. You do this by using either the **Customize** dialog box or Visual Basic.

Using the Customize Dialog Box

The **Customize** dialog box provides a convenient way to add a custom toolbar.

▶ **To add a toolbar**

1 If the **Customize** dialog box isn't already open, point to **Toolbars** on the **View** menu, and then click **Customize**.

2 On the **Toolbars** tab, click **New**.

3 In the **Toolbar name** box, type a name for the new toolbar, and then click **OK**.

An empty, floating toolbar with the name you typed is displayed.

The new toolbar is added to the list in the **Toolbars** box on the **Toolbars** tab.

Using Visual Basic

You use the **Add** method of the **CommandBars** collection to create a new toolbar; setting the *Position* argument of the **Add** method to **msoBarLeft**, **msoBarTop**, **msoBarRight**, **msoBarBottom**, or **msoBarFloating** indicates whether the **CommandBar** object you're creating is a floating toolbar or a docked toolbar. The following example creates and displays a new toolbar named "Custom Tools."

```
Set cstm = CommandBars.Add(Name:="Custom Tools", Position:=msoBarFloating, _
    MenuBar:=False, Temporary:=False)
cstm.Visible = True
```

Adding and Grouping Controls

You can add controls to any built-in or custom toolbar, and you can visually separate them (with lines) into logical groupings.

Using the Customize Dialog Box

The **Customize** dialog box provides an easy method for adding controls to toolbars.

▶ **To add a built-in control to a toolbar**

1 If the **Customize** dialog box isn't already open, point to **Toolbars** on the **View** menu, and then click **Customize**.

2 If the toolbar you want to modify isn't visible, select the check box next to the name of that toolbar in the **Toolbars** box on the **Toolbars** tab.

3 On the **Commands** tab, click a category of commands in the **Categories** box.

The commands in the category you select are now listed in the **Commands** box.

4 Drag a control from the **Commands** box to the position on the menu where you want to add the control.

A vertical I-beam on the toolbar indicates the position where the control will be added when you release the mouse button.

Tip You can easily make a copy of any built-in toolbar control by displaying the toolbar that contains that control and holding down CTRL while you drag the control to another toolbar.

The **Customize** dialog box also provides a quick way to add a custom command to a built-in or custom toolbar. However, each Microsoft Office application has a different technique for using the **Customize** dialog box to do this. The following paragraphs describe these differences.

Microsoft Access   To add a control that runs a macro, follow the same steps as in the procedure for adding a built-in control to a toolbar. In the **Categories** box, click **All Macros**. Drag the macro you want from the **Commands** box to the position on the toolbar where you want it to appear. To add a control that runs a **Function** procedure, follow the same steps as in the procedure for adding a built-in control to a toolbar. In the **Categories** box, click any category and drag any item you want to the position on the toolbar where you want it to appear. Right-click the control, and then click **Control Properties** to open the **Control Properties** dialog box. In the **Caption** box, delete the current name, and then type the new name for your control. In the **On Action** box, type an expression to run your Visual Basic **Function** procedure. The expression must use the following syntax: =*functionname*().

Microsoft Excel   Follow the same steps as in the procedure for adding a built-in control to a toolbar; in the **Categories** box, click **Macros**, and then drag the **Custom Button** control from the **Commands** box to the position on the toolbar where you want the control to appear. Right-click the new control, and then click **Assign Macro**. In the **Assign Macro** dialog box, select the macro you want to run. Use the commands on the shortcut menu to change the image of the control.

Microsoft Word   Follow the same steps as in the procedure for adding a built-in control to a toolbar; in the **Categories** box, click **Macros**, and then drag a macro from the **Commands** box to the position on the toolbar where you want the control to appear. Use the commands on the shortcut menu for the new control to change the control's name, image, and other display properties.

Tip   In Word, if you write a procedure whose name is the same as that of a built-in Word control (or if you write a procedure named "MAIN" in a module whose name is the same as that of a built-in Word command), that procedure will replace the built-in functionality of the control whenever the module that contains it is available in the current context. Every copy of the control on whatever toolbar it appears will run the replacement procedure. For more information about controlling the context of your customizations, see "Scope of Changes to the User Interface" earlier in this chapter. For more information about modifying Word commands, see Chapter 7, "Microsoft Word Objects."

Microsoft PowerPoint   Follow the same steps as in the procedure for adding a built-in control to a toolbar; in the **Categories** box, click **Macros**, and then drag a macro from the **Commands** box to the position on the toolbar where you want it to appear. Use the commands on the shortcut menu for the new control to change the control's name, image, and other display properties.

Modifying the Appearance of a Toolbar Button

The face of a button on a toolbar can be either the button image alone, the button name alone, or the button image displayed next to the name. Whether a button appears with just an image, just a name, or both is determined by its "style." You set a button's style using commands on the shortcut menu while the **Customize** dialog box is open. The following table describes the effect of each style on toolbar buttons.

Style	What appears on a toolbar button
Default Style	Button image only
Text Only (In Menus)	Button image only
Text Only (Always)	Name only
Image And Text	Button image and name

While the **Customize** dialog box is open, you can add or modify the image on a toolbar button. The following table describes the techniques you can use.

To	Do this
Use a predefined image	Right-click the button, point to **Change Button Image**, and then click the image you want.
Copy and paste another button's image	Right-click the button that has the image you want to use, and then click **Copy Button Image**. Right-click the button whose image you're customizing, and then click **Paste Button Image**.
Copy and paste an image from a graphics program	Open the image you want to copy in a graphics program. Select and copy the image (preferably a 16 x 16 pixel image or portion). Switch back to your application. Right-click the button, and then click **Paste Button Image**.
Edit the button's current image	Right-click the button, and then click **Edit Button Image**. In the **Button Editor** dialog box, you can change the color and shape of the image, adjust the image's position on the button, and preview your changes to the image. When you finish editing the image, click **OK**.
Reset a button to use its original image	Right-click the button, and then click **Reset Button Image**.

Tip In Microsoft Access, you can use the **Properties** dialog box to set many other properties of menu commands. For more information, see Chapter 1 in *Building Applications with Microsoft Access 97*.

Grouping Controls

You can separate groups of related controls on a toolbar, using lines. The lines themselves aren't controls; rather, you can set each control on a toolbar to appear with a line before it. Use the **Customize** dialog box to set a command to appear as the first control in a group of controls.

▶ **To begin a group of buttons on a toolbar**

1 If the **Customize** dialog box isn't already open, point to **Toolbars** on the **View** menu, and then click **Customize**.

2 If the toolbar that contains the control you want to modify isn't visible, select the check box next to the name of that toolbar in the **Toolbar** box on the **Toolbars** tab.

3 Right-click the control you want to appear with a line before it, and then click **Begin Group**.

The next time you right-click that control, a check mark will be displayed next to **Begin Group** on the shortcut menu. To remove the line before a control, right-click the control and then click **Begin Group** again (the check mark will no longer appear).

Using Visual Basic

Use the **Add** method of the **CommandBarControls** collection to add a new control to the **CommandBar** object that represents a particular toolbar. To add a built-in control, you specify the ID number of the control by using the *Id* argument of the **Add** method. The following example adds the **Spelling** control to the toolbar named "Quick Tools."

```
Set mySpell = CommandBars("Quick Tools").Controls.Add(Id:=2)
```

For information about determining the built-in command ID numbers of an Office application, see "Menu Item and Toolbar Control IDs" later in this chapter.

To add a custom control, you add a new control and then set the **OnAction** property to specify a Visual Basic procedure to run whenever that control is clicked. Setting the *Type* argument of the **Add** method to **msoControlButton** indicates that a control is a button. Set the **FaceId** value of the control to the ID of a built-in control whose face you want to copy. The following Microsoft Excel example adds a button before the **Save** button on the **Standard** toolbar. Microsoft Excel runs the OpenDatabaseProc Visual Basic procedure whenever the user clicks the menu item. The example also sets the image on the button to a grid (ID 987).

```
Set databaseItem = CommandBars("Standard").Controls. _
    Add(Type:=msoControlButton, Before:=3)
With databaseItem
    .OnAction:="OpenDatabaseProc"
    .FaceId = 987
End With
```

There are many properties of the objects that represent toolbar buttons that you can set in Visual Basic to modify the appearance of a control. For more information, see "Style Property" and "FaceID Property" in Help, as well as the Help topics for other properties and methods of the **CommandBarButton** object.

To set a control to begin a group of controls (that is, to be preceded by a line), just set the **BeginGroup** property of the **CommandBarButton**, **CommandBarPopup**, or **CommandBarComboBox** object that represents that control to **True**. To remove the line, set the **BeginGroup** property of the appropriate object to **False**. Use **Controls**(*index*), where *index* is the caption or index number of a control, to return an object that represents the control.

Adding and Initializing Text Box, List Box, and Combo Box Controls

You can add built-in text box, list box, and combo box controls by using the **Customize** dialog box. Use the same steps that were given earlier in this section for adding built-in controls.

To add and initialize the contents of custom text box, list box, and combo box controls, you must use Visual Basic. You use the **Add** method of the **CommandBarControls** collection to add a text box, list box, or combo box; the *Type* argument indicates the kind of control you're adding, as shown in the following table.

To add this control	Specify this type
Text box	**msoControlEdit**
List box	**msoControlDropDown**
Combo box	**msoControlComboBox**

You can use the **Style** property of the text box, list box, or combo box to indicate whether the caption of the control should appear to the left of the box itself.

The following example adds a combo box with the label "Quarter" to a custom toolbar and assigns the macro named "ScrollToQuarter" to the combo box.

```
Set newCombo = CommandBars("Custom1").Controls _
    .Add(Type:=msoControlComboBox)
With newCombo
    .AddItem "Q1"
    .AddItem "Q2"
    .AddItem "Q3"
    .AddItem "Q4"
    .Style = msoComboNormal
    .OnAction = "ScrollToQuarter"
End With
```

While your Visual Basic application is running, the procedure assigned to the **OnAction** property of the combo box control is called each time the user changes the control. In the procedure, you can use the **ActionControl** property of the **CommandBars** object to find out which control was changed and to return the changed value. The **ListIndex** property will return the item that was entered in the combo box.

Deleting Toolbar Controls

Deleting built-in toolbar controls can help you tailor your Visual Basic application to the needs of the user. For example, you may want to delete a built-in control from a toolbar and replace it with a custom version of that command, which will perform specialized tasks for the user. Or you may want to remove certain controls to simplify the interface or reduce the possibility that inexperienced users will choose commands you didn't intend for them to use.

Note You can restore built-in toolbars or toolbar controls that you've deleted. However, you cannot restore custom toolbars or toolbar controls that you've deleted; you must re-create them.

Using the Customize Dialog Box

With the **Customize** dialog box open, you can delete any toolbar control.

▶ **To delete a toolbar control**

1 If the **Customize** dialog box isn't already open, point to **Toolbars** on the **View** menu, and then click **Customize**.

2 If the toolbar that contains the toolbar control you want to delete isn't visible, select the check box next to the name of that toolbar in the **Toolbars** box on the **Toolbars** tab.

3 Right-click the control you want to delete, and then click **Delete** on the shortcut menu.

To delete an entire custom toolbar, open the **Customize** dialog box, click the name of that toolbar in the **Toolbars** box on the **Toolbars** tab, and then click the **Delete** button. You cannot delete built-in toolbars.

Using Visual Basic

Use the **Delete** method to delete a custom toolbar or a custom or built-in toolbar control. You cannot delete a built-in toolbar.

The following Microsoft Excel example deletes the **Print** control from the **Standard** toolbar.

```
CommandBars("Standard").Controls("Print").Delete
```

The following example deletes the custom toolbar named "Custom Bar."

```
CommandBars("Custom Bar").Delete
```

You can restore built-in toolbar controls that you've deleted. For more information, see the following section.

Restoring Built-in Toolbar Controls

You can restore built-in toolbar controls that you've deleted. However, you cannot restore custom toolbars or toolbar controls that you've deleted; you must re-create them.

Using the Customize Dialog Box

You can use the **Customize** dialog box to restore a built-in toolbar to its built-in set of controls.

▶ To restore a built-in toolbar

1 If the **Customize** dialog box isn't already open, point to **Toolbars** on the **View** menu, and then click **Customize**.

2 On the **Toolbars** tab, select the built-in toolbar you want to restore.

3 Click **Restore**.

Using Visual Basic

Use the **Reset** method to reset the components of a built-in toolbar.

The following Microsoft Excel example resets the **Standard** toolbar to its default set of controls.

```
CommandBars("Standard").Reset
```

Run-Time Modifications to Toolbars

You can program the toolbars you create at design time to respond dynamically to changing conditions at run time. If a particular control is an inappropriate choice in certain contexts, you can remove it or disable it to prevent the user from clicking it. If a control represents an option with two possible states, you can make the control appear pushed down to show that the option is turned on or appear flat to show that it's turned off.

Note that although you can make design-time changes to toolbars by using either the **Customize** dialog box or Visual Basic, you must use Visual Basic to make any run-time changes.

Displaying or Hiding Toolbars and Toolbar Controls

A toolbar takes up screen space that could otherwise be used to display data; you can display a toolbar when necessary and hide it when the user no longer needs it. A toolbar is visible if its **Visible** property is **True**, and it's not visible if this property is **False**. Setting this property to **True** corresponds to selecting the check box next to the name of that toolbar on the **Toolbars** tab in the **Customize** dialog box and then clicking **OK**.

The following Microsoft Excel procedure, which is assigned to the View MyToolbar menu item on the **View** menu, switches the state of the menu item and the **Visible** property of the toolbar every time the user clicks the menu item. When the toolbar is made visible, it reappears in the same position it occupied when it was made invisible.

```
Sub ViewMyAppToolbar()
   With CommandBars("Worksheet Menu Bar").Controls("View").Controls("View MyToolbar")
      If .State = msoButtonUp Then
         .State = msoButtonDown
         CommandBars("MyAppTools").Visible = True
      Else
         .State = msoButtonUp
         CommandBars("MyAppTools").Visible = False
      End If
   End With
End Sub
```

When a toolbar is visible, the user can click any control on it to run that control's assigned procedure.

If you want a specific toolbar control to appear only when certain conditions exist, you can hide or show the toolbar control at run time. By setting the **Visible** property to **True** or **False**, you can effectively add a control to or remove a control from the user's workspace without actually deleting the control.

Note Because Word stores customizations in documents and templates, custom toolbars and toolbar controls are visible when the document or template is available in the current context, and they're hidden when the document or template isn't available. In contrast, because Microsoft Excel stores customizations at the workspace level, you need to use the **Visible** property in event code to dynamically change the interface.

Moving and Resizing Toolbars

You may want to adjust the prominence of a toolbar on the screen in response to changing conditions while your application is running. You can do this by changing the size or position of the toolbar. Toolbars support several properties you can use to resize them; to dock them at the top, bottom, left edge, or right edge of the application window; or to position them elsewhere on the screen (if they're are *floating* toolbars). For more information about the properties and methods you can use with **CommandBar** objects that represent toolbars, see "CommandBar Object" in Help, and use the jumps at the top of the topic to display the lists of properties and methods.

Restoring a Built-in Toolbar

If one of the default toolbars has been modified—either by a user or by a Visual Basic procedure—you can return the toolbar to its default state by using the **Reset** method. Using this method corresponds to selecting the name of the customized built-in toolbar on the **Toolbars** tab in the **Customize** dialog box and then clicking **Reset**.

The following example resets all the toolbars to their default state and simultaneously deletes all the custom toolbars.

```
For Each cb In CommandBars
   If cb.BuiltIn Then
      cb.Reset
   Else
      cb.Delete
   End If
Next
```

Caution   Be careful when you use the **Reset** method; it not only restores any built-in toolbar controls that have been deleted, but it also deletes any custom toolbar controls that have been added. Keep in mind that another macro may have added custom toolbar controls to the toolbar, and resetting the toolbar will remove these controls as well. To avoid these problems, remove any toolbar controls added by your application one by one, without resetting the entire toolbar.

Enabling or Disabling Toolbar Controls

You may want to control the availability of a toolbar control while your application is running, to prevent the user from clicking the button at inappropriate times. To do this, you can dynamically enable and disable the toolbar control. When a toolbar control is disabled, it beeps when it's clicked and doesn't run the procedure associated with it. Use the **Enabled** property to set or return the state (enabled or disabled) of a toolbar control.

The following example disables button three on the **Standard** toolbar.

```
CommandBars("Standard").Controls(3).Enabled = False
```

Indicating the State of Toolbar Buttons

If a toolbar button represents an option with two possible states, you can change the appearance of the button to indicate the current state of the option: When the option is turned on, the associated button appears pushed down; when the option is turned off, the button appears flat.

The **State** property for a toolbar button is **msoButtonDown** if the button appears pushed down; this property is **msoButtonUp** if the button appears flat. The following procedure, which is assigned to the new toolbar control **Database View**, changes the appearance of the control before switching between special views on the worksheet.

```
Sub DatabaseView()
   With CommandBars("MyAppToolbar").Controls(3)
      If .State = msoButtonDown Then
         .State = msoButtonUp
         'Switch to database view
      Else
         .State = msoButtonDown
         'Switch to worksheet view
      End If
   End With
End Sub
```

Modifying Text Box, List Box, and Combo Box Controls

If you add custom text box, list box, or combo box controls to a toolbar, you can make run-time changes such as changing the current value of the text box portion of the control and adding or removing items from the list portion of the control (for list boxes and combo boxes only).

You can set the **Text** property of a text box, list box, or combo box control to reflect a change in the state of your Visual Basic application. For example, if the user clicks a toolbar button that runs a procedure named "MaxZoom" (a custom procedure that displays the active document at maximum zoom), the text box portion of a combo box control that's used to adjust the zoom more precisely and display a percentage value can be set to the maximum zoom percentage.

You can use the **AddItem** and **RemoveItem** methods to add and remove items (by index number) from the list portion of a list box or combo box control. For example, if you created a list box control in Word that tracks the styles the user applies during a session, you can add the name of a style to the list portion of the control each time the user applies a style.

Note Be careful when you add or remove an item in a list box or combo box control; this causes the index numbers of all the items to shift.

You can use other properties and methods of list box and combo box controls to change the appearance of a control at run time. For example, you can add and adjust a header list for the control (a header list is the group of list items at the top of the list portion of a control that are separated from the rest of the list items by a line.) For more information about using text box, list box, and combo box controls, see "Using command bars" in Help.

Menu Item and Toolbar Control IDs

Each Office application contains a unique set of menu bars and toolbars and a unique set of available menu items and toolbar controls. (Note that only a subset of the available menu items and toolbar controls actually appears on an application's built-in menu bars and toolbars.) Each application stores its menu bars and toolbars in a unique way. For information about how menu bars and toolbars are stored, see "Scope of Changes to the User Interface" earlier in this chapter.

Whereas the functionality associated with each built-in menu item and toolbar control belongs to a specific Office application, the caption, button image, width, and other default properties of each menu item and toolbar control are stored in one resource shared by all the applications. You can use ID numbers to find specific menu items and toolbar controls in this resource.

Note This resource also contains the default properties of the pop-up controls that display built-in menus. However, those pop-up controls don't contain the built-in menu items on those menus; that is, the pop-up controls are empty.

Although you can usually ignore the ID of a menu item or control and instead use the **Customize** dialog box to make changes to a built-in or custom menu or toolbar, you may need to refer to the ID of an item to make certain kinds of changes to your custom interface. The following are some of the situations in which you'll need to refer to an item's ID:

- You want to assign an item to a built-in or custom menu or toolbar when that item isn't available anywhere in the **Customize** dialog box at design time.

- You want to add a built-in item to a menu or toolbar at run time.

- You want to copy a particular button's image to another button at run time.

You can assign the ID of a built-in item to the *Id* argument of the **Add** method for the **CommandBarControls** collection, and you can assign the ID of a an item to the **FaceId** property of any custom or built-in control.

Note Even though the shared resource contains information about every menu item and toolbar control in all the Office applications, you can only add items and controls whose functionality is contained in the application you're working in. For example, you cannot add the Microsoft Excel **Delete Rows** toolbar button (ID 293) to a toolbar in Word. You can, however, copy the face of the **Delete Rows** toolbar button from Microsoft Excel to a toolbar control in Word.

To determine the IDs of the built-in menu items and toolbar controls in a specific Office application, you can do any of the following:

- In a module, write code to assign a menu item or toolbar control that already appears on a menu or toolbar to an object variable, and then use debugging tools to inspect the value of the **Id** property of that object. Using that ID, you can add a copy of the item or control to another menu or toolbar by using the **Add** method, or you can copy the image to another button by assigning the ID to another button's **FaceId** property.

- Run the following procedure in one of the Office applications to create a text document that lists the IDs and captions of all the built-in commands in that application.

```
Sub outputIDs()
Const maxId = 4000
Open "c:\ids.txt" For Output As #1
' Create a temporary command bar with every
' available item and control assigned to it.
Set cbr = CommandBars.Add("Temporary", msoBarTop, False, True)
For i = 1 To maxId
    On Error Resume Next
    cbr.Controls.Add Id:=i
Next
On Error GoTo 0
' Write the ID and caption of each control to the output file.
For Each btn In cbr.Controls
    Write #1, btn.Id, btn.Caption
Next
' Delete the command bar and close the output file.
cbr.Delete
Close #1
End Sub
```

- Run the following procedure in one of the Office applications to create a set of custom toolbars that contain as many buttons as there are valid **FaceId** property values in Office; each button's image and ToolTip text is set to one of those values. You can cross-reference the ID of a built-in command (see the preceding procedure) to the **FaceId** property value of a button on one of these toolbars, and vice versa.

```
Sub MakeAllFaceIds()
'Make fourteen toolbars with 300 faces each.
'Note that maxId is greater than last valid ID, so
'error will occur when first invalid ID is used.
Const maxId = 3900
On Error GoTo realMax
For bars = 0 To 13
    firstId = bars * 300
    lastId = firstId + 299
    Set tb = CommandBars.Add
    For i = firstId To lastId
        Set btn = tb.Controls.Add
```

```
            btn.FaceId = i
            btn.TooltipText = "FaceId = " & i
        Next
        tb.Name = ("Faces " & CStr(firstId) & " to " _
            & CStr(lastId))
        tb.Width = 591
        tb.Visible = True
    Next
'Delete the button that caused the error and set toolbar name
realMax:
btn.Delete
tb.Name = ("Faces " & CStr(firstId) & " to " _
    & CStr(i - 1))
tb.Width = 591
tb.Visible = True
End Sub
```

Note   The IDs of the pop-up controls for built-in menus are in the range 30002 to 30426.
Remember that these IDs return empty copies of the built-in menus.

CHAPTER 9

Microsoft Office Assistant

Microsoft Office 97 uses the Office Assistant to provide a single source for online Help. The Office Assistant can offer tips on the task you're performing, answer questions specific to the Office application you're using, and deliver messages from the application. You can use the Office Assistant in your own Visual Basic application to deliver information, guide the user through a task, and even run your procedures in response to the user's selecting a control in the Office Assistant balloon. You control the Office Assistant, the balloon, and all of the items inside the balloon by using the Assistant portion of the Microsoft Office object model.

Note The Office Assistant isn't available in Microsoft Access 97 applications you build using the run-time version of Microsoft Access.

Contents

- Using the Microsoft Office Assistant
- Using the Microsoft Office Assistant Balloon

Using the Microsoft Office Assistant

In an Office application, the user chooses which Assistant he or she wants to see and then specifies the circumstances under which the Assistant is to be displayed. In a Visual Basic application, you can make the Assistant visible, animate it, move its window to a different location on the screen, and display balloons that contain various kinds of information and controls.

Note You cannot record the Assistant's animation or balloon actions, and you cannot record options selected in the **Office Assistant** dialog box.

The first step in implementing the Assistant in your Visual Basic application is to determine how involved your user wants the Assistant to be in delivering information. On the **Options** tab in the **Office Assistant** dialog box, the user sets his or her preferences for the placement of the Assistant, the type of Help topics that the Assistant is to offer, and the Assistant's response to the F1 key.

You can use properties of the **Assistant** object to determine the choices the user has made regarding the Assistant. Each of the user's preferences corresponds to a property of the **Assistant** object. For example, the **AssistWithHelp** property returns **True** if the user has selected the **Respond to F1 key** option on the **Options** tab in the **Office Assistant** dialog box.

If the user's preferences indicate that he or she wants the Assistant's help, you can program your application to make full use of the Assistant by displaying text or prompts inside a balloon that would otherwise be displayed in a message box or input box, and you can make the Assistant available to offer tips that are automatically sent from the application.

There are 34 different animations available for the Assistant. You can program the Assistant to respond to a particular circumstance with a particular animation by assigning one of the **MsoAnimationType** constants to the **Animation** property of the **Assistant** object. Depending on the Assistant the user has chosen, setting the **Animation** property may or may not result in any obvious animation. However, the **MsoAnimationType** constants are valid for all Assistants.

Note You can assign one of the **msoAminationType** constants to the **Balloon** object as well. If you do this, the Assistant will perform the specified animation when the balloon is displayed. For more information, see "Using the Microsoft Office Assistant Balloon" later in this chapter.

The following example has the Assistant display a message if the **Display alerts** option is selected on the **Options** tab in the **Office Assistant** dialog box, or displays a standard message box if this option isn't selected. The Assistant is animated when it displays the message, and after the user closes the balloon, the **Visible** property of the Assistant is set to the value it had before the example ran.

```
hdng = "Empty field"
msg = "You need to enter a part number " _
        & "before you can proceed."
If Assistant.AssistWithAlerts = True Then
    With Assistant
    userState = .Visible
    .Visible = True
    Set bln = .NewBalloon
    With bln
        .Mode = msoModeModal
        .Button = msoButtonSetOK
        .Heading = hdng
        .Text = msg
        .Animation = msoAnimationGetAttentionMinor
        ret = .Show
    End With
    .Visible = userState
    End With
```

```
Else
    ret = MsgBox(msg, vbOKOnly, hdng)
End If
```

Using the Microsoft Office Assistant Balloon

The **Balloon** object is the most important part of the Office Assistant object model. You use balloons to deliver messages to your user or to request information from the user that you can use in your Visual Basic application. There are several types of balloons, each of which can contain labels and check boxes, as well as certain types of graphics. Only one balloon can be visible at a time, but you can create multiple **Balloon** objects and store them in variables for use at any time, and you can reuse any **Balloon** object by resetting its properties.

Creating Balloons

To create a balloon, you use the **NewBalloon** property of the **Assistant** object. The balloon that's returned by the property is blank. Use the **Mode** property to specify how you want the balloon to respond to the user's actions. To add a heading to the balloon, you use the **Heading** property, and to add text to the body of the balloon, you use the **Text** property. You can also add controls or graphics if you want. Finally, you use the **Show** method to display the balloon you've designed. The **Show** method displays the balloon as it exists (that is, as you've designed it) at that point in time; therefore, it's important to use the **Show** method after you've set or changed any balloon properties.

There are several types of balloons you can display; the type of balloon a **Balloon** object represents is determined by the **Mode** property, which you can set to one of the following **MsoModeType** constants: **msoModeModal**, **msoModeAutoDown**, or **msoModeModeless**.

A modal balloon (**msoModeModal**) demands the user's complete attention because keyboard or mouse activity is restricted to the balloon while the balloon is displayed. A modal balloon is best used for alerts or critical messages. The following example uses a modal balloon to prompt the user to confirm whether the active file should be closed without changes being saved. You can use the value of the button that's clicked (which is assigned to ret) to determine whether or not the event should continue. You can use this example as part of an event procedure that runs whenever a file is closed, or you can use it in a series of balloons leading the user through a process.

```
Set bln = Assistant.NewBalloon
With bln
    .Mode = msoBalloonModal
    .Heading = "Warning"
    .Text = "If you close this file without saving it, " _
        & "this macro cannot proceed. Close without saving?"
    .Button = msoButtonSetOkCancel
    ret = .Show
End With
```

An AutoDown balloon (**msoModeAutoDown**) is dismissed when the user clicks or types anywhere in the application. This type of balloon is best used for quick messages that aren't critical to the task at hand. The following example displays a tip for using a custom dialog box (the code can run in an event procedure for a dialog box control). Because the balloon is an AutoDown balloon, the message disappears as soon as the user clicks anywhere in the dialog box.

```
hdng = "Selecting a data source"
msg = "In this dialog box, you can specify a workbook " _
        & "or an external table of data to use for input. " _
        & "If you use external data, it must contain delimited " _
        & "fields, rather than fixed-length fields."
With Assistant
    Set bln = .NewBalloon
    With bln
        .Mode = msoModeAutoDown
        .Button = msoButtonSetOK
        .Heading = hdng
        .Text = msg
        ret = .Show
    End With
End With
```

While a modeless balloon (**msoModeModeless**) is displayed, the user can complete a task in the application; that is, the user can type in the document and use menu and toolbar commands. You can use a modeless balloon to display procedures or tips for using your Visual Basic application, for the benefit of the user.

When the user clicks a control or button in a modeless balloon, a *callback procedure* is called. Your Visual Basic application must contain a procedure (whose name is assigned to the **Callback** property) that responds to the action the user takes. For example, if the user clicks the **OK** button, he or she wants to dismiss the modeless balloon; the callback procedure should respond accordingly by applying the **Close** method to the balloon. The following example displays a series of steps for the user to follow while the balloon remains displayed. The callback procedure closes the balloon when the user clicks **OK**.

```
Sub DisplaySteps()
Set bln = Assistant.NewBalloon
With bln
    .Mode = msoModeModeless
    .Callback = "StepsCallback"
```

```
        .BalloonType = msoBalloonTypeNumbers
        .Button = msoButtonSetOK
        .Heading = "To create a new report"
        .Labels(1).Text = "On the File menu, click New Report."
        .Labels(2).Text = "In the New Report dialog box, select the period " _
            & "(monthly, quarterly, or yearly)."
        .Labels(3).Text = "Click the Create button."
        ret = .Show
    End With
End Sub

Sub StepsCallback(bln As Balloon, btn As Long, priv As Long)
    bln.Close
End Sub
```

For more information about the **Callback** property and callback procedures, see
"Using Callback Procedures" later in this chapter.

Managing Multiple Balloons

There isn't a collection of **Balloon** objects. Instead, you can create an array to store
more than one balloon variable. You can create and store empty balloons, or you can
create and store balloons complete with heading, text, and controls. The following
example creates an array and adds three **Balloon** objects, with numbered headings, to
the array.

```
Dim myBlnArray(3) as Balloon

With Assistant
    For i = 1 To 3
        Set myBlnArray(i) = .NewBalloon
        myBlnArray(i).Heading = i
    Next
End With
```

The following example displays the second balloon in the array.

```
myBlnArray(2).Show
```

Alternatively, you can set a separate object variable for each balloon you create; this
way, you can reference the variable at any time. If you declare balloon variables
globally, you can call them from any procedure in your program.

Adding Text and Controls to Balloons

Every balloon can contain a heading and text. By default, a balloon contains an **OK**
button at the bottom, but it can also contain any of a variety of button combinations,
or no buttons at all (although showing no buttons requires a modeless balloon with
button labels; for information about button labels, see "Adding and Modifying
Labels" later in this section).

To provide emphasis or greater detail, you can add an icon to the heading, and you can add bitmaps, Windows metafiles, or Macintosh pict files anywhere text can appear in the balloon. Also, every balloon can contain as many as five numbered, bulleted, or button labels, and as many as five check boxes; you can use these elements to deliver or return detailed information from the user.

Setting the Heading and Text

The most basic elements of a balloon are the heading and the simple text that appear at the top of the balloon. Both the heading and text are optional; you can display a balloon that contains neither one. You set the heading and text by using the **Heading** and **Text** properties. You specify which buttons to display at the bottom of the balloon by setting the **Button** property to one of the **MsoButtonSetType** constants. The following example displays a simple message in a modal balloon.

```
Set bln = Assistant.NewBalloon
With bln
    .Mode = msoModeModal
    .Button = msoButtonSetYesNo
    .Heading = "Empty file"
    .Text = "The file you specified does not contain any data. Quit now?"
    ret = .Show
End With
```

The **Show** method returns a value that indicates which button was clicked to close the balloon. You can use the return value to make a decision about what action to take next. In the preceding example, if the **Show** method set the value of ret to **msoBalloonButtonYes**, the example can proceed to quit the running macro as the user requested.

Adding Icons and Bitmaps

To get the user's attention, you can add icons and bitmaps to Office Assistant balloons. Icons are displayed at the top of the balloon, to the left of the heading text, whereas bitmaps can be displayed anywhere in the balloon. To add an icon, assign one of the **msoIconType** constants to the **Icon** property of the **Balloon** object. The following example displays a simple alert balloon.

```
Set bln = Assistant.NewBalloon
With bln
    .Mode = msoModeModal
    .Heading = "Attention Please"
    .Text = "That command is not available now."
    .Icon = msoIconAlert
    .Show
End With
```

To add a Windows or Macintosh bitmap to a balloon, specify the type (.bmp) and the path of the bitmap. You can insert a bitmap can be inserted the balloon text, the balloon heading, or a label. You can also include braces around text if you format the text as shown in the following example. This example inserts a Windows bitmap file into the text of a balloon; this will produce a balloon error if Circles.bmp doesn't exist in the specified folder. For information about handling balloon errors, see "BalloonError Property" in Help.

```
myBmp = "{bmp c:\Windows\circles.bmp}"
myText1 = "This text is before the picture, "
myText2 = " and this text is after the picture."
myText3 = " {{This is text in braces.}"
Set bln = Assistant.NewBalloon
With bln
    .Mode = msoModeAutoDown
    .Heading = "Displaying a Bitmap."
    .Text = myText1 & myBmp & myText2 & myText3
    .Show
End With
```

You can specify a graphic you want displayed by using the following syntax: {*type location sizing_factor*}. In this syntax, *type* indicates the type of graphic that will be added to the balloon, *location* should be the complete path and can be a network location (*server\folder\picture.bmp*) or a local hard drive (C:*folder\picture.bmp*), and *sizing_factor* represents the width (in characters) of the Windows metafile or the Macintosh picture (it has no effect on a .bmp file). If proportional fonts are being used, *sizing_factor* represents the average character width. You can use *sizing_factor* to reduce a large graphic to fit your balloon, or to enlarge a small graphic to enhance the image. The following example reduces the displayed size of the Windows metafile Clouds.wmf to a 20-character width and inserts it as the heading in a balloon.

```
Set myBln = Assistant.NewBalloon
myWmf = "{wmf c:\graphics\clouds.wmf 20}"
With myBln
    .Mode = msoModeAutoDown
    .Heading = myWmf
    .Text = "Balloon with .wmf in heading"
    .Show
End With
```

Adding and Modifying Labels

There are three types of labels you can add to a balloon: numbered labels, bulleted labels, and button labels. You can add as many as five labels to a given balloon, but they must all be of the same type; you cannot mix numbers, bullets, and buttons in the same balloon. To indicate which type of labels you want, you set the **BalloonType** property of a balloon to one of the following **MsoBalloonType** constants: **msoBalloonTypeNumbers**, **msoBalloonTypeBullets**, or **msoBalloonTypeButtons**. To return a **BalloonLabel** object that represents one of the numbered, bulleted, or button labels, you use **Labels**(*index*), where *index* is a number from 1 through 5. You set the **Text** property of the **BalloonLabel** object to specify the label's text.

Note   If you try to reference a label greater than 5, an error occurs.

You can use numbered labels and bulleted labels to present related information in a meaningful way. That is, rather than creating a complex string to assign the **Text** property of a balloon, you can assign simple strings to the **Text** property of as many as five numbers or bullets. The following example displays a modal balloon with a list of troubleshooting suggestions for a macro.

```
Set bln = Assistant.NewBalloon
With bln
    .Mode = msoBalloonModal
    .Button = msoButtonSetOK
    .BalloonType = msoBalloonTypeBullets
    .Heading = "Tips for locating output"
    .Text = "If you cannot locate the output log, consider the following:"
    .Labels(1).Text = "Check the current folder name in the Save dialog box."
    .Labels(2).Text = "Make sure you type the file name correctly."
    .Labels(3).Text = "If you saw the Empty File message, no log was created."
    ret = .Show
End With
```

You use button labels to let the user make choose from a list of two or more possible actions. Using the return value of the **Show** property (in a modal or AutoDown balloon) or the second argument passed to the callback procedure (in a modeless balloon), you can determine which button label was clicked and take the appropriate action.

The following example displays a list of three button labels. The variable x is set to the return value of the **Show** method, which will be 1, 2 or 3, depending on which button the user clicks (there's no **OK** button). In the example, a simple message box displays the value of the variable x, but you can pass the value to another procedure, or you can use the value in a **Select Case** statement.

```
Set b = Assistant.NewBalloon
With b
    .Mode = msoModeModal
    .Button = msoButtonSetNone
    .Heading = "Balloon heading"
    .Text = "Select one of these things:"
    .Labels(1).Text = "Choice One"
    .Labels(2).Text = "Choice Two"
    .Labels(3).Text = "Choice Three"
    x = .Show
End With
MsgBox x
```

The following example prompts the user to select either a network printer or a local printer before a document is printed. The user can work in the application (because the balloon is a modeless balloon) but is reminded that printing cannot occur until a printer is selected. The ProcessPrinter procedure would determine which button label was clicked, run the appropriate statements, and then close the balloon.

```
Set bln = Assistant.NewBalloon
With bln
    .Mode = msoModeModeless
    .Button = msoButtonSetNone
    .Heading = "Select A Printer"
    .Text = "You must select a printer before printing."
    .Icon = msoIconAlert
    .Labels(1).Text = "Local printer"
    .Labels(2).Text = "Network printer"
    .Callback = "ProcessPrinter"
    ret = .Show
End With
```

For more information about the **Callback** property of a modeless balloon, see "Using Callback Procedures" later in this section.

Adding and Modifying Check Boxes

You use check boxes to let the user select one or more items in a list. By default, each balloon contains five check boxes when it's created; however, you must set the **Text** property for each check box you want to be visible. To return a **BalloonCheckbox** object that represents one of the check boxes, you use **Checkboxes**(*index*), where *index* is a number from 1 through 5.

Note   If you try to reference a check box by using a number greater than 5, an error occurs.

If you display a balloon that contains check boxes, the user can select one or more of the check boxes before clicking a button. You can then use the value of each check box (indicated by the **Checked** property) to control subsequent statements or branching structures in your code. The following example displays a balloon in which the user can select one, two, or three check boxes, or none. A second balloon confirms which check boxes were selected.

```
Set a = Assistant.NewBalloon
Set b = Assistant.NewBalloon
With a
    .Mode = msoModeModal
    .Button = msoButtonSetOkCancel
    .Heading = "Print Regional Sales Data"
    .Text = "Select the region(s) you want to print."
    For i = 1 To 3
        .CheckBoxes(i).Text = "Region " & i
    Next
End With
retA = a.Show
If retA = msoBalloonButtonOK Then
    s = ""
    For i = 1 To 3
        If a.CheckBoxes(i).Checked = True Then
            If s = "" Then
                s = CStr(i)
            Else
                s = s & ", " & CStr(i)
            End If
        End If
    Next
    With b
        .Mode = msoModeModal
        .Heading = "Print Regional Sales Data"
        If s <> "" Then
            .Button = msoButtonSetYesNo
            .Text = "Please confirm that you want to print " & _
                "data for the following region(s): " & s
        Else
            .Button = msoButtonSetOK
            .Text = "You did not select any regions to print."
        End If
        retB = .Show
    End With
End If
```

Using Callback Procedures

If you create a modeless balloon, you must assign to the **Callback** property the name
of a callback procedure. A callback procedure must be written to receive three
arguments: the first argument is a **Balloon** object that represents the balloon that
called the procedure; the second argument is a number that indicates the index number
or constant of the button label or button that was clicked; and the third argument is a
number that's used by wizards to control the Assistant (unless you're developing a
custom wizard, you can ignore the third argument). The following example shows a
valid declaration for a callback procedure. Note that you can use any argument names
you prefer in your declarations.

```
Sub MyCallback(bln As Balloon, btn As Long, priv As Long)
```

Note   You must assign the **Callback** property a string that indicates the correct scope of the callback procedure in relation to the code you're writing, just as if you were writing a statement to call the procedure directly. For example, if you're writing code in a module and the callback procedure is in a Microsoft Excel worksheet (Sheet1) in the same project, you would set the **Callback** property to "Sheet1.MyCallback."

The following example displays a balloon that contains the names of three printers. The callback procedure runs the appropriate printer-specific code and then closes the balloon.

```
Sub TestCallback()
Set bln = Assistant.NewBalloon
With bln
    .Mode = msoModeModeless
    .Callback = "ProcessPrinter"
    .Button = msoButtonSetNone
    .BalloonType = msoBalloonTypeButtons
    .Heading = "Select a Printer"
    .Labels(1).Text = "Network Printer"
    .Labels(2).Text = "Local Printer"
    .Labels(3).Text = "Local Color Printer"
    .Show
End With
End Sub

Sub ProcessPrinter(bln As Balloon, ibtn As Long, _
        iPriv As Long)
    Assistant.Animation = msoAnimationPrinting
    Select Case ibtn
    Case 1
        ' Insert printer-specific code
    Case 2
        ' Insert printer-specific code
    Case 3
        ' Insert printer-specific code
    End Select
    bln.Close
End Sub
```

CHAPTER 10

Shapes and the Drawing Layer

Visual Basic provides a common object model that represents the drawing layer in Microsoft Excel 97, Word 97, and PowerPoint 97. The top-level object in this object model is the **Shapes** collection, which contains all the graphic objects—such as AutoShapes, freeforms, OLE objects, and pictures—that you can add to the drawing layer. (Note that shapes you insert into the text layer in Word aren't included in the **Shapes** collection.)

This chapter covers the principal objects, properties, and methods used to create and modify objects in the drawing layer in Microsoft Excel, Word, and PowerPoint. For information about application-specific enhancements to the drawing layer object model in PowerPoint, see Chapter 6, "Microsoft PowerPoint Objects." For information about ActiveX controls (a special type of shape), see Chapter 12, "ActiveX Controls and Dialog Boxes."

Contents

- Understanding the Shape, ShapeRange, and Shapes Objects
- Drawing a Shape on a Document, Worksheet, or Slide
- Editing a Shape
- Working with OLE Objects on a Document, Worksheet, or Slide
- Working with More Than One Shape

Understanding the Shape, ShapeRange, and Shapes Objects

There are three different objects that represent shapes: the **Shapes** collection, which represents all the shapes in the drawing layer of a Microsoft Excel, Word, or PowerPoint document; the **ShapeRange** collection, which represents a subset of the shapes in the drawing layer; and the **Shape** object, which represents an individual shape. In general, you use the **Shapes** collection when you want to add shapes to the drawing layer or iterate through all the shapes in the drawing layer; you use the **Shape** object when you want to format or manipulate a single shape; and you use the **ShapeRange** collection when you want to format or manipulate multiple shapes the same way you work with multiple selected shapes in the user interface.

Note A **ShapeRange** collection can have as few as one member or as many members as there are shapes in the drawing layer. A **ShapeRange** collection that contains a single member is essentially equivalent to a **Shape** object. You can use a **ShapeRange** collection that contains all the members in the **Shapes** collection to format all the shapes in the drawing layer at at the same time. Properties and methods that apply to the **Shape** object also apply to the **ShapeRange** collection . For information about how these properties and methods behave when they're applied to a **ShapeRange** collection that contains a single shape or to a **ShapeRange** collection that contains multiple shapes, see "Working with More Than One Shape" later in this chapter.

Returning the Shapes Collection

To return the entire collection of shapes in the drawing layer, use the **Shapes** property. The following example selects all the shapes in the drawing layer of myDocument.

```
myDocument.Shapes.SelectAll
```

Returning the Shape Object

Use **Shapes**(*index*), where *index* is the shape's name or the index number, to return a **Shape** object that represents a shape on a slide. The following example duplicates the third shape on myDocument and places it on the Clipboard.

```
myDocument.Shapes(3).Duplicate
```

The following example duplicates the shape named "Red Square" on myDocument.

```
myDocument.Shapes("Red Square").Duplicate
```

Each shape is assigned a default name (for example, "Rectangle 3") when you add it to the **Shapes** collection. To give the shape a more useful, meaningful name, use the **Name** property. The following example adds a rectangle to myDocument and gives the rectangle the name "Red Square."

```
myDocument.Shapes.AddShape(msoShapeRectangle, 144, 144, 72, 72).Name = "Red Square"
```

Tip The methods that add a shape to the drawing layer also return a reference to the added shape, so you can add a shape and apply a property or method to it in a single statement, as shown in the preceding example. For more information, see "Drawing a Shape on a Document, Worksheet, or Slide" later in this chapter.

Returning the ShapeRange Collection

Use **Shapes.Range**(*index*), where *index* is either the shape's name or index number or an array of shape names or shape index numbers (or both), to return a **ShapeRange** collection that represents a subset of the **Shapes** collection. The following example sets the fill for shapes one and three on myDocument.

```
myDocument.Shapes.Range(Array(1, 3)).Fill.PresetGradient _
    msoGradientHorizontal, 1, msoGradientLateSunset
```

Use **Selection.ShapeRange** to return a **ShapeRange** collection that represents all the shapes in the selection. Use **Selection.ShapeRange**(*index*), where *index* is the shape's name or index number, to return a **Shape** object that represents one of the shapes in the selection. The following example sets the fill for the first shape in the selection.

```
ActiveWindow.Selection.ShapeRange(1).Fill.PresetGradient _
    msoGradientHorizontal, 1, msoGradientLateSunset
```

Note   The macro recorder generates selection-based code—that is, when you work with a shape with the macro recorder turned on, it records a step for selecting the shape, records a step for accessing the **ShapeRange** collection in the selection, and then records the properties and methods you apply to the shape. When you write code from scratch or edit recorded code, you can create more efficient code by skipping the selection step and returning shapes directly from the **Shapes** collection.

Drawing a Shape on a Document, Worksheet, or Slide

Use one of the methods of the **Shapes** collection, listed in the following table, to add a shape to a document, worksheet, or slide. For detailed syntax information, see the Help topic for the specific method.

To add this kind of graphic	Use this method
Callout	**AddCallout**
Sticky-note-like comment (PowerPoint only)	**AddComment**
Line or curve that connects two other shapes (Microsoft Excel and PowerPoint)	**AddConnector**
Bézier curve	**AddCurve**
Native Microsoft Excel form control (Microsoft Excel only)	**AddFormControl**
Rectangle with no line and no fill and an attached text frame	**AddLabel**
Line	**AddLine**
Sound or movie (PowerPoint only)	**AddMediaObject**

To add this kind of graphic	Use this method
ActiveX control (Word only; use **AddOLEObject** in Microsoft Excel and PowerPoint)	**AddOLEControl**
Embedded or linked OLE object	**AddOLEObject**
Picture	**AddPicture**
Placeholder for text or for a graphic object (PowerPoint only)	**AddPlaceholder**
Open polyline or closed polygon drawing	**AddPolyline**
AutoShape	**AddShape**
Rectangle with no line and no fill and an attached text frame	**AddTextbox**
WordArt	**AddTextEffect**
Slide title (PowerPoint only)	**AddTitle**
Freeform	**BuildFreeform** and **ConvertToShape**

The following example adds a rectangle to my Document.

```
myDocument.Shapes.AddShape msoShapeRectangle, 50, 50, 100, 200
```

When you add a shape, you usually specify the dimensions of the shape and the position of the upper-left corner of the bounding box for the shape relative to the upper-left corner of the page, worksheet, or slide. Distances in the drawing layer are measured in points (72 points = 1 inch).

The methods that add shapes to the drawing layer return a reference to each added shape. You can therefore add a shape and apply properties and methods to it in a single step, as shown in the following example, which adds a shape to my Document and sets its name it the same statement.

```
myDocument.Shapes.AddShape(msoShapeIsoscelesTriangle, 10, 10, 100, 100).Name = "shpOne"
```

The following example adds a shape to my Document and formats its fill.

```
With myDocument.Shapes.AddShape(msoShapeRectangle, 90, 90, 90, 50).Fill
    .ForeColor.RGB = RGB(128, 0, 0)
    .BackColor.RGB = RGB(170, 170, 170)
    .TwoColorGradient msoGradientHorizontal, 1
End With
```

Editing a Shape

You can use properties and methods of the **Shape** and **ShapeRange** objects to move, resize, or delete a shape; change its appearance; or add text to it.

Finding the Properties and Methods You Need to Perform a Task

Properties and methods that control attributes and behavior common to all types of shapes apply directly to the **Shape** and **ShapeRange** objects. Related properties and methods that apply to specific types of shapes are encapsulated in secondary objects that you return from the **Shape** object.

Common Properties and Methods

Properties and methods that control and attributes and behavior common to shapes of different types apply directly to the **Shape** and **ShapeRange** objects. This group includes properties that control the size and position of the shape (such as **Left**, **Top**, **Height**, and **Width**) and methods that control generic editing behavior (such as **Duplicate** and **ZOrder**). The following example sets the size of shape one on myDocument.

```
With myDocument.Shapes(1)
    .Height = 50
    .Width = 100
End With
```

Properties and Methods for Specific Types of Shapes

Related shape attributes that apply to a specific type of shape are grouped under secondary objects, such as the **FillFormat** object, which contains the properties that apply to shapes with fills, or the **CalloutFormat** object, which contains all the properties that are unique to callouts. To set these kinds of attributes for a shape, you must first return the object that contains them and then set properties of that object. For example, you use the **Fill** property to return the **FillFormat** object, and then you set the **ForeColor** property of the **FillFormat** object to set the fill foreground color for the specified shape. The following example sets the foreground color to red for the fill for shape one on myDocument.

```
myDocument.Shapes(1).Fill.ForeColor.RGB = RGB(255, 0, 0)
```

The following table shows the objects accessible from the **Shape** object that contain functionally related properties and methods. Note that some of the properties that return these secondary objects have the same name as the returned object (for example, the **PictureFormat** property returns the **PictureFormat** object) whereas other properties have the name of the returned object minus the word "Format" (for example, the **Fill** property returns the **FillFormat** object).

Use this property of the Shape object	To return this object	Which contains properties and methods that apply to
Callout	**CalloutFormat**	Callouts
ConnectorFormat (Microsoft Excel and PowerPoint only)	**ConnectorFormat**	Connectors
ControlFormat (Microsoft Excel only)	**ControlFormat**	Native form controls
Fill	**FillFormat**	Shapes that can contain fills (all shapes except lines)
Line	**LineFormat**	All shapes (the **LineFormat** object can represent a line or a shape's border)
LinkFormat	**LinkFormat**	Linked OLE objects, linked pictures (Word only), and linked fields (Word only)
OLEFormat	**OLEFormat**	OLE objects
PictureFormat	**PictureFormat**	Pictures and OLE objects
Shadow	**ShadowFormat**	All shapes
TextEffect	**TextEffectFormat**	WordArt objects
ThreeD	**ThreeDFormat**	Shapes that can be extruded
WrapFormat (Word only)	**WrapFormat**	Shapes that text will wrap around

Trying to return certain secondary objects (such as the **CalloutFormat**, **ConnectorFormat**, **OLEFormat**, **PictureFormat**, or **TextEffectFormat** object) from an inappropriate type of shape can cause an error. For example, if you apply the **OLEFormat** property to a shape that isn't an OLE object, you'll get an error. (Trying to return certain other secondary objects—such as the **FillFormat**, **LineFormat**, **ShadowFormat**, or **ThreeDFormat** object—from an inappropriate type of shape doesn't cause an error.)

To avoid problems, check the **Type** property and, when applicable, the **AutoShapeType** property of a shape before applying a property or method that applies only to certain types of objects, and be sure to include error handling in your code. The following example updates all linked OLE objects on myDocument. Note that you cannot change the type of an existing object; for example, you cannot change an object that's not a picture into a picture.

```
For Each sh In myDocument.Shapes
    If sh.Type = msoLinkedOLEObject Then
        sh.LinkFormat.Update
    End If
Next
```

For information about error handling, see Chapter 14, "Debugging and Error Handling."

Working with the Shape's Fill

The **FillFormat** object represents a shape's fill. You use properties and methods of the **FillFormat** object to set the type, color, and transparency of the fill. Because there are a number of factors that determine a fill's appearance, many individually valid property settings for the **FillFormat** object don't make any sense in combination with other properties or without additional information being supplied. For example, the value **msoPatternDarkVertical** for the **Pattern** property doesn't make much sense in conjunction with the value **msoGradientDiagonalUp** for the **GradientStyle** property, and the value **msoFillPicture** for the **Type** property doesn't make sense if you haven't specified a picture file to use.

So that you don't inadvertently assign incompatible values to individual properties of the **FillFormat** object or neglect to supply a necessary piece of information when you assign a property value, most of the properties are read-only. You can set their values only by using methods that set multiple individual properties to compatible values at the same time. For example, you could not write code that would leave you with the two incompatible settings mentioned in the preceding paragraph, because using the **Patterned** method to set a patterned fill automatically sets the **GradientStyle** property to **msoGradientMixed**, and using the **OneColorGradient**, **PresetGradient**, or **TwoColorGradient** method to set a gradient fill automatically sets the value of the **Pattern** property to **msoPatternMixed**.

Use one of the following methods to set a shape's fill type: **Background** (PowerPoint only), **OneColorGradient**, **Patterned**, **PresetGradient**, **PresetTextured**, **Solid**, **TwoColorGradient**, **UserPicture**, or **UserTextured**. You can also use any of the following read/write properties to control the fill's appearance: **BackColor**, **ForeColor**, **Transparency**, or **Visible**.

The following example adds a rectangle to myDocument and then sets the foreground color, background color, and gradient for the rectangle's fill.

```
With myDocument.Shapes.AddShape(msoShapeRectangle, 90, 90, 90, 50).Fill
    .ForeColor.RGB = RGB(128, 0, 0)
    .BackColor.RGB = RGB(170, 170, 170)
    .TwoColorGradient msoGradientHorizontal, 1
End With
```

Adding Shadows and 3-D Effects

Use the **Shadow** property of the **Shape** object to return the **ShadowFormat** object, and use the properties and methods of the **ShadowFormat** object to edit a shape's shadow. The following example sets the shadow for shape three on myDocument to semitransparent red. If the shape doesn't already have a shadow, this example adds one to it.

```
With myDocument.Shapes(3).Shadow
    .Visible = True
    .ForeColor.RGB = RGB(255, 0, 0)
    .Transparency = 0.5
End With
```

Use the **ThreeD** property of the **Shape** object to return the **ThreeDFormat** object, and use the properties and methods of the **ThreeDFormat** object to edit a shape's extrusion. The following example adds an oval to myDocument and then specifies that the oval be extruded to a depth of 50 points and that the extrusion be purple, orthographic, and lit from the left.

```
Set myShape = myDocument.Shapes.AddShape(msoShapeOval, 90, 90, 90, 40)
With myShape.ThreeD
    .Visible = True
    .Depth = 50
    .ExtrusionColor.RGB = RGB(255, 100, 255)    ' RGB value for purple
    .Perspective = False
    .PresetLightingDirection = msoLightingLeft
End With
```

You cannot apply three-dimensional formatting to certain kinds of shapes. Most of the properties and methods of the **ThreeDFormat** object for such a shape will fail.

Note If you don't see the shadow or extrusion you expect, make sure that the **Visible** property of the **ShadowFormat** or **ThreeDFormat** object is set to **True**.

Adding Text to a Shape

The area within a shape that can contain text is called a *text frame*. The **TextFrame** object of a given shape contains the text in the text frame as well as the properties and methods that control the alignment and anchoring of the text frame.

Note Only built-in, two-dimensional AutoShapes have text frames; lines, connectors, freeforms, pictures, OLE objects, and media objects don't. Before applying the **TextFrame** property to a shape, check to see whether the shape has a text frame. In PowerPoint, you can do this by checking the value of the **HasTextFrame** property. In Microsoft Excel and Word, check the **Type** property of the shape to see whether it's a type of shape that can contain text. You should always include error handling in case the **TextFrame** property gets applied to a shape that doesn't have a text frame.

In Word, use the **TextRange** property of the **TextFrame** object to return a **Range** object that represents the range of text inside the specified text frame. The following example adds text to the text frame for shape one in the active document.

```
ActiveDocument.Shapes(1).TextFrame.TextRange.Text = "My Text"
```

In Microsoft Excel, use the **Characters** property of the a **TextFrame** object to return a **Characters** object that represents the text inside the specified text frame. The following example adds text to the text frame for shape one on the active worksheet.

```
ActiveWorksheet.Shapes(1).TextFrame.Characters.Text = "My Text"
```

In PowerPoint, use the **TextRange** property of the **TextFrame** object to return a **TextRange** object that represents the range of text inside the specified text frame. The following example adds text to the text frame for shape one on slide one in the active presentation.

```
ActivePresentation.Slides(1).Shapes(1).TextFrame.TextRange.Text = "My Text"
```

Working with OLE Objects on a Document, Worksheet, or Slide

You use the properties and methods of the **OLEFormat** object—such as the **Activate** and **DoVerb** methods—to control the OLE object contained in a shape. Use the **OLEFormat** property of the **Shape** object to return the **OLEFormat** object. The following example performs the default verb for shape three on myDocument if this shape contains an OLE object.

```
With myDocument.Shapes(3)
    If .Type = msoEmbeddedOLEObject Or _
            .Type = msoLinkedOLEObject Then
        .OLEFormat.DoVerb
    End If
End With
```

Use the **Object** property of the **OLEFormat** object to return the OLE object contained in the specified shape. (In Microsoft Excel, you must use the **Object** property twice in a row, separated by the dot operator, to return the OLE object.) The following example, run from Word or PowerPoint, adds text to cell A1 on worksheet one in the Microsoft Excel workbook contained in shape three on myDocument.

```
With myDocument.Shapes(3)
    .OLEFormat.Activate
    .OLEFormat.Object.Worksheets(1).Range("A1").Value = "New text"
End With
```

Use the **Application** property of the OLE object returned by the **Object** property to return the top-level object of the application that created the OLE object. The following example, run from Microsoft Excel, displays the name of the application in which each embedded OLE object on the active sheet was created. Notice that you must use the **Object** property twice in a row to return an OLE object in Microsoft Excel.

```
For Each s In ActiveSheet.Shapes
    If s.Type = msoEmbeddedOLEObject Then
        s.OLEFormat.Activate
        MsgBox s.OLEFormat.Object.Object.Application.Name
    End If
Next
```

For information about using ActiveX controls (a special type of interactive OLE object), see Chapter 12, "ActiveX Controls and Dialog Boxes."

Working with More Than One Shape

There are several ways to work with multiple shapes. If you want to set properties for multiple shapes individually, you can loop through a **Shapes** or **ShapeRange** collection and apply properties and methods to the individual **Shape** objects in the collection. If you want to apply a property or method to multiple shapes at the same time, you can construct a **ShapeRange** collection that contains the shapes and then apply the property or method to the **ShapeRange** collection. If you want to form a single shape out of multiple shapes that can then be formatted, sized, and positioned as a single entity, you can group the shapes. If you want to position shapes relative to each other, you can align and distribute them horizontally or vertically.

Constructing a Shape Range That Contains Only Certain Types of Shapes

If you want to construct a shape range that contains only the shapes in the specified collection that possess a certain attribute or attributes, use a conditional statement to test for the attributes you want, and add the names or index numbers of the shapes that satisfy your conditions to a dynamic array. You can then construct a shape range by using this array as an argument. The following example constructs a shape range that contains all the AutoShapes on myDocument and then groups them.

```
With myDocument.Shapes
    numShapes = .Count
    If numShapes > 1 Then
        numAutoShapes = 0
        ReDim autoShpArray(1 To numShapes)
        For i = 1 To numShapes
            If .Item(i).Type = msoAutoShape Then
                numAutoShapes = numAutoShapes + 1
                autoShpArray(numAutoShapes) = .Item(i).Name
            End If
        Next
        If numAutoShapes > 1 Then
            ReDim Preserve autoShpArray(1 To numAutoShapes)
            Set asRange = .Range(autoShpArray)
            asRange.Group
        End If
    End If
End With
```

Tip If you want to include shapes that have one of several possible values for a property in an array—for example, if you want to include all shapes that are of type **msoEmbeddedOLEObject**, **msoLinkedOLEObject**, **msoLinkedPicture**, or **msoPicture**—use a **Select Case** structure instead of an **If...End If** structure to determine which shapes to include in the shape range.

Applying a Property or Method to Several Shapes at the Same Time

In the user interface, there are some operations you can perform with several shapes selected; for example, you can select several shapes and set all their individual fills at once. There are other operations you can only perform with a single shape selected; for example, you can only edit the text in a shape if a single shape is selected.

In Visual Basic, there are two ways to apply properties and methods to a set of shapes. These two ways allow you to perform any operation that you can perform on a single shape on a range of shapes, whether or not you can perform the same operation in the user interface.

- If the operation works on a multiple selected shapes in the user interface, you can perform the same operation in Visual Basic by constructing a **ShapeRange** collection that contains the shapes you want to work with, and applying the appropriate properties and methods directly to the **ShapeRange** collection.

- If the operation doesn't work on multiple selected shapes in the user interface, you can still perform the operation in Visual Basic by looping through the **Shapes** collection or through a **ShapeRange** collection that contains the shapes you want to work with, and applying the appropriate properties and methods to the individual **Shape** objects in the collection.

Important Many properties and methods that apply to the **Shape** object and the **ShapeRange** collection fail if they're applied to certain kinds of shapes. For example, the **TextFrame** property fails if it's applied to a shape that cannot contain text. If you're not positive that each of the shapes in a **ShapeRange** collection can have a certain property or method applied to it, don't apply the property or method to the collection. If you want to apply one of these properties or methods to a collection of shapes, you must loop through the collection and test each individual shape to make sure that it's an appropriate type of shape before applying one of these properties or methods to it.

Applying a Property or Method to a ShapeRange Collection

If you can perform an operation on multiple selected shapes in the user interface at the same time, you can do the programmatic equivalent by constructing a **ShapeRange** collection and then applying the appropriate properties or methods to it. The following example constructs a shape range that contains the AutoShapes named "Big Star" and "Little Star" on myDocument and applies a gradient fill to them.

```
Set myRange = myDocument.Shapes.Range(Array("Big Star", "Little Star"))
myRange.Fill.PresetGradient msoGradientHorizontal, 1, msoGradientBrass
```

The following are general guidelines for how properties and methods behave when they're applied to a **ShapeRange** collection:

- Applying a method to a the collection is equivalent to applying the method to each individual **Shape** object in that collection.

- Setting the value of a property of the collection is equivalent to setting the value of the property of each individual shape in that collection.

- A property of the collection that returns a constant returns the value of the property for an individual shape in the collection if all shapes in the collection have the same value for that property. If not all shapes in the collection have the same value for the property, it returns the "mixed" constant.

- A property of the collection that returns a simple data type (such as **Long**, **Single**, or **String**) returns the value of the property for an individual shape if all shapes in the collection have the same value for that property.

- The value of some properties can be returned or set only if there's exactly one shape in the collection. If there's more than one shape in the collection, a run-time error occurs. This is generally the case for returning or setting properties when the equivalent action in the user interface is possible only with a single shape (actions such as editing text in a shape or editing the points of a freeform).

The preceding guidelines also apply when you are setting properties of shapes that are grouped under secondary objects of the **ShapeRange** collection, such as the **FillFormat** object. If the secondary object represents operations that can be performed on multiple selected objects in the user interface, you will be able to return the object from a **ShapeRange** collection and set its properties. For example, you can use the **Fill** property to return the **FillFormat** object that represents the fills of all the shapes in the **ShapeRange** collection. Setting the properties of this **FillFormat** object will set the same properties for all the individual shapes in the **ShapeRange** collection.

Looping Through a Shapes or ShapeRange Collection

Even if you cannot perform an operation on several shapes in the user interface at the same time by selecting them and then applying a command, you can perform the equivalent action programmatically by looping through the **Shapes** or **ShapeRange** collection that contains the shapes you want to work with and applying the appropriate properties and methods to the individual **Shape** objects in the collection. The following example loops through all the shapes on myDocument and adds text to each shape that's an AutoShape.

```
For Each sh In myDocument.Shapes
    If sh.Type = msoAutoShape Then
            sh.TextFrame.TextRange.InsertAfter " (version 1)"
    End If
Next
```

Grouping, Aligning, Distributing, and Layering Shapes

Use the **Align** and **Distribute** methods of the **ShapeRange** object to align or evenly distribute shapes horizontally or vertically. Use the **ZOrder** method of the **Shape** or **ShapeRange** object to change the layering order of shapes on a document relative to one another. For examples of the syntax you use to perform these operations, see the appropriate Help topics in Microsoft Excel, Word, or PowerPoint.

When you want to work with multiple shapes as a single entity, you can group a range of shapes together into single shape by using the **Group** method of the **ShapeRange** collection. The following example adds two shapes to myDocument, groups the two new shapes together, sets the fill for the group, rotates the group, and then sends it to the back of the drawing layer.

```
With myDocument.Shapes
    .AddShape(msoShapeCan, 50, 10, 100, 200).Name = "shpOne"
    .AddShape(msoShapeCube, 150, 250, 100, 200).Name = "shpTwo"
    With .Range(Array("shpOne", "shpTwo")).Group
        .Fill.PresetTextured msoTextureBlueTissuePaper
        .Rotation = 45
        .ZOrder msoSendToBack
    End With
End With
```

Use the **Ungroup** method of the **Shape** object to ungroup a group of shapes, and use the **Regroup** method of the **ShapeRange** collection to restore a group of shapes that you've ungrouped.

If you want to work with the individual shapes in a group without ungrouping them, use the **GroupItems** property of the **Shape** object that represents the group of shapes to return the **GroupShapes** object, and use the **Item** method of the **GroupShapes** object to return an individual shape within the group of shapes. The following example adds three triangles to myDocument, groups the triangles, sets a color for the entire group, and then changes the color for the second triangle only.

```
With myDocument.Shapes
    .AddShape(msoShapeIsoscelesTriangle, 10, 10, 100, 100).Name = "shpOne"
    .AddShape(msoShapeIsoscelesTriangle, 150, 10, 100, 100).Name = "shpTwo"
    .AddShape(msoShapeIsoscelesTriangle, 300, 10, 100, 100).Name = "shpThree"
    With .Range(Array("shpOne", "shpTwo", "shpThree")).Group
        .Fill.PresetTextured msoTextureBlueTissuePaper
        .GroupItems(2).Fill.PresetTextured msoTextureGreenMarble
    End With
End With
```

CHAPTER 11

Data Access Objects

Microsoft Data Access Objects (DAO) provide a way to control a database from any application that supports Visual Basic for Applications, including Microsoft Access, Microsoft Excel, and Microsoft Visual Basic. Some DAO objects represent the structure of your database, while others represent the data itself. By using DAO, you can create and manage local or remote databases in a variety of formats, and work with their data. This chapter explains how to program with DAO objects from within Microsoft Office applications.

Contents

- Working with DAO Objects
- Using DAO with Microsoft Jet
- Accessing ODBC Data
- Using DAO with ODBCDirect
- Using ODBCDirect

Working with DAO Objects

Microsoft DAO objects provide a way to interact with a database from any application that includes Visual Basic for Applications. DAO objects represent different parts of a database. You can use DAO objects to work with the parts of your database from code. With DAO objects, you can:

- Create a database or change the design of its tables, queries, indexes, and relationships.
- Retrieve, add, delete, or change the data in the database.
- Implement security to protect your data.

- Work with data in different file formats and link tables in other databases to your database.

- Connect to databases on remote servers and build client/server applications.

Note In order to use DAO objects, you must select the **Data Access** check box when you install Microsoft Office. If you haven't installed Data Access with Microsoft Office, run Setup again.

DAO objects are organized in a hierarchical relationship. Objects contain collections, and collections contain other objects. The **DBEngine** object is the top-level object that contains all the other objects and collections in the DAO object hierarchy. The following table summarizes the DAO objects.

Object	Description
Connection	Network connection to an Open Database Connectivity (ODBC) database
Container	Security information for various types of objects in the database
Database	Open database
DBEngine	The top-level object in the DAO object hierarchy
Document	Security information for individual objects in the database
Error	Data access error information
Field	Field in a **TableDef**, **QueryDef**, **Recordset**, **Index**, or **Relation** object
Group	Group account in the current workgroup
Index	Table index
Parameter	Query parameter
Property	Property of an object
QueryDef	Saved query definition in a database
Recordset	Set of records defined by a table or query
Relation	Relationship between two table or query fields
TableDef	Saved table definition in a database
User	User account in the current workgroup
Workspace	Active DAO session

Designing Databases in Microsoft Access

You can design databases in Visual Basic with DAO. However, if you're programming in an application other than Microsoft Access, you may find it faster to design your database in the Microsoft Access user interface, then write DAO code for any additional functionality that you want. With Microsoft Access, you can quickly and easily design tables, queries, indexes, and relationships; link tables from external data sources; and implement security. You can then open the database with DAO from another application that hosts Visual Basic.

There are a few things to keep in mind when you create a database in Microsoft Access:

- When you open an .mdb file created in Microsoft Access from another application, you can't work with Microsoft Access forms, reports, macros, or modules. You should design forms and reports and write all Visual Basic code from the application in which you're working.

- If you write code to work with your database within Microsoft Access, that code will not necessarily run if you copy it to a module in another application, such as Microsoft Excel. You may need to modify the code and remove any Microsoft Access-specific objects, methods, properties, or functions.

- In Microsoft Access, you use the **CurrentDb** function to return a reference to the database that's currently open in the Microsoft Access window. You can then use DAO to work with the current database. If you use this code in an application other than Microsoft Access, you'll need to change code that calls the **CurrentDb** function so that it calls the **OpenDatabase** method of a **Workspace** object instead.

- Microsoft Access creates additional properties for DAO objects. When you create a database with DAO in Visual Basic, then open it in Microsoft Access, you may notice that some new properties are defined for some of your DAO objects. For example, a **Field** object in the **Fields** collection of a **TableDef** object may have a **Description** property, which is created by Microsoft Access. You can see these properties when you enumerate through the **Properties** collection for a DAO object.

Setting a Reference to the Microsoft DAO Object Library

To work with DAO objects from within any application, you must have a reference to the Microsoft DAO 3.5 object library. Microsoft Access sets this reference automatically. You may need to set it yourself if you're working within another Microsoft Office application.

To set a reference to the Microsoft DAO 3.5 object library from a Microsoft Office application other than Microsoft Access, open the Visual Basic Editor, click **References** on the **Tools** menu, and then select the **Microsoft DAO 3.5 Object Library** check box. Once you've set a reference to the DAO object library, you can view the DAO objects in the Object Browser by clicking **DAO** in the **Project/Library** box.

Some objects, properties, and methods that were supported in earlier versions of Microsoft DAO have been replaced by new objects, properties, and methods with more complete functionality, and are no longer supported by DAO version 3.5. If you're working with an application created in an earlier version of Microsoft DAO, you can set a reference to the Microsoft DAO 2.5/3.5 compatibility library rather than to the Microsoft DAO 3.5 object library. The Microsoft DAO 2.5/3.5 compatibility library contains all of the objects, methods, and properties that are in the Microsoft DAO 3.5 object library, plus some that existed in DAO version 2.5, but that are no longer supported in DAO version 3.5.

Code that uses objects, methods, and properties that were available in DAO version 2.5 but are no longer available in DAO version 3.5 will continue to run when you reference the Microsoft DAO 2.5/3.5 compatibility library. However, it's a good idea to update your code to take advantage of the features of DAO version 3.5, and to write new code that uses the objects, properties, and methods provided by the Microsoft DAO 3.5 object library. The Microsoft DAO 2.5/3.5 compatibility library is larger, so it requires more resources. Also, future versions may not support some objects, methods, and properties which are now available in the compatibility library.

To determine whether you need to use the compatibility library, make sure there is a reference set to the Microsoft DAO 3.5 object library and compile all modules that contain DAO code. If your code compiles without any problems, you can use the Microsoft DAO 3.5 object library. If your DAO code generates compile errors, then you should set a reference to the Microsoft DAO 2.5/3.5 compatibility library and try to compile your code again.

For more information about which DAO features are supported in the DAO 2.5/3.5 compatibility library but not in the Microsoft DAO 3.5 object library, search DAO Help for "Obsolete features in DAO," or search Microsoft Access Help for "DAO, compatibility with previous versions."

Referring to DAO Objects in Visual Basic

You refer to DAO objects in code in the same way that you refer to other objects. Because the **DBEngine** object doesn't have a collection, you can refer to it directly. You must refer to other objects within their collections and according to their positions in the object hierarchy.

You can refer to any type of object within a collection in one of two ways: by its **Name** property setting or by its index number, which indicates its position within the collection. DAO objects are indexed beginning with zero. This means that the first object in a collection has an index number of 0, the second object has an index number of 1, and so on. The following examples, which refer to a **Database** object within the **Databases** collection, illustrate both ways to refer to an object within a collection.

```
Databases("database name")
Databases(0)
```

To refer to a **Database** object in code, you also need to refer to it according to its position within the object hierarchy. The following code fragment shows how you can actually refer to a **Database** object in code. The **Database** object is the first member of the **Databases** collection of the default **Workspace** object, which is a member of the **Workspaces** collection of the **DBEngine** object. Note that if you're working in an application other than Microsoft Access, you must open a database with the **OpenDatabase** method before you run this code.

```
Dim dbs As Database
Set dbs = DBEngine.Workspaces(0).Databases(0)
```

When you work with DAO objects from any application other than Microsoft Access, you may want to qualify the object with the Visual Basic name of the DAO object library, which is **DAO**. By qualifying objects when you use them, you ensure that Visual Basic always creates the correct object. The following example declares a DAO object variable of type **Database**:

```
' Qualify object variable type.
Dim dbs As DAO.Database
```

Adding New DAO Objects to a Collection

As stated earlier in this chapter, some DAO objects represent the structure of the database, and others provide a means for you to work with the data stored in the database. Objects that represent the structure of the database are saved with the database. Objects that you use to work with the data in the database generally are not saved, but are created each time you need them.

When you create a new DAO object to be saved with the database, you must append it to the appropriate collection of saved objects by using that collection's **Append** method. The following example creates a new **TableDef** object named ArchivedInvoices with a new **Field** object named OrderID. It appends the new **Field** object to the **Fields** collection of the new **TableDef** object, and it appends the **TableDef** object to the **TableDefs** collection of the **Database** object that represents the open database.

Note   The following example, and other examples in this chapter, use the Northwind sample database to illustrate concepts of DAO programming. In order to try these examples, you need to have installed the Northwind sample database which is included with Microsoft Access. By default, it is installed in the C:\Program Files\Microsoft Office\Office\Samples folder. If you haven't installed the Northwind sample database, you can install it by running Setup again.

```
Function AddTable() As Boolean

    ' Declare object variables and constant.
    Dim dbs As Database, tdf As TableDef, fld As Field
    Const conPath As String = _
        "C:\Program Files\Microsoft Office\Office\Samples\Northwind.mdb"

    On Error GoTo Err_AddTable
    ' Assign current database to database variable.
    Set dbs = DAO.DBEngine.Workspaces(0).OpenDatabase(conPath)
    ' Create new table and field, and assign to table and field variables.
    Set tdf = dbs.CreateTableDef("ArchivedInvoices")
    Set fld = tdf.CreateField("OrderID", dbLong)

    ' Add field to table's Fields collection.
    tdf.Fields.Append fld
    ' Add table to database's TableDefs collection.
    dbs.TableDefs.Append tdf
    dbs.Close
    AddTable = True

Exit_AddTable:
    Exit Function

Err_AddTable:
    MsgBox "Error " & Err & ": " & Err.Description
    AddTable = False
    Resume Exit_AddTable
End Function
```

Note The preceding example uses the **OpenDatabase** method to open the Northwind sample database, return a reference to it, and assign this reference to an object variable of type **Database**. If you're programming within Microsoft Access, use the **CurrentDb** function to return a reference to the database that's currently open in Microsoft Access.

Working with External Data

You can use DAO to work with databases in different formats. There are three different categories of database formats that are accessible through DAO. The first type of format is the Microsoft Jet format. You can use DAO to work with all databases created with the Microsoft Jet database engine, including those created in Microsoft Access, Microsoft Visual Basic, Microsoft Visual C++®, and Microsoft Excel.

The second type of database format is the installable ISAM format. An installable ISAM is a driver that provides access to external database formats through DAO and the Microsoft Jet database engine. You must use your application's Setup program to install any installable ISAMs that you want to use. Installable ISAMs are loaded by Microsoft Jet when you refer to them in code. The individual database formats for which installable ISAMs are available include:

- Microsoft FoxPro®, versions 2.0, 2.5, 2.6, 3.0 (read-only), and DBC

- dBASE III, dBASE IV, and dBASE version 5.0

- Paradox, versions 3.*x*, 4.*x*, and 5.*x*

- Microsoft Excel version 3.0, 4.0, 5.0, 7.0, and 8.0 worksheets

- Microsoft Exchange/Outlook

- Lotus 1-2-3 WK1, WK3, and WKS spreadsheets

- Delimited and fixed-width text files in tabular format

- Tabular data in Hypertext Markup Language (HTML) files

The third type of database format that is accessible through DAO is the Open Database Connectivity (ODBC) data source. ODBC data sources, such as Microsoft SQL Server™ versions 4.2 and later, require an ODBC driver. Often an ODBC data source resides on a network server. ODBC is useful for developing client/server applications. The next section introduces two ways to work with ODBC data sources through DAO.

Using DAO to Work with ODBC Data Sources

There are two different ways to use DAO to work with ODBC data sources: through Microsoft Jet, or by means of a new technology called *ODBCDirect*. If you're working with a database created with the Microsoft Jet database engine or in an external format supported by an installable ISAM, all DAO operations are processed through Microsoft Jet. If you're working with an ODBC data source, you can either process DAO operations through Microsoft Jet, or you can use ODBCDirect to circumvent the Microsoft Jet engine and work directly with the data in the ODBC data source.

Whether you use DAO with Microsoft Jet or with ODBCDirect to work with an ODBC data source depends on what kind of operations you need to perform on the data source. You can use DAO with Microsoft Jet when you need to take advantage of Microsoft Jet's unique features for ODBC operations, such as the ability to create or modify objects or to join data from different database formats.

You can use ODBCDirect when you need to run queries or stored procedures against a back-end server, such as Microsoft SQL Server, or when your client application needs only the specific capabilities of ODBC, such as batch updates or asynchronous queries. ODBCDirect can also make certain client/server operations significantly faster.

Because not all DAO features are available with ODBCDirect, Microsoft DAO still supports ODBC through the Microsoft Jet database engine. You can use ODBC through Microsoft Jet, ODBCDirect, or both, with a single ODBC data source.

Which of these two methods you can use to access an ODBC data source is determined by what type of workspace you're working in. A *workspace*, represented by a **Workspace** object, is an active session for a particular user account. A *session* marks a sequence of operations performed by the database engine. A session begins when a particular user logs on and ends when that user logs off. The operations that a user can perform during a session are determined by the permissions granted to that user. If you don't specifically create a workspace, then DAO creates a default workspace for you.

With Microsoft DAO version 3.5, you can create either of two types of workspaces for ODBC operations. If you create a *Microsoft Jet workspace*, you can use DAO with Microsoft Jet to access ODBC data. If you create an *ODBCDirect workspace*, you can use DAO to work directly with the data in the ODBC data source, without going through the Microsoft Jet database engine.

Each type of workspace has its own object model. The next section of this chapter discusses the object model for the Microsoft Jet workspace. Later sections discuss the advantages of using each type of workspace and describe the object model for ODBCDirect workspaces.

Using DAO with Microsoft Jet

Microsoft Jet workspaces include objects that you can use to define the structure of your database, such as the **TableDef**, **QueryDef**, **Field**, **Index**, **Parameter**, and **Relation** objects. Microsoft Jet workspaces also include objects that you can use to manipulate your data, such as the **Recordset** object. You can use other objects, such as the **User**, **Group**, **Container**, and **Document** objects, to secure your application. The following diagram shows the object model for Microsoft Jet workspaces.

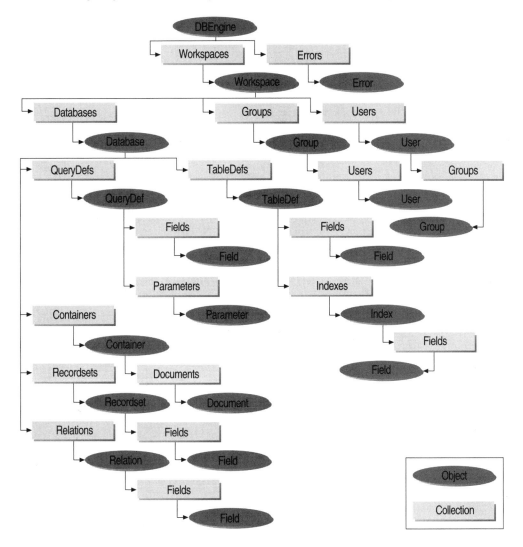

The DBEngine Object

As previously mentioned, the **DBEngine** object is the top-level object in the DAO object hierarchy. It contains all other DAO objects and collections. The **DBEngine** object is the default object in the object model, so in many cases you don't need to refer to it explicitly.

The **DBEngine** object contains two collections: the **Workspaces** collection and the **Errors** collection. The **Workspaces** collection is the default collection of the **DBEngine** object, so you don't need to refer to it explicitly. You can return a reference to the first **Workspace** object in the **Workspaces** collection of the **DBEngine** object in any of the following ways:

```
Set wrk = DBEngine.Workspaces(0)
Set wrk = DBEngine(0)
Set wrk = Workspaces(0)
```

If you don't specifically create a new **Workspace** object, DAO automatically creates a default workspace when you need it. The settings of the **DefaultUser** and **DefaultPassword** properties of the **DBEngine** object specify the default user name and password to be used with the default **Workspace** object. By default, the **DefaultUser** property is set to Admin and the **DefaultPassword** property is set to a zero-length string ("").

The setting for the **DefaultType** property of the **DBEngine** object determines whether the default workspace is a Microsoft Jet workspace or an ODBCDirect workspace. By default, the **DefaultType** property is set to **dbUseJet**, and the default workspace is a Microsoft Jet workspace. When you're creating a workspace, you can override the setting for this property by specifying either **dbUseJet** or **dbUseODBC** as the *type* argument of the **CreateWorkspace** method. For example, if the **DefaultType** property is set to **dbUseJet** and you want to create an ODBCDirect workspace, specify the **dbUseODBC** constant as the *type* argument of the **CreateWorkspace** method. Conversely, if the **DefaultType** property is set to **dbUseODBC** and you want to create a Microsoft Jet workspace, specify the **dbUseJet** constant as the *type* argument of the **CreateWorkspace** method.

You can use some of the methods of the **DBEngine** object to maintain your database. For example, the **CompactDatabase** method copies your database and compacts it. The **RepairDatabase** method attempts to repair a database that's been damaged.

For more information about the **DBEngine** object, search DAO Help for "DBEngine object."

The Workspace Object and the Workspaces Collection

The DAO **Workspace** object defines a session for a user, based on the user's permissions. You use the **Workspace** object to manage the current session. The **Workspace** object contains open databases and provides mechanisms for simultaneous transactions and for securing your application. The **Workspaces** collection contains all active **Workspace** objects of the **DBEngine** object that have been appended to the **Workspaces** collection.

When you begin working with DAO objects in Visual Basic, DAO automatically creates a default workspace. To refer to the default workspace, you can refer to the index number of the first **Workspace** object in the **Workspaces** collection, as shown in the following example:

```
Dim wrk As Workspace
Set wrk = Workspaces(0)
```

DAO workspaces can be shared or hidden. A workspace is hidden until the user marks it as shared by appending the **Workspace** object to the **Workspaces** collection. After a workspace has been appended, you can access it throughout your code simply by referring to it within the **Workspaces** collection. If you need a **Workspace** object only within a particular procedure, you can create the **Workspace** object but not append it to the **Workspaces** collection.

As noted earlier in this chapter, there are two types of **Workspace** objects: Microsoft Jet workspaces and ODBCDirect workspaces. In a Microsoft Jet workspace, you can use DAO with the Microsoft Jet database engine to access data in Microsoft Jet databases, installable ISAM data sources, and ODBC data sources. In an ODBCDirect workspace, you can use DAO to access data in ODBC data sources, without going through the Microsoft Jet database engine. You can work with both Microsoft Jet and ODBCDirect workspaces from within a single application.

For more information about ODBCDirect workspaces, see "Using DAO with ODBCDirect" later in this chapter.

Creating a New Microsoft Jet Workspace

To create a new Microsoft Jet workspace, use the **CreateWorkspace** method of the **DBEngine** object. The following code creates a Microsoft Jet workspace. The constant specified for the *type* argument, **dbUseJet**, specifies that the workspace will be a Microsoft Jet workspace. If the **DefaultType** property of the **DBEngine** object is set to **dbUseJet**, then you don't need to specify a value for the *type* argument; DAO automatically creates a Microsoft Jet workspace.

```
Dim wrk As Workspace
Set wrk = CreateWorkspace("JetWorkspace", "Admin", "", dbUseJet)
```

Newly created **Workspace** objects—those created with the **CreateWorkspace** method—are not automatically appended to the **Workspaces** collection. You can use the **Append** method of the **Workspaces** collection to append a new **Workspace** object if you want it to be part of the collection. However, you can use the **Workspace** object even if it's not part of the collection. Append the new **Workspace** object to the **Workspaces** collection if you want to use the workspace from procedures other than the one in which you created it.

For more information about creating a workspace, search DAO Help for "CreateWorkspace method."

The Error Object and the Errors Collection

The **Error** object contains information about an error that occurred during a DAO operation. More than one error can occur during a single DAO operation; each individual error is represented by a separate **Error** object. The **Errors** collection contains all of the **Error** objects that correspond to a single DAO operation. When a subsequent DAO operation generates an error, the **Errors** collection is cleared, and one or more new **Error** objects are placed in the **Errors** collection. DAO operations that don't generate any errors have no effect on the **Errors** collection.

The first **Error** object in the **Errors** collection represents the lowest level error, the one that occurred closest to the ODBC data source. The second represents the next higher level error, and so forth. For example, if an ODBC error occurs while trying to open a **Recordset** object, the first **Error** object, Errors(0), contains the lowest level ODBC error; other **Error** objects contain the ODBC errors returned by the various layers of ODBC, and the last **Error** object contains the error returned by DAO. In this case, the ODBC driver manager, and possibly the driver itself, return separate **Error** objects. The index number of the last **Error** object in the collection, the DAO error, is one less than the value returned by the **Count** property of the **Errors** collection. The Visual Basic **Err** object contains the same error as the last **Error** object in the DAO **Errors** collection.

The following example tries to insert values into a table that doesn't exist, causing two DAO errors.

Note The following example, and other examples in this chapter, use the Microsoft SQL Server Pubs sample database to illustrate concepts of client/server programming. This database is included with Microsoft SQL Server. If you don't have Microsoft SQL Server, you can adapt the example to your work with your data source, or simply study it to understand the concepts. Before you can work with any ODBC data source, you must register it. For information about registering an ODBC data source, see "Registering an ODBC Data Source" later in this chapter.

```
Private Sub CauseODBCError()
   Dim dbs As Database, errObj As Error

   On Error GoTo Err_CauseODBCError
   Set dbs = OpenDatabase("", 0, 0, "ODBC;UID=sa;PWD=;DATABASE=Pubs;DSN=Publishers")
   dbs.Execute "INSERT INTO SomeTable VALUES (1,2,3)", dbSQLPassThrough
   Exit Sub

Err_CauseODBCError:
   For Each errObj In Errors
      Debug.Print errObj.Number, errObj.Description
   Next
   Resume Next
End Sub
```

The Database Object and the Databases Collection

The **Database** object represents an open database. It can be a Microsoft Jet database or an external data source. The **Databases** collection contains all currently open databases. The following table shows the relationship between the **Database** object and the **Databases** collection and other objects and collections in a Microsoft Jet workspace.

Object or collection	Is contained by	Contains
Database object	**Databases** collection	**Containers** collection
		QueryDefs collection
		Properties collection
		Recordsets collection
		Relations collection
		TableDefs collection
Databases collection	**Workspace** object	**Database** objects

Opening a Database Object

To open a database and return a reference to the **Database** object that represents it in any application other than Microsoft Access, use the **OpenDatabase** method of the **DBEngine** object or of a **Workspace** object. When you use the **OpenDatabase** method of the **DBEngine** object, Microsoft DAO opens the database in the default workspace, as shown in the following example.

```
Function RetrieveRecordset(strDbName As String, strSource As String) As Boolean
    Dim dbs As Database
    Dim rst As Recordset

    On Error GoTo Err_RetrieveRecordset
    Set dbs = OpenDatabase(strDbName)
    Set rst = dbs.OpenRecordset(strSource, dbOpenDynaset)
    ' Perform some operation with recordset.
        .
        .
        .
    RetrieveRecordset = True

Exit_RetrieveRecordset:
    rst.Close
    dbs.Close
    Exit Function

Err_RetrieveRecordset:
    MsgBox "Error " & Err & ": " & Err.Description
    RetrieveRecordset = False
    Resume Exit_RetrieveRecordset
End Function
```

If you're working within Microsoft Access, use the Microsoft Access **CurrentDb** function to return a reference to the database that's currently open. Use the **OpenDatabase** method to open databases other than the one that's currently open, or to open databases in an ODBCDirect workspace. The following example uses the **CurrentDb** function to return a reference to the database that is currently open in Microsoft Access.

```
Dim dbs As Database
Set dbs = CurrentDb
Debug.Print dbs.Name
```

Creating Database Replicas with DAO

If you need to maintain two or more copies of a database, you can replicate the database. When you replicate a database, you designate the database to be the Design Master and create one or more copies of it that are identical in structure and data; the copies are called *replicas*. You can create multiple replicas of a database and maintain them on the same computer or over a network. You can add, change, or delete objects only in the Design Master. You can change data in the Design Master or in any of the replicas. When a user changes data within one replica, the users of other replicas can synchronize their replica, so that the same data is maintained in all replicas.

You can use DAO to make a database replicable, create replicas, synchronize replicas, and manage a set of replicas. You can also use DAO to create partial replicas. *Partial replicas* are replicas that contain only a subset of records in a full replica. By using partial replicas, you can synchronize a replica with only the data that you need, rather than with an entire database. For more information about partial replicas, search Microsoft Access Help for "partial replicas."

To replicate a database with DAO, you must first make the database replicable by setting either the **Replicable** or the **ReplicableBool** property of the **Database** object. These properties don't exist on the **Database** object until you create them and append them to the **Properties** collection. After you've made the database replicable, you can create one or more replicas of it. The following example backs up a database, makes it replicable by setting the **ReplicableBool** property to **True**, and creates a replica by using the DAO **MakeReplica** method.

```
Function ReplicateDatabase(strDBName As String) As Boolean
    Dim dbs As Database, prp As Property
    Dim strBackup As String, strReplica As String
    Const conPropNotFound As Integer = 3270

    On Error GoTo Err_ReplicateDatabase
    If InStr(strDBName, ".mdb") > 0 Then
        strBackup = Left(strDBName, Len(strDBName) - 4)
    Else
        strBackup = strDBName
    End If
```

```
    strReplica = strBackup & "Replica" & ".mdb"
    If MsgBox("Make backup copy of file?", vbOKCancel) = vbOK Then
        strBackup = strBackup & ".bak"
        FileCopy strDBName, strBackup
        MsgBox "Copied file to " & strBackup
    End If

    Set dbs = OpenDatabase(strDBName, True)
    dbs.Properties("ReplicableBool") = True
    dbs.MakeReplica strReplica, "Replica of " & strDBName
    MsgBox "Created replica '" & strReplica & "'."
    dbs.Close
    ReplicateDatabase = True

Exit_ReplicateDatabase:
    Exit Function

Err_ReplicateDatabase:
    If Err = conPropNotFound Then
        Set prp = dbs.CreateProperty("ReplicableBool", dbBoolean, True)
        dbs.Properties.Append prp
        Resume Next
    Else
        MsgBox "Error " & Err & ": " & Err.Description
    End If
    ReplicateDatabase = False
    Resume Exit_ReplicateDatabase
End Function
```

Note   The **Replicable** and **ReplicableBool** properties are functionally identical. The only difference between them is that the **Replicable** property setting is a string, and the **ReplicableBool** property setting is a **Boolean** value.

For more information about database replication and the DAO properties and methods that you can use for replication, search DAO Help for "replication."

The TableDef Object and the TableDefs Collection

A **TableDef** object represents the stored definition of a base table or a linked table in a Microsoft Jet workspace. The **TableDefs** collection contains all stored **TableDef** objects in a database. The following table shows the relationship between the **TableDef** object and the **TableDefs** collection and other objects and collections in a Microsoft Jet workspace.

Object or collection	Is contained by	Contains
TableDef object	**TableDefs** collection	**Fields** collection
		Indexes collection
		Properties collection
TableDefs collection	**Database** object	**TableDef** objects

Creating a Table with Code

To create a table with DAO code, use the **CreateTableDef** method of a **Database** object. After you've created a new **TableDef** object, but before you append it to the database, you must define one or more fields for the table. The following example creates a table that contains some of the error codes and strings used or reserved by Visual Basic in the Northwind sample database.

```
Function CreateErrorsTable() As Boolean
    Dim dbs As Database, tdf As TableDef, fld As Field, idx As Index
    Dim rst As Recordset, intCode As Integer, strErr As String

    Const conAppObjErr = "Application-defined or object-defined error"

    ' Create Errors table with ErrorCode and ErrorString fields.
    Set dbs = CurrentDb

    On Error Resume Next
    ' Delete any existing Errors table.
    dbs.TableDefs.Delete "Errors"

    On Error GoTo Error_CreateErrorsTable
    ' Create table.
    Set tdf = dbs.CreateTableDef("Errors")
    ' Create fields.
    Set fld = tdf.CreateField("ErrorCode", dbInteger)
    tdf.Fields.Append fld
    Set fld = tdf.CreateField("ErrorString", dbMemo)
    tdf.Fields.Append fld
    dbs.TableDefs.Append tdf

    ' Create index.
    Set idx = tdf.CreateIndex("ErrorCodeIndex")
    Set fld = idx.CreateField("ErrorCode")
    With idx
        .Primary = True
        .Unique = True
        .Required = True
    End With
    idx.Fields.Append fld
    tdf.Indexes.Append idx

    ' Open recordset on Errors table.
    Set rst = dbs.OpenRecordset("Errors")
    ' Set recordset's index.
    rst.Index = "ErrorCodeIndex"

    ' Show hourglass pointer.
    DoCmd.Hourglass True

    ' Loop through error codes.
    For intCode = 1 To 32767
        On Error Resume Next
        strErr = ""
```

```
    ' Attempt to raise each error.
    Err.Raise intCode

    ' Check whether error is VBA, DAO, or Access error.
    ' If error is not a VBA error, the Description property
    ' of the Err object contains "Application-defined or object-defined error".
    If Err.Description <> conAppObjErr Then
        strErr = Err.Description

    ' Use AccessError method to return descriptive string for
    ' DAO and Access errors.
    ElseIf AccessError(intCode) <> conAppObjErr Then
        strErr = AccessError(intCode)
    End If

    ' If error number has associated descriptive string, add to table.
    If Len(strErr) > 0 Then
        ' Add new record to recordset.
        rst.AddNew
        ' Add error number to table.
        rst!errorcode = intCode
        ' Add descriptive string to table.
        rst!ErrorString.AppendChunk strErr
        ' Update record.
        rst.Update
    End If
    Next intCode

    DoCmd.Hourglass False
    ' Close recordset.
    rst.Close
    MsgBox "Errors table created."
    ' Show new table in Database window.
    RefreshDatabaseWindow

    CreateErrorsTable = True

Exit_CreateErrorsTable:
    Exit Function

Error_CreateErrorsTable:
    MsgBox Err & ": " & Err.Description
    CreateErrorsTable = False
    Resume Exit_CreateErrorsTable
End Function
```

Linking a Table to a Database

To use tables from an external data source in your database, you can link them to your database. You can link tables that reside in another Microsoft Jet database, or tables from other programs and file formats, such as Microsoft Excel, dBASE, Microsoft FoxPro, Paradox, or previous versions of Microsoft Jet. This is more efficient than opening the external database directly, especially if the table comes from an ODBC data source.

To link a table to your database, use the **CreateTableDef** method to create a new table. Next, specify settings for the **Connect** and **SourceTableName** properties of the **TableDef** object. You can also set the **Attributes** property of the **TableDef** object to specify that the object has certain characteristics. Finally, append the **TableDef** object to the **TableDefs** collection.

For more information about the **Connect**, **SourceTableName**, and **Attributes** properties, search DAO Help for the name of the property.

The following example links a Microsoft Excel version 8.0 worksheet to a database as a table.

Important   Before you run this code, make sure that the Microsoft Excel ISAM driver (Msexcl35.dll) is installed on your system. If it's not, you need to run Setup again to install it. The Microsoft Excel ISAM driver enables Microsoft Excel 97 files to work with the Microsoft Jet database engine. For more information about working with the Microsoft Excel ISAM driver, search Microsoft Access Help for "Microsoft Excel driver."

```
Function LinkExcelTable() As Boolean
    Dim dbs As DAO.Database, tdf As DAO.TableDef

    Const errNoISAM As Integer = 3170
    Const conPath As String = _
       "C:\Program Files\Microsoft Office\Office\Samples\Northwind.mdb"

    On Error GoTo Err_LinkExcelTable
    ' Return a reference to Northwind database.
    Set dbs = OpenDatabase(conPath)
    ' Create new TableDef object.
    Set tdf = dbs.CreateTableDef("LinkedTable")
    ' Specify range that is source table.
    tdf.SourceTableName = "DataRange"
    ' Specify connect string.
    tdf.Connect = "EXCEL 8.0; DATABASE=C:\My Documents\XLTable.xls"
    ' Append new TableDef object.
    dbs.TableDefs.Append tdf
    LinkExcelTable = True

Exit_LinkExcelTable:
    Exit Function

Err_LinkExcelTable:
    If Err = errNoISAM Then
```

```
      Dim strErr As String
      strErr = Err & ": " & Err.Description
      strErr = strErr _
         & " You may not have the ISAM driver installed properly on your computer, " _
         & "or you may have specified the Connect string incorrectly." _
         & " Check the Connect string and the ISAM driver."
      MsgBox strErr, vbOKOnly, "Error!"
   Else
      MsgBox "Error " & Err & ": " & Err.Description
   End If
End Function
```

The Field Object and the Fields Collection

In a Microsoft Jet workspace, the **Field** object represents a field in a table, query, index, relation, or recordset. The **Fields** collection contains all **Field** objects associated with a **TableDef**, **QueryDef**, **Index**, **Relation**, or **Recordset** object. The following table shows the relationship between the **Field** object and the **Fields** collection and other objects and collections in a Microsoft Jet workspace.

Object or collection	Is contained by	Contains
Field object	**Fields** collection	**Properties** collection
Fields collection	**TableDef** object	**Field** objects
	Index object	
	QueryDef object	
	Recordset object	
	Relation object	

The **Fields** collection is the default collection of a **TableDef**, **QueryDef**, **Index**, **Relation**, or **Recordset** object, which means that you don't need to explicitly refer to the **Fields** collection. For example, the following code fragment returns a reference to the LastName field in the Employees table in the Northwind sample database.

```
Dim dbs As Database, tdf As TableDef, fld As Field

Const conPath As String = _
   "C:\Program Files\Microsoft Office\Office\Samples\Northwind.mdb"

Set dbs = OpenDatabase(conPath)
Set tdf = dbs.TableDefs("Employees")
Set fld = tdf!LastName
```

In the **Fields** collection of a **TableDef**, **QueryDef**, **Index**, or **Relation** object, the **Field** object is a structural unit. It represents a column in a table with a particular data type. If you're creating a database in Microsoft Access, you can define fields for any of these objects and set most of their properties in the Microsoft Access user interface, rather than by programming with DAO.

In a **Recordset** object, a **Field** object contains data, and you can use it to read data from a record or write data to a record. You can't work with the fields in a **Recordset** object in the Microsoft Access user interface; you must use DAO.

The **Fields** collection of a **TableDef** object contains all of the fields defined for a particular table. For a **QueryDef** object, the **Fields** collection contains fields that are included in the **QueryDef** object from one or more tables. The **Fields** collection of an **Index** object includes the one or more fields on which the index is defined.

For a **Relation** object, the **Fields** collection contains the fields involved in a relationship. Typically, there are two fields in the **Fields** collection of a **Relation** object. One is the field that is the primary key in the table, specified by the **Table** property of the **Relation** object; the other is the field that is the corresponding foreign key in the table, specified by the **ForeignTable** property of the **Relation** object.

The **Fields** collection of a **Recordset** object contains the fields specified in the *source* argument of the **OpenRecordset** method. The *source* argument specifies the source of the records for the new **Recordset** object and can be a table name, a query name, or an SQL statement that returns records.

The **Value** property of a **Field** object applies only to a **Field** object in the **Fields** collection of a **Recordset** object. The **Value** property returns the value of the data stored in that field for the current record. Because the **Value** property is the default property of a **Field** object, and the **Fields** collection is the default collection of a **Recordset** object, you can return the value of a field without explicitly referring to either the **Fields** collection or the **Value** property. The following code shows three ways you can refer to the **Value** property. It prints the value of the LastName, FirstName, and Title fields for the first record in a table-type **Recordset** object based on the Employees table.

```
Dim dbs As Database, rst As Recordset
Const conPath As String = _
    "C:\Program Files\Microsoft Office\Office\Samples\Northwind.mdb"

Set dbs = OpenDatabase(conPath)
Set rst = dbs.OpenRecordset("Employees")
' Explicitly reference Fields collection and Value property.
Debug.Print rst.Fields("LastName").Value
' Implicitly reference Fields collection, explicitly reference Value property.
Debug.Print rst!FirstName.Value
' Implicitly reference Fields collection and Value property.
Debug.Print rst!Title
```

The Index Object and the Indexes Collection

The **Index** object represents an index on a table in your database in a Microsoft Jet workspace. The **Indexes** collection contains all of the **Index** objects defined for a particular table. The following table shows the relationship between the **Index** object and the **Indexes** collection and other objects and collections in a Microsoft Jet workspace.

Object or collection	Is contained by	Contains
Index object	**Indexes** collection	**Fields** collection
		Properties collection
Indexes collection	**TableDef** object	**Index** objects

An index speeds up searching and sorting on a table. You can improve query performance in your database by indexing fields on both sides of joins, fields that are sorted, or fields that are used to specify criteria for a query. However, indexes add to the size of your database, and they can slow performance when you update data in indexed fields, or when you add or delete data. They can also reduce the efficiency of multiuser applications. If you evaluate your performance needs, you can add or omit indexes appropriately.

An index specifies the order in which records are accessed from database tables in a table-type **Recordset** object. For example, suppose that you have an index on the LastName field in the Employees table in the Northwind sample database. If you create a table-type **Recordset** object, then set the **Recordset** object's **Index** property to the name of the new index, the records returned by the **Recordset** object will be ordered alphabetically by last name.

You create an index on one or more fields in the table. When you create an index with DAO, you must create the field or fields to be included in the index and append them to the **Fields** collection of the **Index** object, as shown in the following example.

```
Sub SeekRecord()
    Const conPath As String = _
        "C:\Program Files\Microsoft Office\Office\Samples\Northwind.mdb"
    Dim dbs As Database, tdf As TableDef, idx As Index
    Dim fld As Field, fldLast As Field, fldFirst As Field
    Dim rst As Recordset

    ' Return a reference to Northwind database.
    Set dbs = DBEngine(0).OpenDatabase(conPath)
    ' Return a reference to Employees table.
    Set tdf = dbs.TableDefs("Employees")
    ' Create new index on LastName and FirstName fields.
    Set idx = tdf.CreateIndex("FirstLastName")
    ' Create fields in Fields collection of new index.
    Set fldLast = idx.CreateField("LastName", dbText)
    Set fldFirst = idx.CreateField("FirstName", dbText)
    ' Append Field objects.
    idx.Fields.Append fldLast
    idx.Fields.Append fldFirst
    ' Set Required property.
    idx.Required = True
    ' Append new Index object.
    tdf.Indexes.Append idx
    ' Open table-type recordset.
    Set rst = dbs.OpenRecordset("Employees")
    ' Set Index property of Recordset object.
    rst.Index = idx.Name
    ' Perform seek operation.
    rst.Seek "=", "King", "Robert"

    ' Print values of all fields except Photo.
    For Each fld In rst.Fields
        If fld.Type <> dbLongBinary Then
            Debug.Print fld
        End If
    Next fld
End Sub
```

When you create an index, you can also impose certain restrictions on the data contained in the fields that are indexed. For example, if you want to designate a particular field in a table as the primary key, you can create an **Index** object and set its **Primary** and **Unique** properties to **True**. A primary key is a special type of index. Each value in the field designated as the primary key must be unique. A foreign key is also an index, although it doesn't require special property settings. Other indexes are neither primary nor foreign keys and serve only to speed up searching and sorting operations.

Note If you're designing a database in the Microsoft Access user interface, you can add new indexes, change or delete existing indexes, and set index properties in table Design view. To do so, click **Indexes** on the **View** menu.

For more information about indexes, search DAO Help for "Index object."

The QueryDef Object and the QueryDefs Collection

The **QueryDef** object represents a query in DAO. **QueryDef** objects can be saved with your database, or they can be temporary. The **QueryDefs** collection contains all **QueryDef** objects that are saved with your database and any temporary **QueryDef** objects that are currently open. The following table shows the relationship between the **QueryDef** object and the **QueryDefs** collection and other objects and collections in a Microsoft Jet workspace.

Object or collection	Is contained by	Contains
QueryDef object	**QueryDefs** collection	**Fields** collection
		Parameters collection
		Properties collection
QueryDefs collection	**Database** object	**QueryDef** objects

Creating Persistent Queries

A query that's saved with your database is called a *persistent* query. You can create persistent queries in Visual Basic by using DAO, or you can create them in the Microsoft Access user interface.

To create a persistent query with DAO, use the **CreateQueryDef** method of a **Database** object, as shown in the following example.

```
Const conPath As String = _
    "C:\Program Files\Microsoft Office\Office\Samples\Northwind.mdb"
Dim dbs As Database, qdf As QueryDef, rst As Recordset
Dim strSQL As String

strSQL = "SELECT FirstName, LastName, HireDate FROM Employees " _
    & "WHERE Title = 'Sales Representative' ORDER BY HireDate;"
Set dbs = OpenDatabase(conPath)
Set qdf = dbs.CreateQueryDef("Sales Representatives", strSQL)
Set rst = qdf.OpenRecordset
```

You don't need to append a **QueryDef** object to the **QueryDefs** collection. If you specify a value for the *name* argument of the **CreateQueryDef** method in a Microsoft Jet workspace, DAO automatically appends the new **QueryDef** object to the **QueryDefs** collection of the **Database** object. If you specify a zero-length string ("") for the *name* argument, DAO creates a temporary **QueryDef** object.

Note In an ODBCDirect workspace, **QueryDef** objects are always temporary.

Creating Temporary Queries

You can create a temporary **QueryDef** object when you need to run an SQL statement but don't want to store a new **QueryDef** object in the database. A temporary **QueryDef** object is not appended to the database and exists until the variable that represents it goes out of scope.

The following example creates two temporary **QueryDef** objects to return data from the Microsoft SQL Server Pubs sample database. It first queries the table of titles in the Microsoft SQL Server Pubs sample database and returns the title and title identifier of the best-selling book. It then queries the table of authors and instructs the user to send a bonus check to each author based on his or her royalty share. The total bonus is $1,000 and each author should receive a percentage of that amount.

This example uses ODBC through Microsoft Jet. You can apply the same principles to create a temporary **QueryDef** object on a Microsoft Jet database or an installable ISAM data source, or in an ODBCDirect workspace.

```
Function DetermineBonuses()
    Const conPath As String = _
        "C:\Program Files\Microsoft Office\Office\Samples\Northwind.mdb"
    Dim dbsCurrent As Database, qdfBestSellers As QueryDef
    Dim qdfBonusEarners As QueryDef, rstTopSeller As Recordset
    Dim rstBonusRecipients As Recordset, strAuthorList As String

    ' Open database from which QueryDef objects can be created.
    Set dbsCurrent = OpenDatabase(conPath)

    ' Create temporary QueryDef object to retrieve data from
    ' Microsoft SQL Server database.
    Set qdfBestSellers = dbsCurrent.CreateQueryDef("")
    qdfBestSellers.Connect = "ODBC;DATABASE=Pubs;UID=sa;PWD=;DSN=Publishers"
    qdfBestSellers.SQL = "SELECT title, title_id FROM titles ORDER BY ytd_sales DESC;"
    Set rstTopSeller = qdfBestSellers.OpenRecordset()
    rstTopSeller.MoveFirst

    ' Create temporary QueryDef to retrieve data from SQL Server database
    ' based on results from first query.
    Set qdfBonusEarners = dbsCurrent.CreateQueryDef("")
    qdfBonusEarners.Connect = "ODBC;DATABASE=Pubs;UID=sa;PWD=;DSN=Publishers"
    qdfBonusEarners.SQL = "SELECT * FROM titleauthor WHERE title_id = '" & _
        rstTopSeller!title_id & "'"
    Set rstBonusRecipients = qdfBonusEarners.OpenRecordset()

    ' Build string containing names of authors to whom bonuses are owed.
    Do While Not rstBonusRecipients.EOF
        strAuthorList = strAuthorList & rstBonusRecipients!au_id & ": $" & _
            CStr(10 * rstBonusRecipients!royaltyper) & vbCr
        rstBonusRecipients.MoveNext
    Loop

    ' Display results.
    MsgBox "Please send a check to the following " & _
        "authors in the amounts shown: " & vbCr & _
        strAuthorList & " for outstanding sales of " & _
        rstTopSeller!Title & "."
```

```
        rstBonusRecipients.Close
        rstTopSeller.Close
        dbsCurrent.Close
End Function
```

The Parameter Object and the Parameters Collection

A **Parameter** object represents a value supplied to a query. The **Parameters** collection contains all of the **Parameter** objects defined for a **QueryDef** object. The following table shows the relationship between the **Parameter** object and the **Parameters** collection and other objects and collections in a Microsoft Jet workspace.

Object or collection	Is contained by	Contains
Parameter object	**Parameters** collection	**Properties** collection
Parameters collection	**QueryDef** object	**Parameter** objects

When you want the user or the application to supply a value at run time that limits the set of records returned by a query, you can define parameters for the query. For example, you can create a query on an Orders table that prompts the user to specify the range of records to return based on a range of order dates.

To create a parameter query, use the SQL PARAMETERS declaration to define parameters for the query. The syntax for the PARAMETERS declaration is:

PARAMETERS *name datatype* [, *name datatype* [, ...]]

The PARAMETERS declaration precedes the rest of the SQL statement and is separated from the SQL statement by a semicolon (;). The following SQL statement defines two parameters, Beginning OrderDate and Ending OrderDate, whose *datatype* is DATETIME.

```
PARAMETERS [Beginning OrderDate] DATETIME,[Ending OrderDate] DATETIME;
SELECT * FROM Orders
WHERE (OrderDate Between [Beginning OrderDate] And [Ending OrderDate]);
```

For a list of data types you can use for parameters, search Microsoft Access Help for "data types, SQL."

Each parameter that you define in the SQL statement is represented by a **Parameter** object in the **Parameters** collection of the **QueryDef** object based on that SQL statement. You specify the value of a parameter by setting the **Value** property of the **Parameter** object. The following example creates a new parameter query.

```
Function NewParameterQuery(dteStart As Date, dteEnd As Date) As Boolean
   Dim dbs As Database, qdf As QueryDef, rst As Recordset
   Dim strSQL As String

   On Error Resume Next
   ' Return reference to current database.
   Set dbs = CurrentDb
   ' Construct SQL string.
   strSQL = "PARAMETERS [Beginning OrderDate] DateTime, " _
      & "[Ending OrderDate] DateTime; SELECT * FROM Orders " & _
      "WHERE (OrderDate Between [Beginning OrderDate] " _
      & "And [Ending OrderDate]);"

   ' Delete query if it already exists.
   dbs.QueryDefs.Delete "ParameterQuery"

   On Error GoTo Err_NewParameterQuery
   ' Create new QueryDef object.
   Set qdf = dbs.CreateQueryDef("ParameterQuery", strSQL)

   ' Supply values for parameters.
   If dteStart > dteEnd Then
      MsgBox "Start date is later than end date."
      Exit Function
   End If
   qdf.Parameters("Beginning OrderDate") = dteStart
   qdf.Parameters("Ending OrderDate") = dteEnd

   ' Open recordset on QueryDef object.
   Set rst = qdf.OpenRecordset
   rst.MoveLast
   MsgBox "Query returned " & rst.RecordCount & " records."
   NewParameterQuery = True

Exit_NewParameterQuery:
   rst.Close
   Set dbs = Nothing
   Exit Function

Err_NewParameterQuery:
   MsgBox "Error " & Err & ": " & Err.Description
   NewParameterQuery = False
   Resume Exit_NewParameterQuery
End Function
```

You can call this function from the Debug window as follows:

```
? NewParameterQuery(#6-30-95#, #6-30-96#)
```

Note If you're creating a database in Microsoft Access, you can define parameters for a query in query Design view. For more information, search Microsoft Access Help for "parameter queries."

The Relation Object and the Relations Collection

The **Relation** object represents a relationship between fields in tables and queries. The **Relations** collection contains all stored **Relation** objects in a database. The following table shows the relationship between the **Relation** object and the **Relations** collection and other objects and collections in a Microsoft Jet workspace.

Object or collection	Is contained by	Contains
Relation object	**Relations** collection	**Fields** collection
		Properties collection
Relations collection	**Database** object	**Relation** objects

You can use the **Relation** object to create, delete, or change relationships between fields in tables and queries in your database. You can use the properties of the **Relation** object to specify the type of relationship, which tables supply the fields that participate in the relationship, whether to enforce referential integrity, and whether to perform cascading updates and deletes.

A **Relation** object has a **Fields** collection that contains two fields, one in each of the tables in the relationship. The fields that make up the relationship must be of the same data type, and they must have common values. In most cases, a relationship consists of a field that is the primary key in one table and a foreign key in another table.

You use the **Table** and **ForeignTable** properties of the **Relation** object to specify which tables take part in the relation and how they are related. If you are creating a one-to-many relationship, it is important that you set these properties correctly. In a one-to-many relationship, the table on the "one" side of the relationship is the table in which the field to be joined is the primary key. The setting for the **Table** property must be the name of this table. The table on the "many" side of the relationship is the table in which the field to be joined is the foreign key. The setting for the **ForeignTable** property must be the name of this table.

For example, consider the relationship between the Employees table and the Orders table in the Northwind sample database. The two tables are joined on the EmployeeID field. In the Employees table, this field is the primary key; all values in this field must be unique. In the Orders table, the EmployeeID field is a foreign key. The same value can occur more than once in this field. For the **Relation** object that represents this relationship, the value of the **Table** property is the table on the "one" side of the relationship; the Employees table. The value of the **ForeignTable** property is the table on the "many" side of the relationship; the Orders table.

The following example shows how to create a **Relation** object in Visual Basic. The procedure deletes the existing relationship between the Employees table and the Orders table in the Northwind sample database, then re-creates it.

```
Function NewRelation() As Boolean
    Dim dbs As Database
    Dim fld As Field, rel As Relation
    Const conPath As String = _
       "C:\Program Files\Microsoft Office\Office\Samples\Northwind.mdb"

    On Error GoTo Err_NewRelation
    ' Return reference to current database.
    Set dbs = OpenDatabase(conPath)

    ' Find existing EmployeesOrders relation.
    For Each rel In dbs.Relations
       If rel.Table = "Employees" And rel.ForeignTable = "Orders" Then
          ' Prompt user before deleting relation.
          If MsgBox(rel.Name & " already exists. " & vbCrLf _
             & "This relation will be deleted and re-created.", vbOK) = vbOK Then
                dbs.Relations.Delete rel.Name
          ' If user chooses Cancel, exit procedure.
          Else
             Exit Function
          End If
       End If
    Next rel

    ' Create new relationship and set its properties.
    Set rel = dbs.CreateRelation("EmployeesOrders", "Employees", "Orders")
    ' Set Relation object attributes to enforce referential integrity.
    rel.Attributes = dbRelationDeleteCascade + dbRelationUpdateCascade
    ' Create field in Fields collection of Relation object.
    Set fld = rel.CreateField("EmployeeID")
    ' Provide name of foreign key field.
    fld.ForeignName = "EmployeeID"

    ' Append field to Relation object and Relation object to database.
    rel.Fields.Append fld
    dbs.Relations.Append rel
    MsgBox "Relation '" & rel.Name & "' created."
    Set dbs = Nothing
    NewRelation = True

Exit_NewRelation:
    Exit Function

Err_NewRelation:
    MsgBox "Error " & Err & ": " & Err.Description
    NewRelation = False
    Resume Exit_NewRelation
End Function
```

Note If you're designing a database in Microsoft Access, you can view and change the relationships in your database in the Relationships window. In the Database window, click **Relationships** on the **Tools** menu.

For more information about **Relation** objects, search DAO Help for "Relation object."

The Recordset Object and the Recordsets Collection

The **Recordset** object represents a set of records within your database. The **Recordsets** collection contains all open **Recordset** objects. The following table shows the relationship between the **Recordset** object and the **Recordsets** collection and other objects and collections in a Microsoft Jet workspace.

Object or collection	Is contained by	Contains
Recordset object	**Recordsets** collection	**Fields** collection
		Properties collection
Recordsets collection	**Database** object	**Recordset** objects

DAO offers five types of **Recordset** objects: table-type, dynaset-type, snapshot-type, forward-only-type, and dynamic-type. Table-type **Recordset** objects are supported only in Microsoft Jet workspaces. Dynamic-type **Recordset** objects are available only in ODBCDirect workspaces. For more information, see "Dynamic-Type Recordset Objects" later in the chapter.

The sections that follow discuss some characteristics of each of the other four types of **Recordset** objects. For more information about each type of **Recordset** object, search DAO Help for the name of the particular type of **Recordset** object.

Note that you should always close a **Recordset** object after you have finished working with it, and before you close the **Database** object in which the recordset was created. Use the **Close** method to close a **Recordset** object.

Table-Type Recordset Objects

The table-type **Recordset** object represents a base table in your database. All of the fields and records in the table are included in a table-type **Recordset** object. You can use a table-type **Recordset** object to add, delete, or change records in a table in a Microsoft Jet workspace. You can open a table-type **Recordset** object on base tables in a Microsoft Jet database, but not on tables in ODBC data sources or linked tables. You can also use the table-type **Recordset** object with installable ISAM databases (such as FoxPro, dBASE, or Paradox) to open tables directly, rather than linking them to your database.

The **RecordCount** property of a table-type **Recordset** object returns the number of records in the table. You can return the value of the **RecordCount** property as soon as you've created the recordset; you don't need to use the **MoveLast** method to move to the end of the recordset.

The table-type **Recordset** object can use the indexes defined for the table. When you create a table-type **Recordset** object, you can set the recordset's **Index** property to the name of an index that is defined for the table. You can then use the **Seek** method to search for a particular record based on the ordering criteria specified by the index.

Note   You can't open a table-type **Recordset** object on a linked table from an external data source. Instead, you must use the **OpenDatabase** method to open the external data source, and then open a table-type **Recordset** object.

To create a table-type **Recordset** object, specify the **dbOpenTable** constant for the *type* argument of the **OpenRecordset** method. The following example creates a table-type **Recordset** object and then uses the **Seek** method to locate a particular record and make that record the current record.

```
Function ReturnEmployeesRecord(strKey As String) As Boolean
    Dim dbs As Database, rst As Recordset
    Const conPath As String = _
        "C:\Program Files\Microsoft Office\Office\Samples\Northwind.mdb"

    On Error GoTo Err_ReturnEmployeesRecord
    ' Return reference to Northwind database.
    Set dbs = OpenDatabase(conPath)
    ' Open table-type recordset on Employees table.
    Set rst = dbs.OpenRecordset("Employees", dbOpenTable)
    ' Set Index property of recordset.
    rst.Index = "LastName"
    ' Perform seek operation.
    rst.Seek "=", strKey
    ' Check whether match is found.
    If rst.NoMatch = False Then
        ' Print values of fields in first record found.
        Debug.Print rst!EmployeeID, rst!FirstName & " " & rst!LastName, rst!Title
        ReturnEmployeesRecord = True
    Else
        ReturnEmployeesRecord = False
    End If

Exit_ReturnEmployeesRecord:
    ' Close recordset and database.
    rst.Close
    dbs.Close
    Exit Function

Err_ReturnEmployeesRecord:
    MsgBox "Error " & Err & ": " & Err.Description
    ReturnEmployeesRecord = False
    Resume Exit_ReturnEmployeesRecord
End Function
```

Dynaset-Type Recordset Objects

The dynaset-type **Recordset** object represents the result of a query on one or more tables. A dynaset-type **Recordset** object is a dynamic set of records that you can use to add, change, or delete records from an underlying database table or tables. With a dynaset-type **Recordset** object, you can extract and update data in a multiple-table join, including linked tables from multiple databases. You can create a dynaset-type **Recordset** object in a Microsoft Jet workspace or an ODBCDirect workspace.

A dynaset-type **Recordset** object on a remote data source consists of a series of bookmarks. Each bookmark uniquely identifies one record in the recordset. The actual data in the fields of the recordset is not returned until you specifically refer to the record that contains that data. Microsoft DAO uses the bookmark to find the appropriate record and return the requested data. To improve performance, Microsoft DAO returns only the records that you explicitly refer to in your code; it doesn't necessarily return data from every record in the recordset.

In order to return the value of the **RecordCount** property for a dynaset-type **Recordset** object, you must first use the **MoveLast** method to move to the end of the recordset. Moving to the end of the recordset retrieves all of the records in the recordset.

A dynaset-type **Recordset** object may be updatable, but not all fields can be updated in all dynaset-type **Recordset** objects. To determine whether you can update a particular field, check the setting of the **DataUpdatable** property of the **Field** object.

A dynaset-type **Recordset** object may not be updatable if:

- The data page the user is trying to update is locked by another user.
- The record has changed since it was last read.
- The user doesn't have permission to update the recordset.
- One or more of the tables or fields are read-only.
- The database is opened for read-only access.
- The **Recordset** object was created from multiple tables without a JOIN statement.
- The **Recordset** object includes fields from an ODBC data source, or Paradox table or tables, and there isn't a unique index on those table or tables.

To create a dynaset-type **Recordset** object, specify the **dbOpenDynaset** constant for the *type* argument of the **OpenRecordset** method, as shown in the following example.

```
Sub PrintHireDates()
    Dim dbs As Database, rst As Recordset
    Dim strSQL As String
    Const conPath = "C:\Program Files\Microsoft Office\Office\Samples\Northwind.mdb"

    ' Open database and return reference to Database object.
    Set dbs = DBEngine.Workspaces(0).OpenDatabase(conPath)
    ' Initialize SQL string.
    strSQL = "SELECT FirstName, LastName, HireDate FROM Employees " & _
        "WHERE HireDate <= #1-1-93# ORDER BY HireDate;"
    ' Open dynaset-type recordset.
    Set rst = dbs.OpenRecordset(strSQL, dbOpenDynaset)
    ' Print records in recordset.
    Do Until rst.EOF
        Debug.Print rst!FirstName, rst!LastName, rst!HireDate
        rst.MoveNext
    Loop
    ' Close recordset and database.
    rst.Close
    dbs.Close
End Sub
```

Snapshot-Type Recordset Objects

A snapshot-type **Recordset** object is a static set of records that represents the results of a query. A snapshot-type **Recordset** object includes all values for all the requested fields in your query, whether you refer to them in code or not. A snapshot-type **Recordset** object requires fewer resources than the dynaset-type **Recordset** object, but the data in a snapshot-type **Recordset** object cannot be updated.

As you move through a snapshot-type **Recordset** object for the first time, all data is copied first into memory and then, if the recordset is large, into a temporary Microsoft Jet database on the user's computer. You can scroll forward and backward through the resulting set of data.

To create a snapshot-type **Recordset** object, specify the **dbOpenSnapshot** constant for the *type* argument of the **OpenRecordset** method.

Forward-Only-Type Recordset Objects

A forward-only-type **Recordset** object is identical to a snapshot, except that you can only scroll forward through its records. This improves performance in situations where you only need to make a single pass through a result set.

When working with a forward-only-type **Recordset** object, you cannot use the **MovePrevious** or **MoveFirst** methods, or the **Move** method with a negative integer for the *rows* argument. In a forward-only-type **Recordset** object, only one record exists at any given time. Therefore, you cannot use the **MoveLast** method because it implies that you have a set of records. Forward-only-type **Recordset** objects offer less flexibility than other **Recordset** objects, but they usually provide the greatest speed.

To create a forward-only-type **Recordset** object, specify the **dbOpenForwardOnly** constant for the *type* argument of the **OpenRecordset** method.

The Group Object and the Groups Collection

The **Group** object represents a group of user accounts that have common access permissions in a particular workspace. The **Groups** collection contains all **Group** objects in a workspace or a user account. The following table shows the relationship between the **Group** object and the **Groups** collection and other objects and collections in a Microsoft Jet workspace.

Object or collection	Is contained by	Contains
Group object	**Groups** collection	**Group** objects
		Properties collection
		Users collection
Groups collection	**Workspace** object	**Group** objects
	User object	

You can use the **Group** object, along with the **User**, **Container**, **Document**, and **Workspace** objects, to secure your database. The **Group** object represents a group of user accounts, and the **User** object represents an individual user account. Users can be members of groups. When you establish security in your database, you secure a particular object or set of objects by specifying what type of permissions a user or group has for that object. If a group has certain permissions for an object, all users in the group have the same permissions. Conversely, if a user has permissions for an object, the group to which that user belongs has the same permissions.

Note   The easiest way to secure your database is through the Microsoft Access user interface. From Microsoft Access, you can manage user and group accounts and assign permissions for objects with relative ease. For more information about securing a database in Microsoft Access, search Microsoft Access Help for "security," or see Chapter 14, "Securing Your Application," in *Building Applications with Microsoft Access 97.*

Both a **Workspace** object and a **User** object have a **Groups** collection. When you create a **Group** object, you should first append it to the **Groups** collection of a **Workspace** object. This notifies Microsoft Jet that the group exists.

After you've created a group and added it to the **Groups** collection of the **Workspace** object, you need to specify which users belong to that group. To do so, you can append the new **Group** object to the **Groups** collection of a **User** object. In this way, you specify that a particular user belongs to this group. Alternatively, you can append a **User** object to the **Users** collection in a **Group** object to give a particular user account the permissions held by that group. In either case, the existing **Group** object must already be a member of the **Groups** collection of the current **Workspace** object.

The following example creates a new group, the Managers group, and appends it to the **Groups** collection of the default workspace.

```
Function AddNewGroup() As Boolean
    Dim wrk As Workspace, grp As Group

    Const conAccountExists As Integer = 3390

    On Error GoTo Err_AddNewGroup
    Set wrk = DBEngine.Workspaces(0)
    Set grp = wrk.CreateGroup("Managers", "123abc")
    wrk.Groups.Append grp
    AddNewGroup = True

Exit_AddNewGroup:
    Exit Function

Err_AddNewGroup:
    If Err <> conAccountExists Then
        MsgBox "Error " & Err & ": " & Err.Description
        AddNewGroup = False
    Else
        AddNewGroup = True
    End If
    Resume Exit_AddNewGroup
End Function
```

After you've run this example, the Managers group exists, but no user accounts belong to it. The example in the following section adds user accounts to the Managers group.

The User Object and the Users Collection

The **User** object represents a user account with particular access permissions. The **Users** collection contains all **User** objects in a given workspace or group. The following table shows the relationship between the **User** object and the **Users** collection and other objects and collections in a Microsoft Jet workspace.

Object or collection	Is contained by	Contains
User object	**Users** collection	**Groups** collection
		Properties collection
		User objects
Users collection	**Workspace** object	**User** objects
	Group object	

Like the **Groups** collection, the **Users** collection is a member of a **Workspace** object. Each **User** object in the **Users** collection of a **Workspace** object also has a **Groups** collection, in the same way that each **Group** object in the **Groups** collection of a **Workspace** object has a **Users** collection. To make a user a member of a particular group, you can append a **User** object to the **Users** collection of that **Group** object.

You can achieve the same result by appending the **Group** object to the **Groups** collection of that **User** object. In either case, the existing **User** object must already be a member of the **Users** collection of the current **Workspace** object.

The following example creates a new **User** object and appends it to the **Users** collection of the default workspace. Next, it appends the **User** object to the **Users** collection of the Managers group created in the previous example. Note that because the **User** object doesn't already exist in the **Users** collection of the **Group** object, you must use the **CreateUser** method a second time to create the object there. However, you don't need to specify the *pid* and *password* arguments a second time.

```
Function AddNewUser() As Boolean
    Dim wrk As Workspace, grp As Group, usr As User

    Const conAccountExists As Integer = 3390

    On Error GoTo Err_AddNewUser
    Set wrk = DBEngine.Workspaces(0)
    Set usr = wrk.CreateUser("Joe Manager", "efg456", "")
    wrk.Users.Append usr
    Set grp = wrk.Groups("Managers")
    Set usr = grp.CreateUser("Joe Manager")
    grp.Users.Append usr
    AddNewUser = True

Exit_AddNewUser:
    Exit Function

Err_AddNewUser:
    If Err <> conAccountExists Then
        MsgBox "Error " & Err & ": " & Err.Description
        AddNewUser = False
    Else
        AddNewUser = True
    End If
    Resume Exit_AddNewUser
End Function
```

The Container Object and the Containers Collection

The **Container** object represents a particular set of objects in a database for which you can assign permissions in a secure workgroup. The **Containers** collection contains all the **Container** objects in the database. The following table shows the relationship between the **Container** object and the **Containers** collection and other objects and collections in a Microsoft Jet workspace.

Object or collection	Is contained by	Contains
Container object	**Containers** collection	**Documents** collection
		Properties collection
Containers collection	**Database** object	**Container** objects

DAO provides three types of **Container** objects; every database contains at least these three **Container** objects. The following table describes the types of **Container** objects provided by DAO.

Container name	Contains information about
Databases	Saved databases
Tables	Saved tables and queries
Relationships	Saved relationships

Each **Container** object can contain a **Documents** collection. The **Documents** collection contains individual **Document** objects, each of which represents a document in your database. For more information about **Document** objects, see the following section, "The Document Object and the Documents Collection."

In addition to the **Container** objects provided by DAO, an application may define its own **Container** objects. For example, the following table lists the **Container** objects defined by Microsoft Access.

Container name	Contains information about
Forms	Saved forms
Modules	Saved modules
Reports	Saved reports
Scripts	Saved macros

You use **Container** objects to establish permissions on a set of objects for a user or group. The following example establishes permissions for a group, and any users that belong to it, for the Tables container. To establish permissions, the function first sets the **UserName** property of the Tables container to the name of a group, then sets the **Permissions** property to the appropriate permissions.

```
Function SetGroupPermissions(strGroupName As String) As Boolean
   Dim dbs As Database, ctr As Container

   Const conPath As String = _
      "C:\Program Files\Microsoft Office\Office\Samples\Northwind.mdb"

   On Error GoTo Err_SetGroupPermissions
   Set dbs = DBEngine(0).OpenDatabase(conPath)
   ' Return a reference to the Databases container.
   Set ctr = dbs.Containers("Databases")
   ' Set UserName property to name of group.
   ctr.UserName = strGroupName
   ' Set permissions for the group on the Databases container.
   ctr.Permissions = dbSecDBOpen

   ' Return a reference to the Tables container.
   Set ctr = dbs.Containers("Tables")
   ' Set UserName property to name of group.
   ctr.UserName = strGroupName
   ' Set permissions for the group on the Tables container.
   ctr.Permissions = dbSecRetrieveData or dbSecInsertData or _
      dbSecReplaceData or dbSecDeleteData
   SetGroupPermissions = True

Exit_SetGroupPermissions:
   Exit Function

Err_SetGroupPermissions:
   MsgBox "Error " & Err & ": " & Err.Description
   SetGroupPermissions = False
   Resume Exit_SetGroupPermissions
End Function
```

To establish permissions for the Managers group on the Tables container, you can call the SetGroupPermissions function as follows.

```
Sub SetManagerPermissions()
   If SetGroupPermissions("Managers") = True Then
      MsgBox "Permissions for Managers group set successfully."
   Else
      MsgBox "Permissions for Managers group not set."
   End If
End Sub
```

The Document Object and the Documents Collection

The **Document** object represents an individual object in a database for which you can assign permissions in a secure workgroup. The **Documents** collection contains all of the **Document** objects in a given **Container** object. The following table shows the relationship between the **Container** object and the **Containers** collection and other objects and collections in a Microsoft Jet workspace.

Object or collection	Is contained by	Contains
Document object	**Documents** collection	**Properties** collection
Documents collection	**Container** object	**Document** objects

The following table describes the **Document** objects provided by DAO. It lists the type of object each **Document** object describes, the name of its **Container** object, and what type of information it contains.

Document	Container	Contains information about
Database	Databases	Saved database
Table or query	Tables	Saved table or query
Relationship	Relationships	Saved relationship

Other applications can define additional **Document** objects. For example, the following table lists the **Document** objects defined by Microsoft Access.

Document	Container	Contains information about
Form	Forms	Saved form
Macro	Scripts	Saved macro
Module	Modules	Saved module
Report	Reports	Saved report
SummaryInfo	Databases	Database document summary
UserDefined	Databases	User-defined properties

The following example establishes permissions for a particular user on all the existing Table **Document** objects in the **Documents** collection of the Tables **Container** object. Table **Document** objects represent either tables or queries.

```
Function SetPermissionsOnDocument(strUserName As String) As Boolean
    Dim dbs As Database, ctr As Container, doc As Document

    Const conPath As String = _
        "C:\Program Files\Microsoft Office\Office\Samples\Northwind.mdb"

    On Error GoTo Err_SetPermissionsOnDocument
    ' Return reference to Northwind sample database.
    Set dbs = DBEngine(0).OpenDatabase(conPath)
    ' Return reference to Tables container.
    Set ctr = dbs.Containers("Tables")
```

```
' Enumerate through documents in Tables container.
For Each doc In ctr.Documents
   ' Set UserName property to name of user.
   doc.UserName = strUserName
   ' Set permissions for that user on the document.
   doc.Permissions = dbSecRetrieveData or dbSecInsertData or _
      dbSecReplaceData or dbSecDeleteData
Next doc
SetPermissionsOnDocument = True

Exit_SetPermissionsOnDocument:
   Exit Function

Err_SetPermissionsOnDocument:
   MsgBox "Error " & Err & ": " & Err.Description
   SetPermissionsOnDocument = False
   Resume Exit_SetPermissionsOnDocument
End Function
```

The Properties Collection

Most DAO objects contain a **Properties** collection. Each **Property** object in the **Properties** collection corresponds to a property of the object. You can use an object's **Properties** collection either to determine which properties apply to a particular object or to return their settings. For example, the following procedure loops through the properties that apply to the **Database** object, which represents the current database. The procedure displays the name of each property in the Debug window.

```
Sub DisplayProperties()
   Dim dbs As Database, prp As Property

   Const conPath As String = _
      "C:\Program Files\Microsoft Office\Office\Samples\Northwind.mdb"

   ' Open database and return reference.
   Set dbs = OpenDatabase(conPath)
   Debug.Print "Current Database Properties"
   ' Enumerate Properties collection.
   For Each prp In dbs.Properties
      Debug.Print prp.Name
   Next prp
   dbs.Close
End Sub
```

Some properties of DAO objects don't automatically exist in the **Properties** collection for that object. Before you can set a property of this type, you must create a **Property** object to represent the property and append the new **Property** object to the **Properties** collection. After you create the property and append it to the collection, you can set or read it as you would any other property.

When you're writing code that uses this type of property, it's a good idea to implement error handling in case the property does not yet exist in the collection. The following function is a generic procedure that you can use to set any property that doesn't automatically exist in an object's **Properties** collection. It implements error handling. The first time you call the procedure, an error occurs because the property does not yet exist within the **Properties** collection. Within the error handler, the procedure creates the new **Property** object and appends it to the collection. The next time you call the procedure, the error does not occur because the property already exists, and the property is set with the value you've specified.

```vba
Function SetProperty(obj As Object, strName As String, _
        intType As Integer, varSetting As Variant) As Boolean
    Dim prp As Property

    Const conPropNotFound As Integer = 3270

    On Error GoTo Error_SetProperty
    ' Explicitly refer to Properties collection.
    obj.Properties(strName) = varSetting
    SetProperty = True

Exit_SetProperty:
    Exit Function

Error_SetProperty:
    If Err = conPropNotFound Then
        ' Create property, denote type, and set initial value.
        Set prp = obj.CreateProperty(strName, intType, varSetting)
        ' Append Property object to Properties collection.
        obj.Properties.Append prp
        obj.Properties.Refresh
        SetProperty = True
        Resume Exit_SetProperty
    Else
        MsgBox Err & ": " & vbCrLf & Err.Description
        SetProperty = False
        Resume Exit_SetProperty
    End If
End Function
```

To set the **ReplicableBool** property of a **Database** object, you can call the preceding function as follows.

```vba
Sub ReplicateDatabase()
    Dim dbs As Database

    Const conPath As String = _
        "C:\Program Files\Microsoft Office\Office\Samples\Northwind.mdb"

    Set dbs = OpenDatabase(conPath, True)
    If SetProperty(dbs, "ReplicableBool", dbBoolean, True) Then
        Debug.Print "Database replicated successfully."
    Else
```

```
      Debug.Print "Database not replicated."
   End If
End Sub
```

The SetProperty function shown in the previous example is a generic procedure that you can use to set any property, including those that must first be appended to the **Properties** collection. You can compare this function to the ReplicateDatabase function shown earlier in this chapter, in "Creating Database Replicas with DAO." Both functions achieve the same end, but the SetProperty function can be used to set any property, while the ReplicateDatabase function sets only the **ReplicableBool** property.

Each time you set or read a property that doesn't automatically exist in the **Properties** collection for an object, you must refer to the **Properties** collection explicitly. For example, each time you refer to the **ReplicableBool** property after it has been set, you must refer to it within the **Properties** collection, as shown in the following example.

```
Dim dbs As Database
Const conPath As String = _
   "C:\Program Files\Microsoft Office\Office\Samples\Northwind.mdb"
Set dbs = OpenDatabase(conPath)
Debug.Print dbs.Properties("ReplicableBool")
```

You can also use the SetProperty function shown in the previous example to define custom properties on DAO objects. For example, you may want to define a property that stores the name of the user who last modified a particular table. When you set or read a custom property, you must refer to the **Properties** collection explicitly, as shown in the previous examples.

Some applications define their own properties for DAO objects. For example, Microsoft Access defines properties for DAO **TableDef**, **QueryDef**, **Field**, and **Document** objects. If you're working with a database that has been opened in Microsoft Access, some of these properties may be defined for DAO objects.

For more information about the **Properties** collection, search DAO Help for "properties, collection" and "CreateProperty method."

Accessing ODBC Data

When you're working with an ODBC data source, you'll need to decide whether you should use ODBC with Microsoft Jet, ODBCDirect, or both. This section discusses the advantages of both ODBC with Microsoft Jet and ODBCDirect. It also explains how to register an ODBC data source, whether you're working with a Microsoft Jet workspace or with an ODBCDirect workspace.

Accessing ODBC Data with Microsoft Jet

The following capabilities are supported in Microsoft Jet workspaces, but not in ODBCDirect workspaces:

- **Updatable Joins**   You can update data in **Recordset** objects based on multiple-table joins.

- **Support for Linked Tables**   You can store persistent links to server data in a local Microsoft Jet database. When you link a table, you can cache information about the table's structure, including field and index information, in your local database. The next time you access that table, the connection is quicker because you don't need to retrieve the structural information from the data source again.

- **Support for the Find Methods**   You can use the **FindFirst**, **FindNext**, **FindPrevious**, and **FindLast** methods with **Recordset** objects in a Microsoft Jet workspace.

- **Partial Failures of Update Queries**   If you have a bulk-operation query, and it fails for some reason, the query stops, giving you the opportunity to decide whether or not you want to commit the changes made up to the point of failure.

- **User-Defined Properties**   You can customize DAO objects by adding persistent properties to existing objects. For example, you can add a Description property to an object so that you can store descriptive text about the object.

- **Crosstab Queries**   You can use the SQL TRANSFORM statement to create crosstab queries that summarize data.

- **Heterogeneous Data Access**   You can work with server data, native Microsoft Jet database (.mdb file) data, and external installable ISAM data such as FoxPro, Paradox, and dBASE data. You can perform joins on tables in different data sources.

- **Programmatic Data Definition Language (DDL)**   You can use DAO to perform operations that affect the structure of your database. For example, you can create, delete, and modify tables.

- **Form and Control Binding**   If your application requires that forms or controls be bound to data in an ODBC data source, you must use Microsoft Jet. Data accessed within an ODBCDirect workspace cannot be bound to forms or controls because ODBCDirect does not support linked tables.

Accessing ODBC Data with ODBCDirect

With ODBCDirect, you can access server data by using the existing DAO object model directly on top of the ODBC application programming interface (API). ODBCDirect implements a thin code layer over the ODBC API that establishes connections, creates cursors, and runs complex procedures using minimal workstation resources, without going through Microsoft Jet. ODBCDirect offers the following advantages:

- **Direct Access**   Your application can access ODBC data sources directly. You can improve performance, reduce network traffic, and take advantage of the server's capabilities by processing more data on the server.

- **Reduced Resource Requirements**   You don't have to go through the Microsoft Jet database engine, so your application requires fewer resources at the workstation. If you're using ODBCDirect from Microsoft Access, keep in mind that Microsoft Access always loads Microsoft Jet, even though ODBCDirect operations don't go through Microsoft Jet.

- **Improved Access to Server-Specific Functionality**   You can take advantage of features specific to the ODBC server that aren't available if you're using ODBC through Microsoft Jet. For example, in an ODBCDirect workspace, you can specify where cursors are located—on the client or on the server—for servers that support different types of cursors. In addition, to interact with stored procedures on the server, you can specify input values and check return values; operations that are not possible in a Microsoft Jet workspace.

- **Asynchronous Queries**   You can run a query and perform other operations without waiting for the query to finish. You can then check properties to keep track of the query's progress. You can enhance concurrency and optimize performance with asynchronous queries.

- **Batch Optimistic Updating**   With batch optimistic updating, you can cache **Recordset** changes locally and then submit these changes to the server in a single batch.

- **Flexible Stored Procedure Execution**   You can handle output parameters and return values from stored procedures.

Note   You can't perform DDL operations with DAO in an ODBCDirect workspace, but you can run SQL DDL statements to modify the structure of the database.

Registering an ODBC Data Source

Before you can use ODBC in a Microsoft Jet workspace or in an ODBCDirect workspace, you must register the ODBC data source. Registering the data source stores information about the data source in the Windows Registry and makes this information available to applications. You can register a data source from the ODBC data source manager or from Visual Basic.

▶ To register a SQL Server data source by using the ODBC data source manager

1 In Windows Control Panel, double-click the 32bit ODBC icon.

2 Click **Add** and then double-click the ODBC driver for the data source you want to access. For example, double-click **SQL Server**.

3 In the **Data Source Name** box, type a data source name (DSN). This can be any string, such as SalesDB or Pubs. The string doesn't have to correspond to the actual name of a database or table you want to access.

4 In the **Description** box, type a description of the database, such as Sales Data for 1996. You can enter any text.

5 In the **Server** box, type the name of the network server where your data source resides. Do not include a double-backslash (\\) before the name.

6 Click **Options**, and then type the name of the database you want to access in the **Database Name** box. For example, to specify the Microsoft SQL Server Pubs sample database, type **Pubs**.

Note This procedure describes the steps for registering a Microsoft SQL Server data source. The steps for registering other ODBC data sources may vary because each data source driver requires a different set of information. If the dialog box for the data source you selected has values not described in the preceding steps, click the **Help** button for more information.

In some cases, you may want to register the data source in Visual Basic code instead of relying on users to register it with the ODBC data source manager. To do this, use the **RegisterDatabase** method of the **DBEngine** object. The following example registers a data source named Pubs.

```
Function RegisterDB() As Boolean
   Dim str As String

   On Error GoTo Err_RegisterDB
   ' Build keywords string.
   str = "Description=SQL Server on Server Publishers" & _
      vbCr & "OemToAnsi=No" & _
      vbCr & "Network=(Default)" & _
      vbCr & "Address=(Default)" & _
      vbCr & "Server=Publishers" & _
      vbCr & "Database=Pubs"
   ' Register database.
   DBEngine.RegisterDatabase "Pubs", "SQL Server", True, str
   RegisterDB = True

Exit_RegisterDB:
   Exit Function

Err_RegisterDB:
   MsgBox "Error " & Err & ": " & Err.Description
   RegisterDB = False
   Resume Exit_RegisterDB
End Function
```

Using DAO with ODBCDirect

The object model for an ODBCDirect workspace includes a subset of the objects in a Microsoft Jet workspace, with the addition of a new object, the **Connection** object. The following diagram shows the object model for ODBCDirect workspaces; the subsequent sections describe the objects themselves, to the extent that they differ from the objects in the Microsoft Jet object model.

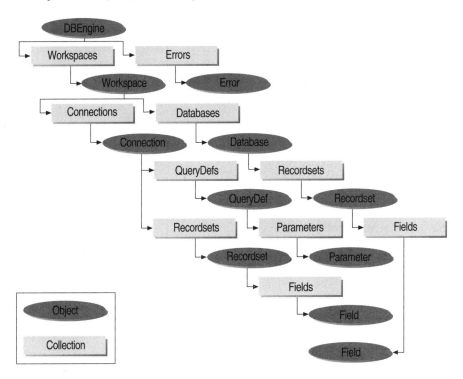

The DBEngine Object

The **DBEngine** object contains both Microsoft Jet and ODBCDirect workspaces. As mentioned earlier in this chapter, the **DefaultType** property of the **DBEngine** object determines what type of **Workspace** object is created by default when you use the **CreateWorkspace** method. If you set the **DefaultType** property to **dbUseODBC**, then the default workspace is an ODBCDirect workspace. When you're creating a workspace, you can override the setting for this property by specifying either **dbUseJet** or **dbUseODBC** as the *type* argument of the **CreateWorkspace** method. For example, if the **DefaultType** property is set to **dbUseJet** and you want to create an ODBCDirect workspace, specify the **dbUseODBC** constant as the *type* argument of the **CreateWorkspace** method. Conversely, if the **DefaultType** property is set to

dbUseODBC and you want to create a Microsoft Jet workspace, specify the **dbUseJet** constant as the *type* argument of the **CreateWorkspace** method.

Note If you're programming in Microsoft Access, avoid setting the **DefaultType** property to **dbUseODBC**. Because Microsoft Access uses DAO and Microsoft Jet for many types of operations, setting the **DefaultType** property to **dbUseODBC** may cause unexpected results.

The following example creates an ODBCDirect workspace.

```
Dim wrkODBC As Workspace
Set wrkODBC = DBEngine.CreateWorkspace("NewODBCWrk", "Admin", "", dbUseODBC)
```

Because you can use both Microsoft Jet and ODBCDirect workspaces in your code, you may need to determine the type of a **Workspace** object after it is created. You can do this by using the **Type** property of the **Workspace** object. The **Type** property is read-only once it is set and returns either **dbUseJet** or **dbUseODBC**.

The Workspace Object and the Workspaces Collection

The **Workspace** object represents an ODBCDirect workspace. The **Workspaces** collection contains the set of all active ODBCDirect workspaces. The following table shows the relationship between the **Workspace** object and the **Workspaces** collection and other objects and collections in an ODBCDirect workspace.

Object or collection	Is contained by	Contains
Workspace object	**Workspaces** collection	**Connections** collection
		Databases collection
		Properties collection
Workspaces collection	**DBEngine** object	**Workspace** objects

The first step in using ODBCDirect is to create an ODBCDirect workspace with the **CreateWorkspace** method. The ODBCDirect workspace routes calls directly to the ODBC application programming interface (API), as opposed to the Microsoft Jet workspace, which first routes calls to the Microsoft Jet database engine, and then to the ODBC API if you're using ODBC.

The Connection Object and the Connections Collection

After you've created an ODBCDirect workspace, you can connect to an ODBC data source. To connect to an ODBC data source, you can use the **OpenConnection** method to open a new **Connection** object, or you can use the **OpenDatabase** method to open a new **Database** object. This section explains how to use the **Connection** object. For information on how to use a **Database** object, see the following section, "The Database Object and the Databases Collection."

A **Connection** object represents a connection to an ODBC database in an ODBCDirect workspace. The **Connections** collection contains all currently open **Connection** objects. When you open a **Connection** object, it is automatically appended to the **Connections** collection of the **Workspace** object. When you close a **Connection** object with the **Close** method, it is removed from the **Connections** collection.

The **Connection** object provides the following advantages for accessing ODBC data:

- **Asynchronous Connection**   Your application can connect to an ODBC data source asynchronously. Rather than pausing execution while the connection is established, your code can continue to perform other operations, and can later check to determine whether the connection was made successfully.

- **Asynchronous Queries**   Your application can run queries against your ODBC data source asynchronously. Rather than pausing execution while a long query runs, your code can perform other tasks, and then check later to determine whether the query has run successfully.

- **QueryDef Objects**   You can define **QueryDef** objects that represent queries in the ODBC data source.

You can use the **OpenConnection** method to create a **Connection** object. The syntax of the **OpenConnection** method is:

Set *connection* = *workspace*.**OpenConnection** (*name*, *options*, *readonly*, *connect*)

The *connection* argument is the name of the new **Connection** object. The *workspace* argument is the name of an ODBCDirect **Workspace** object from which you're creating the new **Connection** object.

The *name* argument indicates the name of the registered data source. You can reference the new **Connection** object by using either the data source name (DSN) or the **Connection** object's ordinal position within its collection. The *options* argument determines if and when to prompt the user to establish the connection, and whether or not to open the connection asynchronously. The *readonly* argument controls the updatability of the data accessed through the connection. Set this argument to **True** to prevent updates; set it to **False** to allow updates.

The *connect* argument is a valid connect string that supplies parameters to the ODBC driver manager. These parameters can include user name, password, default database, and data source name (DSN), which overrides the value provided in the *name* argument.

The connect string must start with `"ODBC;"`, and must contain a series of values needed by the driver to access the data. The actual connect string can vary depending on the data source you're trying to access; different ODBC data sources require different parameters in the *connect* argument. Usually, the minimum requirement is a user ID, a password, and a DSN, as shown in the following example:

```
ODBC;UID=JamesK;PWD=OpenSesame;DSN=MasterData
```

When the ODBC driver processes the connect string and one or more of the parameters required by the data source is missing, the driver displays a dialog box that asks for the information. If you don't want this dialog box displayed, you must make sure that the connect string has all the required information.

Note If you are trying to connect to a Microsoft SQL Server database that uses integrated security, omit the user ID (UID) and password (PWD) values because your Windows NT® user name and password are automatically used. For example, the connect string may look something like the following:

```
ODBC;UID=;PWD=;DATABASE=Pubs;DSN=Pubs
```

For more information about parameters that can be included in a connect string, search DAO Help for "Connect property."

The following example illustrates how to use the **OpenConnection** method to open a new **Connection** object.

```
Function OpenPubsConnection() As Boolean
    Dim wrk As Workspace, cnn As Connection, rst As Recordset, fld As Field
    Dim strConnect As String, strSQL As String

    On Error GoTo Err_OpenPubsConnection
    ' Create connnect string.
    strConnect = "ODBC;DSN=Pubs;UID=SA;PWD=;DATABASE=Pubs"
    ' Create SQL string.
    strSQL = "SELECT * FROM Authors WHERE State = 'MD';"

    ' Create ODBCDirect workspace.
    Set wrk = DBEngine.CreateWorkspace("NewODBCDirect", "sa", "", dbUseODBC)
    ' Open connection.
    Set cnn = wrk.OpenConnection("Pubs", dbDriverNoPrompt, False, strConnect)
    ' Open recordset on connection.
    Set rst = cnn.OpenRecordset(strSQL, dbOpenDynaset)
    ' Print values in recordset.
    Do Until rst.EOF
        For Each fld In rst.Fields
            Debug.Print fld.Name, fld.Value
        Next fld
        Debug.Print
        rst.MoveNext
    Loop
    OpenPubsConnection = True

Exit_OpenPubsConnection:
    rst.Close
    cnn.Close
    Exit Function

Err_OpenPubsConnection:
    MsgBox "Error " & Err & ": " & Err.Description
    OpenPubsConnection = False
    Resume Exit_OpenPubsConnection
End Function
```

After you've created a **Connection** object, you can open **Recordset** objects and run queries on the **Connection** object.

When you open a **Connection** object, a corresponding **Database** object is created and appended to the **Databases** collection in the same workspace. When you open a database in an ODBCDirect workspace, a **Connection** object is likewise created and appended to the **Connections** collection. When you close either the **Connection** object or the **Database** object, the corresponding object is also closed.

Note   Before you close a **Connection** object, close all open **Recordset** objects within it.

Opening Connections Asynchronously

In some cases, opening connections to data sources can take a long time, making it necessary for users to wait until the connection completes or an error occurs. To reduce the amount of time users must wait, you can open a connection asynchronously. This means that your application can complete other tasks while the connection is being established. To open a connection asynchronously, specify the **dbRunAsync** constant for the *options* argument of the **OpenConnection** method, as shown in the following example.

```
Dim wrk As Workspace, cnn As Connection, strConnect As String

Set wrk = DBEngine.CreateWorkspace("NewODBCDirect", "sa", "", dbUseODBC)
strConnect = "ODBC;DSN=Pubs;UID=SA;PWD=;DATABASE=Pubs"
Set cnn = wrk.OpenConnection("",dbDriverNoPrompt + dbRunAsync, False, strConnect)
```

You can use the **StillExecuting** property of the **Connection** object to see if the connection has been established, or use the **Cancel** property of the **Connection** object to cancel the connection attempt if it takes too long.

The Database Object and the Databases Collection

You can also connect to an ODBC data source by using the **OpenDatabase** method to open a **Database** object. However, the **Database** object in an ODBCDirect workspace doesn't support all of the functionality of a **Connection** object. Specifically, if you're using a **Database** object, you can't connect asynchronously, run queries asynchronously, or define **QueryDef** objects that represent queries in the ODBC data source.

To connect to an ODBC data source with the **OpenDatabase** method in an ODBCDirect workspace, specify a valid connect string for the *connect* argument of the **OpenDatabase** method, as shown in the following example.

```
Dim wrk As Workspace, dbs As Database
Dim strConnect As String

strConnect = "ODBC;DSN=Pubs;UID=SA;PWD=;DATABASE=Pubs"
Set wrk = DBEngine.CreateWorkspace("NewODBCDirect", "sa", "", dbUseODBC)
Set dbs = wrk.OpenDatabase("Pubs", dbDriverNoPrompt, False, strConnect)
```

Switching Between Connection and Database Objects

With ODBCDirect, you can open a **Database** object and a **Connection** object against the same ODBC data source, and use both in your code. You can then take advantage of each object for its different capabilities.

Alternatively, you may want to create a single object and then switch to the other type when needed. To do this, use the **Connection** property of the **Database** object or the **Database** property of the **Connection** object. You can use these properties to create **Connection** objects from **Database** objects and to create **Database** objects from **Connection** objects. This is especially useful for adding ODBCDirect capabilities to existing applications that only use **Database** objects.

For example, you can use a **Database** object for most of your ODBC data access needs, but when you need to run an asynchronous query, you can create a **Connection** object from the **Database** object and then run the query on the **Connection** object. The following example illustrates this technique.

```
Sub DeleteRecords()
    Dim dbs As Database, strConnect As String
    Dim cnn As Connection

    ' Open database in default workspace.
    strConnect = "ODBC;DSN=Pubs;DATABASE=Pubs;UID=sa;PWD=;"
    Set dbs = OpenDatabase("", False, False, strConnect)

    ' Try to create Connection object from a Database object. If workspace is an
    ' ODBCDirect workspace, the query runs asynchronously. If workspace is a
    ' Microsoft Jet workspace, an error occurs and the query runs synchronously.

    Err = 0
    On Error Resume Next
    Set cnn = dbs.Connection
    If Err = 0 Then
        cnn.Execute "DELETE FROM Authors", dbRunAsync
    Else
        dbs.Execute "DELETE FROM Authors"
    End If
End Sub
```

The QueryDef Object and the QueryDefs Collection

The **QueryDef** object represents a temporary definition of a query in an ODBCDirect workspace. The **QueryDefs** collection contains all **QueryDef** objects that currently exist in the workspace. The following table shows the relationship between the **QueryDef** object and the **QueryDefs** collection and other objects and collections in an ODBCDirect workspace.

Object or collection	Is contained by	Contains
QueryDef object	**QueryDefs** collection	**Parameters** collection
		Properties collection
QueryDefs collection	**Connection** object	**QueryDef** objects

Unlike **QueryDef** objects created in a Microsoft Jet workspace, **QueryDef** objects created in an ODBCDirect workspace are always temporary—they are not saved within the data source before they run, even if you assign them a name.

Running Asynchronous Queries

Creating and running queries in an ODBCDirect workspace is similar to creating and running queries in a Microsoft Jet workspace. You create the query by invoking the **CreateQueryDef** method on a **Connection** object, and then use the **Execute** or **OpenRecordset** methods on the resulting query.

You can use asynchronous queries so that users can continue using your application while the query runs. You can also give users the ability to cancel asynchronous queries if they are taking too long. The following example runs an asynchronous query.

```
Function DeleteLargeSales() As Boolean
    Dim wrk As Workspace, rst As Recordset
    Dim cnn As Connection, qdf As QueryDef
    Dim strConnect As String, strSQL As String
    Dim errObj As Error

    On Error GoTo Err_DeleteLargeSales
    ' Create ODBCDirect workspace.
    Set wrk = DBEngine.CreateWorkspace("ODBC", "sa", "", dbUseODBC)
    ' Create connect string.
    strConnect = "ODBC;DSN=Publishers;UID=SA;PWD=;DATABASE=Pubs"
    ' Open connection on workspace.
    Set cnn = wrk.OpenConnection("", dbDriverNoPrompt, False, strConnect)
    ' Delete existing QueryDef named DeleteLargeSales.
    For Each qdf In cnn.QueryDefs
        If qdf.Name = "DeleteLargeSales" Then
            cnn.QueryDefs.Delete "DeleteLargeSales"
        End If
    Next qdf

    ' Create QueryDef.
    Set qdf = cnn.CreateQueryDef("DeleteLargeSales")
    strSQL = "DELETE FROM sales WHERE qty = 100"
    qdf.SQL = strSQL

    ' Run query asynchronously.
    qdf.Execute dbRunAsync

    While qdf.StillExecuting
    ' Additional code runs here while query runs.
    ' Check StillExecuting property to determine whether query has finished.
    Wend

    DeleteLargeSales = True

Exit_DeleteLargeSales:
    cnn.Close
    wrk.Close
    Exit Function

Err_DeleteLargeSales:
    For Each errObj In Errors
        Debug.Print errObj.Number, errObj.Description
    Next errObj
    DeleteLargeSales = False
    Resume Exit_DeleteLargeSales
End Function
```

The preceding example uses a **QueryDef** object on a **Connection** object to run an asynchronous query. You can also use the **Execute** method directly on the **Connection** object, as shown in the following example.

```
Dim cnn As Connection, strConnect As String

strConnect = "ODBC;DSN=Pubs;UID=SA;PWD=;DATABASE=Pubs"
Set cnn = OpenConnection("", dbDriverNoPrompt, False, strConnect)
cnn.Execute "DELETE FROM sales WHERE qty = 100", dbRunAsync
cnn.Close
```

When you run a query asynchronously, you can use the **StillExecuting** property to determine if the query has completed. If the value of the **StillExecuting** property is **True**, the query has not yet completed. If you want to cancel an asynchronous query, use the **Cancel** method, as shown in the following example.

```
Function CancelAsynchQuery() As Boolean
    Dim wrk As Workspace, cnn As Connection, strConnect As String
    Dim errObj As Error

    On Error GoTo Err_CancelAsynchQuery
    Set wrk = DBEngine.CreateWorkspace("ODBCDirect", "Admin", "", dbUseODBC)
    strConnect = "ODBC;DSN=Pubs;UID=SA;PWD=;DATABASE=Pubs"
    Set cnn = wrk.OpenConnection("", dbDriverNoPrompt, False, strConnect)

    ' Start transaction in order to roll back if needed.
    wrk.BeginTrans
    cnn.Execute "DELETE FROM sales WHERE qty = 100", dbRunAsync

    ' Perform other operations.
        .
        .
        .

    ' If query is still running, cancel and roll back.
    If cnn.StillExecuting Then
        cnn.Cancel
        wrk.Rollback
    ' If query is complete, commit transaction.
    Else
        wrk.CommitTrans
    End If
    CancelAsynchQuery = True

Exit_CancelAsynchQuery:
    cnn.Close
    wrk.Close
    Exit Function

Err_CancelAsynchQuery:
    For Each errObj In Errors
        Debug.Print errObj.Number, errObj.Description
    Next errObj
    CancelAsynchQuery = False
    Resume Exit_CancelAsynchQuery
End Function
```

You can use the **StillExecuting** property and the **Cancel** method with **QueryDef**, **Connection**, and **Recordset** objects.

A **Connection** object can support only one asynchronous operation at a time. Also, you can't perform another DAO operation, such as recordset manipulation, on a **Connection** object while an asynchronous query runs on the same **Connection** object. After an asynchronous query is complete, you can then begin running another asynchronous query on the same **Connection** object. You must first test the value of the **StillExecuting** property to determine whether you can start the next asynchronous operation. To run multiple asynchronous queries at the same time, you must create separate **Connection** objects and run each asynchronous query on its own **Connection** object.

In most cases, you'll want to run an asynchronous query as part of a transaction. Be aware, however, that if you call the **CommitTrans** method while the asynchronous query is still running, your code will pause at the **CommitTrans** method until the query finishes. For this reason, it is more efficient to periodically check the **StillExecuting** property and continue to perform other work while the query runs. Once the **StillExecuting** property returns **False**, you can then call the **CommitTrans** method. This prevents your code from pausing at the **CommitTrans** method.

Note If you cancel an action query that is not part of a transaction, the query updates records up to the point where you called the **Cancel** method. The operation will be partially complete and will not be rolled back. For this reason, you should use the **Cancel** method only within the scope of a transaction. Additionally, if you start an asynchronous query in a procedure and the procedure exits before the query has completed, the query will continue to run.

To improve performance when you're retrieving data from an ODBC data source, you can cache records locally. A *cache* is a space in local memory that holds the data most recently retrieved from the server. If you're performing repeated operations on a set of data, caching that data makes those operations faster because you don't have to retrieve the data from the server each time you need it.

In ODBCDirect queries, use the **CacheSize** property of the **QueryDef** object to specify the number of records to cache. The default cache size is 100 records. The following example shows how to reset the cache size to 200 records.

```
Sub SetCacheSize()
    Dim wrk As Workspace, qdf As QueryDef, rst As Recordset
    Dim cnn As Connection, strConnect As String

    Set wrk = CreateWorkspace("ODBCDirect", "Admin", "", dbUseODBC)
    Set cnn = OpenConnection("", dbDriverNoPrompt, False, strConnect)
    strConnect = "ODBC;DSN=Pubs;UID=SA;PWD=;DATABASE=Pubs"
    Set qdf = cnn.CreateQueryDef("tempquery")
    qdf.SQL = "SELECT * FROM roysched"
    qdf.CacheSize = 40
    Set rst = qdf.OpenRecordset()
    ' Perform some operations on recordset.
```

```
      rst.Close
      cnn.Close
End Sub
```

The Parameter Object and the Parameters Collection

The **Parameter** object in an ODBCDirect workspace is similar to the **Parameter** object in a Microsoft Jet workspace, with a few differences. In an ODBCDirect workspace, you can change the setting of the **Type** property, which is read-only in a Microsoft Jet workspace. You can also use the **Direction** property to indicate whether a parameter is an input parameter, an output parameter, or both, or the return value from the procedure. The following example specifies parameters for a query in an ODBCDirect workspace.

```
Function RunStoredProc() As Boolean
    Dim wrk As Workspace
    Dim qdf As QueryDef, rst As Recordset, fld As Field
    Dim cnn As Connection, strConnect As String, strSQL As String

    Set wrk = CreateWorkspace("ODBCDirect", "sa", "", dbUseODBC)
    strConnect = "ODBC;DSN=Pubs;UID=sa;PWD=;DATABASE=Pubs"
    Set cnn = wrk.OpenConnection("", dbDriverNoPrompt, False, strConnect)

    strSQL = "CREATE PROCEDURE tamram @lolimit money AS " _
        & "SELECT pub_id, type, title_id, price " _
        & "FROM titles WHERE price >@lolimit"
    cnn.Execute strSQL

    Set qdf = cnn.CreateQueryDef("RunStoredProc")
    qdf.SQL = "{ call tamram (?) }"
    qdf.Parameters(0).Value = CCur(10)
    Set rst = qdf.OpenRecordset()
    Do Until rst.EOF
        For Each fld In rst.Fields
            Debug.Print fld.Name, fld.Value
        Next fld
        rst.MoveNext
    Loop
End Function
```

The Recordset Object and the Recordsets Collection

The **Recordset** object represents the records that result from running a query on a **Connection** object or a **Database** object in an ODBCDirect workspace. The **Recordsets** collection contains all currently open **Recordset** objects on a **Connection** object or a **Database** object. The following table shows the relationship between the **Recordset** object and the **Recordsets** collection and other objects and collections in an ODBCDirect workspace.

Object or collection	Is contained by	Contains
Recordset object	**Recordsets** collection	**Field** objects
		Properties collection
Recordsets collection	**Connection** object	**Recordset** objects
	Database object	

The types of **Recordset** objects supported in an ODBCDirect workspace include the dynaset-type, snapshot-type, forward-only-type, and dynamic-type **Recordset** objects. For more information on all of these **Recordset** objects except the dynamic-type **Recordset** object, see "Table-Type Recordset Objects," "Dynaset-Type Recordset Objects," "Snapshot-Type Recordset Objects," "Forward-Only-Type Recordset Objects" earlier in this chapter. The following section describes dynamic-type **Recordset** objects.

Dynamic-Type Recordset Objects

An additional type of **Recordset** object, the dynamic-type **Recordset** object, is available in ODBCDirect workspaces. Dynamic-type **Recordset** objects behave like dynaset-type **Recordset** objects, but they are updated dynamically as other users make modifications to the underlying tables. To create a dynamic-type **Recordset** object, specify the **dbOpenDynamic** constant for the *type* argument of the **OpenRecordset** method.

Dynamic-type **Recordset** objects are available only if you're using an ODBC driver that supplies its own cursors. Because not all ODBC drivers supply their own cursors, you need to determine whether yours does before you try to open a dynamic-type **Recordset** object. If your ODBC driver doesn't supply its own cursors, then you should open a snapshot-type or forward-only-type **Recordset** object instead. For more information on cursors, see "Using Cursors in ODBCDirect Workspaces" later in this chapter.

The advantage of using a dynamic-type **Recordset** object is that the recordset will immediately reflect any changes to the data, including added or deleted records. For example, if you open a dynamic-type **Recordset** object and another user edits a record in one of the underlying tables, that change will be reflected in the **Recordset** you opened. In order to do this, however, DAO must constantly requery the data source, which may slow performance considerably. Therefore, avoid using dynamic-type **Recordset** objects except in situations where it's crucial to have the most up-to-date data at all times.

Opening Recordset Objects Asynchronously

In addition to running queries asynchronously, you can open **Recordset** objects asynchronously. To do so, specify the **dbRunAsync** constant for the *options* argument of the **OpenRecordset** method. You can then use the **Cancel** method and the **StillExecuting** property directly on the **Recordset** object. For example, if you open a **Recordset** object asynchronously, and it takes a long time to open because more records are returned than expected, you can give users the option of canceling the operation in order to specify more restrictive criteria that returns fewer records.

If you cancel an **OpenRecordset** method, the **Recordset** object becomes invalid and you must reopen it to retrieve a valid **Recordset** object.

Because moving to the last record in a recordset can take a long time, the **MoveLast** method of a **Recordset** object supports asynchronous operation. To perform an asynchronous **MoveLast** operation, use the **dbRunAsync** constant with the **MoveLast** method. Be sure to check the **StillExecuting** property to determine when this operation is complete.

The Field Object and the Fields Collection

In an ODBCDirect workspace, the **Field** object represents a field in a **QueryDef** object or a **Recordset** object. When you're performing batch updates, you can use the **Value**, **VisibleValue**, and **OriginalValue** properties of a **Field** object to verify successful completion of a batch update. For more information, see "Using Batch Optimistic Updating" in the following section.

Using ODBCDirect

The following sections explain how to perform some common operations in an ODBCDirect workspace: using batch optimistic updating, working with cursors, and working with stored procedures.

Using Batch Optimistic Updating

In many client/server applications, optimistic updates occur on a record-by-record basis. This usually happens with the following series of events:

1. A user edits a record.

2. The user tries to save the record.

3. The server attempts to place a lock on that record, and if successful, the record is updated. Otherwise, a lock violation is handled by the application.

4. The user moves to another record and the entire process is repeated.

Although this process works well for many applications, it is often more efficient to have the user edit multiple records that are cached locally and then submit these records to the server in a single batch for updating. This process is called *batch optimistic updating*.

▶ To use batch optimistic updating

1 Create an ODBCDirect workspace.

2 Set the **DefaultCursorDriver** property of the workspace to **dbUseClientBatchCursor**.

3 Open a **Connection** or **Database** object from the ODBCDirect workspace.

4 Use the **OpenRecordset** method on the **Connection** or **Database** object to open a **Recordset** and specify the **dbOptimisticBatch** constant in the *lockedits* argument.

5 Perform any edits to the **Recordset** object. All edits are cached locally.

6 When you are ready to update the data source, call the **Update** method on the **Recordset** object, specifying **dbUpdateBatch** for the *type* argument.

Note If you attempt a batch update while a record in that **Recordset** object is being edited by the user, the record being edited will automatically be updated before the batch update begins.

The following example illustrates how to use batch optimistic updating.

```
Function RunInBatch()
    Dim wrk As Workspace, cnn As Connection, rst As Recordset
    Dim strConnect As String

    ' Create ODBCDirect workspace.
    Set wrk = DBEngine.CreateWorkspace("ODBCDirect", "Admin", "", dbUseODBC)
    ' Set default cursor driver to dbUseClientBatchCursor.
    wrk.DefaultCursorDriver = dbUseClientBatchCursor
    ' Create connect string.
    strConnect = "ODBC;DSN=Pubs;DATABASE=Pubs;UID=sa;PWD=;"
    ' Open connection.
    Set cnn = wrk.OpenConnection("", dbDriverNoPrompt, False, strConnect)
    ' Open recordset on connection.
    Set rst = _
        cnn.OpenRecordset("SELECT * FROM sales", dbOpenDynaset, 0, dbOptimisticBatch)

    ' Change all records in local recordset.
    While Not rst.EOF
        rst.Edit
        rst!qty = rst!qty + 1
        rst.Update
        rst.MoveNext
    Wend

    ' Update all records in data source.
    rst.Update dbUpdateBatch
End Function
```

If multiple records have been edited locally, and you want to update the current record before you perform the batch update, you can call the **Update** method and specify the **dbUpdateCurrentRecord** constant for the *type* argument. This writes the current record to the data source without writing any other batch updates. This is illustrated in the following example.

```
' Edit and update first record.
' Only first record is written back to data source.
rst.MoveFirst
rst.Edit
rst!qty = rst!qty + 2
rst.Update dbUpdateCurrentRecord

' Update remaining records in data source.
rst.Update dbUpdateBatch
```

Handling Collisions

When you attempt to update a group of records in a single batch operation, it is possible that other users are editing one or more records you are trying to update, causing a *collision*. A collision occurs when a batch update attempts to update a record at the same time another user is updating the record.

To handle collisions, examine the **BatchCollisions** property on the **Recordset** object. The **BatchCollisions** property returns an array that stores bookmarks pointing to records in the **Recordset** object on which a collision occurred. Each time a collision occurs during a batch update, a bookmark for the record is added to the array returned by the **BatchCollisions** property. You can then move to each of these bookmarks and examine the following properties of the **Field** object of the current record.

Property	Description
Value	The current value of the field in your **Recordset** object. This corresponds to the value of the field after the **Update** method was called.
OriginalValue	The value of the field in your **Recordset** object before the **Update** method was called.
VisibleValue	The value of the field as it is stored in the database.

After examining these properties, you can choose one of the following options:

- You can force the current value in your **Recordset** object into the database, overwriting the field's original value. To do this, call the **Update** method and specify **True** for the *force* argument.

- You can change the current value in your **Recordset** object to the original value and force the change into the database.

Caution   Calling the **Update** method and specifying the **dbUpdateBatch** constant for the *type* argument and **True** for the *force* argument forces all your changes into the data source and overwrites any changes that other users made to the records. For this reason, it is safer to call the **Update** method without specifying the *force* argument, and then resolve collisions individually by using the array returned by the **BatchCollisions** property along with the **Value**, **OriginalValue**, and **VisibleValue** properties.

The following example shows how to use the array returned by the **BatchCollisions** property to force all changes made to a local **Recordset** object into the database.

```
Function BatchForceChanges()
    Dim rst As Recordset, cnn As Connection, varCollision As Variant

    ' Open recordset for batch optimistic updating.
    Set rst = _
        cnn.OpenRecordset("SELECT * FROM sales", dbOpenDynaset, 0, dbOptimisticBatch)
    ' Change all records in local recordset.
    While Not rst.EOF
        rst.Edit
        rst!qty = rst!qty + 1
        rst.Update
        rst.MoveNext
    Wend
    rst.Update dbUpdateBatch

    ' Check for collisions and force all changes to recordset
    ' into database one record at a time.
    For j = 0 to rst.BatchCollisionCount - 1
        varCollision = rst.BatchCollisions(j)
        rst.BookMark = varCollision
        rst.Update dbUpdateCurrentRecord, True
    Next j
End Function
```

In the preceding example, modifications to the **Recordset** object are written back to the database one record at a time. In the following example, all records are saved in a batch instead of writing one record at a time.

```
' Open recordset.
Set rst = _
    cnn.OpenRecordset("SELECT * FROM sales", dbOpenDynaset, 0, dbOptimisticBatch)
' Change all records in local recordset.
```

```
While Not rst.EOF
    rst.Edit
    rst!qty = rst!qty + 1
    rst.Update
    rst.MoveNext
Wend
rst.Update dbUpdateBatch, True
```

Using Cursors in ODBCDirect Workspaces

A *cursor* indicates the current record position in a result set. Most types of cursors contain a representation of the data in the data source, and are not updatable. *Keysets* are cursors that contain actual data, and are updatable.

You work with a cursor through the DAO **Recordset** object. When you open a **Recordset** object through DAO, ODBCDirect creates the corresponding cursor. Each type of **Recordset** object, except for the table-type **Recordset** object, corresponds to a different type of cursor.

Characteristics of Cursors

You can use cursors to work with sets of data on an ODBC data source. Cursors can:

- Represent some or all records in a single table.
- Represent some or all records in a multiple-table join.
- Represent no records.
- Be read-only or updatable at either the cursor or the field level.
- Be fully scrollable, meaning that you can move forward and backward through the records, or they can be forward-only scrolling.
- Exist on either the client or the server.

Client-Side Cursors vs. Server-Side Cursors

A cursor requires temporary resources to hold its data. These resources can be in the form of RAM, a paging file such as the virtual memory feature of Microsoft Windows, or temporary files or databases. If these resources are stored on the client machine, the cursor is called a *client-side* cursor. With this type of cursor, the server sends the data that the cursor represents across the network to the client, along with the data required by the cursor itself. The client manages the temporary resources needed by the cursor.

Some server database engines, such as Microsoft SQL Server version 6.0, support an additional type of cursor known as *server-side* cursors. With this cursor type, the server manages the result set with resources located on the server itself. The server returns only the requested data to the client over the network. Using this type of cursor can result in significant performance improvements compared to client-side cursors, especially in situations where excessive network traffic or inadequate network bandwidth is a problem. However, because RAM and disk space resources are needed at the server, you must plan accordingly and ensure that your server hardware is capable of managing all cursors requested by clients.

Choosing a Cursor Type

When you open a **Recordset** object on a non-ODBC data source, you can specify a constant for the *type* argument of the **OpenRecordset** method that determines what type of recordset is opened. When you open a **Recordset** object on an ODBC data source, you use this same argument to specify the type of cursor that the **Recordset** object represents. Each type of cursor corresponds to a type of recordset. The following table shows the four constants you can use for the *type* argument, the type of **Recordset** object that is created on a non-ODBC data source, and the type of cursor that is created on an ODBC data source.

Constant	Recordset type	Cursor type
dbOpenDynamic	Dynamic-type	Dynamic
dbOpenDynaset	Dynaset-type	Keyset
dbOpenSnapshot	Snapshot-type	Static
dbOpenForwardOnly	Forward-only-type	Forward-only scrolling (this is the default)

For more information about ODBC cursors, see the *ODBC 3.0 Programmer's Reference*.

Note Table-type **Recordset** objects aren't supported in ODBCDirect workspaces, so they have no corresponding cursor.

The **DefaultCursorDriver** property of a **Workspace** object specifies where ODBCDirect creates the cursor—on the client or on the server. You can set the **DefaultCursorDriver** property to any of the constants listed in the following table.

Constant	Description
dbUseODBCCursor	Use client-side cursors. Client-side cursors give better performance for small result sets, but degrade quickly for larger result sets.
dbUseServerCursor	Use server-side cursors. For most large operations, server-side cursors provide better performance, but may cause more network traffic. Not all ODBC data sources support server-side cursors.
dbUseDefaultCursor	Use server-side cursors if the server supports them; otherwise, use client-side cursors.
dbUseClientBatchCursor	Use client batch cursors. Required for batch updates.
dbUseNoCursor	Open all **Recordset** objects as forward-only-type, read-only, with a rowset size of 1.

Record Locking

When you open a **Recordset** object, you can also specify the type of record locking you want to use by setting the *lockedits* argument of the **OpenRecordset** method to the appropriate constant. The following table lists the five constants you can use for the *lockedits* argument of the **OpenRecordset** method, and describes the ODBC cursor lock type to which they correspond.

Constant	ODBC cursor lock type
dbOptimistic	Uses optimistic locking to determine how changes are made to the **Recordset** object in a multiuser environment. The page containing the record that is being edited is locked only while the record is being updated by the **Update** method.
DbPessimistic	Uses pessimistic locking to determine how changes are made to the **Recordset** object in a multiuser environment. The page containing the record that is being edited is locked as soon as you use the **Edit** method.
DbOptimisticValue	Uses optimistic concurrency based on record values.
DbOptimisticBatch	Uses batch optimistic updating.
DbReadOnly	Default for ODBCDirect workspaces. Prevents users from making changes to the data in the **Recordset** object.

Some combinations of cursors and lock types will not work together. For example, with Microsoft SQL Server version 6.0 cursors, if you specify the **dbOpenSnapshot** constant for the *type* argument of the OpenRecordset method, you must specify the **dbReadOnly** constant for the *lockedits* argument. Static cursors do not support the other types of record locking. Which combinations work together depends on the cursor driver. For specific information about compatible lock types, refer to your cursor driver documentation.

Your cursor driver can handle different combinations of cursor types and lock types in different ways. In some cases, it may return an error if it does not handle a specific combination. In other cases, it may switch to the nearest possible combination that it supports. If an error occurs, DAO places the error information in the **Errors** collection.

Cursor Limitations

In an ODBCDirect workspace, the default recordset is a read-only, forward-only-type **Recordset** object. Therefore, if you create the default **Recordset** object by opening it without specifying a value for the *type* argument, you won't be able to edit data on the server. If you want to edit data on the server, you need to explicitly specify a lock type other than **dbReadOnly** for the *lockedits* argument of the **OpenRecordset** method.

Because you can't open a table-type **Recordset** object in an ODBCDirect workspace, you can't use the **Index** property or the **Seek** method to retrieve data. Also, recordsets opened against ODBC data sources do not support any of the Find methods:

FindFirst, **FindNext**, **FindPrevious**, and **FindLast**. In a client/server environment, it's more efficient to fetch only the data that you need, rather than retrieving more records than you need and then searching through those records for the data that you want. Therefore, design your queries to return only the records that you need.

Retrieving Multiple Result Sets

Any SQL statement can include multiple SELECT statements or stored procedures that invoke one or more SELECT statements. Each SELECT statement generates a result set that must be processed by your code or discarded before the resources are released and the next result set is made available. Because you don't necessarily know how many results sets will be generated by a stored procedure, your code must be prepared to process an unknown number of result sets. Note that when a stored procedure returns multiple result sets, none of the result sets can be updated.

You can use either client-side cursors or server-side cursors to retrieve multiple result sets. If you use client-side cursors, multiple result sets are returned no matter what type of **Recordset** object you open. If you use server-side cursors to retrieve multiple result sets, you must open a forward-only-type **Recordset** object.

▶ **To retrieve multiple results sets**

1 Set the workspace's **DefaultCursorDriver** property to **dbUseServerCursor** to specify server-side cursors.

2 Create a **QueryDef** object and set its **SQL** property to a valid SQL string that returns multiple **Recordset** objects.

3 Set the **CacheSize** property of the **QueryDef** object to 1 to request that the server sends you one record at a time. When you retrieve records in this way, you don't actually utilize the cursor.

4 Open a **Recordset** object on the **QueryDef** object you just created. Specify **dbOpenForwardOnly** for the *type* argument of the **OpenRecordset** method.

5 Use the **NextRecordset** method to access the next **Recordset** object in the group of **Recordset** objects returned by the server. This discards the current **Recordset** object and replaces it with the next **Recordset** object specified in your query's SQL statement. If there are no more **Recordset** objects in the group of **Recordset** objects, then the return value of the **NextRecordset** method will be **False** and the current **Recordset** object will be empty.

The following example prints the values of each field for each record in each result set.

```
Function GetMultipleResults()
    Dim wrk As Workspace, rst As Recordset, cnn As Connection, qdf As QueryDef
    Dim fld As Field, strSQL As String, strConnect As String, fDone As Boolean

    ' Create ODBCDirect workspace.
    Set wrk = DBEngine.CreateWorkspace("ODBCDirect", "Admin", "", dbUseODBC)
    ' Create connect string.
```

```
strConnect = "ODBC;DSN=Pubs;DATABASE=Pubs;UID=sa;PWD=;"
' Open connection.
Set cnn = wrk.OpenConnection("", dbDriverNoPrompt, False, strConnect)
' Create SQL statement.
strSQL = "SELECT au_lname, au_fname FROM Authors; SELECT title FROM Titles;"
' Set default cursor driver.
wrk.DefaultCursorDriver = dbUseServerCursor

' Open recordset.
Set qdf = cnn.CreateQueryDef("", strSQL)
qdf.CacheSize = 1
' Open recordset on QueryDef.
Set rst = qdf.OpenRecordset(dbOpenForwardOnly)

Do Until fDone = True
    ' Print values for each field in each record of recordset.
    While Not rst.EOF
        For Each fld In rst.Fields
            Debug.Print fld.Value
        Next fld
        rst.MoveNext
    Wend
    fDone = Not rst.NextRecordset()
Loop
rst.Close
cnn.Close
wrk.Close
End Function
```

Working with Stored Procedures

You can use ODBCDirect **QueryDef** objects to run stored procedures. ODBCDirect **QueryDef** objects support stored procedures that have both input parameters and return values. Input parameters are the parameter values supplied to the procedure at run time. The procedure's return value is the value that it returns when it has finished running. For example, a stored procedure may return the number of records that have been affected.

The following example creates a stored procedure named GetEmps on the server.

```
strSQL = "CREATE PROCEDURE GetEmps AS "
strSQL = strSQL & "SELECT * FROM EMPLOYEE;"
cnn.Execute strSQL
```

If there is already a stored procedure named GetEmps on the server, you can use the DROP statement to delete it before creating a new one, as shown in the following example.

```
strSQL = "DROP PROCEDURE GetEmps;"
cnn.Execute strSQL
```

You can run the stored procedure by using the **Execute** method of a **Connection** object. To retrieve the return value, create a **QueryDef** object and open a recordset on it.

```
Set qdf = cnn.CreateQueryDef("qry", "{ call GetEmps() }")
Set rst = qdf.OpenRecordset
```

Use the **Parameter** object to work with parameters. The **Direction** property of a **Parameter** object tells DAO how the parameter will function. The ODBC driver tries to determine the parameter direction, but the **Direction** property is read/write, so you can set it if you need to. The following example creates a simple stored procedure with an input parameter and a return value. It then runs the procedure and retrieves the return value.

```
' Create stored procedure on the server.
strSQL = "CREATE PROCEDURE UpdateEmps (@invar int) AS RETURN @invar;"
cnn.Execute strSQL

' Create QueryDef object to run stored procedure.
Set qdf = cnn.CreateQueryDef("qry", "{ ? = call UpdateEmps(?) }")

' Handle parameters.
qdf.Parameters(0).Direction = dbParamReturnValue
qdf.Parameters(1) = 10
qdf.Execute

' Get return value.
var = qdf.Parameters(0).Value
```

ActiveX Controls and Dialog Boxes

Microsoft Excel 97, Word 97, and PowerPoint 97 share powerful new tools for creating custom dialog boxes. Because these applications use the same dialog box tools in the Visual Basic Editor, you only have to learn how to create custom dialog boxes one way for all three applications, and you can share these dialog boxes across applications.

After you've created a custom dialog box, you can add ActiveX controls (previously referred to as OLE controls) to it. You can also place ActiveX controls directly on a document, worksheet, or slide. To determine how custom dialog boxes and controls respond to specific user actions—for example, clicking a control or changing its value—you write event procedures that will run whenever a specific event occurs.

Note For information about designing forms in Microsoft Access, see *Building Applications with Microsoft Access 97*, available in Microsoft Access 97 and Microsoft Office 97, Developer Edition. An online version of *Building Applications with Microsoft Access 97* is available in the ValuPack on CD-ROM in Microsoft Access 97 and Microsoft Office 97, Professional Edition. For information about designing forms in Microsoft Outlook 97, see *Building Microsoft Outlook 97 Applications* by Peter Krebs, available from Microsoft Press.

Contents
- Designing Custom Dialog Boxes
- Using Custom Dialog Boxes
- Working with Controls on a Document, Sheet, or Slide
- Working with Controls Programmatically

Designing Custom Dialog Boxes

To create a custom dialog box, you must create a form (also called a *UserForm*) to contain controls, add controls to the form, set properties for the controls, and write code that responds to form and control events.

Note When you're in the Visual Basic Editor designing your dialog box, you're in design mode. In design mode, you can edit controls. Controls don't respond to events in design mode. When you run your dialog box—that is, when you display it the way users will see it—you're in run mode. Controls do respond to events in run mode.

Creating a New Dialog Box

Every custom dialog box in your project is a form, or UserForm. A new UserForm contains a title bar and an empty area in which you can place controls.

▶ **To create a new UserForm**

- On the **Insert** menu in the Visual Basic Editor, click **UserForm**.

    A new, empty UserForm is displayed. Use the **Properties** window to set properties for the UserForm—that is, to change the name, behavior, and appearance of the form. For example, to change the caption on a form, set the **Caption** property. For more information about the **Properties** window and the Visual Basic Editor, see Chapter 1, "Programming Basics."

Adding Controls to a Custom Dialog Box

Use the **Toolbox** to add controls to a custom dialog box. Click **Toolbox** on the **View** menu to display the **Toolbox** if it's not already visible. To see the name of a particular control in the **Toolbox**, position the mouse pointer over that control.

To add a control to a custom dialog box, find the control you want to add in the **Toolbox**, drag the control onto the form, and then drag one or more of the control's adjustment handles until the control is the size and shape you want. For more information about a specific type of control, add the control to a form, select the control, and then press F1.

Note Dragging a control (or a number of "grouped" controls) from a custom dialog box back to the **Toolbox** creates a template of that control, which you can reuse at any time. This is a useful feature for implementing a standard "look and feel" for your applications.

After you've added controls to the form, use the commands on the **Format** menu or the buttons on the **UserForm** toolbar in the Visual Basic Editor to adjust the alignment and spacing of the controls. Use the **Tab Order** dialog box (**View** menu) to set the tab order of the controls on the form.

Tip   The Visual Basic Editor sets the **TabIndex** property for the controls to determine the tab order. If you want to prevent users from tabbing to a particular control, you can set the **TabStop** property to **False** for that control. To do this, right-click the control, and then click **Properties** to display the Properties window.

▶ Practice 1: Design and run a custom dialog box

1   Create a new UserForm.

2   On the UserForm, insert a **Frame** control.

3   In the **Frame** control, insert three **OptionButton** controls.

4   Click **Run Sub/UserForm** on the **Run** menu.

The custom dialog box is displayed. The option buttons should work when you click them. Because you first created a **Frame** control to contain the option buttons, clicking one option button automatically turns all the other ones off in that control.

5   Click the **Close** button on the UserForm title bar to exit run mode and return to design mode.

Setting Control and Dialog Box Properties at Design Time

You can set some control properties at design time (before any macros are run). In design mode, right-click a control and then click **Properties** on the shortcut menu to display the **Properties** window. Property names are listed in the left-hand column in the window, and property values are listed in the right-hand column. You set a property value by typing the new value in the space to the right of the property name.

Tip   You can view the properties of an object either sorted alphabetically (on the **Alphabetic** tab in the **Properties** window) or sorted into functional categories (on the **Categorized** tab).

▶ Practice 2: Set control properties in design mode

1   Create a new UserForm.

2   Add an **Image** control, a **CommandButton** control, and a few other controls to the UserForm.

3   Right-click the image you added, click **Properties** on the shortcut menu to display the **Properties** window for the image, and then find **Picture** (for the **Picture** property) in the list of properties. To browse for files that you can set this property to, click the ellipsis button (…) in the space to the right of **Picture**. Select a file in the **Load Picture** dialog box, and then click **OK**.

4 Click the **CommandButton** you added; the list of properties in the **Properties** window changes to the properties of command buttons. Find **Caption** and type **Send Order** in the space to the right to set the value of the **Caption** property. The caption is the text that appears on the face of the command button.

5 In the list of properties for the command button, type **CmdSendOrder** in the space to the right of (**Name**). This sets the name you use to refer to the button in your code.

6 In the list of properties for the command button, type **Click here to send order** in the space to the right of **ControlTipText**. When the user positions the mouse pointer over this command button in run mode, this tip will appear, indicating what the button does.

7 In the list of properties for the command button, type **s** in the space to the right of **Accelerator**. Notice that the "S" in the "Send Order" caption on the command button is now underlined. (If you choose as an accelerator key a letter that isn't in the control caption, there will by no visual indication that the control has an accelerator key.) While any dialog box is running, the user can press ALT+the accelerator key (in this case, "S") to move the focus directly to the control.

8 On the **Run** menu, click **Run Sub/UserForm**, and then move the focus to a control other than the **Send Order** button. You can press ALT+S to move the focus to the **Send Order** button.

9 Click the **Close** button on the UserForm title bar to exit run mode and return to design mode.

Tip To set a property for several controls at the same time, select the controls and then change the value for that property in the **Properties** window.

▶ **Practice 3: Set UserForm properties in design mode**

1 Click anywhere in a UserForm except on a control to select the UserForm.

2 In the **Properties** window, type **Book Order Form** in the space to the right of **Caption**.

3 In the space to the right of **BackColor** in the list of properties, click the arrow to see a set of values from which to choose. Click the **Palette** tab, and then click the color you want to set as the background color for the dialog box.

4 To see the results of your new settings, run the dialog box. Click the **Close** button on the title bar to return to design mode.

Creating Tabs in Dialog Boxes

If you need for a single dialog box to handle a large number of controls that can be sorted into categories, you can create a dialog box with two or more tabs and then place different sets of related controls on different tabs in the dialog box. To create a dialog box with tabs, add a **MultiPage** control to the dialog box and then add controls to each tab (or *page*). To add, remove, rename, or move a page in a **MultiPage** control, right-click one of the pages in design mode, and then click a command on the shortcut menu.

Note Don't confuse **MultiPage** controls with **TabStrip** controls. The pages (or tabs) of a **MultiPage** control contain a unique set of controls that you add during design time to each page. Using a **TabStrip** control, which can look like a series of tabs or buttons, you can modify the values of a shared set of controls at run time. For information about using TabStrip controls, see "Displaying a Custom Dialog Box" later in this chapter.

Writing Code to Respond to Dialog Box and Control Events

Each form or control recognizes a predefined set of events, which can be triggered either by the user or by the system. For example, a command button recognizes the Click event that occurs when the user clicks that button, and a form recognizes the Initialize event that occurs when the form is loaded. To specify how a form or control should respond to events, you write *event procedures.*

To write an event procedure for a form or control, open the **Code** window by double-clicking the UserForm or control object, and then click the event name in the **Procedure** box (in the upper-right corner of the window). Event procedures include the name of the UserForm or control. For example, the name of the Click event procedure for the command button Command1 is Command1_Click. For more information about writing event procedures, see Chapter 1, "Programming Basics."

▶ **Practice 4: Write and run an event procedure for a command button**

1   Create a new UserForm, and then add a **CommandButton**, a **CheckBox**, and a **ComboBox** control to it.

2   Click the command button. In the **Properties** window, change the code name of the command button by typing **CmdSendOrder** in the space to the right of **(Name)**.

3   Double-click the command button to view the code associated with it. By default, the Click event procedure will be displayed in the **Code** window.

4   Add a statement to the CmdSendOrder_Click procedure to display a simple message box (use the following example).

```
Private Sub CommandButton1_Click()
    MsgBox "I've been clicked once"
End Sub
```

5   Run the dialog box to see the results. The CmdSendOrder_Click event procedure will run every time this command button is clicked in run mode. Because you haven't written code for the other controls yet, they don't respond to your mouse actions. Click the **Close** button on the title bar to return to design mode.

To see all the events that command buttons recognize, click the down arrow next to the **Procedure** box in the **Code** window. Events that already have procedures written for them appear bold. Click an event name in the list to display its associated procedure.

To see the events for a different control on the same UserForm or for the UserForm itself, click the object name in the **Object** box in the **Code** window, and then click the arrow next to the **Procedure** box.

Tip If you add code to an event procedure before you change the code name of the control, your code will still have its previous code name in any procedures it's used in. For example, assume that you add code to the Click event for the Command1 button and then rename the control as Command2. When you double-click Command2, you won't see any code in the Click event procedure; You'll need to move code from Command1_Click to Command2_Click. To simplify development, it's a good idea to name your controls with the names you really want for them before you write any code.

Using Custom Dialog Boxes

To exchange information with the user by way of a custom dialog box, you must display the dialog box to the user, respond to user actions in the dialog box, and, when the dialog box is closed, get information that the user entered in it.

Displaying a Custom Dialog Box

When you want to display a custom dialog box to yourself for testing purposes, you click **Run Sub/UserForm** on the **Run** menu in the Visual Basic Editor. However, when you want to display a dialog box to a user, you use the **Show** method. The following example displays the dialog box named "UserForm1."

```
UserForm1.Show
```

Getting and Setting Properties at Run Time

If you want to set default values for controls in a custom dialog box, modify controls while the dialog box is visible, and have access to the information that a user enters in the dialog box, you must set and read the values of control properties at run time.

Setting Initial Values for Controls

To set the initial value, or *default value*, that a control will have every time the dialog box that contains it is displayed, add code to the Initialize event procedure for the UserForm that contains the control that sets the value for the control. When you display the dialog box, the Initialize event will be triggered, and the control's value will be initialized.

▶ **Practice 5: Write and run an Initialize event procedure for a UserForm**

1   Create a new UserForm, and then add a **TextBox**, a **ListBox**, and a **CheckBox** control to it.

2   Click the text box. In the **Properties** window, type **txtCustomerName** in the space to the right of **(Name)** to set the code name of the text box. Then change the code name of the list box to "lstRegions," change the code name of the check box to "chkSendExpress," and change the code name of the UserForm itself to "frmPhoneOrders."

3   Double-click the UserForm to display the **Code** window. With **UserForm** selected in the **Object** box of the **Code** window, select **Initialize** in the **Procedure** box. Complete the UserForm_Initialize procedure, as shown in the following example.

```
Private Sub UserForm_Initialize()
    With frmPhoneOrders
        .txtCustomerName.Text = "Grant Clarridge"   'Sets default text
        .chkSendExpress.Value = True   'Checks check box by default
        With .lstRegions
            .AddItem "North"           'These lines populate the list box
            .AddItem "South"
            .AddItem "East"
            .AddItem "West"
            .ListIndex = 3             'Selects the 4th item in the list
        End With
    End With
End Sub
```

Note   Although collections in the Microsoft Excel, Word, and PowerPoint object models are 1-based, arrays and collections associated with forms are 0-based. Therefore, to select the fourth item in the list in the preceding example, you must set the **ListIndex** property to 3.

4   Run the dialog box to see the results. Click the **Close** button on the title bar to return to design mode.

Use Me to Simplify Event Procedure Code

In the preceding example, you can use the keyword **Me** instead of the code name of the UserForm. That is, you can replace the statement With frmPhoneOrders with the statement With Me. The **Me** keyword used in code for a UserForm or a control on the UserForm represents the UserForm itself. This technique lets you use long, meaningful names for controls while still making code easy to write. Many examples in this chapter demonstrate how to use **Me** this way.

If you want to set the initial value (default value) for a control but you don't want that to be the initial value every time you call the dialog box, you can use Visual Basic code to set the control's value before you display the dialog box that contains the control. The following example uses the **AddItem** method to add data to a list box, sets the value of a text box, and displays the dialog box that contains these controls.

```
Private Sub GetUserName()
    With UserForm1
        .lstRegions.AddItem "North"
        .lstRegions.AddItem "South"
        .lstRegions.AddItem "East"
        .lstRegions.AddItem "West"
        .txtSalesPersonID.Text = "00000"
        .Show
        ' ...
    End With
End Sub
```

Setting Values to Modify Controls While a Dialog Box Is Running

You can set properties and apply methods of controls and the UserForm while a dialog box is running. The following example sets the text (the **Text** property) of TextBox1 to "Hello."

```
TextBox1.Text = "Hello"
```

By setting control properties and applying control methods at run time, you can make changes in a running dialog box in response to a choice the user makes. For example, if you want a particular control to be available only while a particular check box is selected, you can write code that enables the control whenever the user selects the check box and disables it whenever the user clears the check box.

Enabling a Control

You can use the **Enabled** property of a control to prevent the user from making changes to the control unless a specified condition is met. For example, a common use of the **Enabled** property is in an event procedure for a text box that enables the **OK** button only when the user has entered a value that conforms to a standard pattern.

Setting the **Enabled** property is often used to make a set of option buttons available only while the user has a particular check box selected, as demonstrated in the following practice. This code is included in the Change event procedure for the check box, and it runs whenever the state of the check box (checked or cleared) changes.

▶ **Practice 6: Enable and disable controls during run time**

1 Create a new UserForm, and then add a **CheckBox** control to it. Add a **Frame** control to the UserForm, and then place three **OptionButton** controls within the frame.

2 Double-click the check box to switch to the **Code** window. With **CheckBox1** selected in the **Object** box in the **Code** window, click **Change** in the **Procedure** box. Complete the CheckBox1_Change procedure as shown in the following example.

```
Private Sub CheckBox1_Change()
    With Me
        If .CheckBox1.Value = True Then
            .OptionButton1.Enabled = False
            .OptionButton2.Enabled = False
            .OptionButton3.Enabled = False
        Else
            .OptionButton1.Enabled = True
            .OptionButton2.Enabled = True
            .OptionButton3.Enabled = True
        End If
    End With
End Sub
```

3   Run the dialog box; select and clear the check box to see how changing the state of the check box enables or disables the three option buttons. Click the **Close** button on the title bar to return to design mode.

Setting the Focus to a Control

You can set the focus to a control in a dialog box by using the **SetFocus** method of that control (the control with the focus is the one that responds to keyboard input from the user).

▶ **Practice 7: Set the control focus during run time**

1   Create a new UserForm, and then add a **CheckBox**, an **Image**, and a few other controls to it. In the **Properties** window, set the **Picture** property of the image to display a graphic.

2   Double-click the image to switch to the **Code** window. With **Image1** selected in the **Object** box in the **Code** window, select **Click** in the **Procedure** box. Complete the Image1_Click procedure as shown in the following example.

```
Private Sub Image1_Click()
    Me.CheckBox1.SetFocus
End Sub
```

3   Run the dialog box. Give the focus to a control other than CheckBox1. When you click Image1, CheckBox1 is given the focus (a dotted rectangle surrounds the check box, and you can press the SPACEBAR to select or clear the check box). Click the **Close** button on the title bar to return to design mode.

Displaying and Hiding Parts of a Dialog Box

You can set properties or apply methods of the UserForm itself while a dialog box is running. A common use for this is to expand a UserForm to reveal additional options when the user clicks a command button.

▶ **Practice 8: Resize a UserForm during run time**

1 Create a new UserForm. The value of its **Height** property (the number to the right of **Height** in the **Properties** window) should be 180.

2 Add a **CommandButton** control at the top of the UserForm, and then add a **CheckBox** control to the bottom of the UserForm (the **Top** property for the check box should be at least 120).

3 Double-click the UserForm to switch to the **Code** window. With **UserForm** selected in the **Object** box of the **Code** window, click **Initialize** in the **Procedure** box. Complete the UserForm_Initialize procedure as shown in the following example. Setting the height of the dialog box to 120 points when it's initially displayed specifies that the control at the bottom of the dialog box will be hidden when the dialog box opens.

```
Private Sub UserForm_Initialize()
    Me.Height = 120
End Sub
```

4 In the **Object** box in the **Code** window, click **CommandButton1**, and then select **Click** in the **Procedure** box. Complete the Image1_Click procedure as shown in the following example. The example toggles the value of the **Height** property of the UserForm between 120 points (the initial value) and 180 points.

```
Private Sub OptionButton1_Click()
    With Me
        .Height = 300 - .Height
    End With
End Sub
```

5 Run the dialog box. To hide or display the bottom section of the dialog box that contains the check box, click the command button. Click the **Close** button on the title bar to return to design mode.

Browsing Data with a TabStrip Control

You can use a **TabStrip** control to view different sets of information in the same set of controls in a dialog box. For example, if you want to use one area of a dialog box to display contact information pertaining to a group of individuals, you can create a **TabStrip** control and then add controls to contain the name, address, and phone number of each person in the group. You can then add a "tab" to the **TabStrip** control for each member of the group. After doing this, you can write code that, when you click a particular tab, updates the controls to display data about the person identified on that tab.

Tip To add, remove, rename, or move a tab in a tab strip, right-click the tab strip in design mode, and then click an item on the shortcut menu.

The following example changes the value of TextBox1 each time a different tab of TabStrip1 is clicked. The index number of the tab that was clicked is passed to the event procedure.

```
Private Sub TabStrip1_Click(ByVal Index As Long)
If Index = 0 Then
    Me.TextBox1.Text = "7710 Betty Jane Lane"
ElseIf Index = 1 Then
    Me.TextBox1.Text = "9523 15th Ave NE"
End If
End Sub
```

Keep in mind that forms-related collections are 0-based, which means that the index of the first member in any collection is 0 (zero).

Note Don't confuse **TabStrip** controls with **MultiPage** controls. Unlike a **TabStrip** control, the pages (or tabs) of a **MultiPage** control contain a unique set of controls that you add during design time to each page. For information about using **MultiPage** controls, see "Creating Tabs in Dialog Boxes" earlier in this chapter.

Data Validation

There are times when you'll want to make sure that the user only enters a value of a specific type in a particular control. For example, if you're using a **TextBox** control, which allows the user to enter any data type, and if your code expects to get a value of type **Integer** back from the text box, you should write code that verifies that the user has entered a valid integer before the dialog box closes. To verify that the user has entered the appropriate type of data in a control, you can check the value of the control either when the control loses the focus or when the dialog box is closed. The following example will prevent the user from moving the focus away from the txtCustAge text box without first entering a valid number.

```
Private Sub txtCustAge_Exit(ByVal Cancel As MSForms.ReturnBoolean)
    If Not IsNumeric(txtCustAge.Text) Then
        MsgBox "Please enter numeric value for the customer's age."
        Cancel = True
    End If
End Sub
```

Notice that you set the *Cancel* argument of a control's Exit event procedure to **True** to prevent the control from losing the focus.

To verify data before a dialog box closes, include code to check the contents of one or more controls in the dialog box in the same routine that unloads the dialog box. If a control contains invalid data, use an **Exit Sub** statement to exit the procedure before the **Unload** statement can be executed. The following example runs whenever the user clicks the cmdOK command button.This procedure prevents the user from closing the dialog box by using the cmdOK button until the txtCustAge text box contains a number.

```
Private Sub cmdOK_Click()
    If Not IsNumeric(txtCustAge.Text) Then
        MsgBox "Please enter numeric value for the customer's age."
        txtCustAge.SetFocus
        Exit Sub
    End If
    custAge = txtCustAge.Text
    Unload Me
End Sub
```

Getting Values When the Dialog Box Closes

Any data that a user enters in a dialog box is lost when the dialog box is closed. If you return the values of controls in a UserForm after the form has been unloaded, you get the initial values for the controls rather than any values the user may have entered.

If you want to save the data entered in a dialog box by a user, you can do so by saving the information to module-level variables while the dialog box is still running. The following example displays a dialog box and saves the data that's been entered in it.

```
'Code in module to declare public variables
Public strRegion As String
Public intSalesPersonID As Integer
Public blnCancelled As Boolean

'Code in form
Private Sub cmdCancel_Click()
    Module1.blnCancelled = True
    Unload Me
End Sub

Private Sub cmdOK_Click()
    'Save data
    intSalesPersonID = txtSalesPersonID.Text
    strRegion = lstRegions.List(lstRegions.ListIndex)
    Module1.blnCancelled = False
    Unload Me
End Sub

Private Sub UserForm_Initialize()
    Module1.blnCancelled = True
End Sub

'Code in module to display form
Sub LaunchSalesPersonForm()
    frmSalesPeople.Show
    If blnCancelled = True Then
        MsgBox "Operation Cancelled!", vbExclamation
    Else
        MsgBox "The Salesperson's ID is: " & _
            intSalesPersonID & _
            "The Region is: " & strRegion
    End If
End Sub
```

Closing a Custom Dialog Box

Dialog boxes are always displayed as *modal*. That is, the user must close the dialog box before returning to the document. Use the **Unload** statement to unload a UserForm when the user indicates that he or she wants to close the dialog box. Typically, you provide a command button in the dialog box that the user can click to close it.

The following example inserts the name of a dialog box into a Word document and then unloads the form. The code appears in the Click event for an **OK** button in the dialog box.

```
Private Sub cmdOK_Click()
    ActiveDocument.Content.InsertAfter txtUserName.Text
    Unload UserForm1
End Sub
```

Using the Same Dialog Box in Different Applications

Microsoft Excel, Word, and PowerPoint share features for creating custom dialog boxes. You can create a UserForm in one of these applications and share it with the other applications.

▶ **To share a UserForm with another application**

1   In the Visual Basic Editor for the application in which you created the UserForm, right-click the UserForm in the **Project Explorer**, and then click **Export File** on the shortcut menu.

2   Choose a name to export the UserForm as, and then click **Save**. The UserForm is saved with the .frm file name extension.

3   In the Visual Basic Editor for the application in which you want to use the UserForm, right-click the project where you want to store the form in the Project Explorer, and then click **Import File** on the shortcut menu.

4   Select the name you gave the dialog box when you saved it, and then click **Open**.

Note   Not every UserForm that runs as it's supposed to in one application will run correctly when it's imported into another application. For example, if you import a UserForm that contains Word-specific code into Microsoft Excel, the UserForm won't run correctly.

Working with Controls on a Document, Sheet, or Slide

Just as you can add ActiveX controls to custom dialog boxes, you can add controls directly to a document, sheet, or slide to make it interactive. For example, you might add text boxes, list boxes, option buttons, and other controls to a document to turn it into an online form; you might add a button to a sheet that runs a commonly used macro; or you might add buttons and other controls to the slides in a presentation to help the user navigate the slide show.

Although working with a control on a document, sheet, or slide is very similar to working with a control in a custom dialog box, there are a few differences. Among those differences are the following:

- On a document, sheet, or slide, you add controls by using the **Control Toolbox**, not the **Toolbox**. To display the **Control Toolbox**, point to **Toolbars** on the **View** menu, and then click **Control Toolbox**.

- When you're designing a custom dialog box, you run a dialog box to switch to run mode, where your controls will respond to events, and you close a dialog box and return to the Visual Basic Editor to switch back to design mode, where you can work with the controls without having them respond to events. When you're working with controls on documents or in workbooks, you click the **Exit Design Mode** button on the **Visual Basic** toolbar to switch to run mode, and you click the **Design Mode** button to switch back to design mode. In PowerPoint, you run a slide show to switch to run mode, and you switch to any editing view to switch back to design mode.

- A control may not have the same set of events on a document, sheet, or slide as it does on a UserForm. For example, a command button on a UserForm has an Exit event, whereas a command button on a document doesn't.

Using ActiveX Controls on Word Documents

You can add controls to documents to create interactive documents, such as online forms. Keep the following points in mind when you're working with controls on documents:

- You can add ActiveX controls to either the text layer or the drawing layer. To add a control to the text layer, hold down the SHIFT key while you click the control on the **Control Toolbox** toolbar that you want to add to the document. To add a control to the drawing layer, click the control on the **Control Toolbox** toolbar without holding down the SHIFT key.

- A control you add to the text layer is an **InlineShape** object to which you gain access programmatically through the **InlineShapes** collection. A control you add to the drawing layer is a **Shape** object to which you gain access programmatically through the **Shapes** collection.

- Controls in the text layer are treated like characters and are positioned as characters within a line of text. For example, if you place controls in the cells within a table, the controls will be automatically moved when you resize any columns in the table.

- You cannot drag controls from the **Control Toolbox** onto a Word document. When you press SHIFT and click a control to add it to the text layer, the control is automatically added at the insertion point. When you click a control to add it to the drawing layer, the position of the control is based on the position of the insertion point, but may not match it. If you add multiple controls to the drawing layer without moving the insertion point, the controls will all be placed in the same position, one on top of the other, so that you only see the last one you added.

- In design mode, ActiveX controls in the drawing layer are visible only in page layout view or online layout view.

- ActiveX controls in the drawing layer are always in run mode (so that they can receive input from a user) in page layout view or online layout view.

- If you want the user to be able to move between controls in an online form by pressing TAB, add the controls to the text layer, and protect the form by clicking the **Protect Form** button on the **Forms** toolbar.

- If you want to add form fields instead of ActiveX controls to your document to create an online form, use the **Forms** toolbar.

Using ActiveX Controls on Microsoft Excel Sheets

You can add controls to worksheets or chart sheets next to the data the controls are linked to so that they're easy for the user to find and understand, and so that using them causes only minimal interruptions during a work session. For example, you can add to a worksheet a button that runs a procedure that formats the active cell when the button is clicked.

Keep the following points in mind when you're working with controls on sheets:

- In addition to the standard properties available for ActiveX controls, you can use the following properties with ActiveX controls in Microsoft Excel: **BottomRightCell**, **LinkedCell**, **ListFillRange**, **Placement**, **PrintObject**, **TopLeftCell**, and **ZOrder**.

You can set and return these properties by using the ActiveX control name. The following example scrolls through the workbook window until CommandButton1 is in the upper-left corner of the window.

```
Set t = Sheet1.CommandButton1.TopLeftCell
With ActiveWindow
    .ScrollRow = t.Row
    .ScrollColumn = t.Column
End With
```

- Some Microsoft Excel Visual Basic methods and properties are disabled when an ActiveX control is activated. For instance, you cannot use the **Sort** method when a control is active; thus, the following example will fail in a Click event procedure (because the control is still active after the user clicks it).

```
Private Sub CommandButton1_Click
    Range("a1:a10").Sort Key1:=Range("a1")
End Sub
```

You can work around this problem by activating some other element on the sheet before you use the property or method that failed. For instance, the following example sorts the range.

```
Private Sub CommandButton1_Click
    Range("a1").Activate
    Range("a1:a10").Sort Key1:=Range("a1")
    CommandButton1.Activate
End Sub
```

- Controls in a Microsoft Excel workbook embedded in a document in another application won't work if the user double-clicks the workbook to edit it. The controls will work if the user right-clicks the workbook and then clicks the **Open** command on the shortcut menu.

- When you save a Microsoft Excel 97 workbook by using the Microsoft Excel 5.0/95 Workbook file format, all ActiveX control information is lost.

- The **Me** keyword in an event procedure for an ActiveX control on a sheet refers to the sheet, not to the control.

Using ActiveX Controls on PowerPoint Slides

Adding controls to your PowerPoint slides provides a sophisticated way for you to exchange information with the user while a slide show is running. For example, you can use controls on slides so that viewers of a show designed to be run in a kiosk have a way to choose options and then run a custom show based on the viewer's choices.

Keep the following points in mind when you're working with controls on slides:

- A control on a slide is in design mode except when the slide show is running.

- If you want a particular control to appear on all the slides in a presentation, add the control to the slide master.

- The **Me** keyword in an event procedure for a control on a slide refers to the slide. The **Me** keyword in an event procedure for a control on a master refers to the master, not to the slide that's being displayed when the control event is triggered.

- Writing event code for controls on slides is very similar to writing event code for controls in dialog boxes. The following example (the Click event procedure for the command button named "cmdChangeColor") sets the background for the slide the button is on.

```
Private Sub cmdChangeColor_Click()
    With Me
        .FollowMasterBackground = Not .FollowMasterBackground
        .Background.Fill.PresetGradient msoGradientHorizontal, 1,
msoGradientBrass
    End With
End Sub
```

- You may want to use controls to provide your slide show with navigation tools that are more complex than those built into PowerPoint. For instance, if you add two buttons named "cmdBack" and "cmdForward" to the slide master and write the code in the following example for them, all slides based on the master (and set to show master background graphics) will have these professional-looking navigation buttons, which will be active during a slide show.

```
Private Sub cmdBack_Click()
    Me.Parent.SlideShowWindow.View.Previous
End Sub

Private Sub cmdForward_Click()
    Me.Parent.SlideShowWindow.View.Next
End Sub
```

- To work with all the ActiveX controls on a particular slide without affecting the other shapes on the slide, you can construct a **ShapeRange** collection that contains only controls. You can then either apply properties and methods to the entire collection or iterate through the collection to work with each control individually. The following example aligns all the controls on slide one in the active presentation and arranges them vertically.

```
With ActivePresentation.Slides(1).Shapes
    numShapes = .Count
    If numShapes > 1 Then
        numControls = 0
        ReDim ctrlArray(1 To numShapes)
        For i = 1 To numShapes
            If .Item(i).Type = msoOLEControlObject Then
                numControls = numControls + 1
                ctrlArray(numControls) = .Item(i).Name
            End If
        Next
        If numControls > 1 Then
            ReDim Preserve ctrlArray(1 To numControls)
            Set ctrlRange = .Range(ctrlArray)
            ctrlRange.Distribute msoDistributeVertically, True
            ctrlRange.Align msoAlignLefts, True
        End If
    End If
End With
```

Working with Controls Programmatically

To gain access to a control programmatically, you can either refer to the control by its code name or get to it through the collection it belongs to. (The code name of a control is the value of the **(Name)** property for that control in the **Properties** window.)

The following example sets the caption for the control named "CommandButton1."

```
CommandButton1.Caption = "Run"
```

Note that when you use a control name outside the class module for the document, sheet, or slide that contains the control, you must qualify the control name with the code name of the document, sheet, or slide. The following example changes the caption on the control named "CommandButton1" on the Sheet1.

```
Sheet1.CommandButton1.Caption = "Run"
```

You can also gain access to ActiveX controls through the **Shapes**, **OLEObjects**, or **InlineShapes** collection. ActiveX controls you add to the drawing layer of a document, sheet, or slide are contained in **Shape** objects and can be programmatically controlled through the **Shapes** collection. In Microsoft Excel, ActiveX controls are also contained in **OLEObject** objects that can be controlled through the **OLEObjects** collection. In Word, ActiveX controls you add to the text layer of a document are contained in **InlineShape** objects and can be controlled through the **InlineShapes** collection.

Important   You use the name of the **Shape** object that contains a particular control, not the code name of the control, to gain access to the control programmatically through a collection. In Microsoft Excel and PowerPoint, the name of the object that contains a control matches the code name of the control by default. This isn't true in Word, however; the name of the object that contains a control (which will be something like "Control 1" by default) is unrelated to the code name of a control (which will be something like "CommandButton1" by default). To change the code name of a control, select the control and change the value to the right of **(Name)** in the **Properties** window. To change the name of the **Shape** object, **OLEObject** object, or other object that contains the control, change the value of its **Name** property.

The following example adds a command button to worksheet one.

```
Worksheets(1).OLEObjects.Add "Forms.CommandButton.1", _
    Left:=10, Top:=10, Height:=20, Width:=100
```

The following example sets the **Left** property for CommandButton1 on worksheet one.

```
Worksheets(1).OLEObjects("CommandButton1").Left = 10
```

The following example sets the caption for CommandButton1.

```
Worksheets(1).OLEObjects("CommandButton1").Object.Caption = "Run"
```

The following example adds a check box to the active document's text layer.

```
ActiveDocument.InlineShapes.AddOLEControl ClassType:="Forms.CheckBox.1"
```

The following example sets the **Width** property for the first shape in the active document's text layer.

```
ActiveDocument.InlineShapes(1).Width = 200
```

The following example sets the **Value** property for the first shape in the active document's text layer.

```
ActiveDocument.InlineShapes(1).OLEFormat.Object.Value = True
```

The following example adds a combo box to the active document's drawing layer.

```
ActiveDocument.Shapes.AddOLEControl ClassType:="Forms.ComboBox.1"
```

The following example sets the **Left** property for a combo box contained in Control 1 in the active document's drawing layer.

```
ActiveDocument.Shapes("Control 1").Left = 100
```

The following example sets the **Text** property for a combo box contained in Control 1 in the active document's drawing layer.

```
ActiveDocument.Shapes("Control 1").OLEFormat.Object.Text = "Reed"
```

The following example adds a command button to slide one in the active presentation.

```
ActivePresentation.Slides(1).Shapes.AddOLEObject Left:=100, Top:=100, _
    Width:=150, Height:=50, ClassName:="Forms.CommandButton.1"
```

The following example sets the **Left** property for the control contained in CommandButton1 on slide one in the active presentation.

```
ActivePresentation.Slides(1).Shapes("CommandButton1").Left = 100
```

The following example sets the **Caption** property for the control contained in CommandButton1 on slide one in the active presentation.

```
ActivePresentation.Slides(1).Shapes("CommandButton1") _
    .OLEFormat.Object.Caption = "Run"
```

CHAPTER 13

Optimizing for Size and Speed

Visual Basic is an extremely flexible programming language: there are often several ways to accomplish the same task. When you first start to program, or when you write a macro that will run only once, you'll probably be satisfied with simply "getting the job done." When you write a macro that will be used many times—such as a macro that prepares a weekly report, or an Auto_Open macro that runs every time you open a workbook or document—or when you write a macro that will be used by other people, you'll probably want to *optimize* the macro so that it requires less time and memory to run. The techniques described in this chapter will help you write smaller, faster macros.

Note For information about optimizing Visual Basic in Microsoft Access, see *Building Applications with Microsoft Access 97*, available in Microsoft Access 97 and Microsoft Office 97, Developer Edition. An online version of *Building Applications with Microsoft Access 97* is available in the ValuPack on CD-ROM in Microsoft Access 97 and Microsoft Office 97, Professional Edition.

Contents

- General Optimization Strategies
- Strategies for Optimizing Microsoft Excel
- Strategies for Optimizing Microsoft Word

General Optimization Strategies

Use the following techniques for optimizing your Microsoft Excel, Word, and PowerPoint code.

Note Most of the example code in this section was written in Microsoft Excel, but the principles also apply to Word and PowerPoint. For information about optimizing Visual Basic in Microsoft Access, see *Building Applications with Microsoft Access 97*.

Minimizing OLE References

Every Visual Basic method or property call requires one or more calls through the OLE IDispatch interface. These OLE calls take time. Minimizing the number of method or property calls is one of the best ways to make your macro run faster.

Because you use a period (a "dot") to separate the parts of a Visual Basic statement, an easy way to keep track of the number of method and property calls is to "count the dots." For example, the following statement contains three dots.

```
Workbooks(1).Sheets(1).Range("c5").Value = 10
```

The following statement contains only one dot.

```
ActiveWindow.Left = 200
```

The examples in the following sections demonstrate how reducing the number of dots creates faster-running code.

Using Object Variables

If you find that you're using the same object reference over and over, you can set a variable for the object and subsequently use the variable in place of the object reference. This way, you'll only need to call the object accessor once, when you set the variable, instead of calling it each time you want to refer to the object. The following example calls the **Workbooks** method and the **Sheets** method twice each.

```
Workbooks(1).Sheets(1).Range("c5").Value = 10
Workbooks(1).Sheets(1).Range("d10").Value = 12
```

You can optimize the preceding example by setting an object variable. The following example calls the **Workbooks** method and the **Sheets** method only once each.

```
Set sheet = Workbooks(1).Sheets(1)
sheet.Range("c5").Value = 10
sheet.Range("d10").Value = 12
```

Using the With Statement

You can use the **With** statement to eliminate the need for repetitive object references, without setting an explicit object variable. The example in the preceding section could be rewritten as follows, using the **With** statement. The following example calls the **Workbooks** method and the **Sheets** method only once each.

```
With Workbooks(1).Sheets(1)
    .Range("c5").Value = 10
    .Range("d10").Value = 12
End With
```

Using the **With** statement eliminates the need for the intermediate variable used in the example in the preceding section; otherwise, this code is the same as in that example.

Using a For Each...Next Loop

Using a **For Each...Next** loop to iterate through a collection or array is faster than using an indexed loop. In most cases, using a **For Each...Next** loop is also more convenient and makes your macro smaller and easier to read and debug.

The following example is slow because it sets the row variable `thisRow` by calling `r.Rows(i)` each time through the loop.

```
Set r = Worksheets(1).Range("a1:a200")
For i = 1 To r.Rows.Count
    Set thisRow = r.Rows(i)
    If thisRow.Cells(1, 1).Value < 0 Then
        thisRow.Font.Color = RGB(255, 0, 0)
    End If
Next
```

The following example is faster and smaller than the preceding one because the **For Each...Next** loop keeps track of the row count and position.

```
For Each thisRow In Worksheets(1).Range("a1:a200").Rows
    If thisRow.Cells(1, 1).Value < 0 Then
        thisRow.Font.Color = RGB(255, 0, 0)
    End If
Next
```

Keeping Properties and Methods Outside Loops

Your code can get variable values faster than it can get property values. Therefore, if your code gets the value of a property within a loop, it will run faster if you assign the property to a variable outside the loop and use the variable instead of the property inside the loop. The following example is slow because it gets the **Value** property each time through the loop.

```
For iLoop = 2 To 200
    Cells(iLoop, 1).Value = Cells(1, 1).Value
Next
```

The following example is faster than the preceding one because the value of one property has been assigned to the variable `cv` before the loop begins. Visual Basic must therefore access only one property value (instead of two) each time through the loop.

```
cv = Cells(1, 1).Value
For iLoop = 2 To 200
    Cells(iLoop, 1).Value = cv
Next
```

If you're using an object accessor inside a loop, try to move it outside the loop. The following example calls the **ActiveWorkbook** property, the **Sheets** property, and the **Cells** property each time through the loop.

```
For c = 1 To 1000
   ActiveWorkbook.Sheets(1).Cells(c, 1) = c
Next
```

Rewriting this example by using the **With** statement moves the **ActiveWorkbook** property and **Sheets** property calls outside the loop. You could also move these calls outside the loop by using an object variable.

```
With ActiveWorkbook.Sheets(1)
   For c = 1 To 1000
      .Cells(c, 1) = c
   Next
End With
```

Using Collection Index Numbers

With most object accessor methods and properties, you can specify an individual object in a collection either by name or by number. Using the object's index number is usually faster. If you use the object's name, Visual Basic must resolve the name to the index value; if you use the index value, you avoid this extra step.

There are, however, some significant advantages to specifying an object in a collection by name. One advantage is that using an object's name makes your code easier to read and debug. In addition, specifying an object by name is safer than specifying it by index number, because the index value for an object can change while your code is running. For example, a menu's index number represents the menu's position on the menu bar; therefore, the index number can change if menus are added to or deleted from the menu bar. This is one instance where faster isn't necessarily better. You should use this technique only when you're sure that the index value cannot change.

Minimizing Object Activation and Selection

Most of the time, your code can operate on objects without activating them. If you learned Visual Basic programming by using the macro recorder, you're probably accustomed to activating or selecting an object before you do anything to that object. The macro recorder does this because it must follow your keystrokes as you activate windows and select their contents. However, you can usually write much simpler and faster Visual Basic code that produces the same results without activating or selecting each object before working with it. For example, filling cells C1:C20 on Sheet5 with random numbers (using the **AutoFill** method) produces the macro recorder output shown in the following example.

```
Sheets("Sheet5").Select
Range("C1").Select
ActiveCell.FormulaR1C1 = "=RAND()"
Selection.AutoFill Destination:=Range("C1:C20"), Type:=xlFillDefault
Range("C1:C20").Select
```

All of the **Select** method calls are unnecessary. You can use the **With** statement to write code that operates directly on the worksheet and the range, as shown in the following example.

```
With Sheets("Sheet5")
    .Range("C1").FormulaR1C1 = "=RAND()"
    .Range("C1").AutoFill Destination:=.Range("C1:C20"), _
        Type:=xlFillDefault
End With
```

Keep in mind that the macro recorder records exactly what you do—it cannot optimize anything on its own. The recorded macro uses the **AutoFill** method because that's how the user entered the random numbers. This isn't the most efficient way to fill a range with random numbers. You can do the same thing with a single line, as shown in the following example.

```
Sheets("Sheet5").Range("C1:C20").Formula = "=RAND()"
```

When you optimize recorded code, think about what you're trying to do with the macro. Some of the operations you can perform in the user interface (such as dragging a formula from a single cell into a range) are recorded as methods (such as **AutoFill**) that can be eliminated in the optimized code because there's a faster way to perform the same operation in Visual Basic.

Removing Unnecessary Recorded Expressions

Another reason why the macro recorder produces inefficient code is that it cannot tell which options you've changed in a dialog box. The recorder therefore explicitly sets all available options when you close the dialog box. For example, selecting cells B2:B14 and then changing the font style to bold in the **Format Cells** dialog box produces the recorded macro shown in the following example.

```
Range("B2:B14").Select
With Selection.Font
    .Name = "Arial"
    .FontStyle = "Bold"
    .Size = 10
    .Strikethrough = False
    .Superscript = False
    .Subscript = False
    .OutlineFont = False
    .Shadow = False
    .Underline = xlNone
    .ColorIndex = xlAutomatic
End With
```

You can set the font style for the specified cell to bold with a single line of code and without selecting the range, as shown in the following example.

```
Range("B2:B14").Font.FontStyle = "Bold"
```

Again, if you think about what you're trying to do with the macro and you look through the lists of properties and methods that apply to the **Font** object, you'll see that you could also write this macro using the **Bold** property, as shown in the following example.

```
Range("B2:B14").Font.Bold = True
```

You can also experiment with the macro recorder by recording the same operation performed different ways in the user interface. For example, if you format a range by using the **Bold** button on the **Standard** toolbar, the macro recorder uses the **Bold** property.

Minimizing the Use of Variant Variables

Although you may find it convenient to use **Variant** variables in your code, Visual Basic requires more time to process a value stored in a **Variant** variable than it needs to process a value stored in a variable declared with an explicit data type. Your code can perform mathematical computations that don't involve fractional values faster if you use **Integer** or **Long** variables rather than **Variant** variables. **Integer** or **Long** variables are also the best choice for the index variable in **For...Next** loops. The speed you gain using explicit variable types can come at the expense of flexibility. For example, when using explicit data types, you may encounter cases of overflow that **Variant** variables handle automatically.

Using Specific Object Types

References to objects and their methods and properties are resolved either when your macro is compiled or when it runs. References that are resolved when the macro is compiled are faster than references that must be resolved while the macro is running.

If you declare variables and arguments as specific object types (such as **Range** or **Worksheet**), Visual Basic can resolve references to the properties and methods of those objects when your macro is compiled. For a list of specific object types, see the Object Browser.

In addition, you should use fully qualified object references. This eliminates ambiguity and ensures that the variable has the intended type. A fully qualified object reference includes the library name, as shown in the following examples.

```
Dim wb As Excel.Workbook
Dim dc As Word.Document, cb As MSForms.CommandButton
```

If you declare variables and arguments with the generic **Object** data type, Visual Basic may have to resolve references to their properties and methods when it encounters them at run time, resulting in a significantly slower process.

Using Constants

Using constants in an application makes the application run faster. Constants are evaluated once and are stored when your code is compiled. Variables can change, though, so Visual Basic must get the current variable value each time the macro runs. Constants also make your macros more readable and easier to maintain. If there are strings or numbers in a macro that don't change, declare them as constants.

Turning Off Screen Updating

A macro that makes changes to the appearance of a document—such as a macro that changes the color of every other cell in a large range or that creates a large number of graphic objects—will run faster when screen updating is turned off. You won't be able to watch the macro run (the changes will appear all at once when you turn screen updating back on), but it will run much faster. You may want to leave screen updating turned on while you write and debug the macro, and then turn it off before you run the macro.

To turn off screen updating, set the **ScreenUpdating** property to **False**, as shown in the following example.

```
Application.ScreenUpdating = False
```

Remember to set the **ScreenUpdating** property back to **True** when your macro finishes running (older versions of Microsoft Excel automatically reset this property, but Microsoft Excel 97 and Word 97 don't).

Tip You can sometimes achieve the same effect by not activating the object you're changing. For example, if you create graphic objects on a sheet without first activating the document, you don't need to turn screen updating off because the changes won't be visible anyway.

Strategies for Optimizing Microsoft Excel

In addition to the general information discussed in this chapter, you can use the following techniques to create smaller and faster macros in Microsoft Excel.

Using Worksheet Functions

A Microsoft Excel worksheet function that operates on a range of cells is usually faster than a Visual Basic macro that accomplishes the same task. For example, the SUM worksheet function is much faster than Visual Basic code that iterates a range and adds the values in the range's cells. For example, the following code runs relatively slowly.

```
For Each c In Worksheets(1).Range("A1:A200")
    totVal = totVal + c.Value
Next
```

The following code runs faster than the preceding example.

```
totVal = Application.WorksheetFunction.Sum(Worksheets(1).Range("a1:a200"))
```

Function that produce aggregrate results (such as PRODUCT, COUNT, COUNTA, and COUNTIF) are good candidates for replacing slower Visual Basic code, as are worksheet functions (such as MATCH and LOOKUP) that can take a range as an argument.

Using Special-Purpose Visual Basic Methods

There are also several special-purpose Visual Basic methods that offer a concise way to perform a specific operation on a range of cells. Like worksheet functions, these specialized methods are faster than the general-purpose Visual Basic code that accomplishes the same task.

The following example changes the value in each cell in the range A1:A200 in a relatively slow way.

```
For Each c In Worksheets(1).Range("a1:a200").Cells
    If c.Value = 4 Then c.Value = 4.5
Next
```

The following example, which uses the **Replace** method, performs the same operation much faster.

```
Worksheets(1).Range("a1:a200").Replace "4", "4.5"
```

The following example shows a relatively slow way to add a blue oval to each cell in the range A1:A500 that contains the value 4.

```
For Each c In Worksheets(1).Range("a1:a500").Cells
    If c.Value = 4 Then
        With Worksheets(1).Ovals.Add(c.Left, c.Top, c.Width, c.Height)
            .Interior.Pattern = xlNone
            .Border.ColorIndex = 5
        End With
    End If
Next
```

The following example, which uses the **Find** and **FindNext** methods, performs the same task much faster.

```
With Worksheets(1).Range("a1:a500")
    Set c = .Find(4)
    If Not c Is Nothing Then
        firstAddress = c.Address
        Do
            With Worksheets(1).Ovals.Add(c.Left, c.Top, _
                c.Width, c.Height)
                .Interior.Pattern = xlNone
```

```
            .Border.ColorIndex = 5
        End With
        Set c = .FindNext(c)
    Loop While Not c Is Nothing And c.Address <> firstAddress
    End If
End With
```

For more information about special-purpose Visual Basic methods, see the topic in Help that pertains to the object you're working with, and examine the list of that object's methods. You can also examine the list of all Visual Basic methods on the **Contents** tab in the **Help Topics** dialog box.

Strategies for Optimizing Microsoft Word

In addition to the general information discussed in this chapter, you can use the following techniques to create smaller and faster macros in Word.

Using Range Objects

Working with **Range** objects is faster than working with the **Selection** object. You can define and use multiple **Range** objects, which are invisible to the user.

Using Next and Previous

Whenever possible, use **Next** and **Previous** to return the next or previous item in a collection. For example, using `myRange.Next Unit:=wdWord` is faster than indexing the collection of words (`myRange.Words(10)`).

Avoiding Using the WordBasic Object

Methods of the **WordBasic** object are slower than methods and properties of other Visual Basic objects. For example, `WordBasic.FileOpen` is slower than `Documents.Open`.

Executing Built-in Dialog Boxes

A **With** statement is an efficient way to set many properties of a single object. Another technique for setting multiple properties is to set the properties of a built-in dialog box and then execute the dialog box. Executing a built-in dialog box is faster than using the **With** statement because the built-in dialog box stores the property values and then sets them all at once (using the **Execute** method), whereas the **With** statement sets properties one at a time. The following example sets a number of paragraph formatting properties by using a **With** statement.

```
With Selection.ParagraphFormat
    .Alignment = wdAlignParagraphCenter
    .KeepWithNext = True
    .LeftIndent = InchesToPoints(0.5)
End With
```

The following example sets the same properties as the preceding example, but runs faster because it executes a built-in dialog box.

```
Set dlg = Dialogs(wdDialogFormatParagraph)
dlg.Alignment = wdAlignParagraphCenter
dlg.KeepWithNext = True
dlg.LeftIndent = "0.5"
dlg.Execute
```

CHAPTER 14

Debugging and Error Handling

No matter how carefully crafted your code, errors can (and probably will) occur. Ideally, Visual Basic procedures wouldn't need error-handling code at all. Unfortunately, sometimes files are mistakenly deleted, disk drives run out of space, or network drives disconnect unexpectedly. Such possibilities can cause run-time errors in your code. To handle these errors, you need to add error-handling code to your procedures.

Sometimes errors can also occur within your code; this type of error is commonly referred to as a *bug*. Minor bugs can be frustrating or inconvenient. More severe bugs can cause an application to stop responding to commands, possibly requiring the user to restart the application, losing whatever work hasn't been saved.

The process of locating and fixing bugs in your application is known as *debugging*. Visual Basic provides several tools to help analyze how your application operates. These debugging tools are particularly useful in locating the source of bugs, but you can also use the tools to experiment with changes to your application or to learn how other applications work.

This chapter shows how to use the debugging tools included in Visual Basic and explains how to handle *run-time errors*—errors that occur while your code is running and that result from attempts to complete an invalid operation.

Note The information in this chapter applies to the Visual Basic Editor in Microsoft Excel 97, Word 97, and PowerPoint 97. For information about debugging Visual Basic code and handling errors in Microsoft Access 97, see *Building Applications with Microsoft Access 97*, available in Microsoft Access 97 and Microsoft Office 97, Developer Edition. An online version of *Building Applications with Microsoft Access 97* is available in the Value Pack on CD-ROM in Microsoft Access 97 and Microsoft Office 97, Professional Edition.

Contents

- How to Handle Errors
- Designing an Error Handler
- The Error-Handling Hierarchy
- Testing Error Handling by Generating Errors
- Inline Error Handling
- Centralized Error Handling
- Turning Off Error Handling
- Handling Errors in Referenced Objects
- Approaches to Debugging
- Avoiding Bugs
- Design Time, Run Time, and Break Mode
- Using the Debugging Windows
- Using Break Mode
- Running Selected Portions of Your Application
- Monitoring the Call Stack
- Testing Data and Procedures with the Immediate Window
- Special Debugging Considerations
- Tips for Debugging

How to Handle Errors

Ideally, Visual Basic procedures wouldn't need error-handling code at all. Reality dictates that hardware problems or unanticipated actions by the user can cause run-time errors that halt your code, and there's usually nothing the user can do to resume running the application. Other errors might not interrupt code, but they can cause it to act unpredictably.

For example, the following procedure returns **True** if the specified file exists and **False** if it does not, but doesn't contain error-handling code.

```
Function FileExists (filename) As Boolean
    FileExists = (Dir(filename) <> "")
End Function
```

The **Dir** function returns the first file matching the specified file name (given with or without wildcard characters, drive name, or path); it returns a zero-length string if no matching file is found.

The code appears to cover either of the possible outcomes of the **Dir** call. However, if the drive letter specified in the argument is not a valid drive, the error "Device unavailable" occurs. If the specified drive is a floppy disk drive, this function will work correctly only if a disk is in the drive and the drive door is closed. If not, Visual Basic presents the error "Disk not ready" and halts execution of your code.

To avoid this situation, you can use the error-handling features in Visual Basic to intercept errors and take corrective action. (Intercepting an error is also known as *trapping* an error.) When an error occurs, Visual Basic sets the various properties of the error object, **Err**, such as an error number, a description, and so on. You can use the Err object and its properties in an error-handling routine so that your application can respond intelligently to an error situation.

For example, device problems, such as an invalid drive or an empty floppy disk drive, could be handled by the following example.

```
Function FileExists (filename) As Boolean
    Dim Msg As String
    ' Turn on error trapping so error handler responds
    ' if any error is detected.
    On Error GoTo CheckError
        FileExists = (Dir(filename) <> "")
        ' Avoid executing error handler if no error occurs.
        Exit Function


CheckError:                     ' Branch here if error occurs.
    ' Define constants to represent intrinsic Visual Basic error
    ' codes.
    Const mnErrDiskNotReady = 71, mnErrDeviceUnavailable = 68
    ' vbExclamation, vbOK, vbCancel, vbCritical, and vbOKCancel are
    'constants defined in the VBA type library.
    If (Err.Number = MnErrDiskNotReady) Then
        Msg = "Put a floppy disk in the drive and close the door."
        ' Display message box with an exclamation mark icon and with
        ' OK and Cancel buttons.
        If MsgBox(Msg, vbExclamation & vbOKCancel) = vbOK Then
            Resume
        Else
            Resume Next
        End If
    ElseIf Err.Number = MnErrDeviceUnavailable Then
        Msg = "This drive or path does not exist: " & filename
        MsgBox Msg, vbExclamation
        Resume Next
    Else
        Msg = "Unexpected error #" & Str(Err.Number) & " occurred: " _
        & Err.Description
        ' Display message box with Stop sign icon and OK button.
        MsgBox Msg, vbCritical
        Stop
    End If
    Resume
End Function
```

In this code, the **Err** object's **Number** property contains the number associated with the run-time error that occurred; the **Description** property contains a short description of the error.

When Visual Basic generates the error "Disk not ready," this code presents a message telling the user to choose one of two buttons—**OK** or **Cancel**. If the user chooses **OK**, the **Resume** statement returns control to the statement at which the error occurred and attempts to re-run that statement. This succeeds if the user has corrected the problem; otherwise, the program returns to the error handler.

If the user chooses **Cancel**, the **Resume Next** statement returns control to the statement following the one at which the error occurred (in this case, the **Exit Function** statement).

Should the error "Device unavailable" occur, this code presents a message describing the problem. The **Resume Next** statement then causes the function to continue execution at the statement following the one at which the error occurred.

If an unanticipated error occurs, a short description of the error is displayed and the code halts at the **Stop** statement.

The application you create can correct an error or prompt the user to change the conditions that caused the error. To do this, use techniques such as those shown in the preceding example. The next section discusses these techniques in detail.

Designing an Error Handler

An *error handler* is a routine for trapping and responding to errors in your application. You'll want to add error handlers to any procedure where you anticipate the possibility of an error (you should assume that any Visual Basic statement can produce an error unless you explicitly know otherwise). The process of designing an error handler involves three steps:

1. Set, or *enable*, an error trap by telling the application where to branch to (which error-handling routine to run) when an error occurs.

   The **On Error** statement enables the trap and directs the application to the label marking the beginning of the error-handling routine.

   In the preceding example, the FileExists function contains an error-handling routine named CheckError.

2. Write an error-handling routine that responds to all errors you can anticipate. If control actually branches into the trap at some point, the trap is then said to be *active*.

   The CheckError routine handles the error using an **If...Then...Else** statement that responds to the value in the **Err** object's **Number** property, which is a numeric code corresponding to a Visual Basic error. In the example, if "Disk not ready" is generated, a message prompts the user to close the drive door. A different message is displayed if the "Device unavailable" error occurs. If any other error is generated, the appropriate description is displayed and the program stops.

3. Exit the error-handling routine.

   In the case of the "Disk not ready" error, the **Resume** statement makes the code branch back to the statement where the error occurred. Visual Basic then tries to re-run that statement. If the situation has not changed, then another error occurs and execution branches back to the error-handling routine.

   In the case of the "Device unavailable" error, the **Resume Next** statement makes the code branch to the statement following the one at which the error occurred.

Details on how to perform these steps are provided in the remainder of this topic. Refer to the FileExists function in the preceding example as you read through these steps.

Setting the Error Trap

An error trap is enabled when Visual Basic runs the **On Error** statement, which specifies an error handler. The error trap remains enabled while the procedure containing it is active—that is, until an **Exit Sub**, **Exit Function**, **Exit Property**, **End Sub**, **End Function**, or **End Property** statement is run for that procedure. While only one error trap can be enabled at any one time in any given procedure, you can create several alternative error traps and enable different ones at different times. You can also disable an error trap by using a special case of the **On Error** statement—**On Error GoTo 0**.

To set an error trap that jumps to an error-handling routine, use a **On Error GoTo** *line* statement, where *line* indicates the label identifying the error-handling code. In the FileExists function example, the label is CheckError. (Although the colon is part of the label, it isn't used in the **On Error GoTo** *line* statement.)

Writing an Error-Handling Routine

The first step in writing an error-handling routine is adding a line label to mark the beginning of the error-handling routine. The line label should have a descriptive name and must be followed by a colon. A common convention is to place the error-handling code at the end of the procedure with an **Exit Sub**, **Exit Function**, or **Exit Property** statement immediately before the line label. This allows the procedure to avoid executing the error-handling code if no error occurs.

The body of the error-handling routine contains the code that actually handles the error, usually in the form of a **Select Case** or **If...Then...Else** statement. You need to determine which errors are likely to occur and provide a course of action for each, for example, prompting the user to insert a disk in the case of a "Disk not ready" error. An option should always be provided to handle any unanticipated errors by using the **Else** or **Case Else** clause—in the case of the FileExists function example, this option warns the user then ends the application.

The **Number** property of the **Err** object contains a numeric code representing the most recent run-time error. By using the **Err** object in combination with the **Select Case** or **If...Then...Else** statement, you can take specific action for any error that occurs.

Exiting an Error-Handling Routine

The FileExists function example uses the **Resume** statement within the error handler to re-run the statement that originally caused the error, and uses the **Resume Next** statement to return execution to the statement following the one at which the error occurred. There are other ways to exit an error-handling routine. Depending on the circumstances, you can do this using any of the statements shown in the following table.

Statement	Description
Resume [0]	Program execution resumes with the statement that caused the error or the most recently run call out of the procedure containing the error-handling routine. Use it to repeat an operation after correcting the condition that caused the error.
Resume Next	Resumes program execution at the statement immediately following the one that caused the error. If the error occurred outside the procedure that contains the error handler, execution resumes at the statement immediately following the call to the procedure wherein the error occurred, if the called procedure does not have an enabled error handler.
Resume *line*	Resumes program execution at the label specified by *line*, where *line* is a line label (or nonzero line number) that must be in the same procedure as the error handler.
Err.Raise Number:= *number*	Triggers a run-time error. When this statement is run within the error-handling routine, Visual Basic searches the calls list for another error-handling routine. (The *calls list* is the chain of procedures invoked to arrive at the current point of execution. For more information, see "The Error-Handling Hierarchy" later in this chapter.)

The Difference Between Resume and Resume Next

The difference between **Resume** and **Resume Next** is that **Resume** continues running the application from the statement that generated the error (the statement is re-run), while **Resume Next** continues running the application from the statement that follows the one that generated the error. Generally, you would use **Resume** whenever the error handler can correct the error, and **Resume Next** when the error handler cannot. You can write an error handler so that the existence of a run-time error is never revealed to the user or to display error messages and allow the user to enter corrections.

The following example uses error handling to perform "safe" division on its arguments without revealing errors that might occur. The errors that can occur when performing division are described in the following table.

Error	Cause
"Division by zero"	Numerator is nonzero, but the denominator is zero.
"Overflow"	Both numerator and denominator are zero (during floating-point division).
"Illegal procedure call"	Either the numerator or the denominator is a nonnumeric value (or can't be considered a numeric value).

In all three cases, the following example traps these errors and returns **Null**.

```
Function Divide (numer, denom) as Variant
    Const mnErrDivByZero = 11, mnErrOverFlow = 6, mnErrBadCall = 5
    On Error GoTo MathHandler
        Divide   = numer / denom
        Exit Function
MathHandler:
    If Err.Number = MnErrDivByZero Or Err.Number = ErrOverFlow _
    Or Err = ErrBadCall Then
        Divide = Null      ' If error was Division by zero, Overflow,
                           ' or Illegal procedure call, return Null.
    Else
        ' Display unanticipated error message.
        MsgBox "Unanticipated error " & Err.Number & ": " & _
        Err.Description, vbExclamation
    End If             ' In all cases, Resume Next continues
    Resume Next          ' execution at the Exit Function statement.
End Function
```

Resuming Execution at a Specified Line

Resume Next can also be used where an error occurs within a loop, and you need to restart the operation. Or, you can use **Resume** *line*, which returns control to a specified line label.

The following example illustrates the use of the **Resume** *line* statement. A variation on the FileExists example shown earlier, this function allows the user to enter a file specification that the function returns if the file exists.

```
Function VerifyFile As String
   Const mnErrBadFileName = 52, mnErrDriveDoorOpen = 71
   Const mnErrDeviceUnavailable = 68, mnErrInvalidFileName = 64
   Dim strPrompt As String, strMsg As String, strFileSpec As String
   strPrompt = "Enter file specification to check:"
StartHere:
   strFileSpec = "*.*"            ' Start with a default specification.
   strMsg = strMsg & vbCRLF & strPrompt
   ' Let the user modify the default.
   strFileSpec = InputBox(strMsg, "File Search", strFileSpec, 100, _
   100)
   ' Exit if user deletes default.
   If strFileSpec = "" Then Exit Function
   On Error GoTo Handler
      VerifyFile = Dir(FileSpec)
      Exit Function
Handler:
   Select Case Err.Number        ' Analyze error code and load message.
      Case ErrInvalidFileName, ErrBadFileName
         strMsg = "Your file specification was invalid; try _
         another."
      Case MnErrDriveDoorOpen
         strMsg = "Close the disk drive door and try again."
      Case MnErrDeviceUnavailable
         strMsg = "The drive you specified was not found. Try _
         again."
      Case Else
         Dim intErrNum As Integer
         intErrNum = Err.Number
         Err.Clear                        ' Clear the Err object.
         Err.Raise Number:= intErrNum ' Regenerate the error.
   End Select
   Resume StartHere          ' This jumps back to StartHere label so
                             ' the user can try another file name.
End Function
```

If a file matching the specification is found, the function returns the file name. If no matching file is found, the function returns a zero-length string. If one of the anticipated errors occurs, a message is assigned to the strMsg variable and execution jumps back to the label StartHere. This gives the user another chance to enter a valid path and file specification.

If the error is unanticipated, the **Case Else** segment regenerates the error so that the next error handler in the calls list can trap the error. This is necessary because if the error wasn't regenerated, the code would continue to run at the Resume StartHere line. By regenerating the error you are in effect causing the error to occur again; the new error will be trapped at the next level in the call stack.

The Error-Handling Hierarchy

An *enabled* error handler is one that was activated by executing an On Error statement and hasn't yet been turned off—either by an **On Error GoTo 0** statement or by exiting the procedure where it was enabled. An *active* error handler is one in which execution is currently taking place. To be active, an error handler must first be enabled, but not all enabled error handlers are active. For example, after a **Resume** statement, a handler is deactivated but still enabled.

When an error occurs within a procedure lacking an enabled error-handling routine, or within an active error-handling routine, Visual Basic searches the calls list for another enabled error-handling routine. The calls list is the sequence of calls that leads to the currently executing procedure; it is displayed in the **Call Stack** dialog box. You can display the **Call Stack** dialog box only when in break mode (when you pause the execution of your application), by clicking **Call Stack** on the **View** menu.

Searching the Calls List

Suppose that the following sequence of calls occurs:

1. An event procedure calls Procedure A.

2. Procedure A calls Procedure B.

3. Procedure B calls Procedure C.

While Procedure C is executing, the other procedures are pending. If an error occurs in Procedure C and this procedure doesn't have an enabled error handler, Visual Basic searches backward through the pending procedures in the calls list—first Procedure B, then Procedure A, then the initial event procedure (but no farther)—and runs the first enabled error handler it finds. If it doesn't encounter an enabled error handler anywhere in the calls list, it presents a default unexpected error message and halts execution.

If Visual Basic finds an enabled error-handling routine, execution continues in that routine as if the error had occurred in the same procedure that contains the error handler. If a **Resume** or a **Resume Next** statement is run in the error-handling routine, execution continues as shown in the following table.

Statement	Result
Resume	The call to the procedure that Visual Basic just searched is re-run. In the calls list given earlier, if Procedure A has an enabled error handler that includes a **Resume** statement, Visual Basic re-runs the call to Procedure B.

Statement	Result
Resume Next	Execution returns to the statement following the last statement run in that procedure. This is the statement following the call to the procedure that Visual Basic just searched back through. In the calls list given earlier, if Procedure A has an enabled error handler that includes a **Resume Next** statement, execution returns to the statement after the call to Procedure B.

Notice that the statement run is in the procedure where the error-handling procedure is found, not necessarily in the procedure where the error occurred. If you don't take this into account, your code may perform in ways you don't intend. To make the code easier to debug, you can simply go into break mode whenever an error occurs, as explained in the section "Turning Off Error Handling" later in this chapter.

If the error handler's range of errors doesn't include the error that actually occurred, an unanticipated error can occur within the procedure with the enabled error handler. In such a case, the procedure could run endlessly, especially if the error handler runs a **Resume** statement. To prevent such situations, use the **Err** object's **Raise** method in a **Case Else** statement in the handler. This actually generates an error within the error handler, forcing Visual Basic to search through the calls list for a handler that can deal with the error.

The effect of the search back through the calls list is hard to predict, because it depends on whether **Resume** or **Resume Next** is run in the handler that processes the error successfully. **Resume** returns control to the most recently run call out of the procedure containing the error handler. **Resume Next** returns control to whatever statement immediately follows the most recently run call out of the procedure containing the error handler.

For example, in the calls list discussed earlier, if Procedure A has an enabled error handler and Procedure B and C don't, an error occurring in Procedure C will be handled by Procedure A's error handler. If that error handler uses a **Resume** statement, upon exit, the program continues with a call to Procedure B. However, if Procedure A's error handler uses a **Resume Next** statement, upon exit, the program will continue with whatever statement in Procedure A follows the call to Procedure B. In both cases the error handler does not return directly to either the procedure or the statement where the error originally occurred.

Guidelines for Complex Error Handling

When you write large Visual Basic applications that use multiple modules, the error-handling code can get quite complex. Keep these guidelines in mind:

- While you are debugging your code, use the **Err** object's **Raise** method to regenerate the error in all error handlers for cases where no code in the handler deals with the specific error. This allows your application to try to correct the error in other error-handling routines along the calls list. It also ensures that Visual Basic will display an error message if an error occurs that your code doesn't handle. When you test your code, this technique helps you uncover the errors you aren't handling adequately.

- Use the Clear method if you need to explicitly clear the **Err** object after handling an error. This is necessary when using inline error handling with **On Error Resume Next**. Visual Basic calls the **Clear** method automatically whenever it runs any type of **Resume** statement, **Exit Sub**, **Exit Function**, **Exit Property**, or any **On Error** statement.

- If you don't want another procedure in the calls list to trap the error, use the **Stop** statement to force your code to terminate. Using **Stop** lets you examine the context of the error while refining your code in the development environment.

- Write a fail-safe error-handling procedure that all your error handlers can call as a last resort for errors they cannot handle. This fail-safe procedure can perform an orderly termination of your application by unloading forms and saving data.

Testing Error Handling by Generating Errors

Simulating errors is useful when you are testing your applications, or when you want to treat a particular condition as being equivalent to a Visual Basic run-time error. For example, you might be writing a module that uses an object defined in an external application, and want errors returned from the object to be handled as actual Visual Basic errors by the rest of your application.

In order to test for all possible errors, you may need to generate some of the errors in your code. You can generate an error in your code with the **Raise** method of the **Err** object. The **Raise** method takes a list of named arguments that can be passed with the method. When the code reaches a **Resume** statement, the **Clear** method of the **Err** object is invoked. It is necessary to regenerate the error in order to pass it back to the previous procedure on the call stack.

You can also simulate any Visual Basic run-time error by supplying the error code for that error.

Defining Your Own Errors

Sometimes you may want to define errors in addition to those defined by Visual Basic. For example, an application that relies on a modem connection might generate an error when the carrier signal is dropped. If you want to generate and trap your own errors, you can add your error numbers to the **vbObjectError** constant.

The **vbObjectError** constant reserves the numbers ranging from its own offset to the sum of its offset and 512. Using a number higher than this will ensure that your error numbers will not conflict with future versions of Visual Basic.

To define your own error numbers, you add constants to the declarations section of your module.

```
' Error constants
Const gLostCarrier = 1 + vbObjectError + 512
Const gNoDialTone = 2 + vbObjectError + 512
```

You can then use the **Raise** method as you would with any of the intrinsic errors. In this case, the description property of the **Err** object will return a standard description—"Application-defined or object defined error." To provide your own error description, you will need to add it as a parameter to the **Raise** method.

Inline Error Handling

When you check for errors immediately after each line that may cause an error, you are performing *inline error handling*. Using inline error handling, you can write functions and statements that return error numbers when an error occurs; raise a Visual Basic error in a procedure and handle the error in the calling procedure; or write a function to return a **Variant** data type, and use the **Variant** to indicate to the calling procedure that an error occurred.

Returning Error Numbers

There are a number of ways to return error numbers. The simplest way is to create functions and statements that return an error number, instead of a value, if an error occurs. The following example shows how you can use this approach in the FileExists function example, which indicates whether or not a particular file exists.

```
Function FileExists (p As String) As Long
    If Dir (p) <> " " Then
        FileExists = conSuccess ' Return a constant indicating
    Else                        ' the file exists.
        FileExists = conFailure ' Return failure constant.
    End If
End Function

Dim ResultValue As Long
ResultValue = FileExists ("C:\Testfile.txt")
If ResultValue = conFailure Then
    .
    .   ' Handle the error.
    .
Else
    .
    .   ' Proceed with the program.
    .
End If
```

The key to inline error handling is to test for an error immediately after each statement or function call. In this manner, you can design a handler that anticipates exactly the sort of error that might arise and resolve it accordingly. This approach does not require that an actual run-time error arise.

Handling Errors in the Calling Procedure

Another way to indicate an error condition is to raise a Visual Basic error in the procedure itself, and handle the error in an inline error handler in the calling procedure. The next example shows the same FileExists procedure, raising an error number if it is not successful. Before calling this function, the **On Error Resume Next** statement sets the values of the **Err** object properties when an error occurs, but without trying to run an error-handling routine.

The **On Error Resume Next** statement is followed by error-handling code. This code can check the properties of the **Err** object to see if an error occurred. If Err.Number doesn't contain zero, an error has occurred, and the error-handling code can take the appropriate action based on the values of the **Err** object's properties.

```
Function FileExists (p As String)
   If Dir (p) <> " " Then
      Err.Raise conSuccess          ' Return a constant indicating
   Else                             ' the file exists.
      Err.Raise conFailure          ' Raise error number conFailure.
   End If
End Function

Dim ResultValue As Long
On Error Resume Next
ResultValue = FileExists ("C:\Testfile.txt")
If Err.Number = conFailure Then
   .
   .   ' Handle the error.
   .
Else
   .
   .   ' Continue program.
   .
End If
```

The next example uses both the return value and one of the passed arguments to indicate whether or not an error condition resulted from the function call.

```
Function Power (X As Long, P As Integer, ByRef Result As Integer) _
As Long
    On Error GoTo ErrorHandler
    Result = x^P
    Exit Function
ErrorHandler:
    Power = conFailure
End Function

' Calls the Power function.
Dim lngReturnValue As Long, lngErrorMaybe As Long
lngErrorMaybe = Power (10, 2, lngReturnValue)
If lngErrorMaybe Then
    .
    .    ' Handle the error.
    .
Else
    .
    .    ' Continue program.
    .
End If
```

If the function was written simply to return either the result value or an error code, the resulting value might be in the range of error codes, and your calling procedure would not be able to distinguish them. By using both the return value and one of the passed arguments, your program can determine that the function call failed, and take appropriate action.

Using Variant Data Types

Another way to return inline error information is to take advantage of the Visual Basic **Variant** data type and some related functions. A **Variant** has a tag that indicates what type of data is contained in the variable, and it can be tagged as a Visual Basic error code. You can write a function to return a **Variant**, and use this tag to indicate to the calling procedure that an error has occurred.

The following example shows how the Power function can be written to return a
Variant.

```
Function Power (X As Long, P As Integer) As Variant
    On Error GoTo ErrorHandler
    Power = x^P
    Exit Function

ErrorHandler:
    Power = CVErr(Err.Number)  ' Convert error code to tagged Variant.
End Function

' Calls the Power function.
Dim varReturnValue As Variant
varReturnValue = Power (10, 2)
If IsError (varReturnValue) Then
    .
    .  ' Handle the error.
    .
Else
    .
    .  ' Continue program.
    .
End If
```

Centralized Error Handling

When you add error-handling code to your applications, you'll quickly discover that
you're handling the same errors over and over. With careful planning, you can reduce
code size by writing a few procedures that your error-handling code can call to handle
common error situations.

The following FileErrors function shows a message appropriate to the error that
occurred and, where possible, allows the user to choose a button to specify what
action the program should take next. It then returns code to the procedure that called
it. The value of the code indicates which action the program should take. Note that
user-defined constants such as MnErrDeviceUnavailable must be defined
somewhere (either globally, or at the module level of the module containing the
procedure, or within the procedure itself).

```
Function FileErrors As Integer
   Dim intMsgType As Integer, strMsg As String
   Dim intResponse As Integer
   ' Return Value     Meaning
   ' 0                Resume
   ' 1                Resume Next
   ' 2                Unrecoverable error
   ' 3                Unrecognized error
   intMsgType = vbExclamation
   Select Case Err.Number
      Case MnErrDeviceUnavailable                           ' Error 68
         strMsg = "That device appears unavailable."
         intMsgType = vbExclamation + 4
      Case MnErrDiskNotReady                                ' Error 71
         strMsg = "Insert a disk in the drive and close the door."
      Case MnErrDeviceIO                            ' Error 57
         strMsg = "Internal disk error."
         intMsgType = vbExclamation + 4
      Case MnErrDiskFull                           ' Error 61
         strMsg = "Disk is full. Continue?"
         intMsgType = vbExclamation + 3
      Case ErrBadFileName, ErrBadFileNameOrNumber    ' Error 64 & 52
         strMsg = "That filename is illegal."
      Case ErrPathDoesNotExist                          ' Error 76
         strMsg = "That path doesn't exist."
      Case ErrBadFileMode                              ' Error 54
         strMsg = "Can't open your file for that type of access."
      Case ErrFileAlreadyOpen                      ' Error 55
         strMsg = "This file is already open."
      Case ErrInputPastEndOfFile                       ' Error 62
         strMsg = "This file has a nonstandard end-of-file marker, "
         strMsg = strMsg & "or an attempt was made to read beyond "
         strMsg = strMsg & "the end-of-file marker."
      Case Else
         FileErrors = 3
         Exit Function
   End Select
   intResponse = MsgBox (strMsg, strMmsgType, "Disk Error")
   Select Case intRresponse
      Case 1, 4    ' OK, Retry buttons.
         FileErrors = 0
      Case 5       ' Ignore button.
         FileErrors = 1
      Case 2, 3    ' Cancel, End buttons.
         FileErrors = 2
      Case Else
         FileErrors = 3
   End Select
End Function
```

This procedure handles common file and disk-related errors. If the error is not related to disk Input/Output, it returns the value 3. The procedure that calls this procedure should then either handle the error itself, regenerate the error with the **Raise** method, or call another procedure to handle it.

Note   As you write larger applications, you'll find that you are using the same constants in several procedures in various forms and modules. Making those constants public and declaring them in a single standard module may better organize your code and save you from typing the same declarations repeatedly.

You can simplify error handling by calling the FileErrors procedure wherever you have a procedure that reads or writes to disk. For example, you've probably used applications that warn you if you attempt to replace an existing disk file. Conversely, when you try to open a file that doesn't exist, many applications warn you that the file does not exist and ask if you want to create it. In both instances, errors can occur when the application passes the file name to the operating system.

Turning Off Error Handling

If an error trap has been enabled in a procedure, it is automatically disabled when the procedure finishes running. However, you may want to turn off an error trap in a procedure while the code in that procedure is still running. To turn off an enabled error trap, use the **On Error GoTo 0** statement. After Visual Basic runs this statement, errors are detected but not trapped within the procedure. You can use **On Error GoTo 0** to turn off error handling anywhere in a procedure—even within an error-handling routine itself.

Debugging Code with Error Handlers

When you are debugging code, you may find it confusing to analyze its behavior when it generates errors that are trapped by an error handler. You could comment out the **On Error** line in each module in the project, but this is also cumbersome.

Instead, while debugging, you could turn off error handlers so that every time there's an error, you enter break mode. To do this, select the **Break on All Errors** option on the **General** tab in the **Options** dialog box (**Tools** menu). With this option selected, when an error occurs anywhere in the project, you will enter break mode and the **Watch** window will display the code where the error occurred. If this option is not selected, an error may or may not cause an error message to be displayed, depending on where the error occurred. For example, it may have been raised by an external object referenced by your application. If it does display a message, it may be meaningless, depending on where the error originated.

Handling Errors in Referenced Objects

In procedures that reference one or more objects, it becomes more difficult to determine where an error occurs, particularly if it occurs in another application's object. For example, consider an application that consists of a form module (MyForm), that references a class module (MyClassA), that in turn references a Microsoft Excel **Worksheet** object.

If the **Worksheet** object does not handle a particular error arising in the worksheet, but regenerates it instead, Visual Basic will pass the error to the referencing object, MyClassA. Visual Basic automatically remaps untrapped errors arising in objects outside of Visual Basic as error code 440.

The MyClassA object can either handle the error (which is preferable), or regenerate it. The interface specifies that any object regenerating an error that arises in a referenced object should not simply propagate the error (pass as error code 440), but should instead remap the error number to something meaningful. When you remap the error, the number can either be a number defined by Visual Basic that indicates the error condition, if your handler can determine that the error is similar to a defined Visual Basic error (for instance, overflow or division by zero), or an undefined error number. Add the new number to the Visual Basic constant **vbObjectError** to notify other handlers that this error was raised by your object.

Whenever possible, a class module should try to handle every error that arises within the module itself, and should also try to handle errors that arise in an object it references that are not handled by that object. However, there are some errors that it cannot handle because it cannot anticipate them. There are also cases where it is more appropriate for the referencing object to handle the error, rather than the referenced object.

When an error occurs in the form module, Visual Basic raises one of the predefined Visual Basic error numbers.

Note If you are creating a public class, be sure to clearly document the meaning of each non-Visual Basic error-handler you define. Other programmers who reference your public classes will need to know how to handle errors raised by your objects.

When you regenerate an error, leave the **Err** object's other properties unchanged. If the raised error is not trapped, the **Source** and **Description** properties can be displayed to help the user take corrective action.

Handling Errors Passed from Reference Objects

A class module could include the following error handler to accommodate any error it might trap, regenerating those it is unable to resolve.

```
MyServerHandler:
   Select Case ErrNum
      Case 7    ' Handle out-of-memory error.
         .
         .
         .

      Case 440    ' Handle external object error.
         Err.Raise Number:=vbObjectError + 9999
      ' Error from another Visual Basic object.
      Case Is > vbObjectError and Is < vbObjectError + 65536
         ObjectError = ErrNum
      Select Case ObjectError
         ' This object handles the error, based on error code
         ' documentation for the object.
         Case vbObjectError + 10
            .
            .
            .

         Case Else
             ' Remap error as generic object error and regenerate.
             Err.Raise Number:=vbObjectError + 9999
      End Select
      Case Else
         ' Remap error as generic object error and regenerate.
         Err.Raise Number:=vbObjectError + 9999
   End Select
   Err.Clear
   Resume Next
```

The Case 440 statement traps errors that arise in a referenced object outside the Visual Basic application. In this example, the error is simply propagated using the value 9999, because it is difficult for this type of centralized handler to determine the cause of the error. When this error is raised, it is generally the result of a fatal automation error (one that would cause the component to end execution), or because an object didn't correctly handle a trapped error. Error 440 shouldn't be propagated unless it is a fatal error. If this trap were written for an inline handler as discussed previously in "Inline Error Handling," it might be possible to determine the cause of the error and correct it.

The statement Case Is > vbObjectError and Is < vbObjectError + 65536 traps errors that originate in an object within the Visual Basic application, or within the same object that contains this handler. Only errors defined by objects will be in the range of the **vbObjectError** offset.

The error code documentation provided for the object should define the possible error codes and their meaning, so that this portion of the handler can be written to intelligently resolve anticipated errors. The actual error codes may be documented without the **vbObjectError** offset, or they may be documented after being added to the offset, in which case the **Case Else** statement should subtract **vbObjectError**, rather than add it. On the other hand, object errors may be constants, shown in the type library for the object, as shown in the Object Browser. In that case, use the error constant in the **Case Else** statement, instead of the error code.

Any error not handled should be regenerated with a new number, as shown in the **Case Else** statement. Within your application, you can design a handler to anticipate this new number you've defined. If this were a public class, you would also want to include an explanation of the new error-handling code in your application's documentation.

The last **Case Else** statement traps and regenerates any other errors that are not trapped elsewhere in the handler. Because this part of the trap will catch errors that may or may not have the **vbObjectError** constant added, you should simply remap these errors to a generic "unresolved error" code. That code should be added to **vbObjectError**, indicating to any handler that this error originated in the referenced object.

Debugging Error Handlers in Referenced Objects

When you are debugging an application that has a reference to an object created in Visual Basic or a class defined in a class module, you may find it confusing to determine which object generates an error. To make this easier, you can select the **Break in Class Module** option on the **General** tab in the **Options** dialog box (**Tools** menu). With this option selected, an error in a class module will cause that class to enter the debugger's break mode, allowing you to analyze the error.

Approaches to Debugging

The debugging techniques presented in this chapter use the analysis tools provided by Visual Basic. Visual Basic cannot diagnose or fix errors for you, but it does provide tools to help you analyze how execution flows from one part of the procedure to another, and how variables and property settings change as statements are run. Debugging tools let you look inside your application to help you determine what happens and why.

Visual Basic debugging support includes breakpoints, break expressions, watch expressions, stepping through code one statement or one procedure at a time, and displaying the values of variables and properties. Visual Basic also includes special debugging features, such as edit-and-continue capability, setting the next statement to run, and procedure testing while the application is in break mode.

Kinds of Errors

To understand how debugging is useful, consider the three kinds of errors you can encounter, described in the following paragraphs.

Compile errors   These result from incorrectly constructed code. If you incorrectly type a keyword, omit some necessary punctuation, or use a **Next** statement without a corresponding **For** statement at design time, Visual Basic detects these errors when your code compiles.

Run-time errors   These occur while the application is running (and are detected by Visual Basic) when a statement attempts an operation that is impossible to carry out. An example of this is division by zero.

Logic errors   These occur when an application doesn't perform the way it was intended. An application can have syntactically valid code, run without performing any invalid operations, and yet produce incorrect results. Only by testing the application and analyzing results can you verify that the application is performing correctly.

How Debugging Tools Help

Debugging tools are designed to help you with troubleshooting logic and run-time errors and observing the behavior of code that has no errors.

For instance, an incorrect result may be produced at the end of a long series of calculations. In debugging, the task is to determine what and where something went wrong. Perhaps you forgot to initialize a variable, chose the wrong operator, or used an incorrect formula.

There are no magic tricks to debugging, and there is no fixed sequence of steps that works every time. Basically, debugging helps you understand what's going on while your application runs. Debugging tools give you a snapshot of the current state of your application, including the values of variables, expressions, and properties, and the names of active procedure calls. The better you understand how your application is working, the faster you can find bugs.

Among its many debugging tools, Visual Basic provides several helpful buttons on the **Debug** toolbar, shown in the following illustration.

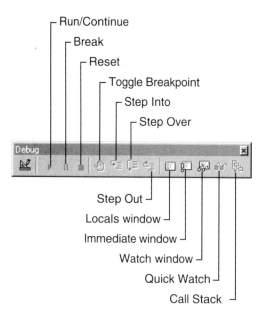

The following table briefly describes each tool's purpose. This chapter discusses situations where each of these tools can help you debug or analyze an application more efficiently.

Debugging tool	Purpose
Run/Continue	Switches from design time to run time (**Run**) or switches from break mode to run time (**Continue**). (In break mode, the name of the button changes to **Continue**.)
Break	Switches from run time to break mode.
Reset	Switches from break mode or run time to design time.
Toggle Breakpoint	Defines a line in a module where Visual Basic suspends execution of the application.
Step Into	Runs the next executable line of code in the application and steps into procedures.
Step Over	Runs the next executable line of code in the application without stepping into procedures.
Step Out	Runs the remainder of the current procedure and breaks at the next line in the calling procedure.
Locals Window	Displays the current value of local variables.
Immediate Window	Allows you to run code or query values while the application is in break mode.
Watch Window	Displays the values of selected expressions.

Debugging tool	Purpose
Quick Watch	Lists the current value of an expression while the application is in break mode.
Call Stack	While in break mode, displays a dialog box that shows all procedures that have been called but not yet run to completion.

Avoiding Bugs

There are several ways to avoid creating bugs in your applications:

- Design your applications carefully by writing down the relevant events and the way your code will respond to each one. Give each event procedure and each general procedure a specific, well-defined purpose.

- Include numerous comments. As you go back and analyze your code, you'll understand it much better if you state the purpose of each procedure in comments.

- Explicitly reference objects whenever possible. Declare objects as they are listed in the **Classes** box in the Object Browser, rather than using a **Variant** or the generic **Object** data types.

- Develop a consistent naming scheme for the variables and objects in your application.

- One of the most common sources of errors is incorrectly typing a variable name or confusing one control with another. You can use **Option Explicit** to avoid misspelling variable names.

Design Time, Run Time, and Break Mode

To test and debug an application, you need to understand which of three modes you are in at any given time. You use Visual Basic at design time to create an application, and at run time to run it. In *break mode*, the execution of the program is suspended so you can examine and alter data. The Visual Basic title bar always shows you the current mode.

The characteristics of the three modes and techniques for moving among them are listed in the following table.

Mode	Description
Design time	Most of the work of creating an application is done at design time. You can design forms, draw controls, write code, and use the **Properties** window to set or view property settings. You cannot run code or use debugging tools, except for setting breakpoints and creating watch expressions.
	To switch to run time, click the **Run** button. To switch to break mode, click **Step Into** on the **Run** menu; the application enters break mode at the first executable statement.
Run time	When an application takes control, you interact with the application the same way a user would. You can view code, but you cannot change it.
	To switch back to design time, click the **Reset** button. To switch to break mode, click the **Break** button.
Break mode	Execution is suspended while running the application. You can view and edit code, examine or modify data, restart the application, end execution, or continue execution from the same point.
	To switch to run time, click the **Continue** button (in break mode, the **Run** button becomes the **Continue** button). To switch to design time, click the **Reset** button.
	You can set breakpoints and watch expressions at design time, but other debugging tools work only in break mode. See "Using Break Mode" later in this chapter.

Using the Debugging Windows

Sometimes you can find the cause of a problem by running portions of code. More often, however, you'll also have to analyze what's happening to the data. You might isolate a problem in a variable or property with an incorrect value, and then have to determine how and why that variable or property was assigned an incorrect value.

With the debugging windows, you can monitor the values of expressions and variables while stepping through the statements in your application. There are three debugging windows: the **Immediate** window, the **Watch** window, and the **Locals** window. To display one of these windows, either click the corresponding command on the **View** menu, or click the corresponding button on the **Debug** toolbar.

The **Immediate** window shows information that results from debugging statements in your code, or that you request by typing commands directly into the window.

The **Watch** window shows the current *watch expressions*, which are expressions whose values you decide to monitor as the code runs. A *break expression* is a watch expression that will cause Visual Basic to enter break mode when a certain condition you define becomes true. In the **Watch** window, the **Context** column indicates the procedure, module, or modules in which each watch expression is evaluated. The **Watch** window can display a value for a watch expression only if the current statement is in the specified context. Otherwise, the **Value** column shows a message indicating the statement is not in context.

The **Locals** window shows the value of any variables within the scope of the current procedure. As the execution switches from procedure to procedure, the contents of the **Locals** window changes to reflect only the variables applicable to the current procedure.

Tip   A variable that represents an object appears in the **Locals** window with a plus sign (+) to the left of its name. You can click the plus sign to expand the variable, displaying the properties of the object and their current values. If a property of the object contains another object, that can be expanded as well. The same holds true for variables that contain arrays or user-defined types.

Using Break Mode

At design time, you can change the design or code of an application, but you cannot see how your changes affect the way the application runs. At run time, you can watch how the application behaves, but you cannot directly change the code.

Break mode halts the operation of an application and gives you a snapshot of its condition at any moment. Variable and property settings are preserved, so you can analyze the current state of the application and enter changes that affect how the application runs. When an application is in break mode, you can do the following:

- Modify code in the application.
- Observe the condition of the application's interface.
- Determine which active procedures have been called.
- Watch the values of variables, properties, and statements.
- Change the values of variables and properties.
- View or control which statement the application will run next.
- Run Visual Basic statements immediately.
- Manually control the operation of the application.

Note   You can set breakpoints and watch expressions at design time, but other debugging tools work only in break mode.

Entering Break Mode at a Problem Statement

When debugging, you may want the application to halt at the place in the code where you think the problem might have started. This is one reason Visual Basic provides breakpoints and **Stop** statements. A *breakpoint* defines a statement or set of conditions at which Visual Basic automatically stops execution and puts the application in break mode without running the statement containing the breakpoint.

You can enter break mode manually if you do any of the following while the application is running:

- Press CTRL+BREAK.

- Choose **Break** from the **Run** menu.

- Click the **Break** button on the toolbar.

It's possible to break execution when the application is idle (when it is between processing of events). When this happens, execution does not stop at a specific line, but Visual Basic switches to break mode anyway.

You can also enter break mode automatically when any of the following occurs:

- A statement generates an untrapped run-time error.

- A statement generates a run-time error and **Break on All Errors** was selected in the **General** tab on the **Options** dialog box (**Tools** menu).

- A break expression defined in the **Add Watch** dialog box changes or becomes true, depending on how you defined it.

- Execution reaches a line with a breakpoint.

- Execution reaches a **Stop** statement.

Fixing a Run-Time Error and Continuing

Some run-time errors result from simple oversights when entering code; these errors are easily fixed. Frequent errors include misspelled names and mismatched properties or methods with objects.

Often you can enter a correction and continue program execution with the same line that halted the application, even though you've changed some of the code. Simply choose **Continue** from the **Run** menu or click the **Continue** button on the toolbar. As you continue running the application, you can verify that the problem is fixed.

If you select the **Break on All Errors** option, Visual Basic disables error handlers in code, so that when a statement generates a run-time error, Visual Basic enters break mode. If **Break on All Errors** is not selected, and if an error handler exists, it will intercept code and take corrective action.

Some changes (most commonly, changing variable declarations or adding new variables or procedures) require you to restart the application. When this happens, Visual Basic presents a message that asks if you want to restart the application.

Monitoring Data with Watch Expressions

As you debug your application, a calculation may not produce the result you want or problems might occur when a certain variable or property assumes a particular value or range of values. Many debugging problems aren't immediately traceable to a single statement, so you may need to observe the behavior of a variable or expression throughout a procedure.

Visual Basic automatically monitors watch expressions—expressions that you define—for you. When the application enters break mode, these watch expressions appear in the **Watch** window, where you can observe their values.

You can also direct watch expressions to put the application into break mode whenever the expression's value changes or equals a specified value. For example, instead of stepping through perhaps tens or hundreds of loops one statement at a time, you can use a watch expression to put the application in break mode when a loop counter reaches a specific value. Or you may want the application to enter break mode each time a flag in a procedure changes value.

Adding, Editing, or Deleting a Watch Expression

You can add, edit, or delete a watch expression at design time or in break mode. To add watch expressions, you can use the **Add Watch** dialog box (**Debug** menu).

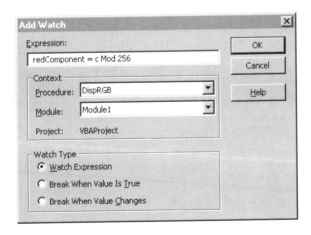

You use the **Edit Watch** dialog box (**Debug** menu) to modify or delete an existing watch expression. The **Add Watch** and **Edit Watch** dialog boxes share the same components (except the **Delete** button, which only appears in the **Edit Watch** dialog box). These shared components are described in the following table.

Component	Description
Expression box	Contains the expression that the watch expression evaluates. The expression is a variable, a property, a function call, or any other valid expression. When you display the **Add Watch** dialog box, the **Expression** box contains the current expression (if any).
Context option group	Sets the scope of variables watched in the expression. Use if you have variables of the same name with different scope. You can also restrict the scope of variables in watch expressions to a specific procedure or to a specific form or module, or you can have it apply to the entire application by selecting All Procedures and All Modules. Visual Basic can evaluate a variable in a narrow context more quickly.
Watch Type option group	Sets how Visual Basic responds to the watch expression. Visual Basic can watch the expression and display its value in the **Watch** window when the application enters break mode. Or you can have the application enter break mode automatically when the expression evaluates to a true (nonzero) statement or each time the value of the expression changes.

Tip You can add a watch expression by dragging an expression from a module to the **Watch** window.

Using Quick Watch

While in break mode, you can check the value of a property, variable, or expression for which you have not defined a watch expression. To check such expressions, use the **Quick Watch** dialog box (**Debug** menu or toolbar). The **Quick Watch** dialog box shows the value of the selected expression in a module. To continue watching this expression, click the **Add** button; the **Watch** window, with relevant information from the **Instant Watch** dialog box already entered, is displayed. If Visual Basic cannot evaluate the value of the current expression, the **Add** button is disabled.

Using a Breakpoint to Selectively Halt Execution

At run time, a breakpoint tells Visual Basic to halt just before executing a specific line of code. When Visual Basic is executing a procedure and it encounters a line of code with a breakpoint, it switches to break mode.

You can set or remove a breakpoint in break mode or at design time, or at run time when the application is idle. To set or remove a breakpoint, click in the margin (the left edge of the module window) next to a line of code. When you set a breakpoint,

Visual Basic highlights the selected line in bold, using the colors that you specified on the **Editor Format** tab in the **Options** dialog box (**Tools** menu).

In a module, Visual Basic indicates a breakpoint by displaying the text on that line in bold and in the colors specified for a breakpoint. A rectangular highlight surrounds the *current statement*, or the next statement to be run. When the current statement also contains a breakpoint, only the rectangular outline highlights the line of code. After the current statement moves to another line, the line with the breakpoint is displayed in bold and in color again. The following illustration shows a procedure with a breakpoint on the fourth line.

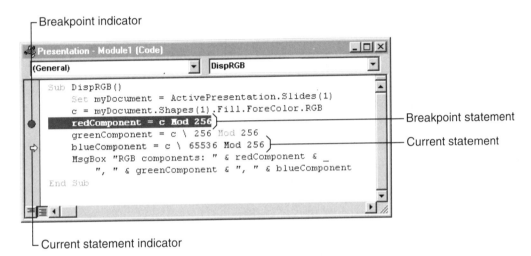

After you reach a breakpoint and the application is halted, you can examine the application's current state. Checking results of the application is easy, because you can move the focus among the forms and modules of your application and the debugging windows.

A breakpoint halts the application just before executing the line that contains the breakpoint. If you want to observe what happens when the line with the breakpoint runs, you must run at least one more statement. To do this, use Step Into or Step Over.

When you are trying to isolate a problem, remember that a statement might be indirectly at fault because it assigns an incorrect value to a variable. To examine the values of variables and properties while in break mode, use the **Locals** window, **Quick Watch**, watch expressions, or the **Immediate** window.

Using Stop Statements

Placing a **Stop** statement in a procedure is an alternative to setting a breakpoint. Whenever Visual Basic encounters a **Stop** statement, it halts execution and switches to break mode. Although **Stop** statements act like breakpoints, they aren't set or cleared the same way.

Remember that a **Stop** statement does nothing more than temporarily halt execution, while an **End** statement halts execution, resets variables, and returns to design time. You can always click **Continue** on the **Run** menu to continue running the application.

Running Selected Portions of Your Application

If you can identify the statement that caused an error, a single breakpoint might help you locate the problem. More often, however, you know only the general area of the code that caused the error. A breakpoint helps you isolate that problem area. You can then use Step Into and Step Over to observe the effect of each statement. If necessary, you can also skip over statements or back up by starting execution at a new line.

Step Mode	Description
Step Into	Run the current statement and break at the next line, even if it's in another procedure.
Step Over	Run the entire procedure called by the current line and break at the line following the current line.
Step Out	Run the remainder of the current procedure and break at the statement following the one that called the procedure.

Note   You must be in break mode to use these commands. They are not available at design time or run time.

Using Step Into

You can use Step Into to run code one statement at a time. (This is also known as single stepping.) When you use Step Into to step through code one statement at a time, Visual Basic temporarily switches to run time, runs the current statement, and advances to the next statement. Then it switches back to break mode. To step through your code this way, click the **Step Into** button on the **Debug** toolbar.

Note   Visual Basic allows you to step into individual statements, even if they are on the same line. A line of code can contain two or more statements, separated by a colon (:). Visual Basic uses a rectangular outline to indicate which of the statements will run next. Breakpoints apply only to the first statement of a multiple-statement line.

Using Step Over

Step Over is identical to Step Into, except when the current statement contains a call to a procedure. Unlike Step Into, which steps into the called procedure, Step Over runs it as a unit and then steps to the next statement in the current procedure. To step through your code this way, click the **Step Over** button on the **Debug** toolbar.

Suppose, for example, that the statement calls the procedure SetAlarmTime. If you choose Step Into, the module shows the SetAlarmTime procedure and sets the current statement to the beginning of that procedure. This is the better choice only if you want to analyze the code within SetAlarmTime. If you use Step Over, the module continues to display the current procedure. Execution advances to the statement immediately after the call to SetAlarmTime, unless SetAlarmTime contains a breakpoint or a Stop statement. Use Step Over if you want to stay at the same level of code and don't need to analyze the SetAlarmTime procedure.

You can alternate freely between Step Into and Step Over. The command you use depends on which portions of code you want to analyze at any given time.

Using Step Out

Step Out is similar to Step Into and Step Over, except it advances past the remainder of the code in the current procedure. If the procedure was called from another procedure, it advances to the statement immediately following the one that called the procedure. To step through your code this way, click the **Step Out** button on the **Debug** toolbar.

Bypassing Sections of Code

When your application is in break mode, you can select a statement further down in your code where you want execution to stop and then click **Run To Cursor** on the **Debug** menu. This lets you "step over" uninteresting sections of code, such as large loops.

Setting the Next Statement to Be Run

While debugging or experimenting with an application, you can select a statement anywhere in the current procedure and then click **Set Next Statement** on the **Debug** menu to skip a certain section of code—for instance, a section that contains a known bug—so you can continue tracing other problems. Or you may want to return to an earlier statement to test part of the application using different values for properties or variables.

Showing the Next Statement to Be Run

You can click **Show Next Statement** on the **Debug** menu to place the insertion point on the line that will run next. This feature is convenient if you've been executing code in an error handler and aren't sure where execution will resume. The **Show Next Statement** command is available only in break mode.

Monitoring the Call Stack

The **Call Stack** dialog box (**Debug** menu or toolbar) shows a list of all active procedure calls; you can display the **Call Stack** dialog box only when the application is in break mode. *Active procedure calls* are the procedures in the application that were started but not completed. You can use the list of active procedure calls to help trace the operation of an application as it runs a series of nested procedures. For example, an event procedure can call a second procedure, which can call a third procedure—all before the event procedure that started this chain is completed. Such nested procedure calls can be difficult to follow and can complicate the debugging process.

Tracing Nested Procedures

The **Call Stack** dialog box lists all the active procedure calls in a series of nested calls. It places the earliest active procedure call at the bottom of the list and adds subsequent procedure calls to the top of the list. The information given for each procedure begins with the module name, followed by the name of the called procedure. You can click the **Show** button in the **Call Stack** dialog box to display the statement in a procedure that passes control of the application to the next procedure in the list.

Note   Because the **Call Stack** dialog box doesn't indicate the variable assigned to an instance of a class, it does not distinguish between multiple instances of classes.

Testing Data and Procedures with the Immediate Window

Sometimes when you are debugging or experimenting with an application, you may want to run individual procedures, evaluate expressions, or assign new values to variables or properties. You can use the **Immediate** window to accomplish these tasks. You evaluate expressions by printing their values in the **Immediate** window.

Printing Information in the Immediate Window

There are two ways to print to the **Immediate** window:

- Include `Debug.Print` statements in the application code.
- Enter statements that use the **Print** method directly in the **Immediate** window.

These printing techniques offer the following advantages over watch expressions:

- You don't have to break execution to get feedback on how the application is performing. You can see data or other messages displayed as you run the application.

- Feedback is displayed in a separate area (the **Immediate** window), so it does not interfere with output that a user sees.

Printing from Application Code

The **Print** method sends output to the **Immediate** window whenever you include the **Debug** object qualifier. For example, the following statement prints the value of Salary to the **Immediate** window every time it is run.

```
Debug.Print "Salary = "; Salary
```

This technique works best when there is a particular place in your application code at which the variable (in this case, Salary) is known to change. For example, you might put the previous statement in a loop that repeatedly alters Salary.

Printing from the Immediate Window

After you're in break mode, you can move the focus to the **Immediate** window to examine data. You can evaluate any valid expression in the **Immediate** window, including expressions involving properties. The currently active module determines the scope. Type a statement that uses the **Print** method and then press ENTER to see the result. A question mark (?) is useful shorthand for the **Print** method.

Assigning Values to Variables and Properties

As you start to isolate the possible cause of an error, you may want to test the effects of particular data values. In break mode, you can set values with statements like the following in the **Immediate** window.

```
VScroll1.Value = 100
MaxRows = 50
```

The first statement alters a property of the VScroll1 object, and the second assigns a value to the variable MaxRows.

After you set the values of one or more properties and variables, you can continue execution to see the results or you can test the effect of the change on procedures.

Testing Procedures with the Immediate Window

The **Immediate** window evaluates any valid Visual Basic executable statement, but it doesn't accept data declarations. You can enter calls to procedures, however, which allows you to test the possible effect of a procedure with any given set of arguments. Simply enter a statement in the **Immediate** window (while in break mode) as you would in a module, as shown in the following statements.

```
X = Quadratic(2, 8, 8)
DisplayGraph 50, Arr1
Form_MouseDown 1, 0, 100, 100
```

When you press the ENTER key, Visual Basic switches to run time to run the statement, and then returns to break mode. At that point, you can see results and test any possible effects on variables or property values.

If **Option Explicit** is in effect (requiring all variable declarations to be explicit), any variables you enter in the **Immediate** window must already be declared within the current scope. Scope applies to procedure calls just as it does to variables. You can call any procedure within the currently active form. You can always call a procedure in a module, unless you define the procedure as **Private**, in which case you can call the procedure only while executing in the module.

You can use the **Immediate** window to run a procedure repeatedly, testing the effect of different conditions. Each separate call of the procedure is maintained as a separate instance by Visual Basic. This allows you to separately test variables and property settings in each instance of the procedure. The **Call Stack** dialog box maintains a listing of the procedures run by each command from the **Immediate** window. Newer listings are at the top of the list. You can use the **Call Stack** dialog box to select any instance of a procedure, and then print the values of variables from that procedure in the **Immediate** window.

Note Although most statements are supported in the **Immediate** window, a control structure is valid only if it can be completely expressed on one line of code; use colons to separate the statements that make up the control structure.

Checking Error Numbers

You can use the **Immediate** window to display the message associated with a specific error number. For example, if you enter the statement `Error 58` in the **Immediate** window and then press ENTER to run the statement, the appropriate error message ("File already exists") is displayed.

Tips for Using the Immediate Window

Here are some shortcuts you can use in the **Immediate** window:

- After you enter a statement, you can run it again by moving the insertion point back to that statement and pressing ENTER anywhere on the line.

- Before pressing ENTER, you can edit the current statement to alter its effects.

- You can use the mouse or the arrow keys to move around in the **Immediate** window. Don't press ENTER unless you are at a statement you want to run.

- CTRL+HOME will take you to the top of the **Immediate** window; CTRL+END will take you to the bottom.

- The HOME and END keys move to the beginning and end of the current line.

Special Debugging Considerations

Certain events that are a common part of using Microsoft Windows can pose special problems for debugging an application. It's important to be aware of these special problems so they don't confuse or complicate the debugging process.

If you remain aware of how break mode can put events at odds with what your application expects, you can usually find solutions. In some event procedures, you may need to use `Debug.Print` statements to monitor values of variables or properties instead of using watch expressions or breakpoints. You may also need to change the values of variables that depend on the sequence of events. This is discussed in the following topics.

Breaking Execution During a MouseDown or KeyDown Event Procedure

If you break execution during a MouseDown event procedure, you may release the mouse button or use the mouse to do any number of tasks. When you continue execution, however, the application assumes that the mouse button is still pressed down. You don't get a MouseUp event until you press the mouse button down again and then release it.

When you press the mouse button down during run time, you break execution in the MouseDown event procedure again, assuming you have a breakpoint there. In this scenario, you never get to the MouseUp event. The solution is usually to remove the breakpoint in the MouseDown procedure.

If you break execution during a KeyDown procedure, similar considerations apply. If you retain a breakpoint in a KeyDown procedure, you may never get a KeyUp event.

Breaking Execution During a GotFocus or LostFocus Event Procedure

If you break execution during a GotFocus or LostFocus event procedure, the timing of system messages can cause inconsistent results. Use a `Debug.Print` statement instead of a breakpoint in GotFocus or LostFocus event procedures.

Tips for Debugging

There are several ways to simplify debugging:

- When your application doesn't produce correct results, browse through the code and try to find statements that may have caused the problem. Set breakpoints at these statements and restart the application.

- When the program halts, test the values of important variables and properties. Use **Quick Watch** or set watch expressions to monitor these values. Use the **Immediate** window to examine variables and expressions.

- Select **Break on All Errors** on the **General** tab of the **Options** dialog box (**Tools** menu) to determine where an error occurred. Step through your code, using watch expressions and the **Locals** window to monitor how values change as the code runs.

- If an error occurs in a loop, define a break expression to determine where the problem occurs. Use the **Immediate** window together with **Set Next** statement to re-run the loop after making corrections.

CHAPTER 15

Developing Applications for the Internet and World Wide Web

This chapter shows you how to use Microsoft Office 97 to develop applications that retrieve, publish, and share information on the Internet or a local area network (LAN). For example, you can create applications that display Hypertext Markup Language (HTML) documents, or you can publish or share information located on a Web server. You can also create hyperlinks that you click to open Microsoft Office documents or objects located on a local hard disk or a LAN.

Contents

- Developing Internet Applications
- Internet Terms and Concepts
- Working with Hyperlinks
- Saving Documents and Objects as HTML
- Opening and Importing HTML Data
- Using the WebBrowser Control
- Using the Internet Transfer Control
- Using the WinSock Control
- Setting Up a Personal Web Server

Developing Internet Applications

The Internet provides an effective solution for broadcasting information across different platforms. For example, many organizations use the Internet to distribute product information, directories, or company policy manuals to people both within and outside of the organization. By applying Internet technologies to their internal network, organizations can help their employees share, analyze, and find information more easily.

Microsoft Office 97 is a flexible and robust tool for creating Internet content. By using the Microsoft Office Internet features, you can create applications to publish and distribute information to peers, management, and other functional groups in a timely manner, regardless of where they are located. For example, you can enter data into a Microsoft Access database, and then publish that database on your company's Web server so that users on a variety of platforms can access that data with a Web browser.

In Microsoft Word, Microsoft Excel, Microsoft PowerPoint, and Microsoft Access, you can use Visual Basic for Applications to automate and extend Internet features in your custom applications.

Internet Terms and Concepts

In all likelihood, you are well aware of what the Internet is, and you've had a chance to take advantage of its many resources. Even if you have used the Internet, the following overview will help to make sure you understand the terms used to describe it in this chapter.

The *Internet* is a collection of computer networks that connects millions of computers around the world. The *World Wide Web* is a client/server technology used to access a vast variety of digital information from the Internet. By using a software client called a *Web browser*, such as Microsoft Internet Explorer, and a modem or other connection to an Internet Service Provider (ISP), you can easily access text, graphics, sound, and other digital information from practically any computer in the world that is running the appropriate server software on the Internet.

Internet Protocols

A Web browser uses a variety of standardized methods for addressing and communicating with Internet servers. These methods are called *protocols*. The most common protocol is *Hypertext Transfer Protocol* (HTTP), which was originally created to publish and view linked text documents, but has been extended to display and run a growing variety of graphics, sound, video, and other multimedia content. Other common protocols include File Transfer Protocol (FTP), Gopher, telnet, RealAudio, as well as protocols used to start other applications such as e-mail and Usenet newsreaders.

The following table describes many of the protocols commonly in use today.

Protocol	Protocol name	Description
http	Hypertext Transfer Protocol	Goes to Web pages that contain text, graphics, sound, and other digital information from a Web server on the World Wide Web.
ftp	File Transfer Protocol	Transfers files between computers on the Internet.

Protocol	Protocol name	Description
gopher	Gopher protocol	Displays information on a Gopher server.
wais	WAIS protocol	Accesses a Wide Area Information Servers database.
file	File protocol	Opens a file on a local hard disk or LAN.
https	Hypertext Transfer Protocol with privacy	Establishes an HTTP connection that uses Secure Sockets Layer (SSL) encryption.
mailto	MailTo protocol	Opens your electronic mail program to send a message to the specified Internet e-mail address.
msn	Microsoft Network protocol	Goes to a location on MSN™, The Microsoft Network.
news	News protocol	Starts a newsreader and opens the specified Usenet newsgroup.
nntp	Network News Transfer Protocol	Performs the same function as News protocol.
mid	Musical Instrument Digital Interface (MIDI) protocol	Plays MIDI sequencer files if the user's computer has a sound card.
cid	CompuServe Dialer (CID) protocol	Establishes a point-to-point protocol (PPP) connection with the Internet through CompuServe's network.
prospero	Prospero protocol	Opens files on the Prospero distributed file system.
telnet	Telnet protocol	Starts a telnet *terminal emulation program*. A terminal emulation program is a command-line interface that you can use to issue commands on a remote computer. For example, by using telnet to connect to a UNIX server, you can issue UNIX commands to perform operations on that server.
rlogin	Rlogin protocol	Starts an Rlogin terminal emulation program.
tn3270	TN3270 protocol	Starts a TN3270 terminal emulation program.
pnm	RealAudio protocol	Plays RealAudio streaming audio from a RealAudio server. Streaming audio and other streaming media formats establish a connection to the server and start playing immediately without downloading an entire file.

Protocol	Protocol name	Description
mms	Microsoft Media Server (MMS) protocol	Plays media such as ActiveMovie™ streaming format files (.asf) from an MMS server.

Uniform Resource Locators

To run or display Internet content with a Web browser, you type an address called a *Uniform Resource Locator* (URL) into its address box. You can enter a URL that points to any Internet file type or resource supported by the browser that will be used to display or run it. You enter most URLs in the following format:

*protocol***://***serveraddress***/***path*

Protocol specifies the Internet protocol used to establish the connection to the server, and is generally followed by a colon and two slash marks. *Serveraddress* specifies what is usually called the *domain name* of the Internet server. *Path* specifies the location and name of the page or file on the Internet server. For example, this is the URL for the What's New page on the Microsoft Access Developer Forum Web site:

http://www.microsoft.com/accessdev/whatsnew.htm

Note   For some protocols, URLs have a different format. For example, the format for a URL that uses the MailTo protocol is **mailto:***username***@***domain*; the format for a URL that uses the News protocol is **news:***newsgroupname*; the format for a URL that uses the Network News Transfer Protocol is **nntp://***newsgroupname*.

Hypertext Markup Language and Hyperlinks

Most files you download and open with a Web browser are pages formatted with *Hypertext Markup Language (HTML) tags*. HTML tags are codes enclosed in angle brackets that are used by a Web browser to determine the structure and appearance of an HTML document, such as graphic elements and text formatting. For example, the two HTML tags in the following sentence:

Make <B>this text</B> look bold.

Cause the text to display like this when viewed with a Web browser:

Make **this text** look bold.

To navigate to other pages or multimedia content, a user clicks a *hyperlink* on a Web page. A hyperlink is colored and underlined text, or a graphic, that uses the path specified by a URL to download and open another file, such as another Web page or some form of multimedia content, such as a picture or sound file.

You can use HTML tags called *anchors* to create hyperlinks. An anchor with an HREF attribute goes to a file outside of the current document. For example, the following anchor creates a hyperlink that goes to the Microsoft home page:

<A HREF="http://www.microsoft.com/">Microsoft Home Page</A>

An anchor with a NAME attribute creates a bookmark at a location within the same document. Other hyperlinks can go to the bookmark created with this type of anchor.

HTML was originally a simple system for publishing documents on the Web, but it's rapidly evolving to include features that you can use to create sophisticated, interactive applications.

Tip   You can view an HTML reference that describes the most commonly used HTML tags as well as recent additions supported by Microsoft Internet Explorer and Netscape Navigator at http://www.microsoft.com/workshop/author/newhtml/.

Extensions to Standard Web Browser Functionality

Standard Web browser functionality is evolving through the addition of a variety of new technologies such as *helper applications*, *plug-ins*, *ActiveX controls*, *Java*™ *applets*, and *scripting languages*. If your Web browser doesn't support these technologies, you may need to install additional components to be able to use them.

Helper Applications

Helper applications are typically used to play audio or video files, or to display certain graphic formats. You may need to install helper applications before you can play or display certain content in your Web browser. In more recent browsers, such as Microsoft Internet Explorer version 3.0 and Netscape Navigator version 3.0, many of these functions are built into the browser itself, or are being replaced by one of the other technologies described in this section.

Plug-Ins

By using plug-ins, Web page authors can embed content that uses additional player or reader modules directly within Web pages. For example, there are plug-ins used to display Macromedia Director and Apple QuickTime® movies in a Web page. In order to use Web pages containing content that requires a plug-in, the plug-in must be installed beforehand. Microsoft Internet Explorer version 3.0 and Netscape Navigator versions 2.0 and 3.0 can run plug-ins.

ActiveX Controls

By using ActiveX controls, Web page authors can extend the kinds of content that can be displayed on a Web page. They can also enhance their Web pages with sophisticated formatting features, animation, and embedded programs that perform operations such as background downloading. ActiveX controls don't need to be installed beforehand—they can be downloaded when a user first opens a Web page.

Microsoft Internet Explorer version 3.0 has built-in support for Web pages that contain ActiveX controls. To use a Web page that contains ActiveX controls in Netscape Navigator version 3.0, you must use the NCompass ScriptActive plug-in.

Java Applets

By using the Java programming language, Web page authors can produce applications called applets, which can perform functions similar to plug-ins and ActiveX controls. To display or run a Java applet from a Web page, a Web browser must be able to compile and run Java code. Microsoft Internet Explorer version 3.0 and Netscape Navigator versions 2.0 and 3.0 can run Java applets.

Scripting Languages

Scripting languages are interpreted programming languages that Web page authors can use to perform a variety of operations. They are often used in conjunction with ActiveX controls or Java applets. Three common examples of scripting languages are VBScript, JScript™, and JavaScript. To use a page that contains scripting language code, a Web browser must be able to interpret the code. Microsoft Internet Explorer version 3.0 can run both VBScript and JScript code, as well as most JavaScript code. Netscape Navigator versions 2.0 and 3.0 can run JavaScript code. Netscape Navigator version 3.0 can run VBScript code if you have the NCompass ScriptActive plug-in installed.

In addition to scripting languages, there are a variety of *server-side scripting languages*, such as CGI, PERL, and ActiveX Scripting that extend the functionality of servers. In Microsoft Access, you can create Active Server Pages (ASP) that use ActiveX Scripting to bind data to Web page controls. By using Active Server Pages, your Web pages can perform many of the same functions as Microsoft Access forms.

Intranets

If you install Internet server software, such as Microsoft Internet Information Server, on servers connected by a local area network (LAN), you can use these same Internet technologies to share data within an organization. Such a system is called an *intranet* or *internal Web*. For example, your organization could post human resources information for all employees on a Web page, or a project team could post information about its members and provide hyperlinks to important documentation about the project. All the features in Microsoft Office that are designed for the Internet can also be used on an intranet. For more information about Microsoft Internet Information Server, see http://www.microsoft.com/ntserver/.

You can also set up a *personal web server* to test your Web application or to publish small-scale intranet applications. If you are using Windows 95, you can install Microsoft Personal Web Server. If you are using Windows NT Workstation

version 4.0, you can install Microsoft Peer Web Services. For more information about
Personal Web Server or Peer Web Services, see "Setting Up a Personal Web Server"
later in this chapter.

Working with Hyperlinks

In all Microsoft Office 97 applications, you can create hyperlinks to display and run
standard Internet content. Additionally, in all Office applications except Outlook, you
can create hyperlinks to move between Microsoft Word documents, Microsoft Excel
workbooks, Microsoft PowerPoint presentations, and Microsoft Access databases that
are stored on a local hard disk or on a LAN. You don't need Internet connections or
Web servers to use hyperlinks to move between Office documents or files. You can
use both kinds of hyperlinks in the same application.

A hyperlink to a Microsoft Office document can also go to a specific location or
object within another document or the current document. The following table lists the
objects that a hyperlink can go to within each Microsoft Office application.

Application	Object
Microsoft Access	A table in Datasheet view. A query in Datasheet view. A form in Form view or Datasheet view, depending on the form's **DefaultView** property setting. A report in Print Preview. A macro. Using a hyperlink to go to a macro runs the macro. A module.
Microsoft Excel	A worksheet. A specified range of cells in a worksheet. A named range of cells in a worksheet.
Microsoft PowerPoint	A slide.
Microsoft Word	A bookmark.

When you follow a hyperlink, either by clicking it or by using the **Follow** or
FollowHyperlink method, the Office application may open a cached copy of the
document, depending on the Internet settings in Control Panel. To view or change
these settings, double-click the **Internet** icon in Control Panel, then click **Settings** on
the **Advanced** tab. For more information about the **Follow** and **FollowHyperlink**
methods, see "The Follow Method" and "The FollowHyperlink Method" later in this
chapter.

Specifying a Hyperlink Address

When specifying a hyperlink address, you can use either of two forms:

- A valid URL that points to a resource on the Internet or an intranet.

- A path on a local hard disk, or a path on a LAN.

Specifying a URL as a Hyperlink Address

To create a hyperlink that goes to a Web page or other Internet content, you must enter a valid URL as the hyperlink address. You can enter a URL that points to any Internet file type or resource supported by the browser or to an ActiveX control, such as the WebBrowser control, that will be used to display or run it. For example, the URL to the home page of the Microsoft Office Developer Forum is:

http://www.microsoft.com/officedev/

When you enter a URL like the previous example that doesn't specify a particular file name, be sure to include a slash mark (/) at the end of the address. Although URLs that do not end in a slash mark generally work, they require the server to perform additional operations that add to the overall network load and slow down the opening of the hyperlink. When you specify a file name at the end of a URL, you do not end the URL with a slash mark. For example:

http://www.microsoft.com/default.asp

If your users have Microsoft Internet Explorer version 3.0 or if your application uses the WebBrowser control, your application can open a Microsoft Excel workbook, Word document, or PowerPoint presentation within the browser or control. To do this, the corresponding Office application or viewer (Microsoft Excel Viewer, Word Viewer, or PowerPoint Viewer) must also be installed on the user's computer. In this case, a URL can point directly to an Office document on a Web or intranet server. For example:

http://*YourIntranetServer*/*YourWordDoc*.doc

You can also open an Office document in Microsoft Internet Explorer version 3.0 or in the WebBrowser control directly from the standard file system, without using a Web server. To do so, use the File protocol, as follows:

file://c:\my documents\sales.doc

Specifying a UNC or Standard Path as a Hyperlink Address

To create a hyperlink that starts a Microsoft Office 97 application and opens one of its documents from a LAN, enter a universal naming convention (UNC) path as the hyperlink address. This ensures that the hyperlink continues to work if the document or the application that contains the hyperlink is moved to another computer. A UNC path starts with two backslashes (\\) and supplies the server name, share name, and full path to the file. For example, a UNC path to a Microsoft Excel workbook would be in the following format:

*server**share**path**workbook*.**xls**

You can also specify a network path that uses a mapped drive letter, such as E:*path**workbook*.xls. However, because the path is specific to that drive letter, the hyperlink only works if the user's computer has the drive letter mapped to the appropriate server and share. If you want to create a hyperlink that goes to a file on a local drive, you can use a standard file path starting with a drive letter, such as C:*path**workbook*.xls. In this case, if the application is moved to another computer, the hyperlink only works if the file specified in the address is stored on the same drive and in the same folder on the new computer.

You can also enter a UNC or standard file path as a hyperlink address to open any file type that is registered on the computer running your document or application. For example, if Notepad is installed and registered to open text (.txt) files, you could enter a UNC path to open a text file in the following format:

*server**share**path**filename*.**txt**

Absolute vs. Relative Links

When you create a hyperlink, you can use a path based on either an *absolute link* or a *relative link*. A path based on an absolute link points to a fixed file location. Absolute links identify the destination of a hyperlink by its full address such as C:\\My Documents\\Sales.doc or http:\\\\www.microsoft.com\\default.htm. Use an absolute link for hyperlinks to destinations that won't be moved or that require a full path. For example, use absolute links in hyperlinks to other Web sites, such as a list of your favorite Web sites.

A path based on a relative link points to a destination relative to the file the hyperlink is located in. When the first part of the path is shared by both the file that contains the hyperlink and the destination file, that part is called a *hyperlink base*. For example, if the path to the file that contains the hyperlink is C:\\My Documents\\Databases and the path to the destination file is C:\\My Documents\\Workbooks, then C:\\My Documents is the hyperlink base. The hyperlink base address is automatically added to the beginning of the path for all relative links. You can specify the hyperlink base on the **Summary** tab of the document's property sheet. To open a document's property sheet in Microsoft Excel, Word, or PowerPoint, click **Properties** on the File menu. To open the property sheet for a Microsoft Access database, click **Database Properties** on the **File** menu.

When a hyperlink uses a path based on a relative link, you can move the file that contains the hyperlink and the destination file without breaking the hyperlink if you move the destination file to an identically named location. For example, if you set the hyperlink base to C:\\My Documents and then create a relative link to a document in C:\\My Documents\\Workbooks, and you move the document that contains the relative link to a new computer, you must copy the destination file into an identically named folder in C:\\My Documents on the new computer. Alternatively, you can move the destination file to a folder named Workbooks within another folder (for example, D:\\Applications), and then open the document that contains the relative link and update the hyperlink base to the new folder's name.

If you save a document or database object that contains relative links as an HTML document, the hyperlink base is omitted from the anchor tags created for those relative links. For example, suppose you create a relative link to a database called Names.mdb in C:\My Documents\Databases, and set the hyperlink base to C:\My Documents. When you save the document as an HTML document, the anchor tag created is <A HREF="Databases\Names.mdb">. To keep the hyperlink from breaking in the HTML document, you must create a Databases folder in the folder that contains the HTML document on the HTTP server, and then copy the Names.mdb database into that folder.

Using Objects and Collections to Work with Hyperlinks

All Office 97 applications except Outlook provide objects and collections that you can use to work with hyperlinks in Visual Basic code. Although there are a great number of similarities across each application, in some cases the objects and collections that hyperlinks are associated with differ slightly in each Office application.

To work with hyperlinks in Visual Basic code, you use the **Hyperlink** object. In all Office 97 applications except Microsoft Access, the **Hyperlink** object is a member of the **Hyperlinks** collection. In Microsoft Access, the **Hyperlink** object is a member of the **Controls** collection. The objects that can contain a **Hyperlinks** collection differ for each application. They are listed in the following table.

Application	Objects that can contain a Hyperlinks collection
Microsoft Word	**Document**, **Range**, or **Selection** objects
Microsoft Excel	**Worksheet** or **Range** objects
Microsoft PowerPoint	**Slide** or **Master** objects
Microsoft Access	None. Microsoft Access doesn't have a **Hyperlinks** collection. All **Hyperlink** objects are members of the **Controls** collection. In addition, you can have a set of records that contains fields with the Hyperlink data type and use Visual Basic to work with the records as if they were a collection.

The objects that can have a **Hyperlink** object associated with them differ for each application. The following table summarizes which objects can have an associated **Hyperlink** object.

Application	Objects that can have a Hyperlink object associated with them
Microsoft Word	**Shape**, **InlineShape**, **Selection**, or **Range** objects
Microsoft Excel	**Shape**, **Selection**, or **Range** objects
Microsoft PowerPoint	**Shape.ActionSettings** or **TextRange.ActionSettings** objects
Microsoft Access	**CommandButton**, **ComboBox**, **Image**, **Label**, **ListBox**, or **TextBox** objects

Adding New Hyperlink Objects to the Hyperlinks Collection

In Microsoft Excel and Word, use the **Add** method to create a **Hyperlink** object and add it to the **Hyperlinks** collection. To create a hyperlink with the **Add** method, use the following syntax:

object.**Add**(*anchor*, *address*, *subaddress*)

The following table describes the arguments of the **Add** method.

Argument	Description
object	Required. An expression that returns a **Hyperlink** object.
anchor	Required. The anchor for the hyperlink. Can be either a **Range** or a **Shape** object.
address	Required. The address of the hyperlink.
subaddress	Optional. The subaddress of the hyperlink.

Microsoft Word Examples

In Word, you can use the **Add** method to add a hyperlink to either a **Range** object (a range or selection of text), a **Shape** object (a graphic object), or an **InlineShape** object (a graphic object within a line of text).

Creating a Hyperlink for a Microsoft Word Range Object

The following example inserts the text "Microsoft Web Site" at the beginning of the active document, selects the inserted text, and then adds a hyperlink to the text that goes to the Microsoft home page at http://www.microsoft.com/.

```
Sub AddHyperlinkRange()
   Dim r As Range

   Set r = ActiveDocument.Range(Start := 0, End := 0)
   r.InsertBefore "Microsoft Web Site"
   Selection.MoveRight Unit := wdWord, Count := 3, Extend := wdExtend
   ActiveDocument.Hyperlinks.Add Anchor := Selection.Range, _
      Address := "http://www.microsoft.com/"
End Sub
```

Creating a Hyperlink for a Microsoft Word Shape Object

The following example creates a beveled shape, adds the text "Microsoft Web Site" to the shape, and then adds a hyperlink to the shape that goes to the Microsoft home page at http://www.microsoft.com/.

```
Sub AddHyperlinkShape()
   ActiveDocument.Shapes.AddShape(msoShapeBevel, 150, 150, 100, 30).Select
   With Selection
      .ShapeRange.TextFrame.TextRange.Select
      .Collapse
      .TypeText Text:="Microsoft Web Site"
      .ShapeRange.Select
   End With
   ActiveDocument.Hyperlinks.Add Anchor:=Selection.ShapeRange, _
      Address:= "http://www.microsoft.com/"
End Sub
```

Creating a Hyperlink Associated with a Command Button

In addition to creating **Hyperlink** objects in Visual Basic code, you can create a command button by using the user interface and then add code to the command button's Click event procedure to make it follow a hyperlink. This doesn't create a **Hyperlink** object so the hyperlink isn't available in the document's **Hyperlinks** collection. To create a command button that follows a hyperlink in Microsoft Excel, Word, and PowerPoint, use the following procedure.

▶ **To create a command button that follows a hyperlink**

1 Right-click the menu bar and then click **Control Toolbox** on the shortcut menu.

2 In the toolbox, click the **Command Button** tool, and then click where you want to place the command button.

3 Right-click the command button, and then click **Properties** on the shortcut menu.

4 In the **Caption** property box, enter the text you want on the button. Set any other properties you want to control the button's appearance and then close the **Properties** dialog box.

5 Right-click the command button, and then click **View Code**. Enter a procedure that uses the **FollowHyperlink** method in the button's Click event. For example:

```
Private Sub CommandButton1_Click()
    FollowHyperlink "http://www.microsoft.com/"
End Sub
```

6 Save the code, and exit Design mode to test the button.

Note When using this method, the command button doesn't display blue underlined text or the hand cursor when the mouse is over the button.

For more information about the **FollowHyperlink** method, see "The FollowHyperlink Method" later in this chapter.

Microsoft Excel Examples

In Microsoft Excel, you can use the **Add** method to add a hyperlink to either a **Range** object (a range of one or more cells) or a **Shape** object (a graphic).

Creating a Hyperlink for a Microsoft Excel Range Object

The following example adds the display text "MSN Web site" to cell A1 in the first worksheet in the current workbook, and then adds a hyperlink to that range that goes to the Web site at http://www.msn.com/.

```
Sub AddHyperlink_Range()
    Dim wrk As Worksheet

    Set wrk = ActiveWorkbook.Sheets(1)
    wrk.Range("A1").Value = "MSN Web site"
    wrk.Hyperlinks.Add Address := "http://www.msn.com/", _
        Anchor := wrk.Range("A1")
End Sub
```

Creating a Hyperlink for a Microsoft Excel Shape Object

The following example adds a rounded rectangle labeled "Click Here" to the first worksheet in the current workbook, and then adds a hyperlink to the rectangle that goes to cell C6 on the first sheet of Book2.xls.

```
Sub AddHyperlink_Shape()
    Dim wrk As Worksheet
    Dim shp As Shape

    Set wrk = ActiveWorkbook.Sheets(1)
    Set shp = wrk.Shapes.AddShape(msoShapeRoundedRectangle, 50, 50, 100, 50)
    shp.Select
    Selection.Characters.Text = "Click Here"
    wrk.Hyperlinks.Add Anchor := shp, Address := "C:\My Documents\Book2.xls", _
        SubAddress := "Sheet1!C6"
End Sub
```

Microsoft PowerPoint Examples

PowerPoint doesn't use the **Add** method to create a new hyperlink. Instead, you create a hyperlink by working with the **ActionSettings** collection of a **Shape** object (a graphic) or a **TextRange** object (text associated with a **Shape** object). A **Shape** or **TextRange** object can have two different hyperlinks assigned to it: one that's followed when the user clicks the object during a slide show, and another that's followed when the user passes the mouse pointer over the object during a slide show.

To specify which mouse action to work with, first use the **ActionSettings** property to return the **ActionSettings** collection, then use **ActionSettings**(*index*), where index is either **ppMouseClick** or **ppMouseOver**. Set the **Action** property to **ppActionHyperlink** to specify that the action is a hyperlink. After a hyperlink is created, it's available from the **Hyperlinks** collections for the **Shape**, **TextRange**, and **Slide** objects.

Creating a Hyperlink for a Microsoft PowerPoint Shape Object

The following example adds a Custom action button with text that reads "Microsoft.com" to the first slide in the active presentation, and then adds a hyperlink to the button that goes to the Microsoft home page.

```
Sub AddHyperlinkButton()
   Dim sld As Slide, shp As Shape

   Set sld = ActivePresentation.Slides(1)
   Set shp = sld.Shapes.AddShape(msoShapeActionButtonCustom, 50, 50, 160, 30)
   With shp.TextFrame
      .TextRange.Text = "Microsoft.com"
      .MarginBottom = 5
      .MarginLeft = 5
      .MarginRight = 5
      .MarginTop = 5
   End With
   With shp.ActionSettings(ppMouseClick)
      .Action = ppActionHyperlink
      .Hyperlink.Address = "http://www.microsoft.com/"
   End With
End Sub
```

Creating a Hyperlink for a Microsoft PowerPoint TextRange Object

The following example adds a rectangle to the first slide in the active presentation,
adds text to the rectangle, and then adds a hyperlink to the text. This example defines
a hyperlink for all the text in the text range. It is possible to define more than one
hyperlink within a text range for selected characters.

```
Sub AddHyperlinkText()
   Dim sld As Slide, shp As Shape, txt As Text

   Set sld = ActivePresentation.Slides(1)
   Set shp = sld.Shapes.AddShape(msoShapeRectangle, 0, 0, 250, 140)
   shp.TextFrame.TextRange.Text = "Microsoft Web Site"
   Set txt = shp.TextFrame.TextRange
   With txt.ActionSettings(ppMouseClick)
      .Action = ppActionHypertext
      .Hyperlink.Address = "http://www.microsoft.com/"
   End With
End Sub
```

Microsoft Access Example

Microsoft Access doesn't provide a **Hyperlinks** collection or use the **Add** method to
create a hyperlink on a form or report. Instead, you create hyperlinks for label,
command button, and image controls by setting either the **HyperlinkAddress**
property or the **HyperlinkSubAddress** property, or both, of the control.

Note You can also create a field with the Hyperlink data type to store hyperlink addresses in a
table, and then bind that field to a text box, list box, or combo box on a form. For more
information, see "Storing Hyperlinks in Microsoft Access Tables" later in this chapter.

Creating a Hyperlink Control in Microsoft Access

The following example creates a new label on a form and then sets the
HyperlinkAddress and **HyperlinkSubAddress** properties to create a hyperlink.
When you create a hyperlink in Visual Basic, and you want it to be colored and
underlined, you must also explicitly set the **ForeColor** and **FontUnderline** properties.

```
Sub CreateHyperlinkLabel(strForm As String, xPos As Integer, _
    yPos As Integer, strCaption As String, Optional strAddress As String, _
    Optional strSubAddress As String)
  Dim ctlLabel As Control

  ' Open form, hidden in Design view.
  DoCmd.OpenForm strForm, acDesign,,,,acHidden

  ' Create label control with text specified by strCaption, at
  ' the position specified by xPos and yPos.
  Set ctlLabel = CreateControl(strForm, acLabel, , "", _
    strCaption, xPos, yPos)

  ' Set hyperlink address, text color, and underline.
  With ctlLabel
    .HyperlinkAddress = strAddress
    .HyperlinkSubAddress = strSubAddress
    .ForeColor = "1279872587"
    .FontUnderline = True
  End With

  ' Save form.
  DoCmd.Save acForm, strForm
End Sub
```

To use this example to create a hyperlink, you must specify the form, position, display text, and hyperlink address. For example, enter the following code into the Debug window:

```
CreateHyperlinkLabel "Form1",100,100,"Microsoft Web Site","http://www.microsoft.com/"
```

You can use similar code to create image and command button controls and set properties to create a hyperlink.

Referring to Hyperlink Objects

Use the **Hyperlink** property to return a reference to a **Hyperlink** object. The objects that can have a **Hyperlink** object associated with them differ somewhat for each application.

Microsoft Word Example

Use the **Hyperlink** property to return the hyperlink for a shape. Note that a shape can have only one hyperlink associated with it. The following example follows the hyperlink associated with the first shape in the active document.

```
ActiveDocument.Shapes(1).Hyperlink.Follow
```

Selection and **Range** objects can have multiple **Hyperlink** objects associated with them. For these objects, you must either loop through the object's **Hyperlinks** collection or specify a member of the object's **Hyperlinks** collection by using the **Item** method. The following example loops through the hyperlinks in the current selection.

```
Dim H As Hyperlink, hLinks As Hyperlinks
Set hLinks = Selection.Hyperlinks

For Each H In hLinks
    MsgBox H.Address
Next H
```

The following example displays the address of the first hyperlink in the first 20 characters of the current document in the Immediate window.

```
Debug.Print ActiveDocument.Range(0,20).Hyperlinks(1).Address
```

Microsoft Excel Example

Use the **Hyperlink** property to return the hyperlink for a shape. Note that a shape can have only one hyperlink associated with it. The following example follows the hyperlink associated with the first shape on the first worksheet.

```
Worksheets(1).Shapes(1).Hyperlink.Follow NewWindow:=True
```

Microsoft PowerPoint Example

As mentioned earlier in this chapter, a shape in PowerPoint can have up to two different hyperlinks assigned to it: one that's followed when the user clicks the shape during a slide show, and another that's followed when the user passes the mouse pointer over the shape during a slide show. To return a hyperlink for a shape, you must first reference the appropriate member of the **ActionSettings** collection (**ppMouseOver** or **ppMouseClick**), and then use the **Hyperlink** property.

The following example displays the address for the mouse-click hyperlink of the third shape on the first slide of the active presentation in the Immediate window.

```
Debug.Print ActivePresentation.Slides(1).Shapes(3). _
    ActionSettings(ppMouseClick).Hyperlink.Address
```

Microsoft Access Example

In Microsoft Access, you can use the **Hyperlink** property to return a reference to the **Hyperlink** object associated with a **CommandButton**, **ComboBox**, **Image**, **Label**, **ListBox**, or **TextBox** control.

The CreateHyperlink procedure in the following example sets the **Address** and **SubAddress** properties for a label, image control, or command button to the values passed to the procedure. The **Address** property setting is optional, because a hyperlink to a database object in the current database uses only the **SubAddress** property.

To try this example, create a form with two text box controls named txtAddress and txtSubAddress, and a command button named cmdFollowLink. Then paste the sample code into the Declarations section of the form's module. Display the form in Form view, enter appropriate values in the txtAddress and txtSubAddress text boxes, and click the cmdFollowLink button.

```
Private Sub cmdFollowLink_Click()
    CreateHyperlink Me!cmdFollowLink, Me!txtSubAddress, Me!txtAddress
End Sub

Sub CreateHyperlink(ctlSelected As Control, txtSubAddress As TextBox, _
    Optional txtAddress As TextBox)
    Dim hlk As Hyperlink

    Select Case ctlSelected.ControlType
        Case acLabel, acImage, acCommandButton
            Set hlk = ctlSelected.Hyperlink
            With hlk
                If Not IsMissing(txtAddress) Then
                    .Address = txtAddress
                Else
                    .Address = ""
                End If
                .SubAddress = txtSubAddress
                .Follow
                .Address = ""
                .SubAddress = ""
            End With
        Case Else
            MsgBox "The control '" & ctlSelected.Name & "' does not support hyperlinks."
    End Select
End Sub
```

Referring to a Hyperlink Object by Its Position in the Hyperlinks Collection

Use the **Item** method (or the **Item** property in Microsoft Excel) of the **Hyperlinks** collection to return a single **Hyperlink** object based on its position in the collection. The first object in the collection has an **Item** value of 1. The **Item** method is the default member of the **Hyperlinks** collection, so you can refer to the **Item** method in either of the following ways:

```
Hyperlinks.Item(1)
Hyperlinks(1)
```

Microsoft Word Example

The following example follows the first hyperlink in the selection.

```
If Selection.Hyperlinks.Count >= 1 Then
    Selection.Hyperlinks(1).Follow
End If
```

Note   The **Count** property for the **Hyperlinks** collection of a **Selection** object returns the number of items in the main story only. To count items in other stories, specify the story in the **StoryRanges** collection. For example, to count all of the hyperlinks in the primary footer story you can use the following code.

```
ActiveDocument.StoryRanges(wdPrimaryFooterStory).Hyperlinks.Count.
```

Microsoft Excel Example

The following example uses the **Follow** method to activate the second hyperlink in the range of cells from E5 to E8.

```
Worksheets(1).Range("E5:E8").Hyperlinks(2).Follow
```

Microsoft PowerPoint Example

The following example sets the **Address** property of the second hyperlink on the first slide in the current PowerPoint presentation.

```
ActivePresentation.Slides(1).Hyperlinks(2).Address = "C:\New\Newsales.ppt"
```

Looping Through the Hyperlinks Collection

You can use the **Hyperlinks** collection in Microsoft Excel, Word, and PowerPoint to loop through the set of **Hyperlink** objects associated with an object. In Microsoft Access, you can loop through the **Controls** collection or a set of records to work with the hyperlinks in your application.

The following examples perform operations on a **Hyperlinks** collection that contains existing **Hyperlink** objects. In the Microsoft Excel, Word, and PowerPoint examples that follow, the object that contains the **Hyperlinks** collection is specific to the application. However, you can modify each example to run in another application by referring to the appropriate object. Because the Microsoft Access examples use the **Controls** collection or a set of records instead of the **Hyperlinks** collection, you can only use them in Microsoft Access.

Microsoft Word Example

If the active document includes hyperlinks, this example inserts a list of the hyperlink destinations at the end of the document.

```
Dim hLink As Hyperlink

Set myRange = ActiveDocument.Range(Start:=ActiveDocument.Content.End - 1)
Count = 0
For Each hLink In ActiveDocument.Hyperlinks
    Count = Count + 1
    With myRange
        .InsertAfter "Hyperlink #" & Count & vbTab
        .InsertAfter hLink.Address
        .InsertParagraphAfter
    End With
Next hLink
```

Microsoft Excel Example

The following example updates all hyperlinks on the first worksheet in the active workbook that have the specified address.

```
Dim hLink As Hyperlink

For Each hLink in ActiveWorkbook.Sheets(1).Hyperlinks
    If LCase(hLink.Address) = "C:\Current Work\Sales.ppt" Then
        hLink.Address = "C:\New\Newsales.ppt"
    End If
Next hLink
```

Note   In Word, you can use the **Hyperlinks** collection to access hyperlinks created by inserting a HYPERLINK field. In Microsoft Excel, however, you cannot use the **Hyperlinks** collection to access hyperlinks created by entering a formula using the HYPERLINK function.

Microsoft PowerPoint Example

The following example updates an outdated Internet address for all hyperlinks in the active presentation.

```
Dim hLink As Hyperlink
Dim S As Slide

oldAddr = InputBox("Old internet address")
newAddr = InputBox("New internet address")
For Each S In ActivePresentation.Slides
    For Each hLink In s.Hyperlinks
        If LCase(hLink.Address) = Lcase(oldAddr) Then hLink.Address = newAddr
    Next hLink
Next S
```

Microsoft Access Examples

Microsoft Access doesn't support the **Hyperlinks** collection, but you can loop through the **Controls** collection on a form or report to work with the hyperlinks associated with any control on the form or report. The following procedure displays the name and hyperlink address values for controls that contain hyperlinks in the Debug window.

```
Sub ListHyperlinks(strForm As String)
    Dim Frm As Form
    Dim Ctl As Control

    DoCmd.OpenForm strForm, acDesign, , , , acHidden
    Set Frm = Forms(strForm)

    ' Ignore controls without hyperlinks.
    On Error Resume Next

    For Each Ctl In Frm.Controls
        If Not (Ctl.ControlType = acTextBox) Then
        Debug.Print "Control:" & Ctl.Name & vbCrLf & _
            "Address:" & Ctl.Hyperlink.Address & vbCrLf & _
            "Subaddress:" & Ctl.Hyperlink.SubAddress & vbCrLf
        Else
        Debug.Print "Control:" & Ctl.Name & vbCrLf & _
            "Text box control bound to Hyperlink field " & _
            Ctl.ControlSource & vbCrLf
        End If
    Next Ctl
    Frm.Close
End Sub
```

In addition to creating **Hyperlink** objects that belong to the **Controls** collection of forms and reports, you can have a set of records that contains fields with the Hyperlink data type and use Visual Basic to work with the records as if they were a collection. For example, you can loop through the records in a table to work with the properties of a field. The following procedure works with the Suppliers table in the Northwind sample database. If a field is a Hyperlink field, the procedure loops through all the records in the table. If a field is not null (empty), it displays the record number, field name, and displayed value in the Debug window.

```
Sub HyperlinkRecordset()
    Dim dbs As Database
    Dim rstSuppliers As Recordset
    Dim fldField As Field

    ' Return reference to current database.
    Set dbs = CurrentDb
    ' Create dynaset-type Recordset object.
    Set rstSuppliers = dbs.OpenRecordset("Suppliers", dbOpenDynaset)

    ' Print displayed value for fields containing hyperlinks.
    For Each fldField In rstSuppliers.Fields
        If (fldField.Attributes And dbHyperlinkField) Then
            With rstSuppliers
                Do While Not .EOF
                    If Not IsNull(fldField.Value) Then
                        Debug.Print rstSuppliers.AbsolutePosition + 1 & " " & _
                        fldField.Name & " " & _
                        HyperlinkPart(fldField.Value, acDisplayedValue)
                    End If
```

```
            .MoveNext
          Loop
        .MoveFirst
      End With
    End If
  Next fldField
  ' Free all object variables.
  rstSuppliers.Close
  Set dbs = Nothing
End Sub
```

For more information about Hyperlink fields, see "Storing Hyperlinks in Microsoft Access Tables" later in this chapter.

Using Methods and Properties to Work with Hyperlinks

The following table summarizes the methods and properties you can use to work with hyperlinks in Visual Basic.

Method or property name	Description
Hyperlink property	Returns a reference to a hyperlink object in code.
Follow method	Follows a hyperlink defined by an existing **Hyperlink** object. The **Follow** method has the same effect as clicking the hyperlink.
FollowHyperlink method	Follows a hyperlink address specified in code or passed to the method from a text box. For example, you can prompt a user to type a hyperlink address in a dialog box or form, and then use the **FollowHyperlink** method to go to that address.
ExtraInfoRequired property (Word only)	A read-only property that returns **True** if extra information is required to resolve the specified hyperlink. You can specify extra information, such as a file name or a query string, by using the *extrainfo* argument with the **Follow** or **FollowHyperlink** methods.
AddToFavorites method	Adds a shortcut to the Favorites folder. The **AddToFavorites** method can reference a **Hyperlink** object or the current document (Microsoft Access database, Microsoft Excel workbook, Microsoft PowerPoint presentation, or Microsoft Word document).
Address property	Returns the address of the specified hyperlink. This property is read/write, except in Word, where it is read-only.

Method or property name	Description
Subaddress property	Returns a named location in the destination of the specified hyperlink. The named location can be a bookmark (Microsoft Word), a named cell or cell reference (Microsoft Excel), a database object (Microsoft Access), or a slide number (Microsoft PowerPoint). This property is read/write, except in Word, where it is read-only.
Type property (Microsoft Excel, Word, and PowerPoint only)	Returns the type of object the hyperlink is associated with. Can be one of the following constants: **msoHyperlinkInlineShape** (Word only) **msoHyperlinkRange** **msoHyperlinkShape**
HyperlinkAddress property (Microsoft Access only)	Sets or returns the address of a hyperlink for a label, image control, or command button. The **HyperlinkAddress** property is equivalent to setting or returning the **Address** property for the control in Visual Basic; for example, *object*.**HyperlinkAddress** is equivalent to *object*.**Hyperlink.Address**. You can also set the **HyperlinkAddress** property in the control's property sheet.
HyperlinkSubAddress property (Microsoft Access only)	Sets or returns the location within the Office document or object specified by the **HyperlinkAddress** property. When no **HyperlinkAddress** property is specified, **HyperlinkSubAddress** specifies a database object in the current database. The **HyperlinkSubAddress** property is equivalent to setting or returning the **SubAddress** property for the control in Visual Basic; for example, *object*.**HyperlinkSubAddress** is equivalent to *object*.**Hyperlink.SubAddress**. You can also set the **HyperlinkSubAddress** property in the control's property sheet.

For more information about these methods and properties, search Help in the appropriate application for the name of the method or property.

The Follow Method

The **Follow** method follows a hyperlink defined by an existing **Hyperlink** object, and has the same effect as clicking the hyperlink. The **Follow** method downloads the document or Web page specified by the hyperlink address associated with a **Hyperlink** object and opens it in the appropriate application. If the hyperlink refers to a file system path or uses the File protocol, the **Follow** method opens the document instead of downloading it.

The syntax for the **Follow** method is:

expression.**Follow**(*newwindow, addhistory, extrainfo, method, headerinfo*)

The following table describes the arguments of the **Follow** method.

Argument	Description
expression	Required. An expression that returns a **Hyperlink** object.
newwindow	Optional. A **Boolean** value where **True** (−1) opens the document in a new window and **False** (0) opens the document in the current window. The default value is **False**.
addhistory	Optional. A **Boolean** value where **True** (−1) adds the hyperlink to the History folder and **False** (0) doesn't add the hyperlink to the History folder. The default value is **True**.
extrainfo	Optional. A string or an array of **Byte** data that specifies additional information for HTTP to use to resolve the hyperlink. For example, you can use the *extrainfo* argument to specify the coordinates of an image map or the contents of a form. The string is either appended or posted, depending on the value of the *method* argument. In Word, you can use the **ExtraInfoRequired** property to determine whether extra information is required.
method	Optional. Specifies the way the *extrainfo* argument is handled. You can set the *method* argument to **msoMethodGet** or **msoMethodPost**.
headerinfo	Optional. A string that specifies header information for the HTTP request. The default value is a zero-length string (" "). You can combine several header lines into a single string by using the following syntax: *"string1"* **& vbCr &** *"string2"* The specified string is automatically converted into ANSI characters. Note that the *headerinfo* argument may overwrite default HTTP header fields.

For the *method* argument of the **Follow** method, you can specify one of the constants described in the following table.

Constant	Description
msoMethodGet	The *extrainfo* argument is a string that's appended to the URL, separated by a question mark, when you use the HTTP GET method from an HTML form. For example, you can submit a query to an HTTP server by using an address in the following format: http://www.web.com/cgi-bin/srch?*item1+item2* *item1+item2* is the extra information that's passed to the srch program on the HTTP server.

Constant	Description
msoMethodPost	The *extrainfo* argument is posted to the server as a string or a byte array when you use the HTTP POST method. For example, data from a form is typically submitted to an HTTP server with a series of name/value pairs in the following format:
	*name1=value1***&***name2=value2*
	This data can be submitted as either a string or byte array, depending on what format the program on the server has been programmed to use. Use the HTTP POST method to submit extra information if the program on the HTTP server is reading the form's data from the standard input stream (STDIN).

For examples that illustrate uses of the **Follow** method, see the code samples in previous sections of this chapter.

The FollowHyperlink Method

The **FollowHyperlink** method follows a hyperlink address specified in code or passed to the method from a variable or object. For example, you can prompt a user to type a hyperlink address in a dialog box, and then use the **FollowHyperlink** method to go to that address. The **FollowHyperlink** method downloads the document or Web page specified by the hyperlink address associated with a **Hyperlink** object and opens it in the appropriate application. If the address refers to a file system path or uses the File protocol, the **FollowHyperlink** method opens the document instead of downloading it.

The syntax for the **FollowHyperlink** method is:

expression.**FollowHyperlink**(*address, subaddress, newwindow, addhistory, extrainfo, method, headerinfo*)

The following table describes the arguments of the **FollowHyperlink** method.

Argument	Description
expression	Required. An expression that returns one of the following objects: Microsoft Word **Document** object Microsoft Excel **Workbook** object Microsoft PowerPoint **Presentation** object Microsoft Access **Application** object
address	A string expression that evaluates to a valid hyperlink address.
subaddress	A string expression that evaluates to a named location in the document specified by the *address* argument. The default is a zero-length string (" "). If no *address* is specified, *subaddress* specifies a named location in the document or database.

For information about the *newwindow, addhistory, extrainfo, method,* and *headerinfo* arguments, see the preceding section, "The Follow Method."

Microsoft Word Examples

This example follows the specified URL and displays the Microsoft home page in a new window.

```
ActiveDocument.FollowHyperlink Address:="http://www.microsoft.com", _
    NewWindow:=True, AddHistory:=True
```

This example opens the HTML document named Default.htm directly from the local hard disk.

```
ActiveDocument.FollowHyperlink Address:="file://C:\Pages\Default.htm"
```

Microsoft Excel Example

This example follows the specified URL address and displays the names of all the topics related to opera.

```
ActiveWorkbook.FollowHyperlink Address:="http://search.Yahoo.com/bin/search", _
    AddHistory:=False, Method:=msoMethodGet, ExtraInfo:="p=Opera"
```

Microsoft PowerPoint Example

This example loads the document at www.gohere.com in a new window and adds it to the History folder.

```
Application.ActivePresentation.FollowHyperlink _
    Address:="http://www.gohere.com", NewWindow:=True, AddToHistory:=True
```

Microsoft Access Examples

The following function prompts a user for a hyperlink address and then follows the hyperlink.

```
Function GetUserAddress() As Boolean
    Dim strInput As String

    On Error GoTo Error_GetUserAddress
    strInput = InputBox("Enter a valid address")
    Application.FollowHyperlink strInput, , True
    GetUserAddress = True

Exit_GetUserAddress:
    Exit Function

Error_GetUserAddress:
    MsgBox Err & ": " & Err.Description
    GetUserAddress = False
    Resume Exit_GetUserAddress
End Function
```

You can call this function with a procedure such as the following.

```
Sub CallGetUserAddress()
    If GetUserAddress = True Then
        MsgBox "Successfully followed hyperlink."
    Else
        MsgBox "Could not follow hyperlink."
    End If
End Sub
```

In Microsoft Access, you can also use the **FollowHyperlink** method to specify a hyperlink for controls that don't support the **HyperlinkAddress** or **HyperlinkSubAddress** properties (controls other than labels, image controls, and command buttons, or text boxes bound to Hyperlink fields).

This example uses the **FollowHyperlink** method to add hyperlink behavior to an unbound object frame control. Add the following code to the Click event of an unbound object frame named OLEUnbound1 to start a Web browser and open the specified hyperlink address when you click the image.

Note You can use similar code in Microsoft Excel, Word, or PowerPoint to create a command button that follows a hyperlink. To do so, add a command button by using the **Control Toolbox**, and then define a Click event procedure for the button. For more information, see "Creating a Hyperlink Associated with a Command Button" earlier in this chapter.

```
Private Sub OLEUnbound1_Click()
    Dim strAddress As String

    On Error GoTo Error_OLEUnbound1

    ' Set reference to hyperlink address.
    strAddress = "http://www.microsoft.com/"

    ' Follow hyperlink address.
    Application.FollowHyperlink strAddress, , True

Exit_OLEUnbound1:
    Exit Sub

Error_OLEUnbound1:
    MsgBox Err & ": " & Err.Description
    Resume Exit_OLEUnbound1
End Sub
```

Tip   Using the **FollowHyperlink** method to add hyperlinks to controls that don't support the **HyperlinkAddress** or **HyperlinkSubAddress** properties doesn't provide any feedback to the user to indicate that the control can follow a hyperlink. One way to inform a user that the control contains a hyperlink is to set the control's **ControlTipText** property so that a text message appears when the user rests the pointer on the control.

Handling Hyperlink Errors

If an error occurs when using the **Follow** or **FollowHyperlink** methods in Visual Basic, an Automation error is displayed that contains only an error number in both decimal and hexadecimal format. For example, if xyz.htm doesn't exist, and you run the following code in Microsoft Access:

```
Application.FollowHyperlink "http://www.microsoft.com/xyz.htm"
```

the error message shown in the following illustration occurs.

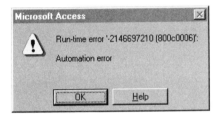

This error number indicates that the requested item could not be found.

You can prevent these error messages from being displayed to users of your application. To do so, check the **Number** property of the **Err** object against a decimal value in the table that follows. Then handle the error by either returning an appropriate message or performing a suitable action. If you want to be certain that all errors are handled, write an error handler that traps the entire set of error numbers.

```
Function GetUserAddress() As Boolean
    Dim strInput As String
    Dim lngErrNumber As Long

    On Error GoTo Error_GetUserAddress
    strInput = InputBox("Enter a valid address")
    Application.FollowHyperlink strInput, , True
    GetUserAddress = True

Exit_GetUserAddress:
    Exit Function

Error_GetUserAddress:
    ' Set variable equal to error number.
    lngErrNumber = Err.Number
    ' Check variable against all possible error numbers.
    Select Case lngErrNumber
        Case -2146697211
            MsgBox "Cannot locate the Internet server or proxy server."
        Case -2146697210
            MsgBox "The site reports that the item you requested " _
            & "could not be found. (HTTP/1.0 404)"
            .
        . ' Repeat for all possible error numbers.
        .
    End Select
    GetUserAddress = False
    Resume Exit_GetUserAddress
End Function
```

The following table lists the error numbers and descriptions for all errors that can occur when using the **Follow** and **FollowHyperlink** methods.

Decimal error number	Hexadecimal error number	Description
–2146697214, –2147221020 and –2147012891	0x800C0002, 0x800401E4 and 0x80072EE5	The address of this site is not valid. Check the address and try again.
–2146697213	0x800C0003	Cannot start an Internet session.
–2146697212 and –2147012867	0x800C0004 and 0x80072EFD	Cannot connect to the Internet server.
–2146697211	0x800C0005	Cannot locate the Internet server or proxy server.
–2146697210 and –2147012868	0x800C0006 and 0x80072EFC	The site reports that the item you requested could not be found. (HTTP/1.0 404)
–2146697209	0x800C0007	The Internet site reports that a connection was established but the data is not available.
–2146697208	0x800C0008	Cannot download the information you requested.
–2146697207	0x800C0009	The item you requested requires proper authentication. (HTTP/1.0 401)

Decimal error number	Hexadecimal error number	Description
−2146697206	0x800C000A	The Internet site cannot return the object you requested. (HTTP/1.0 403)
−2146697205 and −2147012894	0x800C000B and 0x80072EE2	The connection to this Internet site took longer than the allotted time.
−2146697204	0x800C000C	The site reports that the request is not valid.
−2146697203 and −2147012888	0x800C000D and 0x80072EE8	The required Internet protocol is not installed on your computer, or the Internet address you requested may not be valid.
−2146697202	0x800C000E	A security problem has occurred.
−2146697201 and −2147221014	0x800C000F and 0x800401EA	Cannot open the specified file.
−2146697200	0x800C0010	Cannot start the program needed to open this file.
−2147221018 and −2147221164	0x800401E6 and 0x80040154	No program is registered to open this file.
−2147467260	0x80004004	The hyperlink cannot be followed to the destination.

Note   In PowerPoint, one error number is returned for all **Follow** or **FollowHyperlink** method errors: −2147467259 (0x80004005).

The AddToFavorites Method

The **AddToFavorites** method adds a shortcut to the Favorites folder in the Windows program folder.

The syntax for the **AddToFavorites** method is:

expression.**AddToFavorites**

Expression is an expression that returns either a **Hyperlink** object or one of the objects listed in the following table.

Application	Object
Microsoft Word	**Document**
Microsoft Excel	**Workbook**
Microsoft PowerPoint	**Presentation**
Microsoft Access	**Application**

When referring to a **Hyperlink** object, the shortcut is the friendly name of the document. The friendly name is determined by the text in the <TITLE> HTML tag. If the document doesn't have a friendly name, the shortcut name is resolved by the application. If there is an existing shortcut of the same name, it is overwritten without notification.

Microsoft Word Examples

In Word, the shortcut created by the **AddToFavorites** method can refer to a **Document** object or to a **Hyperlink** object.

The following example creates a shortcut to Sales.doc and adds it to the Favorites folder. If Sales.doc isn't currently open, Word opens it from the C:\My Documents folder.

```
Sub AddDocument()
    Dim isOpen As Boolean, doc As Document

    For Each doc In Documents
        If LCase(doc.Name) = "Sales.doc" Then isOpen = True
    Next doc
    If isOpen <> True Then Documents.Open _
        FileName:="C:\My Documents\Sales.doc"
    Documents("Sales.doc").AddToFavorites
End Sub
```

To add an existing hyperlink in the document to the Favorites folder, you must refer to the document's **Hyperlinks** collection. The following example adds all of the hyperlinks in the document to the Favorites folder.

```
Sub AddHyperlinks()
    Dim H As Hyperlink
    Dim Hlinks As Hyperlinks

    Set Hlinks = ActiveDocument.Hyperlinks

    For Each H In Hlinks
        H.AddToFavorites
    Next H
End Sub
```

Microsoft Excel Examples

In Microsoft Excel, the shortcut created by the **AddToFavorites** method can refer to a **Workbook** object or to a **Hyperlink** object.

To create a shortcut to the current workbook and add it to the Favorites folder, use the following code.

```
ActiveWorkbook.AddToFavorites
```

To add an existing hyperlink in the current workbook to the Favorites folder, you must refer to the workbook's **Hyperlinks** collection. For example, to create a shortcut to the address in the first hyperlink in the active workbook and add it to the Favorites folder, use the following code.

```
ActiveWorkbook.Sheets(1).Hyperlinks(1).AddToFavorites
```

Microsoft PowerPoint Examples

In PowerPoint, the shortcut created by the **AddToFavorites** method can refer to a **Presentation** object or to a **Hyperlink** object.

To add a shortcut to the current presentation, use the following code.

```
Application.ActivePresentation.AddToFavorites
```

To add a hyperlink in the current slide to the Favorites folder, you must refer to the slide's **Hyperlinks** collection. The following example adds all of the hyperlinks on the first slide of the current presentation to the Favorites folder.

```
Sub AddHyperlinks()
    Dim H As Hyperlink
    Dim Hlinks As Hyperlinks

    Set Hlinks = ActivePresentation.Slides(1).Hyperlinks

    For Each H In Hlinks
        H.AddToFavorites
    Next H
End Sub
```

Microsoft Access Examples

In Microsoft Access, the shortcut created by the **AddToFavorites** method can refer to the **Application** object, which represents the current database, or to a hyperlink associated with a **Control** object.

To create a shortcut to the current database and add it to the Favorites folder, use the following code.

```
Application.AddToFavorites
```

To refer to a hyperlink associated with a **Control** object, you must use the **Hyperlink** property to access the **Hyperlink** object. For example, to create a shortcut to a hyperlink defined for a command button named Command0 on the current form and add it to the Favorites folder, use the following code.

```
Me!Command0.Hyperlink.AddToFavorites
```

Storing Hyperlinks in Microsoft Access Tables

In Microsoft Access 97, you can create a field with the Hyperlink data type to store hyperlink addresses in a table. You can follow a hyperlink stored in a Microsoft Access table by clicking it in the table. However, typically the field is bound to a text box, list box, or combo box control on a form. Like other bound fields, as the user moves from record to record, the value in the control changes to display the current record's hyperlink value. For example, you can use hyperlinks in this way to create an application in which users can go to Web pages, or to other content on the Internet or an intranet, from a predefined list of addresses.

In addition to storing hyperlinks to Internet addresses, you can also use hyperlinks in Microsoft Access to go to database objects and other Office documents. For example, you could create a document management application that uses a Hyperlink field to store paths to Word documents on a network. Users of such an application could add records to track new documents, or click the hyperlink in a previously added record to open the specified document.

To create a Hyperlink field, add a field in table Design view and set its **DataType** property to Hyperlink. You can also create a Hyperlink field in table Datasheet view by clicking **Hyperlink Column** on the **Insert** menu.

The Hyperlink Field Storage Format

In Microsoft Access, a Hyperlink field stores up to three pieces of information: the *displaytext*, the *address*, and the *subaddress*. Each piece is separated by a pound sign (#), in the following format:

displaytext#address#subaddress

The following table describes each piece of the Hyperlink field storage format.

Piece	Description	Required?
displaytext	The text the user sees in the Hyperlink field in a table, or in a text box bound to the Hyperlink field. You can set the display text to any text string. For example, you may want the display text to be a descriptive name for the Web site or object specified by the *address* and *subaddress*. If you do not specify display text, Microsoft Access displays the value of *address,* or *subaddress* if *address* is also not specified.	No
address	A valid URL that points to a page or file on the Internet or an intranet, or the path to a file on a local hard disk or LAN. If you enter a path on a LAN, you can omit a mapped drive letter and use the universal naming convention (UNC) format: *\\server\share\path\filename.* This prevents the path from becoming invalid if the database is later copied to another computer's hard disk or into a shared network folder.	Yes, unless *subaddress* points to an object in the current database (.mdb) file.
subaddress	The location within a file or document; for example, a database object, such as a form or report. When referring to a database object, the name of the object should be preceded by its type: Table, Query, Form, Report, Macro, or Module. Other possible values for *subaddress* include a bookmark in a Word document, a NAME anchor tag in an HTML document, a PowerPoint slide, or a cell in a Microsoft Excel worksheet.	No

Each piece of the Hyperlink field storage format can be up to 2,000 characters. The maximum length of the entire Hyperlink field value is 6,000 characters.

The following table gives examples of valid Hyperlink field values.

Hyperlink field value	Goes to
Cajun Delights#http://www.cajundelights.com/cajun.htm#	The Cajun Delights Web page. Only the words "Cajun Delights" are displayed in the field or control.
#http://www.cajundelights.com/cajun.htm#	The Cajun Delights Web page. The text "http://www.cajundelights.com" appears in the field or control because no display text is specified.
#http://www.cajundelights.com/cajun.htm#Price	The HTML anchor with the NAME attribute Price on the Cajun Delights Web page. The text "http://www.cajundelights.com/cajun.htm" is displayed.
Resume#c:\windows\personal\resume.doc#	A Microsoft Word file named Resume.doc located in the \Windows\Personal folder. Only the word "Resume" is displayed in the field or control.
#c:\windows\personal\resume.doc#	A Microsoft Word file named Resume.doc located in the \Windows\Personal folder. The text "c:\windows\personal\resume.doc" appears in the field or control because no display text is specified.
#c:\windows\personal\resume.doc#Qualifications	The section in the Resume.doc Word file marked with the bookmark name Qualifications. The text "c:\windows\personal\resume.doc" is displayed.
#\\databases\samples\northwind.mdb#Form Suppliers	The Suppliers form in the Northwind sample application located in the Samples share on the Databases server on a LAN (UNC format path). The text "\\databases\samples\northwind.mdb" is displayed.
Suppliers Form##Form Suppliers	The Suppliers form in the current database. The words "Suppliers Form" are displayed in the field or control.
#c:\windows\personal\1996 Sales.ppt#13	Slide 13 in the 1996 Sales PowerPoint presentation located in the \Windows\Personal folder. The text "c:\windows\personal\1996 Sales.ppt" is displayed.
#c:\windows\personal\budget.xls#Sheet1!A2	The A2 cell in Sheet1 of the Budget.xls file located in the \Windows\Personal folder. The text "c:\windows\personal\budget.xls" is displayed.

You can enter data in a Hyperlink field in three ways: by using the **Insert Hyperlink** dialog box (available through the **Hyperlink** command on the **Insert** menu), by typing an address directly into a Hyperlink field, or by using Data Access Objects (DAO) methods in Visual Basic code. When you use the **Insert Hyperlink** dialog box or type directly into a Hyperlink field, Microsoft Access adds the two pound signs (#) that delimit the parts of the hyperlink data. When you use DAO methods, your code must include the two pound signs to delimit the parts of the hyperlink data.

You can display the stored hyperlink format in a table by moving the insertion point into a Hyperlink field using the keyboard, and then pressing F2. You can edit the stored hyperlink in this form, but be careful to enter pound signs in the appropriate locations. You can add or edit the *displaytext* part of a Hyperlink field by right-clicking a hyperlink in a table, pointing to **Hyperlink** on the shortcut menu, and then typing the display text in the **Display Text** box. You can add or edit the *address* or *subaddress* part of a Hyperlink field by right-clicking a hyperlink in a table, pointing to **Hyperlink** on the shortcut menu, and then selecting **Edit Hyperlink**.

The HyperlinkPart Function

The **HyperlinkPart** function returns information about data stored in a Hyperlink field. The syntax for the **HyperlinkPart** function is:

object.**HyperlinkPart**(*hyperlink* **As Variant,** *part* **As Integer)**

The following table describes the arguments of the **HyperlinkPart** function.

Argument	Description
object	Optional. The **Application** object.
hyperlink	Required. A **Variant** that represents the data stored in a Hyperlink field.
part	Optional. The value for the *part* argument is an intrinsic constant that represents the information you want returned by the **HyperlinkPart** function.

You can set the *part* argument to the following constants.

Constant	Value	Description
acDisplayedValue	0	(Default) The underlined text displayed in a hyperlink.
acDisplayText	1	The *displaytext* part of a Hyperlink field.
acAddress	2	The *address* part of a Hyperlink field.
acSubAddress	3	The *subaddress* part of a Hyperlink field.

Note If you use the **HyperlinkPart** function in an SQL statement or a query, the *part* argument is required and you can't set it to the constants listed in the preceding table—you must use the value instead.

You use the **HyperlinkPart** function to return one of three values stored in a Hyperlink field (*displaytext*, *address*, or *subaddress*) or the displayed value. The value returned depends on the setting of the *part* argument. If you don't use the *part* argument, the **HyperlinkPart** function returns the value Microsoft Access displays for the hyperlink (which corresponds to the **acDisplayedValue** setting for the *part* argument).

When a value is provided in the *displaytext* part of a Hyperlink field, the value displayed by Microsoft Access will be the same as the *displaytext* setting. When there's no value in the *displaytext* part of a Hyperlink field, Microsoft Access displays the value of the *address* or *subaddress* part of the Hyperlink field, depending on which value is first present in the field.

The following table shows the values returned by the **HyperlinkPart** function for data stored in a Hyperlink field.

Hyperlink field data	HyperlinkPart function returned values
#http://www.microsoft.com/#	**acDisplayedValue**: http://www.microsoft.com/ **acDisplayText**: No value returned. **acAddress**: http://www.microsoft.com/ **acSubAddress**: No value returned.
Microsoft#http://www.microsoft.com/#	**acDisplayedValue**: Microsoft **acDisplayText**: Microsoft **acAddress**: http://www.microsoft.com/ **acSubAddress**: No value returned.
Customers##Form Customers	**acDisplayedValue**: Customers **acDisplayText**: Customers **acAddress**: No value returned. **acSubAddress**: Form Customers
##Form Customers	**acDisplayedValue**: Form Customers **acDisplayText**: No value returned. **acAddress**: No value returned. **acSubAddress**: Form Customers

The following example uses all four of the *part* argument constants to display information returned by the **HyperlinkPart** function for each record in a table containing a Hyperlink field. To try this example, paste the DisplayHyperlinkParts procedure into the Declarations section of a module. You can call the DisplayHyperlinkParts procedure from the Debug window, passing to it the name of a table that contains hyperlinks and the name of the field that contains Hyperlink data, as shown in the following example.

```
DisplayHyperlinkParts "MyHyperlinkTableName", "MyHyperlinkFieldName"

Sub DisplayHyperlinkParts(strTable As String, strField As String)
    Dim dbs As Database, rst As Recordset
    Dim strMsg As String

    Set dbs = CurrentDb
    Set rst = dbs.OpenRecordset(strTable)

    While Not rst.EOF     ' For each record in table.
        strMsg = "DisplayValue = " & HyperlinkPart(rst(strField), acDisplayedValue) _
            & vbCrLf & "DisplayText = " & HyperlinkPart(rst(strField), acDisplayText) _
            & vbCrLf & "Address = " & HyperlinkPart(rst(strField), acAddress) _
            & vbCrLf & "SubAddress = " & HyperlinkPart(rst(strField), acSubAddress)
        ' Show parts returned by HyperlinkPart function.
        MsgBox strMsg
        rst.MoveNext
    Wend
End Sub
```

When you use the **HyperlinkPart** function in a query, the *part* argument is required. For example, the following SQL statement uses the **HyperlinkPart** function to return information about data stored as a Hyperlink data type in the URL field of the Links table:

```
SELECT Links.URL, HyperlinkPart([URL],0)
AS Display, HyperlinkPart([URL],1)
AS Name, HyperlinkPart([URL],2)
AS Addr, HyperlinkPart([URL],3) AS SubAddr
FROM Links;
```

For another example of using the **HyperlinkPart** function, see "Displaying a Document in the WebBrowser Control by Using a Hyperlink Stored in a Table" later in this chapter.

Following a Hyperlink in a Text Box Bound to a Hyperlink Field

When you use the **Follow** method in Microsoft Access, you don't need to know the address specified by a control's **HyperlinkAddress** or **HyperlinkSubAddress** property, or by the Hyperlink field that is bound to a text box, list box, or combo box control. You only need to know the name of the control that contains the hyperlink.

This example uses the **Follow** method to automatically open the Web page specified in a text box bound to a Hyperlink field on a form whenever the user moves to a new record. Add the following code to the OnCurrent event of a form.

```
Private Sub Form_Current()
   Dim txt As TextBox

   On Error GoTo Error_Form1

   ' Set reference to the txtAddress text box bound to a Hyperlink field.
   Set txt = txtAddress

   ' Follow the hyperlink.
   txt.Hyperlink.Follow

Exit_Form1:
   Exit Sub

Error_Form1:
   MsgBox Err & ": " & Err.Description
   Resume Exit_Form1
End Sub
```

For another example of following a hyperlink stored in a table, see "Displaying a Document in the WebBrowser Control by Using a Hyperlink Stored in a Table" later in this chapter.

Creating a Hyperlink Field with Visual Basic

You can use Data Access Objects (DAO) code to create a field with the Hyperlink field type. To do so, you must first create a field with the Memo data type and then set the **Attributes** property of the field to **dbHyperlinkField**. The following example creates a table named Hyperlinks that contains a Text field and a Hyperlink field.

```
Sub CreateHyperlinkField()
   Dim db As Database
   Dim tbl As TableDef

   Set db = CurrentDb()

   Set tbl = db.CreateTableDef("Hyperlinks")

   With tbl
      .Fields.Append .CreateField("Text", dbText)
      .Fields.Append .CreateField("Hyperlink", dbMemo)
      .Fields("Hyperlink").Attributes = dbHyperlinkField
   End With

   db.TableDefs.Append tbl
   RefreshDatabaseWindow
End Sub
```

Saving Documents and Objects as HTML

All of the Office 97 applications provide ways to save their data as HTML documents. Microsoft Access and Word provide ways of doing so by using Visual Basic.

Saving Microsoft Access Data as HTML Documents

Microsoft Access has five ways to save data from your database as HTML documents:

Save data as static HTML documents   You can create *static* HTML documents from table, query, and form datasheets, and from reports. When you save data as static HTML documents, the resulting pages reflect the state of the data at the time it was saved, like a snapshot. If your data changes, you must save the pages again to share the new data.

Save table, query, and form datasheets as IDC/HTX files   You can save your table, query, and form datasheets as Internet Database Connector/HTML extension (IDC/HTX) files that generate HTML documents by querying a copy of your database located on a Web server for current data.

Save forms and datasheets as Active Server Pages   You can save your forms as Active Server Pages (ASP) that emulate most of the functionality of your forms and display data from a database located on a Web server. You can also save table, query, and form datasheets as Active Server Pages that display current data from a copy of your database located on a Web server.

Automate the publishing of dynamic and static HTML documents by using the Publish to the Web Wizard   You can use the Publish to the Web Wizard to automate the process of saving multiple objects to any combination of all three file types. In the Publish to the Web Wizard, IDC/HTX files and Active Server Pages (ASP) files are collectively referred to as *dynamic* Web pages because these file types create HTML documents by querying the database to include current data.

Automate the publishing of dynamic and static HTML documents by using the OutputTo method or action   You can use the **OutputTo** method in Visual Basic and the OutputTo action in macros to automate the process of saving objects to any of the three file types.

The following sections discuss each of these options in more detail.

Saving Data as Static HTML Documents

With Microsoft Access, you can save table, query, and form datasheets, and reports as static HTML documents.

▶ **To save a table, query, or form datasheet, or a report as a static HTML document**

1   In the Database window, click the table, query, form, or report you want to save.

2   On the **File** menu, click **Save As/Export**.

3 In the **Save As** dialog box, click **To an External File or Database**, and then click **OK**.

4 In the **Save as type** box, click **HTML Documents (*.html; *.htm)**.

5 If you want to preserve formatting, select the **Save Formatted** check box. To automatically open the resulting HTML document in your Web browser, select the **Autostart** check box.

6 Specify the file name and location to save the file, and then click **Export**.

7 In the **HTML Output Options** dialog box, if you want Microsoft Access to merge an HTML template with the resulting HTML document, specify that as well, and then click **OK**.

For information about HTML templates, see "Using an HTML Template When You Save Data as HTML Documents" later in this chapter.

You can also save data as static HTML documents by using the Publish to the Web Wizard (available through the **Save As HTML** command on the **File** menu), the **OutputTo** method in code, or the OutputTo action in macros. For information about using the **OutputTo** method, see "Saving HTML Documents by Using the OutputTo Method" later in this chapter.

When saving table, query, and form datasheets, Microsoft Access saves each datasheet to a single HTML file. Microsoft Access saves reports as multiple HTML documents, with one HTML file per printed page. To name each page, Microsoft Access uses the name of the object and appends _Page*nn* to the end of each page's file name after the first page; for example, ProductList.htm, ProductList_Page2.htm, ProductList_Page3.htm, and so on.

Saving Table, Query, and Form Datasheets as Static HTML Documents

When you save a table, query, or form datasheet as an HTML document, the HTML document generated is based on the table or query associated with the datasheet, including the current setting of the **OrderBy** or **Filter** property of the table or query. If the datasheet contains a parameter query, Microsoft Access first prompts you for the parameter values, then exports the results.

If you select the **Save Formatted** check box, the HTML document contains an HTML table that reflects as closely as possible the appearance of the datasheet by using the appropriate HTML tags to specify color, font, and alignment. The HTML document follows as closely as possible the page orientation and margins of the datasheet. Whenever you want to use settings that are different from the default orientation and margins for a datasheet, you must first open the datasheet, and then use the **Page Setup** command (**File** menu) to change settings before you save the datasheet as an HTML document.

If you select the **Save Formatted** check box, and a field has a **Format** or **InputMask** property setting, those settings are reflected in the data in the HTML document. For example, if a field's **Format** property is set to Currency, the data in the HTML document is formatted with a dollar sign, a comma as the thousand separator, and two decimal places; for example, $1,123.45.

Saving Reports as Static HTML Documents

When you save a report as HTML documents, the series of HTML documents generated is based on the report's underlying table or query, including the current **OrderBy** or **Filter** property settings of the table or query. If the report contains a parameter query, Microsoft Access first prompts you for the parameter values, then exports the results.

The HTML documents simulate as closely as possible the appearance of the report by creating the appropriate HTML tags to retain attributes such as color, font, and alignment. The proportions and layout of the actual report follow as closely as possible the page orientation and margins set for the report. To change the page orientation and margins, open the report in Print Preview, and then use the **Page Setup** command to change settings before you save the report as HTML documents. These settings are saved from session to session for reports, so if you change them once, they will be used the next time you save the form or report as HTML documents.

Most controls and features of a report, including subreports, are supported except the following: lines, rectangles, OLE objects, and subforms. However, you can use an HTML template file to include report header and footer images in your output files. For an example, see the Nwindtem.htm template file in the C:\Program Files\Microsoft Office\Office\Samples folder.

Navigation Controls When Saving Multiple HTML Documents Per Object

If you specify an HTML template that contains placeholders for navigation controls when you save a report as multiple HTML documents, Microsoft Access creates hyperlinks that the user can use to go to the first, previous, next, and last pages in the publication. Where Microsoft Access places the hyperlinks depends on where you locate the placeholders in the HTML template. For information about HTML templates and placeholders, see "Using an HTML Template When You Save Data as HTML Documents" later in this chapter.

How Microsoft Access Saves Data Types in HTML Format

When you save data as static HTML documents, Microsoft Access saves values from most data types as strings and formats them as closely as possible to their appearance in the datasheet or report. All unformatted data types, except Text and Memo, are saved with right alignment as the default. Text and Memo fields are saved with left alignment by default.

There are two exceptions:

- OLE Object fields are not saved.

- Hyperlink field values are saved as hyperlinks in the HTML document. The hyperlinks use HTML anchor tags with an HREF attribute, as described in the following table.

If	Anchor tag format
The hyperlink doesn't include a subaddress	<A HREF="*address*">*displaytext*</A>
The hyperlink includes a subaddress	<A HREF="*address#subaddress*">*displaytext*</A>
Display text isn't specified	<A HREF="*address*">*address*</A>

Microsoft Access determines the *displaytext*, *address*, and *subaddress* values by parsing the value stored in the Hyperlink field. For information about the *displaytext*, *address*, and *subaddress* values, see "The Hyperlink Field Storage Format" earlier in this chapter.

Using an HTML Template When You Save Data as HTML Documents

When you save data as HTML documents, you can use an HTML template to give a consistent look to the HTML documents you create. For example, you can include your company's logo, name, and address in the page's header, use the background that is used throughout your company, or include standard text in the header or footer of the HTML document.

Note   You can use an HTML template when you save data as static HTML documents, when you save datasheets as IDC/HTX files, when you save a form or datasheet as an Active Server Page, and when you use the Publish to the Web Wizard.

The HTML template can be any HTML document; that is, a text file that includes HTML tags and user-specified text and references. In addition, the HTML template can include placeholders that tell Microsoft Access where to insert certain pieces of data in the HTML documents. When data is saved as HTML documents, the placeholders are replaced with data. The following table describes each of the placeholders that you can use in an HTML template.

Placeholder	Description	Location
<!--AccessTemplate_Title-->	The name of the object being saved	Between <TITLE> and </TITLE>
<!--AccessTemplate_Body-->	The data or object being saved	Between <BODY> and </BODY>
<!--AccessTemplate_FirstPage-->	An anchor tag to the first page	Between <BODY> and </BODY> or after </BODY>

Placeholder	Description	Location
<!--AccessTemplate_PreviousPage-->	An anchor tag to the previous page	Between <BODY> and </BODY> or after </BODY>
<!--AccessTemplate_NextPage-->	An anchor tag to the next page	Between <BODY> and </BODY> or after </BODY>
<!--AccessTemplate_LastPage-->	An anchor tag to the last page	Between <BODY> and </BODY> or after </BODY>
<!--AccessTemplate_PageNumber-->	The current page number	Between <BODY> and </BODY> or after </BODY>

When you install Microsoft Access, sample HTML template files and graphics files are installed in the Access subfolder of the Templates folder. The default location of this folder is C:\Program Files\Microsoft Office\Templates\Access.

Saving Table, Query, and Form Datasheets as IDC/HTX Files

With Microsoft Access, you can save a table, query, or form datasheet as Internet Database Connector/HTML extension (IDC/HTX) files that generate HTML documents by querying a copy of your database located on a Web server. In contrast to static HTML documents, which contain the data that was current at the time the HTML document was created, IDC/HTX files generate an HTML page with current data from your database; therefore, the HTML documents that they generate are called dynamic.

▶ **To save a table, query, or form datasheet as IDC/HTX files**

1 In the Database window, click the table, query, or form you want to save.

2 On the **File** menu, click **Save As/Export**.

3 In the **Save As** dialog box, click **To an External File or Database**, and then click **OK**.

4 In the **Save as type** box, click **Microsoft IIS 1-2 (*.htx;*.idc)**.

5 Specify the file name and location to save the files, and then click **Export**.

6 In the **HTX/IDC Output Options** dialog box, specify:

- The data source name that will be used for the database.

- A user name and password, if required to open the database.

- An HTML template, if you want Microsoft Access to merge one with the HTML extension (HTX) file.

Note   You can specify any of these items later, except the HTML template, by editing the resulting IDC file in a text editor such as Notepad.

7   Click **OK**.

If the datasheet contains a parameter query, Microsoft Access simulates the **Enter Parameter Value** dialog box by creating an additional HTML parameter page that contains an HTML form text box control to enter the parameter value and a button to run the query. You must display this HTML parameter page before you display the datasheet HTML page in your Web application. If you use the Publish to the Web Wizard and you specify a switchboard page, the HTML parameter page is added to the switchboard page. When you export, Microsoft Access runs the query and displays the **Enter Parameter Value** dialog box. You don't need to enter values in this dialog box—just click **OK** to continue.

You can also save a table, query, or form datasheet as IDC/HTX files by using the Publish to the Web Wizard (available through the **Save As HTML** command on the **File** menu), the **OutputTo** method in code, or the OutputTo action in macros. For information about using the **OutputTo** method, see "Saving HTML Documents by Using the OutputTo Method" later in this chapter.

How the Internet Database Connector Works

When you save a table, form, or query datasheet as Internet Connector files, Microsoft Access creates two files: an *Internet Database Connector (IDC) file* and *HTML extension (HTX) file*. These files are used to generate a Web page that displays current data from your database.

An IDC file contains the necessary information to connect to a specified Open Database Connectivity (ODBC) data source and to run an SQL statement that queries the database. The information needed to connect to the database includes the data source name, and if user-level security is established for the database, the user name and password required to open the database. For example, if you save the Current Product List query datasheet from the Northwind sample application as IDC/HTX files, Microsoft Access creates the following IDC file:

```
Datasource:Northwind
Template:Current Product List.htx
SQLStatement:SELECT [Product List].ProductID, [Product List].ProductName
+FROM Products AS [Product List]
+WHERE (((([Product List].Discontinued)=No))
+ORDER BY [Product List].ProductName;

Password:
Username:
```

An IDC file also contains the name and location of an HTML extension (HTX) file. The HTX file is a template for the HTML document; it contains field merge codes that indicate where the values returned by the SQL statement should be inserted. For example, if you save the Current Product List query datasheet from the Northwind sample application as IDC/HTX files, Microsoft Access creates the following HTX file:

```
<HTML>
<TITLE>Current Product List</TITLE>
<BODY>
<TABLE BORDER=1 BGCOLOR=#ffffff><FONT FACE="Arial" COLOR=#000000>
<CAPTION><B>Current Product List</B></CAPTION>
<THEAD>
<TR>
<TD><FONT SIZE=2 FACE="Arial" COLOR=#000000>Product ID</FONT></TD>
<TD><FONT SIZE=2 FACE="Arial" COLOR=#000000>Product Name</FONT></TD>
</TR>
</THEAD>
<TBODY>
<%BeginDetail%>
<TR VALIGN=TOP>
<TD ALIGN=RIGHT><FONT SIZE=2 FACE="Arial" COLOR=#000000><%ProductID%><BR></FONT></TD>
<TD><FONT SIZE=2 FACE="Arial" COLOR=#000000><%ProductName%><BR></FONT></TD>
</TR>
<%EndDetail%>
</TBODY>
<TFOOT></TFOOT>
</BODY>
</HTML>
```

Microsoft Access saves the HTX file to be used with an IDC file with the same name as the IDC file, except with an .htx file name extension rather than an .idc file name extension. After the database information has been merged into the HTML document, it is returned to the Web browser.

If you open Current Product List.idc from a Microsoft Internet Information Server that has an appropriately defined Northwind data source name (DSN), the Web page shown in the following illustration is generated.

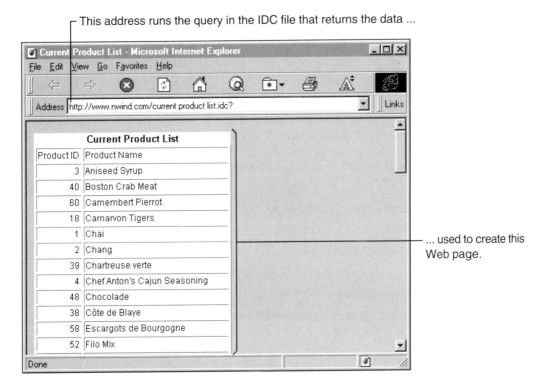

Note   You can also reference an HTML template when you create IDC and HTX files. An HTML template contains additional HTML code to enhance the appearance of the resulting pages. If you specify an HTML template, it is merged with the HTX file. For information about the format of an HTML template, see "Using an HTML Template When You Save Data as HTML Documents" earlier in this chapter.

Requirements for Using IDC/HTX Files

To use IDC/HTX files, your database and the IDC/HTX files must reside on a computer running one of the following operating systems and Internet server platforms:

- Microsoft Windows NT Server version 3.51 or 4.0 running Microsoft Internet Information Server version 1.0, 2.0, or 3.0

- Microsoft Windows NT Workstation version 4.0 and Microsoft Peer Web Services

- Microsoft Windows 95 and Microsoft Personal Web Server

Microsoft Internet Information Server, Microsoft Peer Web Services, and Microsoft Personal Web Server use a component called the Internet Database Connector (Httpodbc.dll) to generate dynamic Web pages from IDC/HTX files.

The Internet Database Connector component requires ODBC drivers to access a database. To access a Microsoft Access database, the Microsoft Access Desktop driver (Odbcjt32.dll) must be installed on your Web server. This driver is installed when you install Microsoft Internet Information Server if you select the **ODBC Drivers And Administration** check box during Setup.

However, the Microsoft Access Desktop driver isn't installed with Microsoft Personal Web Server. If Microsoft Access is installed on the computer you are using to run Microsoft Personal Web Server, and if you selected the driver when you installed Microsoft Access, the driver is already available. If you don't have Microsoft Access installed on the computer you are using to run Microsoft Personal Web Server, you must install the Microsoft Access Desktop driver.

▶ To install the Microsoft Access Desktop driver

1 Run the Microsoft Office or Microsoft Access Setup program.

2 If you are running Setup for the first time, click **Custom**.

 If you are not running Setup for the first time, click **Add/Remove**.

3 Select the **Data Access Controls** check box, and then click **Change Option**.

 Important The **Microsoft Access** check box must also be selected or the driver will not be installed.

4 Select the **Database Drivers** check box, and then click **Change Option**.

5 Select the **Microsoft Access Driver** check box, and then click **OK**.

6 Click **Continue**, and follow the instructions in the remaining Setup dialog boxes.

After the Microsoft Access Desktop driver is installed, you must create either a system DSN or a file DSN that specifies the name and connection information for each database you want to use on the server. You then specify that DSN when you generate the IDC/HTX files.

For information about how to define a system DSN or a file DSN, search the Microsoft Access Help index for "ODBC, setting up data sources." For more information about Microsoft Internet Information Server, see the Microsoft Internet Information Server Web site, located at http://www.microsoft.com/infoserv/iisinfo.htm. For more information about using IDC/HTX files, search the Microsoft Internet Information Server Help index for "database connector."

Tip   You can learn more about applications that use IDC/HTX files by reading about the Job Forum application. For information about the Job Forum application, see the Job Forum white paper, located at http://www.microsoft.com/accessdev/accwhite/jobforpa.htm. For applications that require many users to access the database simultaneously, you should consider upsizing the Microsoft Access database back-end server to Microsoft SQL Server. For information about upsizing a Microsoft Access Web application to Microsoft SQL Server, see http://www.microsoft.com/accessdev/accwhite/upsizeweb.htm.

Saving Forms and Datasheets as Active Server Pages

With Microsoft Access, you can save a form as an Active Server Page (ASP) that emulates much of the functionality of your form. When saving a form as an Active Server Page, Microsoft Access saves most, but not all, controls on the form as ActiveX controls that perform the same or similar functions. Microsoft Access doesn't save or run Visual Basic code behind the form or controls. To copy the layout of your form as closely as possible, Microsoft Access uses the Microsoft HTML Layout control to position the controls on Active Server Pages. The resulting page uses ActiveX Scripting and ActiveX Data Objects to connect the control on the page to a copy of your database on an Internet server. For information about the Microsoft HTML Layout control, see http://www.microsoft.com/workshop/author/layout/layout.htm.

Users who open a form saved as an Active Server Page can browse records, update or delete existing records, and add new records by using a Web browser.

You can also save table, query, and form datasheets as Active Server Pages. When you open a datasheet saved as an ASP, Microsoft Access displays current data from a copy of your database located on an Internet server, much like IDC/HTX files do. However, unlike IDC/HTX files, Active Server Pages require only one file per datasheet. The ASP file uses scripting to establish a connection to the database on the server, and contains information that it uses to format the datasheet. Unlike a form saved as an Active Server Page, users can't update existing records in or add new records to a datasheet saved as an Active Server Page.

▶ **To save a form or datasheet as an Active Server Page**

1   In the Database window, click the form or datasheet you want to save.

2   On the **File** menu, click **Save As/Export**.

3   In the **Save As** dialog box, click **To an External File or Database**, and then click **OK**.

4   In the **Save as type** box, click **Microsoft Active Server Page (*.asp)**.

5   Specify the file name and location to save the file, and then click **Export**.

6 In the **Active Server Page Output Options** dialog box, specify:

- The data source name that will be used for a copy of the current database (required).

- A user name and password, if required to open the database.

- An HTML template, if you want Microsoft Access to merge one with the Active Server Page.

  For information about HTML templates, see "Using an HTML Template When You Save Data as HTML Documents" earlier in this chapter.

- The URL for the server where the Active Server Page will reside.

- The **Session timeout** setting, which determines how long a connection to the server is maintained after the user stops working with the Active Server Page (optional).

7 Click **OK**.

You can also save forms and datasheets as Active Server Pages by using the Publish to the Web Wizard (available through the **Save As HTML** command on the **File** menu), the **OutputTo** method in code, or the OutputTo action in macros. For information about using the **OutputTo** method, see "Saving HTML Documents by Using the OutputTo Method" later in this chapter.

Form Views Supported for Active Server Pages

If the form you save as an Active Server Page has its **DefaultView** property set to Single Form or Continuous Forms, the Active Server Page displays as a single form, unless it is open in Datasheet view when you use the **Save As/Export** command (**File** menu). If the form has its **DefaultView** property set to Datasheet, the Active Server Page displays as a datasheet. Subforms always display as datasheets, regardless of their **DefaultView** property setting. All field data types are saved unformatted, that is, **Format** and **InputMask** property settings aren't saved.

Control Types Supported for Active Server Pages

When Microsoft Access saves a form as an Active Server Page, it replaces Microsoft Access controls with ActiveX controls, as described in the following table.

Microsoft Access control	ActiveX control
Text box	Text box.
Text box control bound to a Hyperlink field	Text box that displays the hyperlink text, but the hyperlink can't be followed.
List box	List box.
Combo box	Combo box.
Label	Label. If the label has **HyperlinkAddress** and/or **HyperlinkSubAddress** properties set, an HTML hyperlink is created for the label.

Microsoft Access control	ActiveX control
Command button	Command button, but any code behind the button isn't saved. If the command button has **HyperlinkAddress** and/or **HyperlinkSubAddress** properties set, an HTML hyperlink is created for the button.
Option group	Option group, but without a group frame.
Option button	Option button.
Check box	Check box.
Toggle button	Toggle button.
ActiveX control	ActiveX control, but any code behind the control isn't saved.
Subform	Subform as datasheet only.

Microsoft Access doesn't support the following controls when saving a form as an Active Server Page:

- Tab control, and anything on a tab control

- Rectangle

- Line

- Page break

- Unbound object frame

- Bound object frame

- Image control

- The background of a form set with the **Picture** property

Note   You can simulate a rectangle or a line by using a Label control without a caption.

Requirements for Using Active Server Pages

To display and use an Active Server Page, a copy of your database and Active Server Pages must reside on a computer running one of the following operating systems and Internet server platforms:

- Microsoft Windows NT Server version 3.51 or 4.0 running Microsoft Internet Information Server version 3.0

- Microsoft Windows NT Workstation version 4.0 and Microsoft Peer Web Services with the Active Server Pages components installed

- Microsoft Windows 95 and Microsoft Personal Web Server with the Active Server Pages components installed

The Microsoft HTML Layout control must be installed on the computer opening the Active Server Page. For more information about installing the Active Server Pages components for Peer Web Services and Personal Web Server, see http://www.microsoft.com/ntserver/. Active Server Pages also require the Microsoft

Access Desktop driver and a valid DSN to access a database. For information about installing the Microsoft Access Desktop driver and defining DSNs, see "Requirements for Using IDC/HTX Files" earlier in this chapter.

Using the Publish to the Web Wizard

With the Publish to the Web Wizard, you can publish a set of Microsoft Access database objects to any combination of static HTML documents, IDC/HTX files, or Active Server Pages (ASP). By using the wizard, you can:

- Pick any combination of tables, queries, forms, or reports to save.

- Specify an HTML template to use for the selected objects.

- Select any combination of static HTML documents, IDC/HTX files, or Active Server Pages.

- Create a home page to tie together the Web pages you create.

- Specify the folder where you save your files.

- Use the Web Publishing Wizard to move the files created by the Publish to the Web Wizard to a Web server.

- Save the answers you provide the wizard as a Web publication profile, and then select that profile the next time you use the wizard. This saves you from having to answer the wizard's questions again.

To run the Publish to the Web Wizard, click **Save As HTML** on the **File** menu. For more information about using the Publish to the Web Wizard, search the Microsoft Access Help index for "Saving database objects, saving in Internet/Web formats."

Saving HTML Documents by Using the OutputTo Method

You can use the **OutputTo** method to save Microsoft Access database objects in the HTML formats described in the previous sections: static HTML documents, IDC/HTX files, or Active Server Pages (ASP).

The syntax of the **OutputTo** method is:

DoCmd.OutputTo *objecttype*, *objectname*, *outputformat*, *outputfile*, *autostart*, *templatefile*

The following table describes the arguments of the **OutputTo** method.

Argument	Description
objecttype	Required. Specifies the type of database object you are going to output. You can use one of the following constants for the *objecttype* argument: **acOutputForm** **acOutputQuery** **acOutputReport** **acOutputTable**

Argument	Description
objectname	Optional. A string expression that's the valid name of an object of the type specified in the *objecttype* argument. If you want to output the active object, specify the object's type for the *objecttype* argument and leave this argument blank.
	If you run Visual Basic code that contains the **OutputTo** method in a library database, Microsoft Access looks for the object with this name first in the library database, then in the current database.
outputformat	Optional. Specifies whether to save the database object as an HTML document, IDC/HTX file, or Active Server Page. You can use one of the following constants for the *outputformat* argument:
	acFormatHTML **acFormatIIS** **acFormatASP**
	If you leave this argument blank, Microsoft Access prompts you for the output format.
outputfile	Optional. A string expression that's the full name, including the path, of the file you want to output the object to.
	You can include the standard file name extension (.asp, .htm, .html, or .htx,) for the output format you select with the *outputformat* argument, but it's not required. If you output to IDC/HTX or ASP files, Microsoft Access always creates files with the standard .htx and .idc or .asp file name extensions.
	If you leave this argument blank, Microsoft Access prompts you for an output file name.
autostart	Optional. Use **True** (−1) to start a Web browser immediately to open the static HTML document specified by the *outputfile* argument. Use **False** (0) if you don't want to start the application. This argument is ignored for IDC/HTX and ASP files.
	If you leave this argument blank, Microsoft Access uses the default value (**False**).
templatefile	Optional. A string expression that's the full name, including the path, of the file you want to use as a template for an HTML, IDC/HTX, or ASP file.

Microsoft Internet Information Server and Microsoft Active Server Pages formats are available only for tables, queries, and forms, so if you specify **acFormatIIS** or **acFormatASP** for the *outputformat* argument, you must specify **acOutputTable**, **acOutputQuery**, or **acOutputForm** for the *objecttype* argument.

You can leave an optional argument blank in the middle of the syntax, but you must include the argument's comma. If you leave a trailing argument blank, don't use a comma following the last argument you specify.

You can't specify the HTML template, data source name, user name and password, server URL, or **Session timeout** setting when you use the **OutputTo** method. Microsoft Access uses the values specified on the **Hyperlinks/HTML** tab of the **Options** dialog box (**Tools** menu) by default. However, you can use the **SetOption** method in your code to temporarily change these settings. For information about using the **SetOption** method, search the Microsoft Access Help index for "SetOption method."

Examples

The following example outputs the Employees table in static HTML document format to the Employee.htm file and immediately opens the file in the default Web browser.

```
DoCmd.OutputTo acOutputTable, "Employees", acFormatHTML, "Employee.htm", True
```

The following example outputs the Employees table in IDC/HTX format to two files named Employee.htx and Employee.idc. It merges the Mc.htm template file into the Employee.htx file.

```
DoCmd.OutputTo acOutputTable, "Employees", acFormatIIS, "Employee",, _
    "C:\Program Files\Microsoft Office\Templates\Access\Mc.htm"
```

The following example outputs the Products form in Active Server Page format to the Products.asp file. It merges the Stones.htm template file into the Products.asp file.

```
DoCmd.OutputTo acOutputFor
321m, "Products", acFormatASP, "Products",, _
    "C:\Program Files\Microsoft Office\Templates\Access\Stones.htm"
```

Saving Microsoft Word Documents as HTML Documents

You can save an existing Word document to HTML format by using the **Save As** command (**File** menu) or by using Visual Basic code. The following example saves the active document as an HTML document.

```
Sub SaveAsHTML
    Dim intFormat As Integer

    intFormat = FileConverters("HTML").SaveFormat
    myDocName = ActiveDocument.Name
    pos = InStr(myDocName, ".")
    If pos > 0 Then
        myDocName = Left(myDocName, pos -1)
        myDocName = myDocName & ".html"
        ActiveDocument.SaveAs FileName:=myDocName, FileFormat:=intFormat
    End If
End Sub
```

When you save an existing Word document to HTML format, formatting and other items that aren't supported by HTML or the Word Web page authoring environment are removed from the file. For more information about what happens when you save a

Word document as a Web page, search Word Help. Instead of saving existing documents as HTML, you may want to create new HTML documents with Microsoft Word Web authoring tools.

Word 97 has many powerful features for creating HTML documents, such as the following:

Word Editing and Formatting Features   Take advantage of advanced Word editing and formatting features—rich-text formatting, spelling and grammar checking, and automatic text correction—when you work with Word Web authoring tools. When you use a Word Web template, you can easily create and format popular Web page items—such as tables, bulleted or numbered lists, and graphic objects—just as you can with a regular Word document.

Word Web Templates   Use the Web Page Wizard or the Blank Web Page template to create new Web pages. The Web Page Wizard gives you different layouts and color themes to choose from, such as a personal home page, a table of contents, a survey, or a registration form. To use the wizard or the template, click **New** on the **File** menu, click the **Web Pages** tab, and then double-click **Web Page Wizard** or **Blank Web Page**. There are several additional Web templates that you can download from the Microsoft Word Web site at http://www.microsoft.com/word/. When you download these templates, they are installed in the same folder as the existing Web templates.

Hyperlinks, Bullets, and Horizontal Lines   By using the **Insert Hyperlink** button on the **Standard** toolbar, you can quickly create hyperlinks on your Web page to link related information in different locations. The hyperlink text is usually blue and underlined. You can also quickly create special graphical bulleted lists and horizontal lines for your Web page. To add a new bullet for selected text, click **Bullets and Numbering** on the **Format** menu, and then select the bullet you want. To add the default bullet to selected text, click **Bullets** on the **Formatting** toolbar. To add a new horizontal line, click **Horizontal Line** on the **Insert** menu, and then select the line style you want.

Forms   You can use forms to collect and present data on your Web page. For example, you can publish a form that collects user feedback or registration information. You can store the input data in a database or a text file for future use. You can quickly create a form by selecting a sample form and then modifying it for your needs by using the **Forms** toolbar. To select a sample form, click **New** on the **File** menu, click the **Web Pages** tab, and then select the sample form you want. To display the **Control Toolbox**, click **Form Design Mode** on the **Standard** toolbar. Use the Web form tools just as you use the regular Word form tools to insert form elements.

Saving Microsoft Excel Worksheets as HTML Documents

To make your Microsoft Excel data available to users on your intranet or the World Wide Web, use the Internet Assistant add-in program to convert worksheet data or charts to HTML Web pages (**Save As HTML** command, **File** menu). Microsoft Excel doesn't support using Visual Basic to save data as HTML documents.

Saving Microsoft PowerPoint Presentations as HTML Documents

To make your Microsoft PowerPoint data available to users on your intranet or the World Wide Web, use the Internet Assistant add-in program to convert presentations to HTML Web pages (**Save As HTML** command, **File** menu). Microsoft PowerPoint doesn't support using Visual Basic to save data as HTML documents.

Opening and Importing HTML Data

Each Office application provides features that you can use to open and import HTML data. You can also use Office applications to open documents and files in a variety formats on your company's intranet. If you have a connection to the Internet, you can open or import data in most of these same formats on Internet sites such as FTP and HTTP servers.

Note In all Office applications except Outlook, you can use Data Access Objects (DAO) code in Visual Basic to access and manipulate data in a variety of formats, including HTML. For more information about using DAO, see Chapter 11, "Data Access Objects."

Opening HTML Data in Microsoft Word

To open HTML documents in Microsoft Word with Visual Basic, use the **Open** method. By default, the **Open** method tries each available file converter until it succeeds. For this reason, as long as the HTML Document converter is installed, the following example opens an HTML document on a local drive.

```
Documents.Open "C:\My Documents\My Document.htm"
```

Similarly, you can specify a URL to open a file located on an HTTP server, as follows.

```
Documents.Open "http://myserver.com/default.htm"
```

To improve performance, you can specify the file converter to use by referring to it in the **FileConverters** collection, as follows.

```
Sub OpenHTML()
    Dim intFormat As Integer

    intFormat = FileConverters("HTML").OpenFormat
    Documents.Open "http://myserver.com/default.htm", Format:=intFormat
End Sub
```

Opening HTML Data in Microsoft Excel

To open HTML documents in Microsoft Excel with Visual Basic, use the **Open** method. You don't need to specify the file converter to use, because the **Open** method tries each available file converter until it succeeds. The following example opens an HTML document on a local drive.

```
Workbooks.Open "C:\My Documents\Product List.htm"
```

Similarly, you can specify a URL to open a file located on an HTTP server, as follows.

```
Workbooks.Open "http://myserver.com/default.htm"
```

You can also get data from an intranet site or from HTTP, FTP, or Gopher sites on the World Wide Web by running a Web query. To run a Web query, point to **Get External Data** on the **Data** menu, and then click **Run Web Query**. For more information about running Web queries, see http://www.microsoft.com/excel/webquery/.

Opening HTML Data in Microsoft PowerPoint

To open HTML documents in PowerPoint with Visual Basic, use the **Open** method. By default, the **Open** method tries each available file converter until it succeeds. For this reason, as long as the HTML Document converter is installed, the following line of code will open an HTML document on a local drive:

```
Presentations.Open "C:\My Documents\My Document.htm"
```

Similarly, you can specify a URL to open a file located on an HTTP server:

```
Presentations.Open "http://myserver.com/default.htm"
```

Importing HTML Data in Microsoft Access

With Microsoft Access, you can import or link data from HTML tables or other data sources on an Internet server. For more information about importing, exporting, and linking HTML data and other data formats on Internet servers, see "Working with HTML Files" in Chapter 18 and "Importing, Linking, and Exporting Data on the Internet" in Chapter 21 in *Building Applications with Microsoft Access 97*.

Using the WebBrowser Control

The Microsoft WebBrowser control is an ActiveX control that you can use to browse Web sites, view Web pages and other documents, and download data located on the Internet from your applications. The WebBrowser control is useful in situations where you don't want to disrupt the work flow in your application by switching to a Web browser or other document-viewing application.

The WebBrowser control can display any Web page that Microsoft Internet Explorer version 3.0 can display. For example, the WebBrowser control can display pages that include any of the following features:

- Standard HTML and most HTML enhancements, such as floating frames and cascading style sheets

- Other ActiveX controls

- Most Netscape plug-ins

- Scripting, such as Microsoft Visual Basic Scripting Edition (VBScript) or JavaScript

- Java applets

- Multimedia content, such as video and audio playback

- Three-dimensional virtual worlds created with Virtual Reality Modeling Language (VRML)

With the WebBrowser control, users of your application can browse sites on the World Wide Web, as well as folders on a local hard disk and on a local area network. Users can follow hyperlinks by clicking them or by typing a URL into a text box. Also, the WebBrowser control maintains a history list that users can browse through to view previously browsed sites, folders, and documents.

In addition to opening Web pages, both Microsoft Internet Explorer version 3.0 and the WebBrowser control can open any ActiveX document, which includes most Office documents. For example, if Office is installed on a user's computer, an application that uses the WebBrowser control can open and edit Microsoft Excel workbooks, Word documents, and PowerPoint presentations from within the control. Similarly, if Microsoft Excel Viewer, Word Viewer, or PowerPoint Viewer is installed, users can open those documents within the WebBrowser control, but they cannot edit them.

You can't open and edit a Microsoft Access database as an ActiveX document within Microsoft Internet Explorer version 3.0 or the WebBrowser control, but a Web page can contain a hyperlink to a Microsoft Access database. Clicking the hyperlink downloads a copy of the database and starts a session of Microsoft Access to open it. Additionally, if you have the server software that supports Internet Database Connector/HTML extension (IDC/HTX) files or Active Server Pages (ASP), you can create Web pages that act as a front-end to an ODBC data source such as a Microsoft

Access or Microsoft SQL Server database. For more information about creating IDC/HTX or ASP files, see "Saving Microsoft Access Data as HTML Documents" earlier in this chapter.

Adding the WebBrowser Control to a Form

Before you can use the WebBrowser control, you must have Microsoft Internet Explorer version 3.0 installed.

If you purchased Microsoft Office 97 on CD-ROM, you can install Microsoft Internet Explorer version 3.0 by running Msie30.exe from the Iexplore subfolder in the ValuPack folder.

If you prefer to install from the Web, you can download and install Microsoft Internet Explorer version 3.0 from http://www.microsoft.com/ie/download/.

Once you have Microsoft Internet Explorer version 3.0 installed, the WebBrowser control is automatically registered and is available in form Design view (Microsoft Access) and in Design mode (Microsoft Excel, Word, and PowerPoint).

▶ To add the WebBrowser control to a document or form

1 In Microsoft Excel, Word, or PowerPoint, open the document or form. In Microsoft Access, open the form in Design view.

2 In Microsoft Excel, Word, or PowerPoint, right-click the menu bar and then click **Control Toolbox**. In Microsoft Access, right-click the menu bar and then click **Toolbox**.

3 In the toolbox, click the **More Controls** tool.

A menu appears that lists all the registered ActiveX controls in your system.

4 On the menu of ActiveX controls, click **Microsoft WebBrowser Control**.

5 On the document or form, click where you want to place the control.

6 Move and size the control to the area you want to display.

In Microsoft Excel, Word, and PowerPoint, you can also add the WebBrowser control to UserForms created with the Visual Basic editor.

▶ To add the WebBrowser control to a UserForm created with the Visual Basic Editor

1 Open a Microsoft Excel, Word, or PowerPoint document.

2 On the **Tools** menu, point to **Macro**, and then click **Visual Basic Editor**.

This starts the Visual Basic Editor or switches to its window if it's already open.

3 On the **Insert** menu, click **UserForm**.

A blank form is created and the toolbox is displayed.

4 Right-click the toolbox, and then click **Additional Controls**.

The **Additional Controls** dialog box is displayed.

5 In the **Available Controls** box, select **Microsoft WebBrowser Control**, and then click **OK**.

A tool icon is added to the toolbox for the WebBrowser Control. You don't need to repeat steps 4 and 5 the next time you use the toolbox.

6 Click the new tool, and then click the form where you want to place the control.

For more information about UserForms, see Chapter 12, "ActiveX Controls and Dialog Boxes."

Tip If the WebBrowser control can't display the full width or height of a Web page or document, it automatically displays scroll bars. However, in most cases, make the control wide enough to display the full width of a typical Web page so that users of your application don't have to scroll horizontally.

Displaying Web Pages or Documents in the WebBrowser Control

To display a Web page or document in the WebBrowser control, use the **Navigate** method in Visual Basic. The syntax for the **Navigate** method is:

object.**Navigate** *URL*

Object is either the name of the WebBrowser control on your form or an object variable that refers to it, and *URL* is a string expression that evaluates to a valid URL or path. *URL* can refer to a Web page or other content on the Internet or an intranet, as well as to an Office document, such as a Word document.

If *URL* refers to an Internet protocol and a location on the Internet, the WebBrowser control must establish a connection before is can display the document. If the computer running your application is connected to a *proxy server* (a secure connection to the Internet through a LAN), or if it has a direct connection to the Internet, the WebBrowser control downloads and displays the Web page or other Internet content immediately. If the computer running your application uses a modem and dial-up connection to the Internet, and that connection hasn't been established beforehand, the WebBrowser control initiates the connection. For example, if the user's computer uses a modem and The Microsoft Network to connect to the Internet, the **Sign In** dialog box is displayed to establish the connection to the Internet before the WebBrowser control can display Internet content.

If *URL* refers to an Internet protocol and a location on an intranet server, the computer running your application must be connected to the intranet and have permission to access that server.

If *URL* refers to a standard file system path on a local hard disk or LAN, the WebBrowser control opens the document and displays it immediately. The WebBrowser control can open Office documents (except Microsoft Access databases), text files, and HTML documents that don't require features supported only by an

Internet/intranet server. For example, the WebBrowser control can't open and run IDC/HTX files or ASP files from the standard file system, but it can open HTML documents that contain only the HTML tags supported by Microsoft Internet Explorer version 3.0.

Note If *URL* refers to a path in the standard file system that doesn't refer to a file name (for example, C:\Windows\System\), the WebBrowser control displays the file system itself, much like My Computer.

The examples and code in the following sections are specific to developing an application that uses the WebBrowser control in Microsoft Access; however, in most cases, you can apply the same basic principles and techniques to using the WebBrowser control in applications developed with other Office applications.

Displaying a Document in the WebBrowser Control by Using an Address in a Text Box

By using the WebBrowser control, you can create a Microsoft Access form that performs most of the functions of Microsoft Internet Explorer version 3.0. For example, the following illustration shows the Custom Browse form (WebBrowseWeb) in the Developer Solutions sample application.

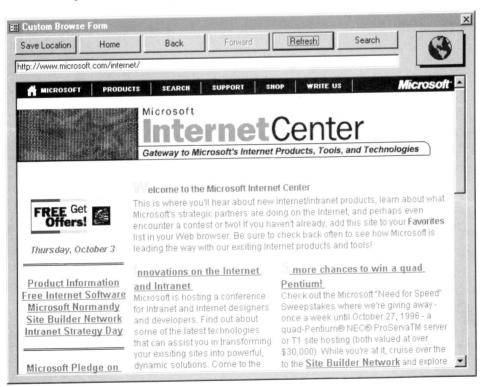

When a user types a valid URL in the text box at the top of the form (txtLinks) and presses ENTER, the WebBrowser control (ActiveXCtl1) displays the Web page or document. Pressing ENTER triggers the AfterUpdate event of the txtLinks text box; the AfterUpdate event contains the following code, which goes to the address specified in the URL that the user entered.

```
Private Sub txtLinks_AfterUpdate()
On Error Resume Next
    ' If the user has entered an address (URL) in this control,
    ' attempt to go to the address.
    If Len(Me!txtLinks) > 0 Then
        Me!ActiveXCtl1.Navigate Me!txtLinks
    End If
End Sub
```

Error handling is passed to the control itself because it displays the same error messages displayed by Microsoft Internet Explorer version 3.0.

If you prefer to start navigation by clicking a command button instead pressing ENTER, you can use similar code in the button's Click event.

The Home, Back, Forward, Refresh, and Search buttons on the Custom Browse form use the corresponding **GoHome**, **GoBack**, **GoForward**, **Refresh**, and **GoSearch** methods of the WebBrowser control. For information about how to view brief descriptions about the properties, methods, and events of the WebBrowser control, see "Viewing Descriptions of the Properties, Methods, and Events of the WebBrowser Control" later in this chapter.

With the Save Location button on the Custom Browse form, you can save the address and a description of the current document to the Links table in the Developer Solutions sample application. When you click the Save Location button, Microsoft Access checks to see if the URL has been saved previously, and if not, uses the following statement to open the **Save Location To Table** dialog box.

```
DoCmd.OpenForm "frmSaveURLDialog", acWindowNormal, , , acFormEdit, acDialog, _
    ctlHyper.LocationName & ";" & ctlHyper.LocationURL
```

The last argument of this statement (ctlHyper.LocationName & ";" & ctlHyper.LocationURL) sets the **OpenArgs** property to a concatenated string that contains the two values returned by the **LocationName** and **LocationURL** properties of the document currently displayed in the Custom Browse form. When the **Save Location To Table** dialog box opens, code in its **Load** event parses the **OpenArgs** property value back into two parts and displays them as the default description and address. When the user clicks **OK**, the description and address in the **Save Location To Table** dialog box form are saved in the Hyperlink and Description fields in the Links table.

For more information about the Custom Browse form, open the Developer Solutions sample application located in the Samples subfolder of your Office folder. To view the Developer Solutions sample application, you must click **Custom** when you install Microsoft Access and then choose to install all sample databases.

Displaying a Document in the WebBrowser Control by Using a Hyperlink Stored in a Table

By using the WebBrowser control, you can create a Microsoft Access form that displays documents specified in hyperlinks stored in a table. For example, the following illustration shows the Browse Saved Hyperlinks form (WebBrowseTable) in the Developer Solutions sample application. You can use the Browse Saved Hyperlinks form to browse addresses saved in the Links table.

When a user clicks a record navigation button at the bottom of the form to move to a new record, the following code in the form's Current event displays the Web page or document whose address is stored in the current record.

```
Private Sub Form_Current()
    Dim varFull As Variant, varDescription As Variant
    Dim HyperlinkAddress As String, HyperlinkSubAddress As String
    Dim msg1 As String, msg2 As String, rst As Recordset, strDisplay As String

    On Error Resume Next

    Set rst = Me.RecordsetClone
    rst.Bookmark = Me.Bookmark
    varFull = rst!HyperLink

    If IsNull(varFull) Then GoTo Current_Err
    varDescription = rst!Description
    Me!ActiveXCtl1.Navigate HyperlinkPart(varFull, acAddress)

    If Err = 438 Then Exit Sub

    gvarBookMark = Me.Bookmark

Current_Bye:
    Exit Sub
Current_Err:

msg1 = "Invalid hyperlink address. Remove the record described as '"
msg2 = "' from the Links table or edit the hyperlink to supply a valid address."

MsgBox msg1 & rst!Description & msg2

    Me.Bookmark = gvarBookMark
    Exit Sub
End Sub
```

This procedure uses the **Navigate** method of the WebBrowser control to display the next hyperlink address. However, don't pass the contents of a Hyperlink field directly to the **Navigate** method. If a user enters or edits data stored in a Hyperlink field from a datasheet or form, it may contain up to three parts of information separated by the pound sign (#). Even if the user doesn't enter all three parts in the datasheet or form, Microsoft Access automatically stores pound signs in the field. If there are pound signs in the Hyperlink field, passing the data from the field directly to the **Navigate** method generates an error. To handle this, the stored value is passed to the **HyperlinkPart** function to extract just the *address* portion of the saved hyperlink, which is then passed to the **Navigate** method. If navigation is successful, the form's **Bookmark** property value is stored in a public variable. This public variable is used to return to the last record if subsequent navigation fails.

Using code to save data in a Hyperlink field doesn't automatically save pound signs in the field. To preserve the proper functioning of a Hyperlink field in other contexts, you may want to write your code to save pound signs before and after a hyperlink address. To see an example of how to do this, view the event procedure set for the Click event of the Save Location button (cmdSaveLocation) on the Custom Browse form.

Note   You don't have to store addresses in a Hyperlink field if you don't need users to be able to navigate to addresses by clicking them in datasheets or forms, or if you don't need to save addresses as HTML anchor tags when saving as HTML. As long as an address doesn't exceed 255 characters, you can store it in a Text field. If an address exceeds 255 characters, you can store it in a Memo field. In either case, you can pass the value stored in the field directly to the **Navigate** method.

For more information about the Browse Saved Hyperlinks form, open the Developer Solutions sample application located in the Samples subfolder of your Office folder. For more information about the format of data stored in a Hyperlink field, see "The Hyperlink Field Storage Format" earlier in this chapter.

Viewing Descriptions of the Properties, Methods, and Events of the WebBrowser Control

Like built-in Office objects, the WebBrowser control has properties that your application can set or read to determine the control's characteristics, methods that your application can use to perform operations on the control, and events your application can respond to. You can view brief descriptions of the properties, methods, and events of the WebBrowser control by using the Object Browser.

Important   In order for these properties, methods, and events to appear in the Object Browser, a reference must be set to the **Microsoft Internet Controls** object library. To set this reference, open a module (Microsoft Access) or open the Visual Basic Editor (Microsoft Excel, Word, or PowerPoint), click **References** on the **Tools** menu, and select the **Microsoft Internet Controls** check box in the **Available References** box.

▶ **To view descriptions of the WebBrowser control's methods, properties, and events**

1   In Microsoft Excel, Word, or PowerPoint, open the Visual Basic Editor. In Microsoft Access, open a module.

2   On the **View** menu, click **Object Browser**.

3   In the **Project/Library** box, click **SHDocVw**.

4   In the **Classes** box, click **WebBrowser**.

The **Members Of** box lists the methods, properties, and events associated with the WebBrowser control.

For more information about the methods, properties, and events of the WebBrowser control, see http://www.microsoft.com/intdev/sdk/docs/iexplore/. If you purchased Microsoft Office 97 on CD-ROM, you can open a Help file named Iexplore.hlp that contains this information in the \ValuPack\Access\WebHelp folder on the CD-ROM.

Distributing the WebBrowser Control with Your Application

Unlike most other ActiveX controls, you can't install the WebBrowser control by itself. For an application that uses the WebBrowser control to work, Microsoft Internet Explorer version 3.0 must also be installed on the computer. Microsoft Internet Explorer version 3.0 can be distributed freely, and doesn't require the payment of royalties or other licensing fees. For information about installing Microsoft Internet Explorer version 3.0, see "Adding the WebBrowser Control to a Form" earlier in this chapter.

Using the Internet Transfer Control

Microsoft Office 97, Developer Edition provides the Internet Transfer control (Msinet.ocx), which you can use to connect to and retrieve files from any Web site that uses either Hypertext Transfer Protocol (HTTP) or File Transfer Protocol (FTP). For example, you could use the Internet Transfer control to:

- Add an FTP browser to any application.

- Create an application that automatically downloads files from a public FTP site.

- Search a World Wide Web site for references to graphics and download only the graphics.

- Retrieve specific pieces of information from a Web page.

Because HTTP and FTP work differently, the operations you can perform with the Internet Transfer control depend on which protocol you are using. For example, the **GetHeader** method only works with HTTP (HTML documents). However, there are a few operations that you can perform with either protocol:

- Set the **AccessType** property of the Internet Transfer control to a valid proxy server.

- Use the **OpenURL** method with a valid URL.

- Use the **Execute** method with a valid URL and command appropriate to the protocol and then use the **GetChunk** method to retrieve data from the buffer.

Tip The Internet Transfer control automatically sets itself to the correct protocol, as determined by the *protocol* portion of the URL. Therefore, when you use the **OpenURL** or **Execute** method, you don't need set the **Protocol** property.

Adding the Internet Transfer Control to a Form

In Microsoft Excel, Word, and PowerPoint, you can add the Internet Transfer control to a UserForm you create with the Visual Basic Editor. Although the Internet Transfer control is available in the toolbox in Microsoft Excel, Word, and PowerPoint, you can't add the control directly to their documents. In Microsoft Access, you can add the Internet Transfer control to a form in Design view. The Internet Transfer control doesn't display when your application is running.

▶ **To add the Internet Transfer control to a Microsoft Excel, Word, or PowerPoint UserForm created with the Visual Basic Editor**

1   Open a Microsoft Excel, Word, or PowerPoint document.

2   On the **Tools** menu, point to **Macro**, and then click **Visual Basic Editor**.

   This starts the Visual Basic Editor or switches to its window if it's already open.

3   On the **Insert** menu, click **UserForm**.

   A blank form is created and the toolbox is displayed.

4   Right-click the toolbox, and then click **Additional Controls**.

   The **Additional Controls** dialog box is displayed.

5   In the **Available Controls** box, select **MSInet Control, version 5.0**, and then click **OK**.

   A tool icon is added to the toolbox for the Internet Transfer control. You don't need to repeat steps 4 and 5 the next time you use the toolbox.

6   Click the new tool, and then click the form where you want to place the control.

   By default, the new control is named Inet*n*, where *n* is some number.

▶ **To add the Internet Transfer control to a Microsoft Access form**

1   Open the form in Design view.

2   In the toolbox, click the **More Controls** tool.

   A menu appears that lists all the registered ActiveX controls in your system.

3   On the menu of ActiveX controls, click **MSInet Control**.

4   On the form, click where you want to place the control.

   By default, the new control is named ActiveXctl*n*, where *n* is some number.

Setting the AccessType Property

In order to make any kind of connection to the Internet, you must determine how your computer is connected to the Internet. If you are on an intranet you will probably be connected to the Internet through a *proxy server*.

When using a proxy server, all computers on an intranet that need to connect to the Internet must do so through the proxy server. By using a proxy server, sometimes called a *firewall*, you can protect your local area network from being accessed by others on the Internet. The proxy server acts as a one-way barrier between your internal network and the Internet, preventing others on the Internet from accessing confidential information on your internal network.

▶ **To determine the proxy server settings on your computer**

Note   The following steps apply only to computers running Windows 95 and Windows NT Workstation version 4.0.

1   On the **Taskbar** of your computer, click **Start**, point to **Settings**, and then click **Control Panel**.

2   Double-click the **Internet** icon.

3   In the **Internet Properties** dialog box, click the **Connection** tab.

4   If the **Connect through a proxy server** check box is selected, click **Settings**.

5   The **Proxy Settings** dialog box shows the name of your intranet's proxy server. If no proxy server is defined, contact your workgroup administrator for available proxy servers.

If you want to use a proxy server other than that named in the **Proxy Settings** dialog box, set the **AccessType** property of the Internet Transfer control to **icNamedProxy** (2). Then set the **Proxy** property to the name of the proxy server you want to use.

If you prefer to use the default proxy server, set the **AccessType** property to **icUseDefault** (0). You don't need to set the **Proxy** property when you use the default proxy server.

The following table describes the settings for the **AccessType** property.

Constant	Value	Description
icUseDefault	0	(Default) The control uses default proxy server settings found in the Windows registry.
IcDirect	1	The control has a direct connection to the Internet.
IcNamedProxy	2	The control uses the proxy server specified in the **Proxy** property.

Using the OpenURL Method

After you have set the **AccessType** property, the most basic operation is to use the **OpenURL** method with a valid URL to retrieve data on the Internet. When you use the **OpenURL** method, the result depends on the target URL. The following example

returns the HTML document found on the Microsoft home page at
http://www.microsoft.com to a text box named Text1.

```
' A TextBox control named Text1 contains the
' return result of the method. The Internet Transfer
' control is named Inet1.
Text1.Text = Inet1.OpenURL("http://www.microsoft.com/")
```

In Microsoft Access, a value assigned to the **Text** property can't be longer than 1,024
characters. Substitute the following line of code that sets the **Value** property of the
text box instead.

```
Text1.Value = ActiveXCtl0.OpenURL("http://www.microsoft.com/")
```

As a result, the text box displays the HTML source code from the Web site, which
may resemble the following illustration.

```
<HTML>
<HEAD>
<TITLE>Microsoft Corporation</TITLE>
<STYLE>
<!-- /*###### start of style sheets #####*/

|BODY {font: 9pt "Arial" "Helvetica"; color: "#000000";}
|A:link {font: 9pt "Arial" "Helvetica"; color: "#000000"; font-weight:bold}
|A:visited {font: 9pt "Arial", "Helvetica"; color: "#000000"; font-weight:bold}
|STRONG {font: 14pt "Arial"; color: "#339933";}
|BIG {font: 10pt "Arial"; color: "#0000A0"; font-weight:bold}|
-->
</STYLE>
```

In this case, the default action was to return the HTML document located at the URL.
However, if the URL specifies a particular text file, the **OpenURL** method retrieves
the actual file. For example, the following code:

```
' In Microsoft Access, substitute Text1.Value
' for Text1.Text in the following line.
Text1.Text = Inet1. OpenURL("ftp://ftp.microsoft.com/disclaimer.txt")
```

retrieves the actual text of the file, as shown in the following illustration.

```
THE INFORMATION IS PROVIDED "AS IS" WITHOUT WARRANTY OF ANY
KIND. MICROSOFT DISCLAIMS ALL WARRANTIES, EITHER EXPRESSED
OR IMPLIED, INCLUDING THE WARRANTIES OF MERCHANTABILITY AND
FITNESS FOR A PARTICULAR PURPOSE. IN NO EVENT SHALL
MICROSOFT CORPORATION OR ITS SUPPLIERS BE LIABLE FOR ANY
DAMAGES WHATSOEVER INCLUDING DIRECT, INDIRECT, INCIDENTAL,
CONSEQUENTIAL, LOSS OF BUSINESS PROFITS OR SPECIAL DAMAGES,
EVEN IF MICROSOFT CORPORATION OR ITS SUPPLIERS HAVE BEEN
ADVISED OF THE POSSIBILITY OF SUCH DAMAGES. SOME STATES DO
NOT ALLOW THE EXCLUSION OR LIMITATION OF LIABILITY FOR
CONSEQUENTIAL OR INCIDENTAL DAMAGES SO THE FOREGOING
LIMITATION MAY NOT APPLY.

Copyright Microsoft Corporation 1993.
```

Finally, you can use the **OpenURL** method with a URL that includes extra data appended to it. For example, many Web sites offer the ability to search a database. To search a database from a Web site, you can send a URL that includes the search criteria. The following example uses the search engine at the www.yahoo.com site with the search criteria p=maui.

```
Dim strURL As String

strURL = "http://www.yahoo.com/bin/search.exe?p=maui"
' In Microsoft Access, substitute Text1.Value
' for Text1.Text in the following line.
Text1.Text = Inet1.OpenURL(strURL)
```

If the search engine finds a match for the criteria, the server returns an HTML document that contains the appropriate information.

Saving Text to a File by Using the OpenURL Method

If you want to save retrieved text to a file, use the **OpenURL** method with the **Open**, **Write**, and **Close** statements, as shown in the following example.

```
Dim strURL As String
Dim intFile As Integer

IntFile = FreeFile()
strURL = "http://www.microsoft.com/"
Open "MSsource.txt" For Output As #IntFile
Write #IntFile, Inet1.OpenURL(strURL)
Close #IntFile
```

You can't save binary files to disk by using the **OpenURL** method. You must use the **Execute** method in conjunction with the **GetChunk** method as described later in this chapter.

Synchronous vs. Asynchronous Transmission

The **OpenURL** method results in a *synchronous* transmission of data. In this context, synchronous means that the transfer operation occurs before any other procedures are run. Thus the data transfer must be completed before you can run any other code.

The **Execute** method, on the other hand, results in an *asynchronous* transmission. When you use the **Execute** method, the transfer operation occurs independently of other procedures. Thus, after the **Execute** method is initiated, other code can run while data is received in the background.

Using the **OpenURL** method results in a direct stream of data that you can save to disk, or view directly in a **TextBox** control (if the data was text). On the other hand, if you are using the **Execute** method to retrieve data, you must monitor the control's connection state by using the StateChanged event. When the appropriate state is reached, use the **GetChunk** method to retrieve data from the control's buffer. This operation is discussed in greater detail in the sections that follow.

Using the Execute Method

You can use the **Execute** method with the FTP and the HTTP protocols to retrieve data or perform operations on Internet servers. The syntax for the **Execute** method is:

*controlname.***Execute** *url, operation, data, requestheaders*

The following table describes the arguments of the **Execute** method.

Argument	Description
controlname	Required. The name of the Internet Transfer control you are working with.
url	Optional. Specifies the URL that you want to connect to.
operation	Optional. Specifies the type of operation to perform.
data	Optional. Specifies additional information needed for HTTP GET, HEAD, POST, and PUT methods.
requestheaders	Optional. Specifies additional headers to be sent from the remote server.

Using the Execute Method with the FTP Protocol

When using the **Execute** method with the FTP protocol, you only use the *operation* argument, and optionally, the *url* argument. The *url* argument is optional because after the first time you invoke the **Execute** method with the *url* argument, the FTP connection remains open. You can perform additional **Execute** method operations on the same URL until a new URL is specified, or until you perform the CLOSE operation. The following example retrieves a file from a remote computer.

```
Inet1.Execute "FTP://ftp.microsoft.com", _
    "GET disclaimer.txt c:\temp\disclaimer.txt"
```

For FTP operations, you do not use the *data* and *requestheaders* arguments. You pass all of the operations and their parameters as a single string in the *operation* argument, with parameters separated by a space, as follows:

operationname parameter1 parameter2

For example, to retrieve a file, the following code includes the operation name (GET), and the two file names required by the operation.

```
' Get the file named Disclaimer.txt and copy it to the
' location C:\Temp\Disclaimer.txt.
Inet1.Execute, "GET Disclaimer.txt C:\Temp\Disclaimer.txt"
```

The *operationname* part of the *operation* argument is an *FTP command*. If you have used FTP to retrieve files from anonymous FTP servers, you are familiar with commands used to navigate through server trees, and to retrieve files to a local hard disk. For example, to change to a different directory with the FTP protocol, you use the **"CD"** command with the path to the directory you want to change to.

For the most common operations, such as putting a file on a server and retrieving a file from a server, the Internet Transfer control uses the same or a similar command with the **Execute** method. The following example uses the "CD" command as an argument of the **Execute** method to change to a different directory.

```
' The txtURL text box contains the path to open. The txtRemotePath
' text box contains the path to change to.
Inet1.Execute txtURL.Text, "CD " & txtRemotePath.Text
```

The following table lists the FTP commands that you can use in the *operation* argument of the **Execute** method.

FTP command	Description	Example
CD *path*	Change Directory. Changes to the directory specified in *path*.	`Inet1.Execute , "CD docs\mydocs"`
CDUP	Changes to parent directory. Same as "CD .."	`Inet1.Execute , "CDUP"`
CLOSE	Closes the current FTP connection.	`Inet.Execute , "CLOSE"`
DELETE *file*	Deletes the file specified in *file*.	`Inet1.Execute , _` `"DELETE discard.txt"`
DIR *path*	Searches the directory specified in *path*. If *path* isn't supplied, the current working directory is searched. Use the **GetChunk** method to return the directory listing.	`Inet1.Execute , "DIR /mydocs"`
GET *file1 file2*	Retrieves the remote file specified in *file1*, and creates a new local file specified in *file2*.	`Inet1.Execute , _` `"GET getme.txt C:\gotme.txt"`
MKDIR *path*	Creates a directory as specified in *path*. Success is dependent on user privileges on the remote host.	`Inet1.Execute , "MKDIR /myDir"`
PUT *file1 file2*	Copies a local file specified in *file1* to the remote host specified in *file2*.	`Inet1.Execute , _` `"PUT C:\putme.txt /putme.txt"`
PWD	Print Working Directory. Returns the current directory name. Use the **GetChunk** method to return the directory name.	`Inet1.Execute , "PWD"`
QUIT	Terminate current connection	`Inet1.Execute , "QUIT"`
RECV *file1 file2*	Same as GET.	`Inet1.Execute , _` `"RECV getme.txt C:\gotme.txt"`
RENAME *file1 file2*	Renames a file. Success is dependent on user privileges on the remote host.	`Inet1.Execute , _` `"RENAME old.txt new.txt"`
RMDIR *path*	Removes a directory. Success is dependent on user privileges on the remote host.	`Inet1.Execute , "RMDIR oldDir"`

FTP command	Description	Example
SEND *file*	Copies a file to the remote host. (same as PUT.)	`Inet1.Execute , _` `"SEND C:\putme.txt /putme.txt"`
SIZE *file*	Returns the size of the file specified in *file*.	`Inet1.Execute _` `"SIZE /largefile.txt"`

Important   If your proxy server is a CERN proxy server, you cannot make direct FTP connections by using the **Execute** method. In that case, to get a file, use the **OpenURL** method with the **Open**, **Put**, and **Close** statements, as described in "Saving Text to a File by Using the OpenURL Method" earlier in this chapter. You can also use the **OpenURL** method to get a directory listing by invoking the method and specifying the target directory as the URL.

Logging On to FTP Servers

FTP servers can be either public or private. Anyone can log on to a public server. To log on to a private server, on the other hand, you must be a registered user of the server. In either case, the FTP protocol requires that you supply a user name and a password.

When logging on to public servers, it is common practice to log on as "anonymous," (UserName = "anonymous") and use your e-mail name as the password. With the Internet Transfer control, the process of logging on is simplified even further. By default, if you do not specify values for the **UserName** and **Password** properties, the Internet Transfer control uses "anonymous" as your user name, and your e-mail name as the password.

If you are logging on to a private server, set the **UserName**, **Password**, and **URL** properties to appropriate values, and use the **Execute** method, as shown in the following example.

```
With Inet1
   .URL = "ftp://ftp.someFTPSite.com"
   .UserName = "John Smith"
   .Password = "mAuI&9$6"
   .Execute ,"DIR"          ' Returns the directory.
   .Execute ,"CLOSE"        ' Close the connection.
End With
```

After you invoke the **Execute** method, the FTP connection remains open. You can then continue to use the **Execute** method to perform other FTP operations such as CD and GET. When you have completed the session, close the connection by using the **Execute** method with the CLOSE operation. You can also close the connection automatically by changing the **URL** property, and invoking either the **OpenURL** or **Execute** method; this closes the current FTP connection and opens the new URL.

Using the Execute Method with the HTTP Protocol

When you use the **Execute** method with the HTTP protocol to request data from the server, you use the GET, HEAD, POST, and PUT methods in the *operation* argument. You can use these methods with the **Execute** method, as shown in the following table.

HTTP method	Description	Example
GET	Retrieves the file specified in the *url* argument.	```Inet1.Execute _ "http://www.microsoft.com" & _ "/default.htm", "GET"```
HEAD	Retrieves only the headers of the file specified in the *url* argument.	```Inet1.Execute , "HEAD"```
POST	Provides additional data to support a request to the remote host.	```Inet1.Execute , "POST", strFormData```
PUT	Replaces data at the specified URL.	```Inet1.Execute , "PUT", "replace.htm"```

Using the Execute Method with the Common Gateway Interface

On many World Wide Web sites, you can search a database for criteria that you specify. Most Web sites accomplish this by using the HTTP protocol, which can send queries that use the Common Gateway Interface (CGI).

It is not in the scope of this section to explain the CGI; however, if you are familiar with the CGI, you can use the **Execute** method to construct an application that simulates the search behavior of these Web sites. The following example shows a typical CGI query string.

```
http://www.yippee.com/cgi-bin/find.exe?find=Hangzhou
```

You could send this same query by using the **Execute** method, as follows.

```
Dim strURL As String, strFormData As String

strURL = "//www.yippee.com/cgi-bin/find.exe"
strFormData = "find=Hangzhou"
Inet1.Execute strURL, "POST", strFormData
```

To retrieve resulting data from a server, you must use the **GetChunk** method, as described in the following section.

Using the GetChunk Method

When you download data from a remote computer by using the **Execute** method, an asynchronous connection is made. For example, if you use the **Execute** method with the HTTP GET method, the server retrieves the requested file. When the entire file has been retrieved, the StateChanged event returns **icResponseCompleted** (12). At that point, you can use the **GetChunk** method to retrieve the data from the buffer. This is shown in the following example.

```
Private Sub Inet1_StateChanged(ByVal State As Integer)
    Dim vtData As Variant      ' Data variable.
    Dim intFile As Integer     ' File number variable.

    intFile = FreeFile()       ' Get free file number.
    Select Case State
    .
    . ' Other cases not shown.
    .
    Case icResponseCompleted
        ' Open a file to write to.
        Open "test.txt" For Binary Access _
            Write As #intFile

        ' Get the first chunk. NOTE: specify a byte
        ' array (icByteArray) to retrieve a binary file.
        vtData = Inet1.GetChunk(1024, icString)

        Do While LenB(vtData) > 0
            Put #intFile, , vtData
            ' Get next chunk.
            vtData = Inet1.GetChunk(1024, icString)
        Loop
        Put #intFile, , vtData
        Close #intFile

    End Select
End Sub
```

Using the WinSock Control

Microsoft Office 97, Developer Edition also provides the WinSock control, which you can use to connect to a remote computer and exchange data. You use the WinSock control with either the Transmission Control Protocol (TCP) or the User Datagram Protocol (UDP). You can use both protocols to create client and server applications. The WinSock control doesn't have a visible interface at run time.

You can use the WinSock control to:

- Create a client application that collects user information before sending it to a central server.

- Create a server application that functions as a central collection point for data from several users.

- Create an application in which uses can exchange messages in real time, or "chat" with each other.

Determining Which Protocol to Use

To use the WinSock control, you must first decide which protocol to use. The major difference between TCP and UDP is their connection state:

- The TCP protocol requires a persistent connection. It is analogous to a telephone—the user must establish a connection before proceeding.

- The UDP protocol is a connectionless protocol. The transaction between two computers is like passing a note—a message is sent from one computer to another, but there is no persistent connection between the two.

Here are a few questions that may help you determine which protocol to use:

- Will the application require acknowledgment from the server or client when data is sent or received? If so, use the TCP protocol because it requires an explicit connection before sending or receiving data.

- Is the integrity of your data critical? If so, use the TCP protocol. Once a connection has been made, the TCP protocol maintains the connection and ensures the integrity of the data. If the integrity of your data is not critical, you can improve performance by using the UDP protocol. Using the UDP protocol can be faster and uses less network bandwidth, but you may experience a certain amount of data loss. However, when transmitting an image or a sound file, the data loss may not even be noticeable.

- Will the data be sent intermittently or in one session? If the data will be sent intermittently, you may want to use the UDP protocol because it requires fewer network resources. For example, use the UDP protocol if you are creating an application that notifies specific computers when certain tasks have completed. If you want the data to be sent in one session, use the TCP protocol because it maintains a persistent connection to the network.

Adding the Control to a Form

In Microsoft Excel, Word, and PowerPoint, you can add the WinSock control to a UserForm you create with the Visual Basic Editor. Although the WinSock control is available in the **Control Toolbox** in Microsoft Excel, Word, and PowerPoint, you can't add the control directly to their documents. In Microsoft Access, you can add the WinSock control to a form in Design view. The WinSock control doesn't display when your application is running.

▶ To add the WinSock control to a Microsoft Excel, Word, or PowerPoint UserForm created with the Visual Basic Editor

1   Open a Microsoft Excel, Word, or PowerPoint document.

2   On the **Tools** menu, point to **Macro**, and then click **Visual Basic Editor**.

This starts the Visual Basic Editor or switches to its window if it's already open.

3   On the **Insert** menu, click **UserForm**.

A blank form is created and the toolbox is displayed.

4   Right-click the toolbox, and then click **Additional Controls**.

The **Additional Controls** dialog box is displayed.

5   In the **Available Controls** box, select **WinSock Control, version 5.0**, and then click **OK**.

A tool icon is added to the toolbox for the WinSock control. You don't need to repeat steps 4 and 5 the next time you use the toolbox.

6   Click the new tool, and then click the form where you want to place the control.

By default, the new control is named Winsock*n*, where *n* is some number.

▶ To add the WinSock control to a Microsoft Access form

1   Open the form in Design view.

2   In the toolbox, click the **More Controls** tool.

A menu appears that lists all the registered ActiveX controls in your system.

3   On the menu of ActiveX controls, click **WinSock Control, version 5.0**.

4   On the form, click where you want to place the control.

By default, the new control is named ActiveXctl*n*, where *n* is some number.

Setting the Protocol Property

After you add the WinSock control to your form, you specify which protocol you are going to use. If you want to use the UDP protocol, set the **Protocol** property to **sckUDPProtocol**. The default setting of the **Protocol** property is **sckTCPProtocol**. You can set the **Protocol** property in the property sheet or in Visual Basic code, as follows.

```
Winsock1.Protocol = sckUDPProtocol
```

Determining the Name of a Computer

To connect to a remote computer, you must know either its Internet Protocol (IP) address or its "friendly name." The IP address is a series of three digit numbers separated by periods (*nnn.nnn.nnn.nnn*). It's much easier to remember the friendly name of a computer.

▶ **To determine the name of a computer**

1 On the **Taskbar** of your computer, click **Start**, point to **Settings**, and then click **Control Panel**.

2 Double-click the **Network** icon.

3 Click the **Identification** tab.

4 The name of your computer is in the **Computer name** box.

After you have determined a computer's name, you can use it as the value for the **RemoteHost** property of a WinSock control, as shown in the examples later in this section.

Creating an Application That Uses the TCP Protocol

When creating an application that uses the TCP protocol, you must first decide if your application will be a client or a server. The client makes a connection request, which the server can then accept to complete the connection. After the connection is complete, the client and server can freely communicate with each other.

▶ **To create a TCP server**

1 Create a Microsoft Excel, Word, or PowerPoint document or a Microsoft Access database.

2 Create a form and name it frmServer.

3 Set the **Caption** property of the form to TCP Server.

4 Add a WinSock control to the form and set its **Name** property to tcpServer.

5 Add two text box controls to the form. Name the first txtSendData, and the second txtOutput.

6 Add the following code to the form.

```
Private Sub Form_Load()
   ' Set the LocalPort property to an integer.
   ' Then invoke the Listen method.
   tcpServer.LocalPort = 1001
   tcpServer.Listen
End Sub

Private Sub tcpServer_ConnectionRequest (ByVal requestID As Long)
   ' Check if the value of the control's State property
   ' is closed. If not, close the connection before
   ' accepting the new connection.
   If tcpServer.State <> sckClosed Then tcpServer.Close
   ' Accept the request with the requestID parameter.
   tcpServer.Accept requestID
End Sub

Private Sub txtSendData_Change()
   ' The TextBox control named txtSendData
```

```
            ' contains the data to be sent. Whenever the user
            ' types into the textbox, the string is sent
            ' using the SendData method.
            tcpServer.SendData txtSendData.Text
        End Sub

        Private Sub tcpServer_DataArrival (ByVal bytesTotal As Long)
            ' Declare a variable for the incoming data.
            ' Use the GetData method and set the Text
            ' property of a TextBox named txtOutput to
            ' the data.
            Dim strData As String
            tcpServer.GetData strData
            ' In Microsoft Access, substitute txtOutput.Value
            ' for txtOutput.Text in the following line.
            txtOutput.Text = strData
        End Sub
```

These procedures create a simple server application. To complete the scenario, you must also create a client application.

▶ To create a TCP client

1   Create a form and name it frmClient.

2   Set the **Caption** property of the form to TCP Client.

3   Add a WinSock control to the form and set its **Name** property to tcpClient.

4   Add two text box controls to the form. Name the first txtSendData, and the second txtOutput.

5   Add a command button control to the form and name it cmdConnect.

6   Set the **Caption** property of the command button control to Connect.

7   Add the following code to the form.

Important   Set the value of the **RemoteHost** property to the name of your computer.

```
Private Sub Form_Load()
   ' The name of the Winsock control is tcpClient.
   ' Note: To specify a remote host, you can use
   ' either the IP address (ex: "121.111.1.1") or
   ' the computer's friendly name, as shown here.
   tcpClient.RemoteHost = "RemoteComputerName"
   tcpClient.RemotePort = 1001
End Sub

Private Sub cmdConnect_Click()
   ' Invoke the Connect method to initiate a
   ' connection.
   tcpClient.Connect
End Sub

Private Sub txtSendData_Change()
   tcpClient.SendData txtSendData.Text
End Sub

Private Sub tcpClient_DataArrival _
(ByVal bytesTotal As Long)
   Dim strData As String
   tcpClient.GetData strData
   ' In Microsoft Access, substitute txtOutput.Value
   ' for txtOutput.Text in the following line.
   txtOutput.Text = strData
End Sub
```

The preceding code creates a simple client/server application. To try the two together, make a copy of the application and put it on another computer. Open the client on one computer and open the server on the other computer. Then click **Connect** on the client form. When you type text into the txtSendData text box on either form, the same text appears in the txtOutput text box on the other form.

Accepting More Than One Connection Request

With Microsoft Word, Microsoft Excel, Microsoft PowerPoint, and Microsoft Access forms, you can only create a server that accepts only one connection request. However, you can use Microsoft Visual Basic version 4.0 or later to create a server application that accepts several connection requests by using the same control. To do so, you create a new instance of the control by setting its **Index** property; this creates a control array. Then you invoke the **Accept** method on the new instance. You do not need to close the connection.

The following code assumes there is a WinSock control on a form named sckServer, and that its **Index** property has been set to 0; thus the control is part of a control array. In the Declarations section, a module-level variable intMax is declared. In the form's Load event, intMax is set to 0, and the **LocalPort** property for the first control in the array is set to 1001. Then the **Listen** method is invoked for the control, making it the control that receives connection requests. As each connection request arrives, the code tests it to see if the **Index** property is 0 (the value of the "listening" control). If so, the listening control increments intMax, and uses that number to create a new control instance. The new control instance then accepts the connection request.

```
Private intMax As Long

Private Sub Form_Load()
    intMax = 0
    sckServer(0).LocalPort = 1001
    sckServer(0).Listen
End Sub

Private Sub sckServer_ConnectionRequest _
    (Index As Integer, ByVal requestID As Long)
    If Index = 0 Then
        intMax = intMax + 1
        Load sckServer(intMax)
        sckServer(intMax).LocalPort = 0
        sckServer(intMax).Accept requestID
        Load txtData(intMax)
    End If
End Sub
```

Creating an Application That Uses the UDP Protocol

Creating a UDP application is even simpler than creating a TCP application because the UDP protocol doesn't require a connection. After you create the forms, add the WinSock controls, and set the **Protocol** property to UDPProtocol, you add code on both computers that performs the following steps:

1. Set the **RemoteHost** property of the WinSock control to the name of the other computer.

2. Set the **RemotePort** property of the WinSock control to the **LocalPort** property of the other WinSock control.

3. Use the **Bind** method to specify the local port to be used by the WinSock control.

The **Bind** method reserves a local port for use by the WinSock control. For example, when you bind the control to port number 1001, no other application can use that port to receive connection requests. This may be useful if you want to prevent another application from using that port.

If there is more than one network adapter on the machine, you can specify which adapter to use in the *LocalIP* argument the **Bind** method. If you do not specify which network adapter to use, the control uses the first adapter listed in the **Network** dialog box, which is available through the computer's Control Panel.

When using the UDP protocol, you can change the setting of the **RemoteHost** and **RemotePort** properties while remaining bound to the same local port. However, with the TCP protocol, you must close the connection before changing the **RemoteHost** and **RemotePort** properties.

In the TCP application created in the previous section, you must set the WinSock control on the client to receive connection requests, and the WinSock control on the server must initiate a connection. In contrast, the two computers in a UDP application do not have such restrictive roles. Both computers can send and receive messages. Because both computers can be considered equal in the relationship, a UDP application is sometimes called a *peer-to-peer application.*

The following procedures create a UDP application that two people can use to exchange messages in real time, or "talk" to each other.

▶ To create a UDP Peer

1 Create a document in Microsoft Excel, Word, or PowerPoint, or create a database in Microsoft Access.

2 Create a form and name it frmPeerA.

3 Set the **Caption** property of the form to Peer A.

4 Add a WinSock control to the form and set its **Name** property to udpPeerA.

5 Set the **Protocol** property to UDPProtocol.

6 Add two text box controls to the form. Name the first txtSendData, and the second txtOutput.

7 Add the following code to the form.

```
Private Sub Form_Load()
   ' The control's name is udpPeerA.
   With udpPeerA
      .Protocol = sckUDPProtocol   ' Set the control to UDP protocol.
      .RemoteHost= "PeerB"         ' Set RemoteHost property to the
                                   ' name of the other computer.
      .RemotePort = 1001           ' Port to connect to.
      .Bind 1002                   ' Bind to the local port.
   End With
   frmPeerB.Show                   ' Show second form.
End Sub

Private Sub txtSendData_Change()
   ' Send text as soon as it's typed.
   udpPeerA.SendData txtSendData.Text
End Sub

Private Sub udpPeerA_DataArrival (ByVal bytesTotal As Long)
   Dim strData As String

   udpPeerA.GetData strData
 ' In Microsoft Access, substitute txtOutput.Value
 ' for txtOutput.Text in the following line.
   txtOutput.Text = strData
End Sub
```

▶ To create a second UDP Peer

1   Create a form and name it frmPeerB.

2   Set the **Caption** property of the form to Peer B.

3   Add a WinSock control to the form and set its **Name** property to udpPeerB.

4   Set the **Protocol** property to UDPProtocol.

5   Add two text box controls to the form. Name the first txtSendData, and the second txtOutput.

6   Add the following code to the form.

```
Private Sub Form_Load()
    ' The control's name is udpPeerB.
    With udpPeerB
        .Protocol = sckUDPProtocol    ' Set the control to UDP protocol.
        .RemoteHost= "PeerA"          ' Set RemoteHost property to the
                                      ' name of the other computer.
        .RemotePort = 1002            ' Port to connect to.
        .Bind 1001                    ' Bind to the local port.
    End With
End Sub

Private Sub txtSendData_Change()
    ' Send text as soon as it's typed.
    udpPeerB.SendData txtSendData.Text
End Sub

Private Sub udpPeerB_DataArrival (ByVal bytesTotal As Long)
    Dim strData As String

    udpPeerB.GetData strData
    ' In Microsoft Access, substitute txtOutput.Value
    ' for txtOutput.Text in the following line.
    txtOutput.Text = strData
End Sub
```

To try this example, make a copy of the application and put it on another computer. Open the first peer on one computer and open the second peer on the other computer. When you type text into the txtSendData text box on either form, the same text appears in the txtOutput text box on the other form.

Setting Up a Personal Web Server

Microsoft provides two products that make it easy to create a personal Web server on your computer for low-volume Web publishing: Microsoft Personal Web Server and Microsoft Peer Web Services. These products are ideal for publishing departmental home pages, personal home pages, or small-scale Web applications on your company's intranet.

Although Personal Web Server and Peer Web Services are intended for small-scale Web publishing, they provide most of the same services and features as Microsoft Internet Information Server, a robust Web server intended for high-volume Web publishing. You can use Personal Web Server or Peer Web Services to develop and test Web applications, and then transfer them to a Web server running Microsoft Internet Information Server.

Both Personal Web Server and Peer Web Services can:

- Publish Web pages on the Internet or over a LAN on an intranet by using the HTTP service.
- Support Microsoft ActiveX controls.
- Transmit or receive files by using the FTP service.
- Run Internet Server API (ISAPI) and Common Gateway Interface (CGI) scripts.
- Send queries to ODBC data sources by using the Internet Database Connector component (Httpodbc.dll).
- Support the Secure Sockets Layer.

In addition, Peer Web Services can:

- Use pass-through security to Windows NT Server and Novell NetWare.
- Use local-user security if Microsoft File and Print Sharing are not installed.
- Perform remote administration by using a Web-based application.
- Distribute documents by using the Gopher service.

Installation Requirements

To run Personal Web Server or Peer Web Services, you must meet the following installation requirements.

Personal Web Server

- A computer with Windows 95 installed.
- A CD-ROM drive for the installation compact disc.
- Adequate disk space for your information content.

Peer Web Services

- A computer with Windows NT Workstation version 4.0 installed.

- A CD-ROM drive for the installation compact disc.

- Adequate disk space for your information content. It is recommended that all drives used with Peer Web Services be formatted with the Windows NT File System (NTFS).

Publication Requirements

When using Personal Web Server or Peer Web Services, each computer you want to access the server must have Transmission Control Protocol/Internet Protocol (TCP/IP) installed. The TCP/IP protocol is included with Windows 95 and Windows NT Workstation version 4.0. To install and configure the TCP/IP protocol and related components, double-click the **Network** icon in Control Panel. Each system must meet additional requirements depending on whether you want to use the server on an intranet or the Internet.

Intranet Publication Requirements

- A network adapter card and local area network (LAN) connection.

- The Windows Internet Name Service (WINS) server or the Domain Name System (DNS) server installed on a computer in your intranet. WINS and DNS run only on Windows NT Server. This step is optional, but it does allow users to use "friendly names" instead of IP addresses when connecting to your server.

Internet Publication Requirements

- An Internet connection and Internet Protocol (IP) address from your Internet Service Provider (ISP).

- DNS registration for that IP address. This step is optional, but it does allow users to use "friendly names" instead of IP addresses when connecting to your server. For example, "microsoft.com" is the friendly domain name registered to Microsoft. Within the microsoft.com domain, Microsoft has named its World Wide Web (WWW) server "www.microsoft.com." Most ISPs can register your domain names for you.

- A network adapter card suitable for your connection to the Internet.

Installing Personal Web Server

The Setup file for the Personal Web Server is available on the Web. To download the Setup program for Personal Web Server for Windows 95, connect to the Microsoft Personal Web Server home page at:

http://www.microsoft.com/ie/iesk/pws.htm

You can install Personal Web Server if you are running Windows 95 or Windows NT Workstation version 4.0. However, if you are using Windows NT, it is recommended that you install Peer Web Services instead.

▶ **To install Personal Web Server from the ValuPack**

1 Connect to the Personal Web Server home page on the Web and download PWS10a.exe.

2 Double-click **PWS10a.exe**.

This starts the installation process. You may be required to supply additional files from your Windows 95 Setup disks.

3 When installation is finished, the Setup program asks if you want to restart your computer. Click **Yes**.

Installing Peer Web Services

The files to install Peer Web Services are provided on the Microsoft Windows NT Workstation version 4.0 Setup CD-ROM.

▶ **To install Peer Web Services**

1 Open **Control Panel**, and then double-click **Network**.

2 Click the **Services** tab, and then click **Add**.

3 In the **Network Service** list, double-click **Peer Web Services**.

This starts the installation process. You may be required to supply additional files from your Windows NT Setup disks.

4 In the first **Microsoft Peer Web Services Setup** dialog box, click **OK**.

5 In the second **Microsoft Peer Web Services Setup** dialog box, select which services you want to install, and then click **OK**.

6 In the **Publishing Directories** dialog box, specify the directories you want to use for each service, or accept the default directories, and then click **OK**.

Getting More Information

For more information about Using Personal Web Server or Peer Web Services, you can refer to their online documentation, which is available once installation is complete.

▶ **To view documentation for Personal Web Server or Peer Web Services**

1 Start your Web browser.

2 To view the documentation for Personal Web Server, in your browser's address box, type:

http://*MyServer*/docs/default.htm

To view the documentation for Peer Web Services, in your browser's address box, type:

http://*MyServer*/iisadmin/htmldocs/inetdocs.htm

where *MyServer* is the name of the computer on which you installed Personal Web Server or Peer Web Services. To determine the name of the computer, open Control Panel, double-click the **Network** icon, and then click the **Identification** tab.

3 Press ENTER.

Switching from the Microsoft Excel 4.0 Macro Language

This appendix introduces users of the Microsoft Excel 4.0 Macro Language to Visual Basic programming. In this appendix, you'll learn how Visual Basic differs from the Microsoft Excel 4.0 Macro Language, how you can continue using your existing Microsoft Excel 4.0 macros, and where to find more information about Visual Basic.

Visual Basic is a true programming language that features variables with scoping, an integrated editor, and enhanced dialog box tools and debugging tools. Learning Visual Basic in Microsoft Excel 97 makes it easier for you to learn programming in other Microsoft Office 97 applications (Microsoft Access, Word, and PowerPoint) as well as Microsoft Project and other Microsoft applications that use Visual Basic. You can also control these other applications easily in your Visual Basic code.

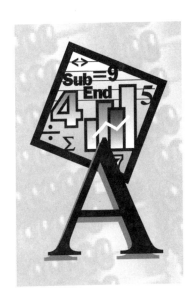

Contents
- Information for Users of Microsoft Excel 4.0 Macros
- Visual Basic Equivalents for Common Macro Functions
- Creating Custom Commands and Dialog Boxes Using Visual Basic

Information for Users of Microsoft Excel 4.0 Macros

This section guides experienced users of Microsoft Excel 4.0 macros to information about learning and using Visual Basic. For more detailed information, see the chapters and Help topics that are cross-referenced in this section.

Acting Directly on Objects in Visual Basic

In Microsoft Excel version 4.0, macros follow the "select, then do" order of actions that pertains to all of Microsoft Excel. With Visual Basic, you don't need to select an object you want your procedure to change; you can change the object directly.

For example, to make a range of text bold in Microsoft Excel version 4.0, you have to first select the range with the SELECT function before changing the format of the text with the FORMAT.FONT function. In Visual Basic, you make a range of text bold by just setting the **Bold** property of the range to **True**. The following example applies bold formatting to cells C1:G5 on Sheet1.

```
Sub MakeSectionBold()
    Worksheets("Sheet1").Range("C1:G5").Font.Bold = True
End sub
```

Note that you can use Visual Basic to change an object (the range C1:G5,in this case) directly, without first selecting it or canceling the current selection. For more information about how to change cells, sheets, and other objects in Microsoft Excel with Visual Basic, see Chapter 4, "Microsoft Excel Objects."

Variables: More Powerful Than Names

To store a value as a variable in Microsoft Excel version 4.0, you'd typically store the value in a name. In Visual Basic, you'd assign the value to a variable instead.

Variables are much more flexible than names. You can make variables available to all procedures, to only the procedures in a given module, or to only a single procedure. You can control the type of data that can be stored in a variable, and you can even create variables that store a combination of data types of your choice.

In Visual Basic, you can also define constants to hold static (constant) values that you can refer to repeatedly. For more information about variables and constants in Visual Basic, see Chapter 1, "Programming Basics."

Using Worksheet Functions in a Procedure

There are many worksheet functions that you can use directly in Visual Basic procedures; the IF function is one exception, though, given that **If** is also a keyword in Visual Basic. You can use the **Application** qualifier to run a Microsoft Excel worksheet function rather than a Visual Basic function. The following example causes a "Sub or Function not defined" error because it doesn't identify ACOS as a worksheet function.

```
Sub MissingObject()
    x = Acos(-1)
End Sub
```

The following example successfully uses the Microsoft Excel worksheet function ACOS because the code first refers to the **Application** object.

```
Sub ReturnArccosine()
    x = Application.Acos(-1)
End Sub
```

The only worksheet function that requires you to explicitly specify that you're referring to either the function's Microsoft Excel version or its Visual Basic version is the LOG function, because both function names are spelled the same way. The Microsoft Excel LOG function returns the logarithm of a specified number to whatever base you indicate. The Visual Basic **Log** function, on the other hand, returns the natural logarithm of a specified number.

Using Your Existing Macros in a Procedure

You can include your existing macros in new Visual Basic procedures by using the **Run** method. When you debug Microsoft Excel 4.0 macros as part of your Visual Basic procedures, the Visual Basic debugger steps into your macros as if they were written in Visual Basic. Your macros can return information to a procedure by using the RETURN macro function.

For more information and an example of the **Run** method, see "Run Method" in Help.

New Tools to Make Debugging Easy

There are numerous tools in Visual Basic to help you debug your code. Visual Basic debugging functionality includes breakpoints, break expressions, watch expressions, stepping through code one statement or one procedure at a time, and displaying the values of variables and properties. Visual Basic also includes special debugging functionality, such as the "edit-and-continue" feature, setting the next statement to run, and procedure testing while the application is in break mode.

For more information about the debugging capabilities of Visual Basic, see Chapter 14, "Debugging and Error Handling."

Visual Basic Equivalents for Common Macro Functions

The easiest way to see the Visual Basic equivalents for common macro functions and Microsoft Excel commands is to use the macro recorder to record macros in Visual Basic. You can arrange the windows on your desktop so that one window shows your Visual Basic module and the other one shows the worksheet or chart you're working on while you're recording a macro. As you work, Microsoft Excel adds Visual Basic statements to your module.

No matter how you write your programs in Microsoft Excel, there are common tasks you'll want to accomplish, such as referring to ranges, controlling how macros run, accessing data in other applications, getting information about workbooks and objects, and creating procedures that run in response to certain events. The following table shows you where to look in this book for information about how to accomplish these tasks with Visual Basic.

For information about	See this chapter
Referring to cells and ranges on worksheets	Chapter 4, "Microsoft Excel Objects"
Controlling the flow of a macro	Chapter 1, "Programming Basics"
Accessing data in other applications	Chapter 11, "Data Access Objects"
Getting information about objects in Microsoft Excel	Chapter 4, "Microsoft Excel Objects"
Running procedures in response to events	Chapter 4, "Microsoft Excel Objects"

Creating Custom Commands and Dialog Boxes Using Visual Basic

Microsoft Excel 97 includes tools for creating custom menus, commands, and dialog boxes. For more information about creating custom commands and dialog boxes using Visual Basic, see Chapter 8, "Menus and Toolbars," and Chapter 12, "ActiveX Controls and Dialog Boxes."

Creating Custom Commands

To create a custom menu or command in Microsoft Excel version 4.0, you first create a menu or command table. You then use the macro function ADD.MENU or ADD.COMMAND to place your custom menu or command on a menu bar or a menu.

To create a custom menu or command in Microsoft Excel 97, you use the **Customize** dialog box to assign custom commands and menus to menu bars. For more information about using the **Customize** dialog box, see Chapter 8, "Menus and Toolbars."

Displaying Built-in Dialog Boxes

In Microsoft Excel version 4.0, to display built-in dialog boxes while running a macro, you use the question-mark form of the macro function corresponding to the dialog box. For example, the DEFINE.STYLE? macro function displays the dialog box in which you define worksheet styles.

In Microsoft Excel 97, to display built-in dialog boxes while running a procedure, you use the **Dialogs** method with the identifier of the dialog box you want displayed. The following example displays the **Open** dialog box (**File** menu).

```
Sub OpenFile()
    Application.Dialogs(xlDialogOpen).Show
End Sub
```

Creating and Displaying Custom Dialog Boxes

To create a custom dialog box in Microsoft Excel version 4.0, you use the Dialog Editor to generate a dialog box definition you place on a macro sheet. You then use the DIALOG.BOX macro function to display your dialog box.

You can use the **DialogBox** method in your Visual Basic procedures to run a Microsoft Excel 4.0 custom dialog box. The following example uses the **DialogBox** method to display such a dialog box and then tests the result. The variable DialogRange refers to the range (on a Microsoft Excel 4.0 macro sheet) that contains the dialog-box definition table.

```
Result = DialogRange.DialogBox
If Not Result Then
    ' User canceled the dialog box
Else
    ' Result is position number of chosen control
End If
```

In Microsoft Excel 97, you create custom dialogs by adding ActiveX controls to forms, or *UserForms*, in the Visual Basic Editor. To create a custom dialog box, you must create a UserForm to contain controls, add whatever controls you want to the UserForm, set properties for the controls, and write code that responds to form and control events. You use the **Show** method in a Visual Basic procedure to display your custom dialog box. For more information about creating dialog boxes in Microsoft Excel 97, see Chapter 12, "ActiveX Controls and Dialog Boxes."

Switching from WordBasic

This appendix is intended to help users switching from the WordBasic programming language to Visual Basic for Applications, the new programming language in Microsoft Word 97 (and other Office 97 applications).

The first step toward making this switch is to convert your existing WordBasic macros. For information about converting your WordBasic macros, see "Converting WordBasic macros to Visual Basic" in Help. This Help topic explains how Word automatically converts macros in Word 6.x or Word 95 templates to Visual Basic.

Although Word converts your macros, you may need to modify parts of them manually to retain the macros' original functionality. In addition to making modifications to converted WordBasic macros, you may need to write new macros in the future. It's possible to continue using WordBasic statements and functions exposed through the WordBasic object, but gradually you'll want to switch over to Visual Basic. For information about the functionality available with Visual Basic, see the introduction in this book.

To help make the switch to Visual Basic an easy one, a table of WordBasic commands and their corresponding Visual Basic syntax is included in Help, in the topic "Visual Basic Equivalents for WordBasic Commands."

Contents

- Logistical Programming Changes in Microsoft Word 97
- Conceptual Differences Between WordBasic and Visual Basic
- Determining Which Properties or Methods to Use
- Selection Object vs. Range Object
- Using WordBasic Statements and Functions
- Miscellaneous Changes
- Example Macros

Logistical Programming Changes in Microsoft Word 97

The introduction in this book discusses the capabilities of Visual Basic. The following paragraphs supplement the information provided in the introduction with references to previous versions of Word.

Macro Editor   The built-in macro editor in previous versions of Word has been replaced by an integrated Visual Basic development environment, which is referred to as the Visual Basic Editor. The Visual Basic Editor runs in its own window and looks exactly the same no matter which Office application you start it from.

Dialog Editor   Previous versions of Word included a separate Dialog Editor application used to design custom dialog boxes. You create custom dialog boxes in Word 97 by creating UserForms in the Visual Basic Editor. For more information about UserForms, see Chapter 12, " ActiveX Controls and Dialog Boxes."

Macro Storage   When you create a new macro in the **Macros** dialog box in Word (point to **Macro** on the **Tools** menu, and then click **Macros**), a new subroutine with the macro name you provide is created in a module. Macros can now be stored in documents as well as templates. You specify the storage location by selecting an item in the **Macros in** box in the **Macros** dialog box. The **Macros in** box includes template names and the name of the active document (for example, "Sales.doc (document)").

Conceptual Differences Between WordBasic and Visual Basic

The primary difference between Visual Basic and WordBasic is that WordBasic consists of a flat list of approximately 900 commands, whereas Visual Basic consists of a hierarchy of objects, each of which exposes a specific set of methods and properties (similar to statements and functions in WordBasic). Objects are the fundamental building block of Visual Basic; almost everything you do in Visual Basic involves modifying objects. Every element of Word—documents, paragraphs, fields, bookmarks, and so on—is represented by an object in Visual Basic. To view a graphical representation of the object model for Word, see "Microsoft Word Objects" in Help.

Whereas most WordBasic commands can be run at any time, Visual Basic instructions drill down through the object model to an object that you can manipulate using properties and methods. There are certain objects that you can get to only from other objects—for instance, the **Font** object, to which you can control from the **Style**, **Selection**, or **Find** object, among others. Before you can change any font-related attributes (such as bold formatting), you need to drill down to the **Font** object.

The programming task of applying bold formatting demonstrates one of the differences between the two programming languages. The following WordBasic example applies bold formatting to the selection.

```
Bold 1
```

Visual Basic doesn't include a **Bold** statement and function; instead, there's a **Bold** property (a property is usually an attribute of an object, such as its size, its color, or whether or not it's bold). The **Bold** property is a property of the **Font** object, which is returned by the **Font** property. The **Font** property is a property of the **Selection** object, which is returned by the **Selection** property. And finally, the **Selection** property is a property of the **Application** object, which is returned by the **Application** property. These relationships are shown in the following object hierarchy.

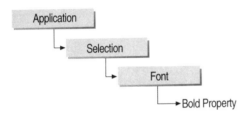

Using this object hierarchy, you can build the instruction shown in the following example to apply bold formatting to the selection.

```
Application.Selection.Font.Bold = True
```

Note   Because the **Selection** property is "global," the **Application** property is optional. To view a list of all the global properties and methods, click **<globals>** at the top of the **Classes** list in the Object Browser.

Instead of being composed of a flat list of commands, Visual Basic consists of a hierarchical arrangement of objects that support a predefined set of properties and methods (as shown in the preceding illustration). The following table shows some common WordBasic instructions and their Visual Basic equivalents.

WordBasic instruction	Equivalent Visual Basic instruction
`FileOpen .Name = "MYDOC.DOC"`	`Documents.Open FileName:= "MYDOC.DOC"`
`Insert "new text"`	`Selection.TypeText Text:="new text"`
`Activate "Document1"`	`Windows("Document1").Activate`
`MsgBox Font$()`	`MsgBox Selection.Font.Name`
`FormatParagraph .Alignment = 3`	`Selection.Paragraphs.Alignment = wdAlignParagraphJustify`

The two instructions in each row of the preceding table are functionally equivalent, but their syntax is dramatically different. Each WordBasic instruction consists of a command name (for example, **FileOpen**) and any applicable arguments (for example, **.Name**). Each Visual Basic instruction, on the other hand, is a combination of one or more properties or methods (for example, **Documents** and **Open**), followed by any applicable arguments for each (for example, *FileName*). The properties and methods you use to drill down through the object model are separated by the dot operator.

The **Open** method in Visual Basic is functionally equivalent to the WordBasic **FileOpen** statement when the **Open** method is used with the **Documents** collection object. The **Documents** collection is returned by the **Documents** property. The following illustration shows the path to the **Open** method.

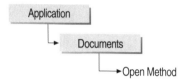

Following this hierarchy, you can build the instruction shown in the following example to open Mydoc.doc.

```
Application.Documents.Open FileName:="MYDOC.DOC"
```

Note   The **Application** property is optional because the **Documents** property is "global."

Visual Basic doesn't include separate statements and functions as in WordBasic. The **Bold** property is a read/write **Boolean** property. This means that the **Bold** property can be set to either **True** or **False** (on or off), or the current value can be returned. The following table shows the Visual Basic equivalents for various versions of the WordBasic **Bold** statement and the WordBasic **Bold** function.

WordBasic Bold statement or function	Equivalent Visual Basic instruction
Bold 1	Selection.Font.Bold = True
Bold 0	Selection.Font.Bold = False
Bold	Selection.Font.Bold = wdToggle
x = Bold()	x = Selection.Font.Bold

Determining Which Properties or Methods to Use

There are a few techniques you can use to determine which Visual Basic properties or methods you need to use to accomplish a particular programming task. When you're first learning Visual Basic, it's usually best to use the macro recorder. The macro recorder is a tool that translates your actions into Visual Basic instructions. For instance, if you turn on the macro recorder and open the document named "Examples.doc" in the current folder, the macro recorder records the following instruction.

```
Documents.Open FileName:="Examples.doc", ConfirmConversions:=False, _
    ReadOnly:=False, AddToRecentFiles:=False, PasswordDocument:="", _
    PasswordTemplate:="", Revert:=False, WritePasswordDocument:="", _
    WritePasswordTemplate:="", Format:=wdOpenFormatAuto
```

To learn more about the preceding instruction, position the insertion point within the word "Open" and then press F1. The Help topic for the **Open** method explains the arguments you can use with that method. For information about the **Documents** property, position the insertion point within the word "Documents" and then press F1.

Until you become somewhat familiar with the Word object model, there are a few tools and techniques you can use to help you drill down through the object hierarchy.

Auto List Members When you type the dot operator after a property or method in the Visual Basic Editor, a list of available properties and methods is displayed. For example, if you type **Application.**, a list containing methods and properties of the **Application** object is displayed. Select the method or property you want to use, and then press TAB to insert the selected item.

Visual Basic Help You can use Help to find out which properties and methods you can use with a particular object. Each object topic in Help includes a **Properties** jump and a **Methods** jump, which display (respectively) a list of properties and a list of methods for the object. To jump to the appropriate Help topic, press F1 in the Object Browser or a module.

Object model For an illustration of how Word objects are arranged in the object hierarchy, see "Microsoft Word Objects" in Help. Click an object in the graphic to display its corresponding Help topic.

Object Browser The Object Browser in the Visual Basic Editor displays the members (properties and methods) of the Word objects.

Using the Object Browser

To perform a task in Visual Basic, you need to determine the appropriate object to use. For example, if you want to apply character formatting found in the **Font** dialog box, use the **Font** object. Then you need to determine how to drill down through the Word object hierarchy from the **Application** object to the **Font** object, through the objects that contain the **Font** object you want to modify.

To see how this is done, open the Visual Basic Editor and click **Object Browser** on the **View** menu. Click **Application** in the **Classes** list. then click **Selection** in the **Members** list. The text at bottom of the Object Browser indicates that **Selection** is a read-only property that returns a **Selection** object. Click **Selection** at the bottom of the Object Browser; **Selection** is now selected in the **Classes** list, and the **Members** list displays the members of the **Selection** object. Scroll through the list of members until you find **Font**, and then click **Font**. The text at the bottom of the Object Browser indicates that **Font** is a read-only property that returns a **Font** object. Click **Font** at the bottom of the Object Browser; **Font** is now selected in the **Classes** list, and the

Members list displays the members of the **Font** object. Click **Bold** in the Members pane. The text at the bottom of the Object Browser indicates that the **Bold** property is a read/write property. For more information about this property, press F1 or click the **Help** button to jump to the Help topic for the **Bold** property.

Given this information, you can write the instruction shown in the following example to apply bold formatting to the selection.

```
Selection.Font.Bold = True
```

As you can see, you use methods or properties to drill down to an object. That is, you return an object by applying a method or property to an object above it in the object hierarchy. After you return the object you want, you can apply the methods and control the properties of that object.

Note A given object often exists in more than one place in the object hierarchy. For an illustration of the Word object model, see "Microsoft Word Objects" in Help. Also, individual properties and methods are often available to multiple objects in the Word object hierarchy. For example, the **Bold** property is a property of both the **Font** and **Range** objects. The following example applies bold formatting to the entire active document (the **Content** property returns a **Range** object).

```
ActiveDocument.Content.Bold = True
```

Selection Object vs. Range Object

Most WordBasic commands modify whatever is selected. For example, the **Bold** command formats the selection with bold formatting, and the **InsertField** command inserts a field at the insertion point. Visual Basic supports this same functionality through the **Selection** object, which you return by using the **Selection** property. The selection can be a block of text or just the insertion point.

The following Visual Basic example inserts the text "Hello World" and a new paragraph after the selection.

```
Selection.InsertAfter Text:="Hello World"
Selection.InsertParagraphAfter
```

In addition to working with the selection, you can define and work with various ranges of text in a document. A **Range** object refers to a contiguous area in a document, with a starting character position and an ending character position. Similar to the way you use bookmarks in a document, you use **Range** objects in Visual Basic to identify portions of a document. For example, you can use Visual Basic to apply bold formatting anywhere in a given document without changing the selection. The following example applies bold formatting to the first 10 characters in the active document.

```
ActiveDocument.Range(Start:=0, End:=10).Bold = True
```

The following example applies bold formatting to the first paragraph.

```
ActiveDocument.Paragraphs(1).Range.Bold = True
```

Both of the preceding example change the formatting in the active document without changing the selection. In most cases, **Range** objects are preferred over the **Selection** object for the following reasons:

- You can define and use multiple **Range** objects, whereas you can have only one **Selection** object per document window.

- Manipulating **Range** objects doesn't change the selection.

- Manipulating **Range** objects is faster than working with the selection.

For more information about working with **Range** and **Selection** objects, see Chapter 7, "Microsoft Word Objects."

Using WordBasic Statements and Functions

You can use WordBasic statements and functions in your Visual Basic macros. When you use a WordBasic macro in Word 97, the macro is automatically modified to work with Visual Basic. The following example is a WordBasic macro in a Word 95 template.

```
Sub MAIN
FormatFont .Name = "Arial", .Points = 10
Insert "Hello World"
End Sub
```

When the template is opened in Word 97, the macro is converted to the code shown in the following example.

```
Public Sub Main()
WordBasic.FormatFont Font:="Arial", Points:=10
WordBasic.Insert "Hello World"
End Sub
```

Each statement in the converted macro begins with the **WordBasic** property. The **WordBasic** property returns an object with methods that correspond to the WordBasic statements and functions; this object makes it possible to run WordBasic macros in Word 97. You can reuse old code (instructions that use the WordBasic property) along with new instructions that you write (instructions that don't use the WordBasic property). The following example is functionally equivalent to the preceding macro; however, the second WordBasic instruction has been changed to use the **TypeText** method of the **Selection** object.

```
Public Sub Main()
WordBasic.FormatFont Font:="Arial", Points:=10
Selection.TypeText Text:="Hello World"
End Sub
```

Using WordBasic Statements

If you still want to use WordBasic statements in Word 97, precede each WordBasic statement with the **WordBasic** property followed by the dot operator. The following Visual Basic example moves the insertion point to the beginning of the document.

```
WordBasic.StartOfDocument
```

The following example sets justified paragraph alignment and adds 1 inch of space above and below each paragraph in the selection.

```
WordBasic.FormatParagraph .Alignment = 3, .Before = "1 in", .After = "1 in"
```

The following example selects all text from the insertion point through the MyMark bookmark. (Notice how the **With** statement is used to specify the **WordBasic** object once for a series of instructions.)

```
With WordBasic
    .ExtendSelection
    .EditGoTo "MyMark"
    .Cancel
End With
```

Using WordBasic Functions

Likewise, to use WordBasic functions in Word 97, precede the WordBasic function with the WordBasic property followed by the dot operator, and use square brackets around the function name. The following table shows the original WordBasic syntax and the corresponding Visual Basic syntax using the WordBasic property.

WordBasic instructions	Equivalent Visual Basic instruction
`MsgBox Font$()`	`MsgBox WordBasic.[Font$]()`
`If Bold() = 0 Then Bold 1`	`If WordBasic.[Bold]() = 0 Then WordBasic.Bold 1`
`x = AppInfo$(1)`	`x = WordBasic.[AppInfo$](1)`

Note Methods of the **WordBasic** object are slower than methods and properties of other Visual Basic objects. For example, `WordBasic.FileOpen` is slower than `Documents.Open`. Also, the WordBasic language won't be updated with new commands in the future. Visual Basic includes objects, properties, and methods that duplicate and improve on WordBasic functionality. If you know which WordBasic command to use to perform a particular task, see the conversion table in "Visual Basic Equivalents for WordBasic Commands" in Help. This will give you a guide as to which Visual Basic methods and properties to use for specific tasks.

Miscellaneous Changes

This section outlines other changes to the programming environment in Word 97.

Syntax Changes

Use the dot operator (.) to separate properties and methods in a Visual Basic instruction. The following example makes the selected text red. The example uses dots to separate the **Selection**, **Font**, and **ColorIndex** properties.

```
Selection.Font.ColorIndex = wdRed
```

Use an equal sign (=) to set property values. The following example makes the first paragraph in the active document bold.

```
ActiveDocument.Paragraphs(1).Range.Bold = True
```

Use a colon followed by an equal sign (:=) to set an argument of a method, and use a comma to separate arguments of a method. The following example opens MyDoc.doc as a read-only document. *FileName* and *ReadOnly* are arguments of the **Open** method.

```
Documents.Open FileName:="C:\MyFiles\MyDoc.doc", ReadOnly:=True
```

Use a space followed by an underscore character (_) to continue a Visual Basic instruction to the next line. (In WordBasic, the continuation character is a backslash character (\).) The following Visual Basic example spans three lines. The first and second lines end with continuation characters. Press ENTER after typing the continuation character.

```
Documents.Open FileName:="C:\MyFiles\MyDoc.doc", _
    ConfirmConversions:=False, ReadOnly:=False, AddToRecentFiles:=True, _
    Revert:=False, Format:=wdOpenFormatAuto
```

Data Types

Visual Basic has many more data types than does WordBasic. You can define and use variables without learning about data types, but if you want to write efficient code you should define variables with the appropriate data type (for instance, **Integer**, **String**, or **Long**). The following example defines the counter variable as an integer.

```
Dim counter As Integer
```

If you don't specify a data type when you define a variable, Visual Basic automatically specifies the **Variant** data type, which takes up the largest amount of memory (a minimum of 16 bytes) of all the data types. For information about the various Visual Basic data types, see Chapter 1, "Programming Basics," or see "Data Type Summary" in Help.

Concatenating Strings and Inserting Special Characters

Use the ampersand character (&) instead of a plus sign (+) to concatenate strings. To insert special characters, you can continue to use the **Chr$()** function in Word 97, or you can use one of the following constants: **vbCr, vbLf, vbCrLf,** or **vbTab.** The following table shows WordBasic instructions that use concatenated strings and special characters, and their Visual Basic equivalents.

WordBasic instruction	Equivalent Visual Basic instruction
`Insert "Hamlet " + Chr$(13)`	`Selection.InsertAfter Text:="Hamlet " & vbCr`
`Msgbox "Hello" + Chr$(32) + "Tom"`	`MsgBox Text:="Hello" & Space & "Tom"`
`Insert Chr$(9)`	`Selection.InsertAfter Text:=vbTab`

Note Use the **ChrW$()** function to return a string that contains the character associated with the specified Unicode character.

Loops and Conditional Statements

Visual Basic and WordBasic have similar conditional and looping statements (also known as *control structures*). Visual Basic includes additional looping statements, which are marked with an asterisk in the following table. For information about using the conditional and looping statements in the following table, see Chapter 1, "Programming Basics."

Statement	Purpose
If...Then...Else	Branching when the specified condition is **True** or **False**
Select Case	Selecting a branch from a set of conditions
Do...Loop*	Looping while or until the specified condition is **True**
While...Wend	Looping while the specified condition is **True** (same as the **Do While...Loop** form of **Do...Loop**)
For...Next	Repeating a group of instructions a specified number of times
For Each...Next*	Repeating a group of instructions for each object in the specified collection

Visual Basic includes a **For...Next** statement for looping through a series of instructions. For looping through objects in a collection, however, the **For Each...Next** statement works more efficiently. The following WordBasic example creates a new document and then inserts the available font names.

```
FileNewDefault
For count = 1 To CountFonts()
    Insert Font$(count)
    InsertPara
Next count
```

The following Visual Basic example is an equivalent for the preceding WordBasic example. Notice how the **With** statement is used to specify the **Selection** object once for a series of instructions.

```
Documents.Add
For i = 1 To FontNames.Count
    With Selection
        .InsertAfter Text:=FontNames(i)
        .InsertParagraphAfter
        .Collapse Direction:=wdCollapseEnd
    End With
Next I
```

The **For Each...Next** statement automatically loops through each item in the collection without using a counter variable that the **For...Next** statement requires. The following Visual Basic example is also an equivalent for the preceding WordBasic example. However, it is more efficient than the preceding Visual Basic equivalent, which uses **For...Next**.

```
Documents.Add
For Each aFont In FontNames
    With Selection
        .InsertAfter Text:=aFont
        .InsertParagraphAfter
        .Collapse Direction:=wdCollapseEnd
    End With
Next aFont
```

Measurements

Often you can specify measurements in WordBasic macros either in points or as a text measurement (that is, a measurement specified as a string). For example, the following WordBasic example sets justified alignment and adds 1 inch of space above and below each paragraph in the selection (1 inch = 72 points).

```
FormatParagraph .Alignment = 3, .Before = 72, .After = "1 in"
```

The following Visual Basic example is equivalent to the preceding WordBasic statement. The **With** statement is used to specify the **Paragraphs** collection object once for a series of instructions that set properties of the **Paragraphs** collection.

```
With Selection.Paragraphs
    .Alignment = wdAlignParagraphJustify
    .SpaceBefore = 72
    .SpaceAfter = InchesToPoints(1)
End With
```

You must specify measurements for Word methods and properties in points. You can do this either by specifying the number of points as a number or by using one of the following conversion methods to convert the measurement to points:

CentimetersToPoints, **InchesToPoints**, **LinesToPoints**, **MillimetersToPoints**, or **PicasToPoints**. The preceding example uses the **InchesToPoints** method to convert 1 inch to points.

Example Macros

This section provides some WordBasic and Visual Basic macros for comparison.

Applying Formatting

The following WordBasic macro applies character and paragraph formatting to the selected text.

```
Sub MAIN
FormatFont .Font = "Times New Roman", .Points = 14, .AllCaps = 1
FormatParagraph .LeftIndent = "0.5"
SpacePara1
End Sub
```

The following Visual Basic macro is the equivalent of the preceding WordBasic macro. This macro uses the **Selection** property to apply character and paragraph formatting to the selected text. It uses the **Font** property to gain access to character-formatting properties, and it uses the **ParagraphFormat** property to gain access to paragraph-formatting properties and methods.

```
Sub Macro1()
With Selection.Font
    .Name = "Times New Roman"
    .Size = 14
    .AllCaps = True
End With
With Selection.ParagraphFormat
    .LeftIndent = InchesToPoints(0.5)
    .Space1
End With
End Sub
```

Deleting to the Beginning of a Sentence

The following WordBasic macro deletes the text between the insertion point and the beginning of the sentence that the insertion point is positioned within. The macro then capitalizes the first letter of the remaining text.

```
Sub MAIN
SentLeft 1, 1
EditCut
ChangeCase 4
End Sub
```

The following Visual Basic macro uses the **MoveStart** method to extend the selection to the beginning of the active sentence. The **Cut** method cuts the selected text and places it on the Clipboard, and the **Case** property changes the capitalization of the character following the selection.

```
Sub Macro1()
With Selection
    .MoveStart Unit:=wdSentence, Count:=-1
    .Cut
    .Range.Case = wdTitleSentence
End With
End Sub
```

Removing Excess Paragraph Marks

Some sources of text include a paragraph mark at the end of every line. This text is difficult to work with in Word because Word treats each line as a separate paragraph and doesn't wrap the text. The following WordBasic macro removes the excess paragraph marks (the end-of-line paragraph marks) but leaves the end-of-paragraph marks.

```
Sub MAIN
EditReplace .Find = "^p^p", .Replace = "@#$#", \
    .Direction = 0, .ReplaceAll, .Format = 0, .Wrap = 1
FileSave
EditReplace .Find = "^p", .Replace = " ", \
    .Direction = 0, .ReplaceAll, .Format = 0, .Wrap = 1
FileSave
EditReplace .Find = "@#$#", .Replace = "^p^p", \
    .Direction = 0, .ReplaceAll, .Format = 0, .Wrap = 1
End Sub
```

The preceding macro assumes that two consecutive paragraph marks signify the end of a paragraph. When you remove paragraph marks from text, you usually want to preserve separate paragraphs. For that reason, this macro replaces two consecutive paragraph marks with the placeholder "@#$#". The macro then replaces each remaining paragraph mark with a space. Finally, it replaces the "@#$#" placeholder with two paragraph marks.

The following Visual Basic macro is the equivalent of the preceding WordBasic macro. The macro uses the **Execute** method of the **Find** object to execute the three find and replace operations. It uses the **Save** method to save the active document after each find and replace operation.

```
Sub Macro1()
With Selection.Find
    .Execute FindText:="^p^p", ReplaceWith:="@#$#", Wrap:=wdFindContinue, _
        Replace:=wdReplaceAll, Format:=False, Forward:=True
    ActiveDocument.Save
    .Execute FindText:="^p", ReplaceWith:=" ", Wrap:=wdFindContinue, _
        Replace:=wdReplaceAll, Format:=False, Forward:=True
    ActiveDocument.Save
    .Execute FindText:="@#$#", ReplaceWith:="^p^p", Wrap:=wdFindContinue, _
        Replace:=wdReplaceAll, Format:=False, Forward:=True
End With
End Sub
```

Counting How Many Times a Word Appears

The following WordBasic macro uses a **While...Wend** loop to count the number of times that a specified word appears in a document. The **InputBox$()** function prompts the user for a search word.

```
Sub MAIN
count = 0
True = -1
searchtext$ = InputBox$("Please type a word to search for:")
StartOfDocument
EditFind .Find = searchtext$, .Direction = 0, .MatchCase = 0, \
    .WholeWord = 0, .Format = 0, .Wrap = 0
While EditFindFound() = True
    count = count + 1
    RepeatFind
Wend
MsgBox searchtext$ + " was found " + count + " times"
End Sub
```

The following Visual Basic macro accomplishes the same task as the preceding WordBasic macro by using a **Do...Loop** statement and the **Execute** method of the **Find** object. Because the macro gets to the **Find** object from a **Range** object (the **Content** property returns a **Range** object), the selection in the document is unchanged. Each time the specified word is found, the count variable is incremented by 1. As soon as the **Do...Loop** statement finishes looping through the document (that it, when it has counted all instances of the specified word), the macro exits the loop and displays the results in a message box.

```
Sub Macro1()
count = 0
searchtext$ = InputBox$("Please type a word to search for:")
With ActiveDocument.Content.Find
    Do While .Execute(FindText:=searchtext$, Format:=False, _
            MatchCase:=False, MatchWholeWord:=False) = True
        count = count + 1
    Loop
End With
MsgBox searchtext$ & " was found " & count & " times"
End Sub
```

Object Model Diagrams

Except where noted, the object model diagrams in this appendix illustrate objects and collections. The following table shows how each type is represented in the diagrams.

This type of item	Is designated this way
object only	
object and collection	

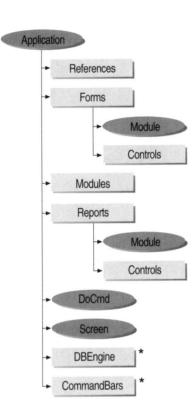

Source (Type Library)

The Microsoft Access 97 object model is provided by MSACC8.OLB, which is included when you install Microsoft Access 97.

Reference information in Help

Help for this object model is available in ACVBA80.HLP

Items marked by a single star (*) designate objects or collections used by this application but whose object model diagram are shown elsewhere in this guide.

Microsoft Excel 97

Default location: \Program Files\Microsoft Office\Office

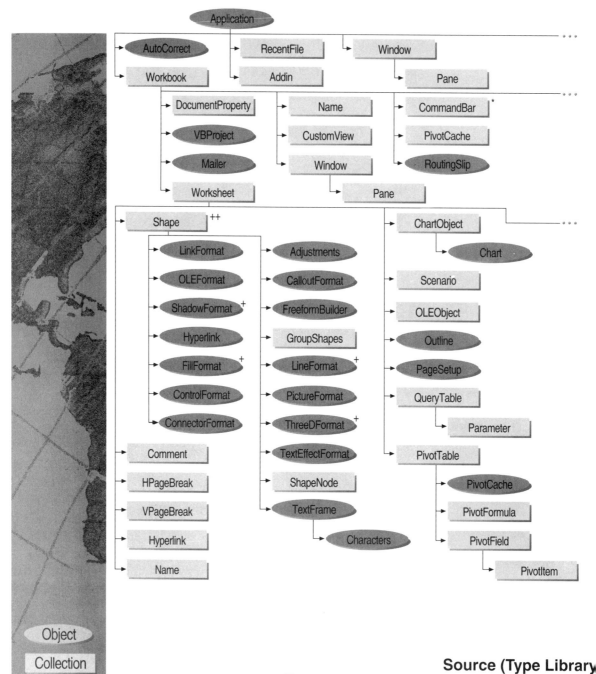

Object

Collection

Source (Type Library)

The Microsoft Excel 97 object model is provided by MSXL8.OLE
which is included when you install Microsoft Excel 97

The dotted line (…) indicates that the diagram continues across page

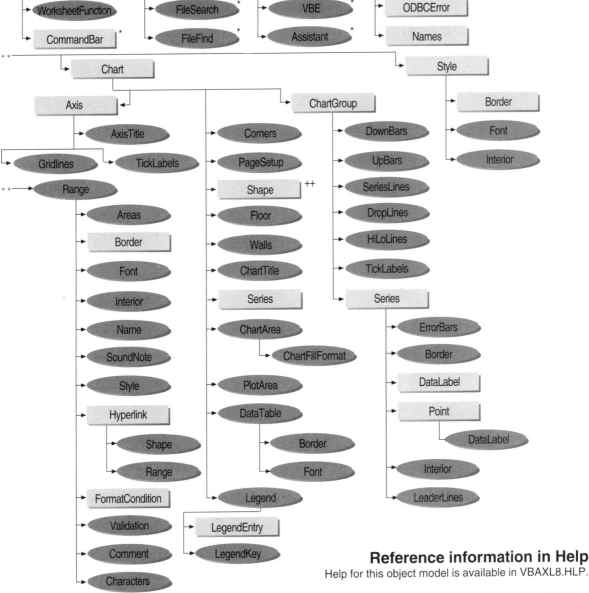

Reference information in Help

Help for this object model is available in VBAXL8.HLP.

Notes

The dotted line (...) indicates that the diagram continues across pages.
Items marked by a single (*) designate objects in the Microsoft Office 97 Library.
Items marked by a double (**) designate objects in the Microsoft Visual Basic Extensibility Object Library.
Items marked by a single (+) designate objects with accessors to the ColorFormat Object.
Items marked by a double (++) note that the ShapeRange Objects have been omitted
from this diagram. For general purposes, you can think of these objects as occupying the
same positions as the Shape object.

Microsoft Outlook 97

Default location: \Program Files\Microsoft Office\Office

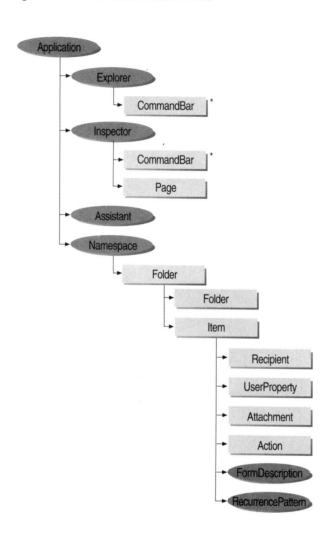

Object

Collection

Source (Type Library

The Microsoft Outlook 97 object model is provided by MSOUTL8.OLE
which is included when you install Microsoft Outlook 97

Reference information in Help

Help for this object model is available in VBAOUTL.HLP

Items marked by a single star (*) designate objects or collections used by thi
application but whose object model diagram are shown elsewhere in this guide

Microsoft Word 97

Default location: \Program Files\Microsoft Office\Office

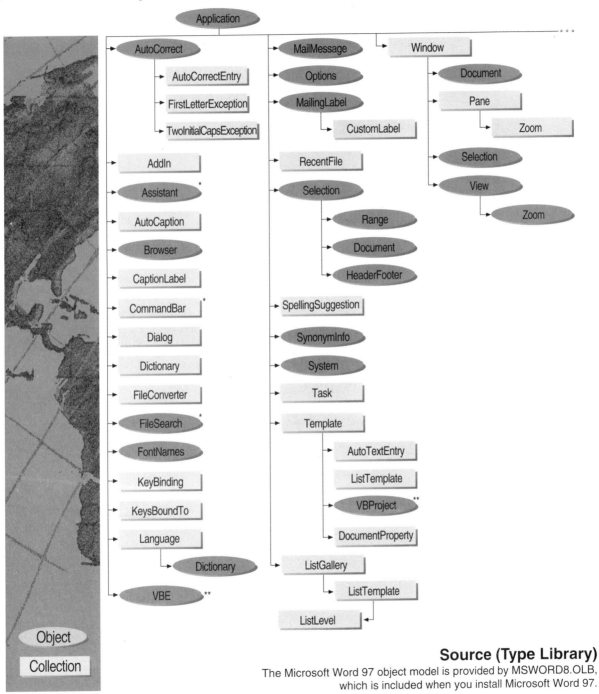

Source (Type Library)

The Microsoft Word 97 object model is provided by MSWORD8.OLB, which is included when you install Microsoft Word 97.

The dotted line (...) indicates that the diagram continues across pages.

491

Microsoft Word 97 (cont.)

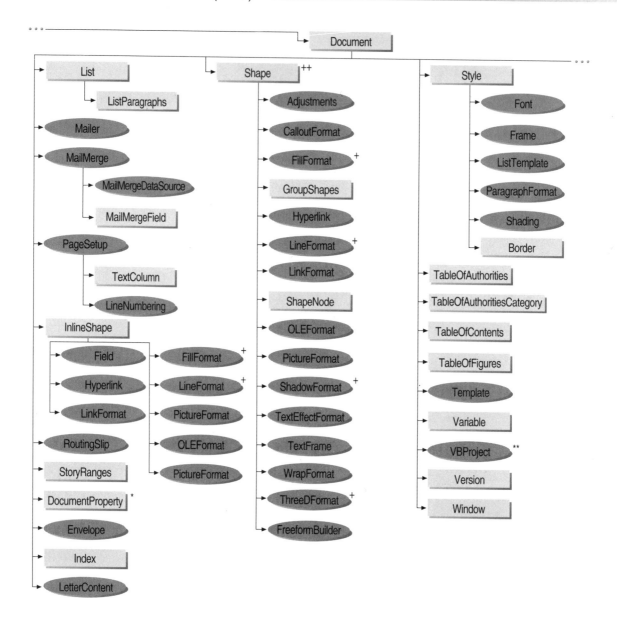

Reference information in Help

Help for this object model is available in VBAWRD8.HLP.

The dotted line (…) indicates that the diagram continues across pages.

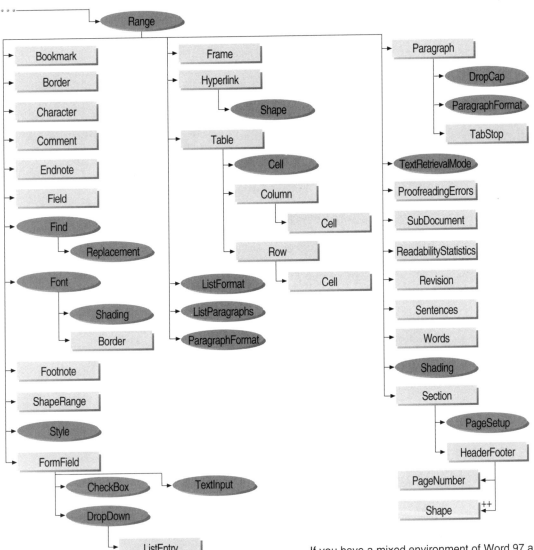

Notes

If you have a mixed environment of Word 97 and Word 95, you can still use the single object, *WordBasic*, through which Word 95 WordBasic macro commands can be accessed. You can obtain the type library (WB70EN32.TLB) from the Microsoft Office Developer Forum at: http://www.microsoft.com/officedev/. Help for WordBasic is available in WRDBASIC.HLP, which is included with Word 95.

The dotted line (…) indicates that the diagram continues across pages. Items marked by a single (*) designate objects in the Microsoft Office 97 Library. Items marked by a double (**) designate objects in the Microsoft Visual Basic Extensibility Object Library. Items marked by a single (+) designate objects with accessors to the ColorFormat Object. Items marked by a double (++) note that the ShapeRange Objects have been omitted from this diagram. For general purposes, you can think of these objects as occupying the same positions as the Shape object.

Microsoft PowerPoint 97

Default location: \Program Files\Microsoft Office\Office

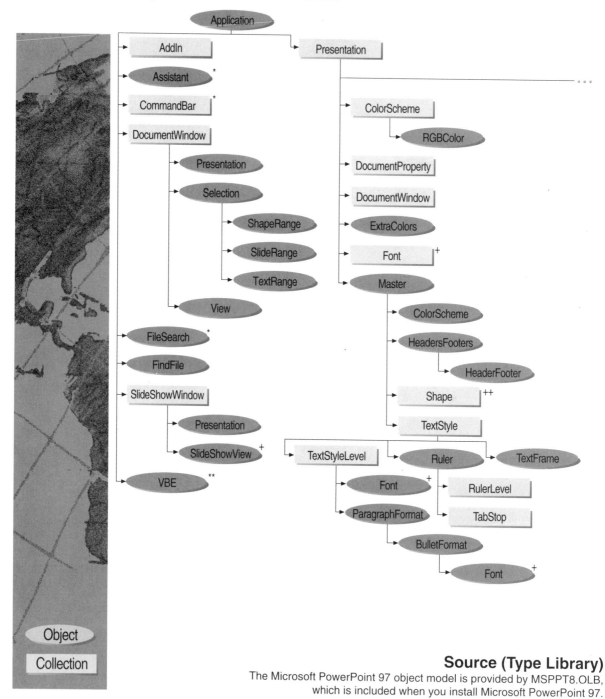

Source (Type Library)

The Microsoft PowerPoint 97 object model is provided by MSPPT8.OLB, which is included when you install Microsoft PowerPoint 97.

The dotted line (…) indicates that the diagram continues across pages.

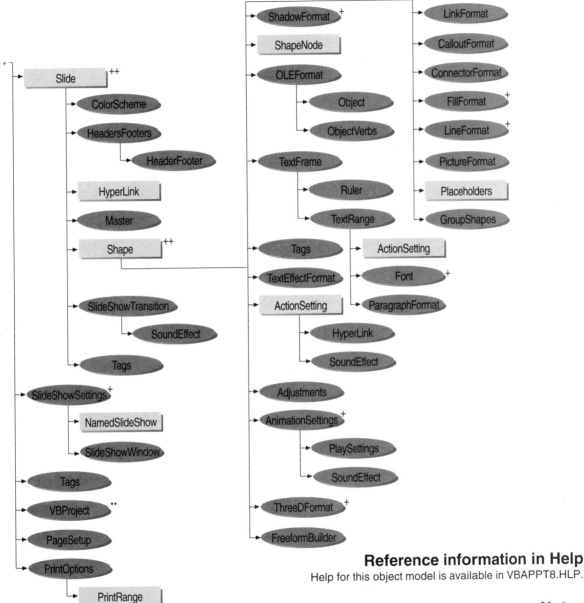

Reference information in Help

Help for this object model is available in VBAPPT8.HLP.

Notes

The dotted line (…) indicates that the diagram continues across pages.
Items marked by a single (*) designate objects in the Microsoft Office 97 Library.
Items marked by a double (**) designate objects in the Microsoft Visual Basic Extensibility Object Library.
Items marked by a single (+) designate objects with accessors to the ColorFormat Object.
Items marked by a double (++) note that the SlideRange and ShapeRange Objects have been omitted from this diagram. For general purposes, you can think of these objects as occupying the same positions as the Slide and Shape objects, respectively.

Microsoft Office Assistant

Default location: \Program Files\Microsoft Office\Office

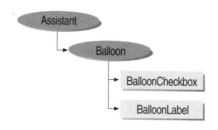

Source (Type Library)

The Microsoft Office Assistant object model is provided by MSO97.DLL, which is included when you install Microsoft Office 97.

Reference information in Help

Help for this object model is available in VBAOFF8.HLP.

Microsoft Binder

Default location: \Program Files\Microsoft Office\Office

Binder

Section

Object

Collection

Source (Type Library)

The Microsoft Office Binder object model is provided by MSBDR8.OLB, which is included when you install Microsoft Office 97.

Reference information in Help

Help for this object model is available in VBABDR8.HLP.

Microsoft Office Command Bars

Default location: \Program Files\Microsoft Office\Office

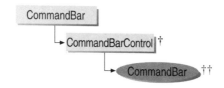

CommandBar

CommandBarControl †

CommandBar ††

Source (Type Library)

The Microsoft Office 97 CommandBars object model is provided by MSO97.DLL. which is included when you install Microsoft Office 97

Reference information in Help

Help for this object model is available in VBAOFF8.HLP

Notes

Items marked by a single (†) indicate the CommandBarControl class has three derived classes which are used to represent a certain subset of control types. The derived classes are CommandBarButton, CommandBarComboBox, and CommandBarPopup. Given a base CommandBarControl object you can determine if it is really one of the derived object types by using the Visual Basic TypeName() function. The derived classes add several properties and methods which only apply to certain control types.

Items marked by a double (††) contain objects that only appear in the CommandBarControlPopup derived class.

Object

Collection

Microsoft Office FileSearch

Default location: \Program Files\Microsoft Office\Office

Object

Collection

Source (Type Library)

The Microsoft Office 97 FileSearch object model is provided by MSO97.DLL, which is included when you install Microsoft Office 97.

Reference information in Help

Help for this object model is available in VBAOFF8.HLP.

Microsoft Graph 97

Default location: \Program Files\Common Files\Microsoft Shared\MSGraph

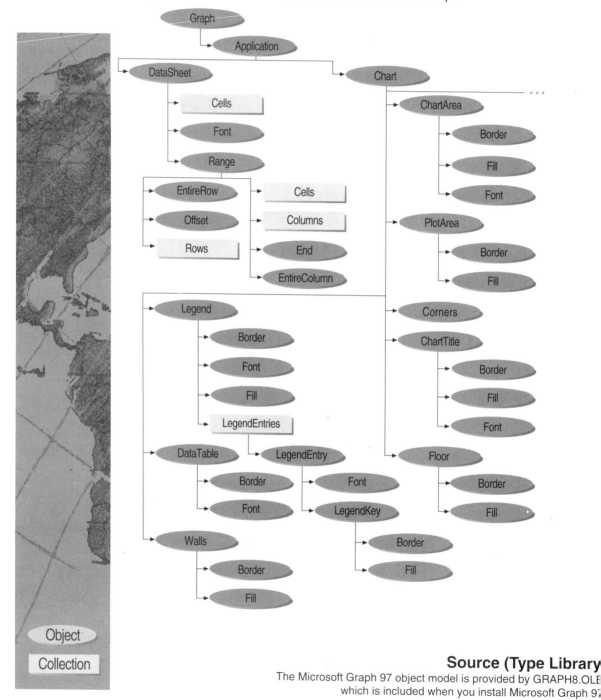

Object

Collection

Source (Type Library

The Microsoft Graph 97 object model is provided by GRAPH8.OLE
which is included when you install Microsoft Graph 97

The dotted line (...) indicates that the diagram continues across pages

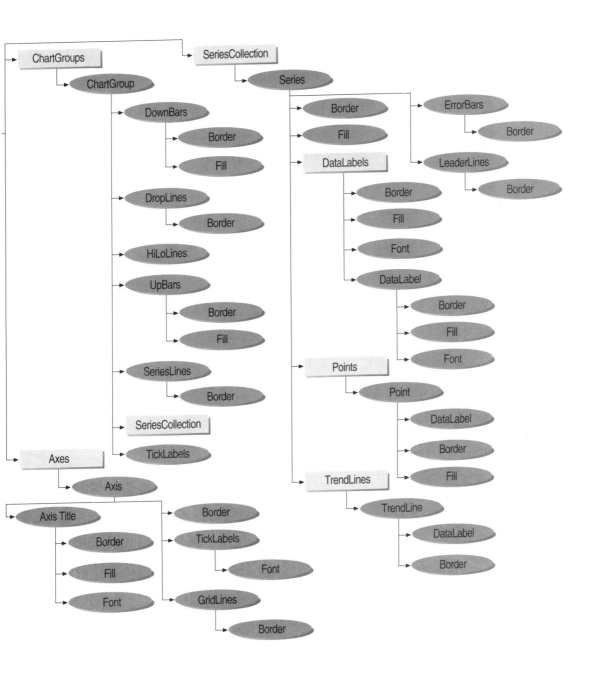

Reference information in Help

Help for this object model is available in VBAGRP8.HLP.

The dotted line (…) indicates that the diagram continues across pages.

Microsoft Data Access for ODBCDirect Workspaces

Default location: \Windows\System

Object

Collection

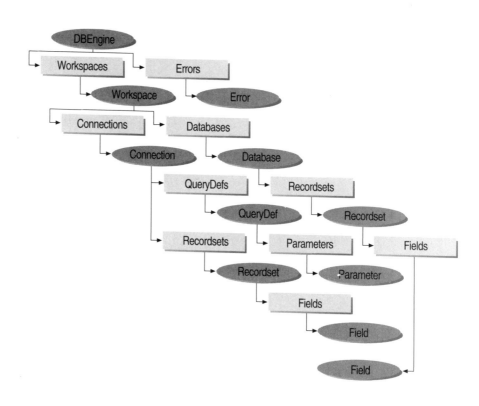

Source (Type Library

The Data Access for ODBCDirect Workspaces object model is provided b
DAO350.DDL, which is included when you install Microsoft Office 9?,
Microsoft Access 97, or Microsoft Excel 9°

Reference information in Hel

Help for this object model is available in DAO35.HLF

Data Access Objects for Microsoft Jet Workspaces

Default location: \Windows\System

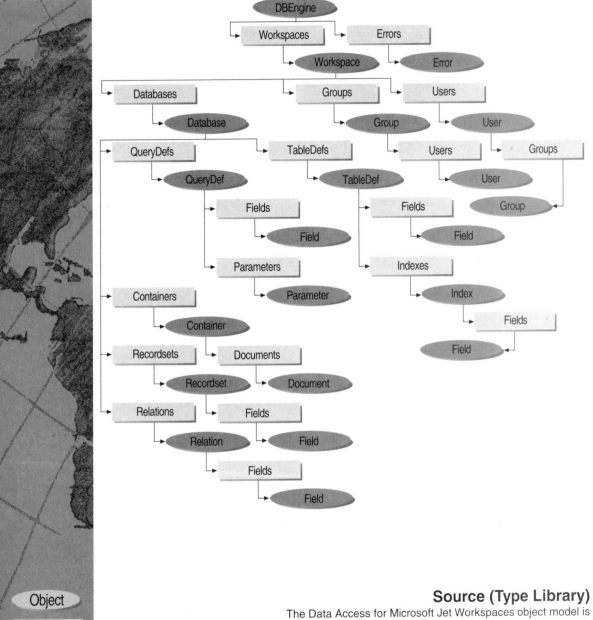

Source (Type Library)

The Data Access for Microsoft Jet Workspaces object model is provided by DAO350.DDL, which is included when you install Microsoft Office 97, Microsoft Access 97, or Microsoft Excel 97.

Reference information in Help

Help for this object model is available in DAO35.HLP.

Microsoft Forms

Default location: \Windows\System32

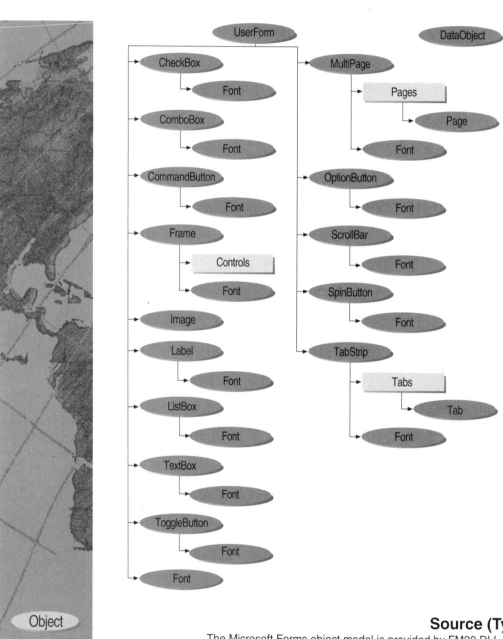

Source (Type Library

The Microsoft Forms object model is provided by FM20.DLL, which is include
when you install Microsoft Office 97, Microsoft Excel 97, Microsoft Outlook 97
Microsoft PowerPoint 97, or Microsoft Word 97

Reference information in Help

Help for this object model is available in FM20.HLP

Microsoft Map 97

Default location: \Program Files\Common Files\Microsoft Shared\Datamap

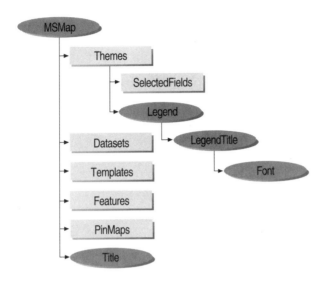

Source (Type Library)

The Microsoft Map object model is provided by MSMAP.TLP,
which is included when you install the Microsoft Map option for Microsoft Excel 97.

Reference information in Help

Help for this object model is available in VBAMAP8.HLP.

Notes

Automation for Microsoft Map works only when Microsoft Map is embedded in
Microsoft Excel 97. It will not work when Microsoft Map is embedded in
other applications, such as Microsoft Visual Basic, version 4.0.

Visual Basic Editor

Default location: \Program Files\Common Files\Microsoft Shared\VBA

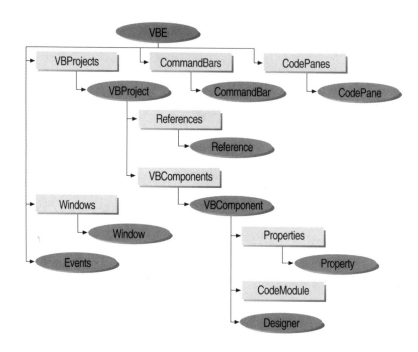

Source (Type Library

The Visual Basic Editor object model is provided by VBEEXT1.OLB, which is included when you install Microsoft Office 97, Microsoft Excel 97 Microsoft Outlook 97, Microsoft PowerPoint 97, or Microsoft Word 97

Reference information in Help

Help for this object model is available in VEENOB3.HLP

Microsoft Project for Windows 95

Default location: \MSOffice\Winproj

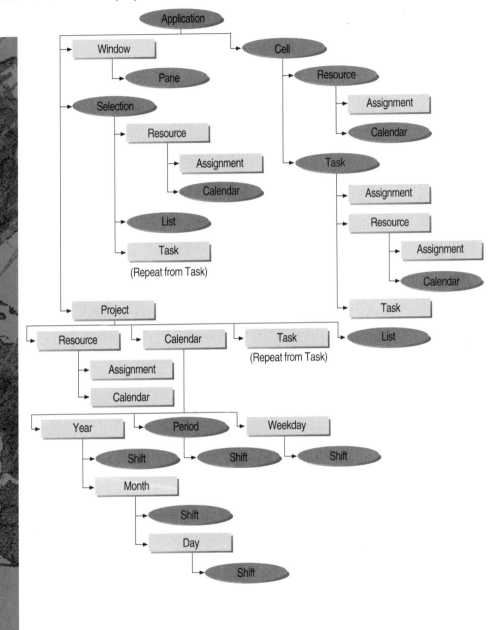

Object
Collection

Source (Type Library)

The Microsoft Project object model is provided by PJ4EN32.OLB, which is included when you install Microsoft Project.

Reference information in Help

Help for this object model is available in VBA_PJ.HLP.

Microsoft Team Manager 97

Default location: \Program Files\Microsoft Team Manager

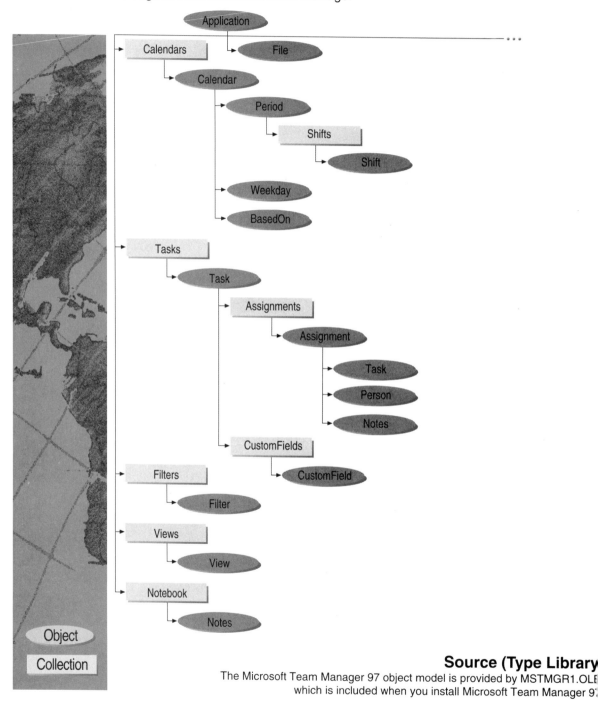

Source (Type Library

The Microsoft Team Manager 97 object model is provided by MSTMGR1.OLE
which is included when you install Microsoft Team Manager 9

The dotted line (…) indicates that the diagram continues across page

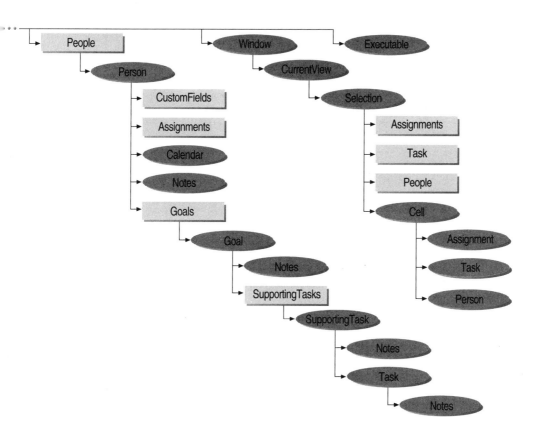

Reference information in Help

Help for this object model is available in TM1VBA.WRI.

The dotted line (...) indicates that the diagram continues across pages.

Microsoft Schedule+ for Windows 95

Default location: \MSOffice\Schedule

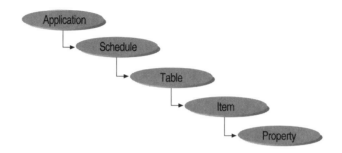

Object

Collection

Source (Type Library)

The Schedule+ object model is provided by SP7EN32.OLE
which is included when you install Microsoft Office for Windows 95

Reference information in Help

Online Help for this object model is available in SPLUSDK.HLP
which is available in the Schedule+ Developer's Kit section
of the Microsoft Exchange Resource Kit. It is also available
on the Microsoft Developer Network (MSDN)

Notes

The Schedule+ Developer's Kit also includes the object model type library
sample code, some Visual Basic calendar utilities, and documentation of the
printing formats available in Schedule+. If you have access to MSDN, you can search the
index to locate articles posted in March, 1996 about Schedule+ programmability

Microsoft Internet Explorer 3.0 Scripting

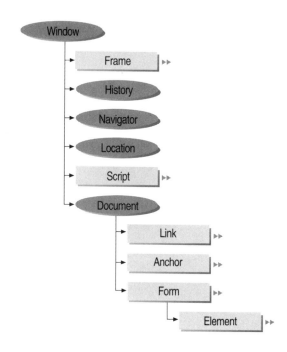

Object

Collection

Source (Type Library)
None. The Microsoft Internet Explorer Scripting object model is generated "on the fly," so there is no need to refer to a specific type library file.

Reference information in Help
The reference is included with the Microsoft ActiveX Software Development Kit (SDK). (Beta 1 is now available from the Microsoft Developer Network. The files are provided in HTML in the \Help\Scripton folder of the SDK.)

Notes
The Scripting Object Model allows you to customize the behavior of individual Web pages that are viewed with Microsoft Internet Explorer. Using the methods, events, and properties associated with the eleven objects found in the object model, you can create scripts with either Visual Basic Script or JScript™. These scripts are typically added to a Web page using the <script> tag and evaluated when the corresponding document is loaded. They can also be specified as attributes of HTML elements.

The double (▶▶) following an object indicates that multiple objects may exist.

Microsoft Windows NT® 4.0 OLE Directory Services

(Class Hierarchy)

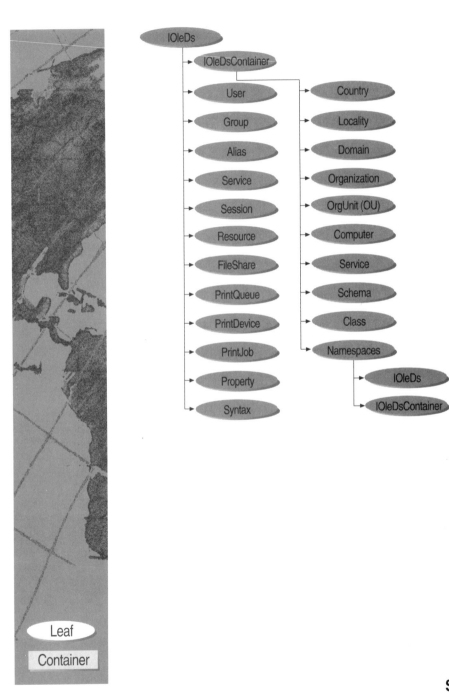

Source (Type Library)

The OLE DS object model is provided by OLEDS.TLB.

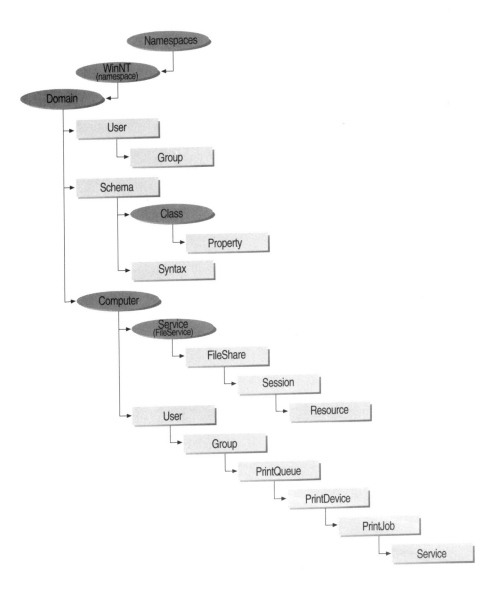

Leaf

Container

Reference information in Help

The OLE DS object model reference information is under development and will be available in the near future through the Microsoft Developer Network (MSDN) and Microsoft's World Wide Web site.

Microsoft Windows NT® 4.0 OLE Directory Services (cont.) ◾
(Object Model)

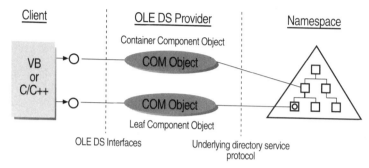

Leaf

Container

Notes

OLE DS provides a framework and implementation for interfaces that abstract
the properties and methods of well-known directory service objects found
within multiple network environments. The OLE DS object model consists of
OLE DS objects and **dependent objects**. An object is manipulated with **interfaces**.
The implementation of an object is found in an **OLE DS provider**. An OLE DS
provider contains the implementation of OLE DS objects and dependent
objects for a particular namespace. OLE DS objects are COM objects that are wrappers
for persistent objects in an underlying directory service. OLE DS objects are divided
into two groups: **directory service leaf objects**, and **directory service container
objects**. A container object can contain other OLE DS objects; a leaf object cannot. Dependent
objects are COM objects that logically divide the functionality of an OLE DS directory service
object. An OLE DS object is typically the host for one or more dependent objects.
Microsoft provides a type library documenting all the standard interfaces supported
by OLE DS (these are the interfaces documented in this specification).
This type library is **OLEDS.TLB**. Provider writers must supply a type library
that contains all of the information found in OLEDS.TLB and additional type
information documenting any provider-specific extensions.

OLE Messaging

Default location: \Windows\System

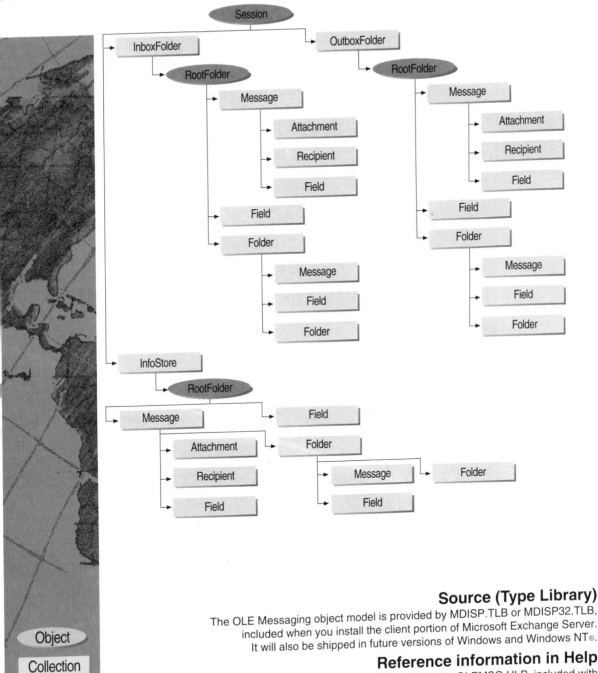

Source (Type Library)

The OLE Messaging object model is provided by MDISP.TLB or MDISP32.TLB, included when you install the client portion of Microsoft Exchange Server. It will also be shipped in future versions of Windows and Windows NT®.

Reference information in Help

Help for this object model is available in OLEMSG.HLP, included with Microsoft Exchange Forms Designer and the Microsoft Solutions Development Kit version 2.0.

Index

Welcome to the
administrator's
shop manual *for*

Microsoft
Office 97.

If you're an administrator or an IS professional, this book was written for you. Here you'll find the hands-on, in-depth information you need to roll out, support, and get the most from Microsoft Office 97 throughout your organization.

For systems running Microsoft Windows® 95 and Microsoft Windows NT® 3.51 and 4.0, this book covers it all—updating from earlier versions of Microsoft Office, switching from other applications such as Lotus 1-2-3 and WordPerfect, and coexistence among different versions of Microsoft Office. Of course, you get full information on network installation, plus the timesaving Network Installation Wizard on the companion CD-ROM. And like all the tools and utilities on the CD-ROM, this wizard is a tested, supported application designed to make your job easier.

No other volume is so packed with authoritative information, straight from the insiders who actually developed Microsoft Office 97. And you can easily update all this information through the Microsoft Office Resource Kit site on the World Wide Web. Get MICROSOFT OFFICE 97 RESOURCE KIT. And help your organization get the most from the newest version of the world's most popular office suite.

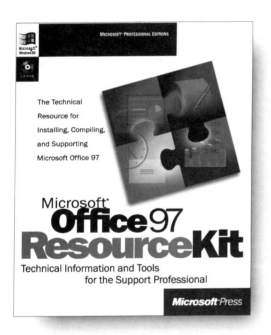

Microsoft® Office 97 Resource Kit
U.S.A. $59.99
U.K.   £56.49 [V.A.T. included]
Canada $80.99
ISBN 1-57231-329-3

How to **build** groupware applications in **less than** a **day.**

With this results-oriented, step-by-step guide and Microsoft® Exchange, you can do it. In fact, with this volume, even nonprogrammers can learn to quickly create professional-quality mail-enabled groupware applications. And Visual Basic® programmers can give those applications more power. The secret for customizing Microsoft Exchange is in three built-in components— public folders, the Exchange Forms Designer, and Visual Basic for Applications. This book shows you how to put them to work. Get BUILDING MICROSOFT EXCHANGE APPLICATIONS. And start saving time.

Building Microsoft Exchange Applications

Workgroup Applications You Can Build In A Day

Peter J. Krebs

Microsoft Press

U.S.A.	**$39.95**
U.K.	£37.49 [V.A.T. included]
Canada	$54.95
ISBN 1-57231-334-X	

Microsoft®Press

Register Today!

Return this
Microsoft® Office 97 / Visual Basic®
Programmer's Guide
registration card for
a Microsoft Press® catalog

U.S. and Canada addresses only. Fill in information below and mail postage-free. Please mail only the bottom half of this page.

1-57231-340-4A *MICROSOFT® OFFICE 97 / VISUAL BASIC®* *Owner Registration Card*
PROGRAMMER'S GUIDE

_____

NAME

_____

INSTITUTION OR COMPANY NAME

_____

ADDRESS

_____

_____

CITY   STATE   ZIP

Microsoft® Press
Quality Computer Books

**For a free catalog of
Microsoft Press® products, call
1-800-MSPRESS**